THE GREATEST COLLEGE FOOTBALL RIVALRIES OF ALL TIME

THE GREATEST COLLEGE FOOTBALL RIVALRIES OF ALL TIME

The Civil War, the Iron Bowl, and Other Memorable Matchups

Martin Gitlin

ROWMAN & LITTLEFIELD
Lanham • Boulder • New York • London

Published by Rowman & Littlefield
A wholly owned subsidary of The Rowman & Littlefield Publishing Group,
Inc.
4501 Forbes Boulevard, Suite 200, Lanham, Maryland 20706
www.rowman.com

16 Carlisle Street, London W1D 3BT, United Kingdom

British Library Cataloguing in Publication Information Available

Library of Congress Cataloging-in-Publication Data

Gitlin, Marty.
The greatest college football rivalries of all time : the Civil War, the Iron Bowl, and other memor-
able matchups / Martin Gitlin.
pages cm.
Includes bibliographical references and index.
ISBN 978-1-4422-2983-9 (cloth : alk. paper) -- ISBN 978-1-4422-2984-6 (ebook) 1. Football--
United States--History. 2. Sports rivalries--United States. I. Title.
GV950.G57 2014
796.332'63--dc23
2014009231

Printed in the United States of America

CONTENTS

INTRODUCTION

Thousands of football games are played on college campuses every fall. Winter bowl games eventually produce champions. But only a comparatively few bring fans to an emotional crescendo regardless of importance to conference standing or drive for a title.

Those battles are part of the greatest rivalries in the history of the sport. They are the annual showdowns backed by tradition. The motivation is not merely victory but bragging rights for a year. Greatness of team and talent has certainly added to the legend of particular rivalries, but others have remained as vibrant as ever to their participants and fans despite gridiron mediocrity and national insignificance.

The magnitude of the college football rivalries that have earned a place in this book have often been based on geography. The Iron Bowl battle between Auburn and Alabama or small-college clash between Pennsylvania neighbors Lehigh and Lafayette would have never grown to such epic proportions had they not been backyard brawls. It can also be argued that such rivalries as Ohio State–Michigan, Georgia–Florida, and Texas–Oklahoma have been fueled in part by proximity. But tradition has proven to be the fuel that drives even those rivalries and certainly those without geographic ties, such as Southern California vs. Notre Dame and Army vs. Navy.

This is not to discount the influence of great players, coaches, and teams in raising the status of particular rivalries to the level of legend. Dozens of future College Football Hall of Fame and even NFL Hall of Fame talents have peppered the rosters of many teams included in this book. Many of the greatest teams in college football history steamrolled to championships, some by virtue of historic victories over their archrivals. Classic clashes on the football field have done more to establish and maintain the greatest rivalries in the history of the sport than anything else. This book highlights those games.

It also highlights fan passion and the intensity of the rivalry participants. Everyone involved in college football gives of himself or herself emotionally to every game on a schedule. But that level of interest and emotional investment is raised to a fever pitch when rivalry week rolls around. To many players, coaches, and fans, a season cannot be a success without a victory over their traditional rival. The dates for that battle alone are circled on the calendar.

So to those who do or do not feel a personal attachment to a particular rivalry, this book should prove entertaining and enlightening. Enjoy.

I

OHIO STATE VS. MICHIGAN: WOODY, BO, AND BEYOND

No Big Ten title clash has ever been viewed as a more likely mismatch than the one played at Michigan Stadium on November 22, 1969.

The Wolverines entered their annual showdown against Ohio State as a 15-point underdog despite the home venue. Coach Woody Hayes had been firmly established as a legend. His Buckeyes were considered by many the finest college football team ever assembled. They had won 22 consecutive games. They were the defending national champions. They had not merely defeated their first nine opponents that season— they had annihilated one and all by an average score of 41–8. They were coming off a 42–14 trouncing of explosive, 10th-ranked Purdue, which had been averaging 37 points a game. They had been ranked first in the nation from the first kickoff of the first game. They had not lost in more than two years.

Michigan, on the other hand, was a pedestrian 7–2 under rookie head coach Bo Schembechler. The Wolverines had experienced lop-sided defeats to Missouri and Michigan State. They forged losing records in four of their previous seven seasons and were no longer considered a national power.

But, to paraphrase a rock-and-roll hit from the era, something was happening here. While the Buckeyes were rolling merrily along, the Wolverines were hitting their stride. They rolled into the showdown on a dominant four-game winning streak in which they had outscored their opponents 178–22. It had taken them half a season to embrace the offensive and defensive systems, grueling practices, and win-at-all-costs mind-set demanded by Schembechler. But they were playing as well as any team in the nation by November 22—at least any team not housed in Columbus, Ohio.

Schembechler was a man possessed heading into the showdown against the Buckeyes. He forced wife Millie to sleep in the baby's room so neither would disturb his concentration as he prepared a game plan. He barely showed any gratitude the Thursday before the game when she prepared his favorite dinner—Southern-style chicken and dumplings.[1]

The stage was set. More than 103,000 streamed into the mammoth bowl in Ann Arbor, Michigan. Millions more settled in to watch the game on national television. Schembechler claimed he knew his team would win after it had clobbered Iowa, 51–6, the previous week. But he could not express such confidence to the media lest he awaken what he hoped was a sleeping giant and overconfident Ohio State bunch. "We can't lay an egg today," Schembechler merely exclaimed. "We have come to win."[2]

Schembechler had designed his defense to stymie versatile All-American quarterback Rex Kern at the expense of limiting battering-ram fullback Jim Otis. But Kern rolled left and raced 25 yards to the Michigan 31 to start the game. Indeed, the Buckeye steamroller appeared to be in full throttle. But this was not the same Wolverines team that had lost to Ohio State the previous two years, including a 50–14 shellacking in 1968. Schembechler made certain of that by having that score stenciled on the scarlet-and-white jerseys worn by the scout team in practices.[3] They halted that drive, fell behind 6–0 on an Otis touchdown run, then forged ahead 7–6 on a 55-yard march engineered by quarterback Don Moorhead. It marked the first deficit faced by the Buckeyes all season.

The team traded touchdowns before Wolverines defensive back Barry Pierson played hero in another role. He scooted 60 yards on a punt return to the 3-yard line to set up a touchdown that gave his team a 21–12 lead and put the Buckeyes on their heels for the first time that year. Playing in comeback mode was not a strong suit for an offense saddled with the "three yards and a cloud of dust" philosophy that had been the signature of Ohio State coach Woody Hayes since he took over the program in 1951.

The result was that Michigan dominated the game defensively in a scoreless second half. Forced to throw, Kern and replacement Ron Maciejowski finished with six interceptions combined, including three from Pierson, two from Tom Curtis, and one from Thom Darden, all of whom went on to ply their trades in the NFL. Schembechler called the effort by Pierson "one of the greatest performances I have ever seen in a single game."[4]

The 24–12 Michigan victory sent shock waves through the American sports world and prompted a joyous celebration in Ann Arbor. On a highly political campus during the height of the unpopular Vietnam War, students temporarily left their activism behind and rejoiced over their gridiron heroes. And Wolverines fullback Garvie Craw, who had scored two touchdowns, roared his approval. "Unbelievable . . . fantastic . . . the greatest victory in the history of the world!" Craw crowed after the final gun signaled a Rose Bowl berth for Michigan against Southern California.[5]

The Wolverines would lose that game, but their victory over Ohio State launched in earnest what is undoubtedly the finest period in the history of an Ohio State–Michigan rivalry generally considered the most intense in college football. Little could anyone have imagined that the era actually began the moment Schembechler blew his first whistle as coach of the Wolverines. He understood Hayes and his football strategy. He realized that if he could keep games against Ohio State close or forge ahead, the Buckeyes could be beaten.

"Bo came in knowing what Woody would do," Pierson said years after the momentous upset. "And the Buckeyes were true to form. We put them in a bind, forcing them to pass, and that wasn't in their books. It backfired on them."[6]

The rivalry between Schembechler and Hayes quickly became one of the most passionate in the annals of American sports. The rivalry between the two football programs, however, had been established before either was born. Around the turn of the 20th century, the Wolverines forged the first dynasty in college football and regularly victimized a Buckeyes bunch that nevertheless won Ohio Athletic Conference championships every year from 1906 to 1912. The Michigan teams of that era were marked by a dominant defense that pitched more shutouts every year than some Major League Baseball teams.

Michigan football was born on May 30, 1879, with a dominant victory over Racine College. The Wolverines were quickly established as a force, winning all 10 games they played from 1884 to 1887 while not surrendering a point and earning a mark of 39–7 from 1894 to 1896, despite playing for three different coaches. The 1898 team was 10–0, with six shutouts. The carousel continued until arguably the first coaching legend in college football history arrived in 1901. That dedicated, highly competitive man was Fielding Yost.

The Wolverines lost just one game in their first five years under Yost. They outscored their opponents by a combined total of 2,821–42 during that stretch. They scored so quickly in at a time of generally offensive malaise in the sport that he was nicknamed "Hurry Up" Yost and his team was known as the "Point-a-Minute" Wolverines. But their defense was equally impressive. They did not give up a point in 1902. They so thoroughly thrashed Stanford in the 1902 Rose Bowl that the Cardinals walked off the field in the third quarter, never to return. The game was never completed.

Michigan boasted many of the premier standouts in the sport following the turn of the century, the greatest of which was halfback Willie Heston, who rushed for 170 yards in the defeat of Stanford and finished his career with 71 touchdowns.

Ohio State was an annual victim before and during the Yost years. The Wolverines beat the Buckeyes 13 times with two ties from 1897 to 1918, including an 86–0 rout in 1902. The combined score of those games was 371–21. Ohio State was blanked the first five times they met and in 11 of those matchups.

The launching of the rivalry on October 16, 1897, prompted little pomp and circumstance. College football had yet to grab hold of America, and the game drew limited attention, even at host Regents Field in Ann Arbor. But it was big enough news to be covered by the University of Michigan campus paper, which predicted a close game.

Each team featured about 20 players. Among them were Michigan running backs James Hogg, George Stuart, and Frederic Hannan, all of whom pierced the Ohio State defense through large holes opened up by their offensive linemen. Of course, all either team did was run the ball—the forward pass was banned until 1906. Touchdowns and field goals at the time were both worth four points and an extra point two. So when Hannan scored the first touchdown in Ohio State–Michigan history on a 10-yard run and Hogg added the extra point, his team led 6–0. By halftime, Stuart had added three touchdowns and the Wolverines had blown it open at 36–0, which proved to be the final score. The Buckeyes lost their last six games that season and finished with a record of 1–7–1 that still stands as their worst ever.[7] That dominance of the Wolverines that afternoon was to become a familiar theme of the rivalry well into the next century.

Of course, the Wolverines had gotten a head start. The Buckeyes launched their football program with a 20–14 defeat of Ohio Wesleyan on May 3, 1890. The immediate success achieved by Michigan eluded Ohio State, which managed just two winning seasons through 1898. They could not beat the Wolverines, but they did slug it out with them toe-to-toe in the first classic clash between the two teams on a cold, snowy Saturday in Ann Arbor on November 24, 1900. Unlike the 1897 game, which was played in front of a solely partisan crowd, this battle drew 900 Ohio State fans, which created a sense of competition both on the field and off it. But the arrival of 157-pound halfback Chic Harley in 1916 transformed the Buckeyes into a national power. They lost just once in four years with Harley at the helm.

The talent of Harley was so inspiring that legendary writer and Ohio native James Thurber was moved years later to describe him as "the greatest football player we Ohioans had never seen and we like to add, belligerently, we have seen them all." He added that Harley's running style was "a kind of cross between music and cannon fire, and it brought your heart up under your ears."[8]

The Buckeyes' record with Harley, however, was a bit tainted. The annual Michigan–Ohio State battles were halted during World War I and did not resume until 1918. Ohio State had joined the Big Ten in 1912, but charter member Michigan had dropped out in 1908 before returning in 1917, so it was not until 1918 that the teams met as conference rivals. The Buckeyes finally broke through with their first victory against the Wolverines the following year to kick off a three-game winning streak. There can be no rivalry without parity. The rise of the Ohio State program gave the clashes a competitive edge that would be maintained for the most part throughout the century and beyond.

Folks were beginning to take notice of the intensity of the rivalry by the 1920s. A few hours before one clash between the teams in Columbus that decade, fans had gathered in a downtown hotel to sell tickets and make bets. One Ohio State fan strolled across the lobby and shouted, "We don't give a damn about the whole state of Michigan!" Soon a band in the lobby began laying a tune called "The Old Gray Mare," to which the fans substituted the new lyrics: "Oh, we don't give a damn for the whole state of Michigan, we're from O-HI-O." A chant was born that would remain a Buckeye put-down of "that state up north" for generations.

A more official declaration of gridiron war was uttered in 1928 by Ohio governor Vic Donahey, who referred to the Buckeyes and Wolverines as "historic rivals" and claimed a "long struggle for athletic supremacy between these two neighboring states."[9]

Ohio State fans were all bark, but their team had no bite against powerful Michigan during the Roaring Twenties. The Buckeyes could not match the talent level of their Big Ten rivals. Two Bennies—Friedman and Oosterbaan—helped the Wolverines reestablish their dominance from 1922 to 1927, during which time they beat the Buckeyes six straight times, including four shutouts, and outscored them, 106–22.

Friedman, who ironically came from an Orthodox Jewish family in northeast Ohio, helped revolutionize college football by bringing the forward pass to that school up north. His talent and touch as a passer was so impressive that *New York Daily News* sportswriter Paul Gallico took notice. "When a Friedman pass reaches the receiver it has gone its route," he wrote. "The ball is practically dead. The receiver has merely to reach up and take hold of it like picking a grapefruit off a tree. That is Benny's secret, and that is why so many of his passes are completed. He is the greatest forward passer in the history of the game."[10]

Oosterbaan caught many of those passes as one of the finest receivers in the history of college football. He led the Big Ten in scoring, with eight touchdowns in 1925, the first of three seasons in which he earned All-American honors.

Both Oosterbaan and Friedman were involved in what many consider the kickoff of the Michigan–Ohio State rivalry in 1926. The Big Ten title was at stake in front of a crowd of 90,000 in Columbus. The Buckeyes raced to a 10–0 lead in the first quarter, but a scoring strike from Friedman to Oosterbaan and a field goal tied it. The Wolverines caught a break late in the game when Ohio State fumbled deep in its own territory. The staunch Buckeyes defense shadowed Oosterbaan and stopped Michigan on three straight plays, so Friedman went another direction on fourth down. He hit Leo Hoffman on a lob pass in the end zone to give his team a 17–10 lead.

The Buckeyes weren't done. They marched downfield for a touchdown. One measly extra point was about to tie the game, but it was botched to the dismay of Buckeye Nation. Game over. Michigan 17, Ohio State 16. The most storied rivalry in major college football had begun in earnest.

The teams took the momentum of that game and ran with it to heighten the conflict in 1927. Oosterbaan was a senior in 1927, a year after Yost retired as coach after 27 seasons, handed the reins to former Wolverines star halfback Harry Kipke, and assumed the job of athletic director. Among Yost's dreams had been to oversee the construction of the biggest college football stadium in the nation. The university administration fought against it, and Yost was forced to overcome financing issues, but Michigan Stadium was finally unveiled for the third home game of that season. And what better opponent to fill the 84,401 seats than Ohio State. The Wolverines rose to the occasion, blanking the Buckeyes, 21–0, to thrill the sellout crowd. It was their sixth consecutive win over Ohio State and ran their overall record in the series to 19–3–2.

The teams split their next six games, but the Ohio State program was about to hit its stride under new coach Francis Schmidt, a Texan who took over in 1934 with an innovative offensive flair. Though he was eventually overshadowed by Woody Hayes in the annals of Buckeyes football, Schmidt was the man who transformed the team into a nation-

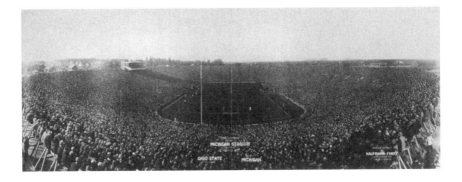

Figure 1.1. Formal opening of the new Michigan Stadium, Ann Arbor, October 22, 1927. Ohio State University vs. University of Michigan. *Source: Library of Congress*

al power for the first time. He shed the team of its reliance on the ground game and let quarterback Tippy Dye loose on the Wolverines that season. Upon his arrival at the school, Schmidt coined one of the most famous sports-related clichés when he offered logically to his team that the Wolverines players also "put their pants on one leg at a time just like everybody else."[11]

His offensive style was known as "razzle dazzle" and featured a wide array of formations. His inspirational leadership trickled down from his players to Ohio State fans everywhere. And when the Buckeyes thrashed Michigan, 34–0, in their first meeting under Schmidt, the crowd stormed the field at Ohio Stadium and tore down the goalposts for the first time in school history. They had witnessed thorough dominance. Their Buckeyes had earned 24 first downs to just three for the Wolverines and had 319 yards rushing to a mere six for the team from that state up north.

Schmidt's comment about the Wolverines and their pants was quickly adopted as folklore when Ohio businessmen and VIPs launched the Ohio Pants Club the following April. The boosters thereby began a tradition in which they would host a banquet to honor the players and coaches after every win over Michigan, during which they presented them with a miniature pair of metal golden pants engraved with the date and score of the triumph. The presentation of the "golden pants" remains a tradition at Ohio State to this day.

That 1934 victory, which was and would remain the most lopsided by the Buckeyes over Michigan until 1968, also launched their first dominant stretch in the series. It marked the first of four consecutive shutouts over the team from "that school up north."

But Schmidt's first win over the Wolverines was a bit tainted since the rise of his program coincided with a sudden and shocking collapse of Michigan, which was coming off successive national championships. Michigan finished dead last in the Big Ten that season under a cloud of controversy. It began when Week 3 opponent Georgia Tech, which was housed in the staunchly segregated South, threatened to boycott the game if Wolverines star Willis Ward played. The first black Michigan player in 40 years was embraced by his teammates and Michigan fans, who protested when Kipke relented and benched him. About 1,500 Michigan students and fans signed a petition demanding that Ward be reinstated, and some of his teammates—including future United States president Gerald Ford—threatened to quit if he wasn't.

Kipke refused to budge. He kept Ward out. And though his team won that game, they lost the rest of them that season and could not recover. Perhaps the greatest program to date in college football lost 22 of 32 games from 1934 to 1937 and were outscored by Ohio State, 114–0, in those four years. Those defeats spelled the end of Kipke at Michigan. He was replaced by Fritz Crisler, but before he left, he recruited a player that would quickly turn the fate of the program around. That player was Tom Harmon.

Harmon blossomed into arguably the most dominant college football player in history. A photo of the lantern-jawed, electrifying halfback was splashed on the cover of *Time* magazine in 1939. The accompanying article referred to his "Tarzan physique" and ability to run "with the power of a wild buffalo and the cunning of a hounded fox."[12]

Such plaudits were far from unwarranted. Harmon transformed the Wolverines into a winner again with his prolific production. He rushed for 2,134 yards, scored 33 touchdowns, and even tossed 16 scoring strikes in his three years at Michigan. He led the nation in scoring in 1939 and 1940, earning the coveted Heisman Trophy during a senior season that might be the greatest in the annals of the sport. Harmon began that year against the University of California by returning the opening kickoff 94 yards for a touchdown, taking his first carry 86 yards into the end zone, and later scoring on jaunts of 70 and 65 yards. One drunken California fan became so frustrated that he jumped out of the stands to try to tackle Harmon. He had no more success than his team.

Harmon led the Wolverines to victories over the Buckeyes in each of his three seasons. He put the cherry on top in 1940 by rushing for 139 yards, completing 10 of 11 passes for 151 yards and two touchdowns, intercepting three passes, and running one of them back for a score in a 40–0 dismantling of Ohio State. Harmon even averaged 50 yards a punt return in a triumph that marked his team's third consecutive shutout of their rival and a rebuke to the embarrassing defeat six years earlier. Following Harmon's last score, a blast through the Buckeyes line, every one of the Ohio State players shook his hand in congratulating him for an incredible game and career. Even the bitterest rivals were moved to show appreciation for what Harmon had accomplished in three seasons.

The Ohio State–Michigan rivalry had gained such importance at both schools that defeat proved motivation enough for a firing or resignation. Such was the case for Schmidt after his team had suffered its third consecutive shutout loss to the Wolverines. The same coach that had been revered after guiding the Buckeyes to four thrashings of Michigan in the previous decade called it quits before he could be canned and died three years later. He was replaced by one of the most legendary coaches in the history of the sport.

Paul Brown had earned a reputation for coaching brilliance at nearby Massillon High School. He had guided his team to six state championships, but critics scoffed at the notion of a prep coach taking over a prominent college program. They were scoffing no longer in 1942 when he clinched a national title with a 21–7 defeat of Michigan. By that time, however, many of the premier players on both teams had enlisted or been drafted into World War II, and attention had shifted away from college football.

Brown left to join the navy after the 1943 season. He was expected to return to the Buckeyes when the war ended but was lured away to coach the fledgling Cleveland Browns. New coach Carroll Widdoes guided Ohio State to one of its most dramatic defeats of the Wolverines in school history a year later. The hero in that 1944 victory was diminutive senior quarterback and future Heisman Trophy winner Les Horvath, who scored the game-winning touchdown late in the fourth quarter. Teammate Dick Flanagan intercepted a pass to seal the 18–14 victory and a Big Ten championship.

One can only speculate as to the future of the Buckeyes had Brown stayed. He became the first coach in football history to use playbooks and utilize a full-time coaching staff. He invented the draw play and instituted a system in which plays were called in from the sideline via a messenger. Such innovations, had Brown decided they were appropriate at the college level, could have dramatically altered the direction of the Ohio State–Michigan rivalry. His departure slanted fortunes in a northern direction. The 1944 win would be the last for Ohio State in the series for the next eight years.

Included in that run for the Wolverines was a notable triumph in 1950. The date was November 23. The temperature at Ohio Stadium was a stinging five degrees. The wind was blowing at 40 miles an hour. The blizzard conditions held up car and train traffic heading to the

Horseshoe. A blanket of snow covered the ground and was still falling at a furious pace. It was deemed the worst snowstorm throughout Ohio since 1913.

The Wolverines were playing for nothing but pride as they entered with an uncharacteristic 4–4 record. They were forced to stay in Toledo the night before and waited for the athletic directors of both schools to decide whether the game should be canceled. Crisler, who now served in that role for Michigan as Oosterbaan toiled as coach, reportedly offered that the game should go on with the notion that the miserable conditions would favor the underdog Wolverines. Ohio State athletic director Dick Larkins yielded to his suggestion that refunding 87,000 tickets would prove disastrous logistically and financially. What became known as the Snow Bowl would be played.

Even the ravenous Michigan haters in Columbus stayed away in droves. Those who braved the elements swathed themselves in layers of clothing, huddled under blankets, and even slipped cardboard boxes over their heads with slits cut out so they could see the action. And after a 140-minute delay to make the field playable, there wasn't much action. Typical plays simply could not be run through the blinding blizzard and icy footing. The players and officials struggled to see the yard lines. The teams shattered a conference record by kicking the ball away 45 times.

One of those punts cost Ohio State the game. With his team leading by a weirdly appropriate score of 3–2, Buckeyes star Vic Janowicz was instructed by coach Wes Fesler to punt the ball away on first down! Wolverines player Tony Momsen somehow stayed on his feet long enough to charge through the line and block it. He followed the bouncing ball into the end zone and tried to squash it down with his body into the snow, but it squirted. He finally grabbed it for a touchdown.

After a halftime in which both bands miraculously performed, both teams traded punts the rest of the game. As Ohio State fans were left to lament the decision by Fesler to punt on first down and the resulting defeat, a shocking upset by Northwestern over Illinois earned Michigan an improbable trip to the Rose Bowl despite earning zero first downs in Columbus and misfiring on all nine pass attempts. The teams combined for 45 punts and 10 fumbles. But it was the tearful Buckeyes that spoke of their sorrow following the game.

"It's like a nightmare," said Ohio State linebacker Sonny Gandee, whose uniform was splattered with blood. "It couldn't have happened, and you're going to wake up and find it was a bad dream."[13]

What Fesler wished was a bad dream turned into a real-life nightmare for him. Making matters worse was that it was his fourth straight loss to Michigan. The fans and media were brutal in their criticism. And two weeks later, he succumbed to the pressure and resigned as coach of the Buckeyes.

The revolving door had to stop for Ohio State to return to its status as a national power. Four head coaches had come and gone in the previous 10 years. The Buckeyes were 2–9–2 against the Wolverines since 1938. A local newspaper polled fans on who they wanted to be hired. The clear winner was Paul Brown, but that was not destined to happen. He was firmly established with the Cleveland Browns team that was taking the NFL by storm, but he accepted an interview. Others wrote in with humorous suggestions such as Lassie the dog, actress Lana Turner, or President Truman. Meanwhile, a little-known coach at Miami of Ohio was impressing the hiring committee in a three-hour interview. That coach was Wayne Woodrow Hayes, who considered the opening at Ohio State as his dream job.

The fiery Hayes beat out future College Football Hall of Fame coaches Sid Gillman and Don Faurot for the job. He understood the importance of beating Michigan but refused to allow himself or his players think beyond the immediate task of their next opponent. When asked about that school up north, he replied, "We'll consider Michigan a little later. Right now, I'm beginning to think about our opener against Southern Methodist."[14]

The Buckeyes indeed beat SMU after entering the season as the third-ranked team in the nation. But they performed poorly under their new coach and concluded a mediocre year with a 7–0 loss to Michigan. His team stumbled to a 16–9–2 record in his first three seasons, which included two defeats to the Wolverines. His boring "three yards and a cloud of dust" offense proved unpopular with his players, as did the discipline he required from them. His players showed a lack of respect for him, even locking him out of the locker room once during his first year at the helm. Soon a familiar cry rang out in Columbus. Disgruntled fans and media members wanted Hayes to be fired.

What Hayes needed was a running back with the talent to make his offensive philosophy a success and a blocker to open holes for him. He recruited the former in Howard "Hopalong" Cassady, whose nickname was borrowed from a Western film star and who blossomed into stardom in 1954. He recruited the latter in Jim Parker, who emerged as one of the premier offensive linemen in the history of college and professional football.

The Buckeyes steamrolled into Michigan week undefeated. The Wolverines were suffering through a 15-year drought in which they compiled an uninspiring record of 74–56–4, but they had lost just twice heading into their 1954 showdown against Ohio State. They were No. 12 in the nation and primed for an upset with a conference crown on the line. The key point of the game occurred after Michigan drove the ball to the Buckeyes' 1-yard line. Fullback Dave Hill slipped as he took the handoff on fourth down, recovered, and dove for the end zone. The Wolverines believed he crossed it, but the officials did not.

Soon Cassady was sprinting 60 yards for a touchdown to cap a 99-yard drive, and the Buckeyes were celebrating a 21–7 victory and Big Ten championship. A triumph over Southern California on New Year's Day gave Hayes and his Buckeyes a national title. Nobody was complaining any more about his disciplinary tactics, offensive conservatism, and temper. Suddenly all were justified. What had made Hayes a candidate for a canning the previous three years was now considered coaching brilliance. And it would remain so well into the 1970s.

Michigan, meanwhile, would not find their Woody for another decade. The Wolverines stumbled along year after year with mediocre records, even falling to 2–7 and last place in the Big Ten in 1962 under embattled coach Bump Elliott. His teams had lost all but one game to Ohio State heading into 1964. The Wolverines had sunk to the lowest depths in their glorious football history. Those depths to which they sunk were about to sink Elliott. But that year, behind such talent as quarterback Bob Timberlake, running back Mel Anthony, and defensive back Rick Volk, Michigan produced its finest season since 1948. They ended a four-game losing streak to the Buckeyes with a 10–0 victory and destroyed Oregon State in the Rose Bowl.

Alas, that Michigan team was merely a one-year wonder. They reverted to mediocrity, suffering through losing seasons in 1965 and 1967 and losses to the Buckeyes in three of the next four years. And when they were crushed by the eventual national champions in 1968 by a score of 50–14—their most lopsided loss to Ohio State since 1935—Bump was bumped.

New coach Bo Schembechler had battled with Hayes in the past. Figuratively, not literally. Their relationship began when the former was a junior offensive tackle at Miami of Ohio. Schembechler was happy as that season approached until Hayes was hired as his head coach. He had the same immediate feeling toward Hayes as his teammates. "I despised him," Schembechler said. "Most of us did."[15]

The intensity and strong personalities of both led to bitterness but also mutual respect. Schembechler quickly gained an admiration of Hayes, who saw coaching potential in his pupil. After Hayes landed the job at Ohio State, he hired Schembechler as a graduate assistant for one year. The protégé soaked in everything he could from Hayes, who ran his team like the military leaders he loved. Schembechler embraced Hayes as a tactician despite the shunning of a passing game that other college and professional coaches were beginning to develop with growing complexity.

Schembechler learned his craft well and moved up the coaching ladder from head position at Presbyterian College in South Carolina to Bowling Green State University to an assistant job at Northwestern. Hayes held him in high enough esteem to hire him as an assistant with the Buckeyes in 1958. Their passionate desire to win and stubbornness resulted in epic clashes during coaches meetings, in which they screamed at each other and kicked chairs. Hayes even fired Schembechler in fits of rage, only to rehire him immediately. They were like two peas fighting in a pod. Schembechler was on his way to earning the nickname "Little Woody." But he didn't want to adopt all his mentor's coaching methods, particularly in regard to discipline.

"It was tough coaching under Woody," Schembechler wrote in his book *Man in Motion*. "Some of the players just couldn't take it. He was too demanding in some things. He would argue about ridiculous things and there was no way you were ever going to win an argument with him."[16]

The same, however, was expressed by Schembechler's players in later years. He felt frustrated at being relegated to an assistant behind Hayes for five years at Ohio State. Hayes informed him that he would be the next head coach after he retired in three to five years. But Hayes outlived his own estimation by more than a decade. The antsy Schembechler decided to hightail it to his alma mater. He accepted the head coaching position at Miami of Ohio, which he guided to a 40–17–3 record and successive Mid-American Conference cochampionships in 1965 and 1966.

It took all of fifteen minutes of an interview for Michigan athletic director Don Canham to hire Schembechler after Elliott was fired. And in that same amount of time, his players knew they were in for a change from his mild-mannered predecessor.

"When you are you going to get that 270 pounds of lard moving?" Schembechler screamed in the face of one lineman during an August practice. One of his players exclaimed, "He's like an animal; he wants us to be like animals." But Schembechler was exactly what a staid Michigan football program needed: a kick in the pants. The Wolverines had become at best a second banana and at worst an afterthought in the Big Ten.

Not after November 22, 1969. The stunning upset of the top-ranked Buckeyes and satisfying victory for pupil over mentor on the sideline thrust the Wolverines back into the college football limelight and raised the Ohio State–Michigan rivalry to its most intense level. For the first time in the history of the two programs, it was coach vs. coach, not just team vs. team. The Wolverines and Buckeyes both thrived in the 1970s, and their annual showdowns became epic battles.

The 1970 Buckeyes played under the inspiration of three words: Remember Ann Arbor. That constant reminder of the fateful afternoon in which the Wolverines denied them a second straight national championship could be seen on bumper stickers and anywhere else an Ohio State fan, student, or player might be leading into the rematch in Columbus. If the Buckeyes needed reinforcement, it came from Hayes, who remained enraged over the 1969 defeat. He was obsessed with revenge for the next year. And when the Wolverines indeed invaded the following November, the Buckeyes were ready.

The importance of the showdown was heightened by the fact that both teams entered undefeated. Ohio State sat atop the national rankings, with Michigan next in line. But what was expected to be a taut battle never materialized. Michigan's Lance Scheffer fumbled the opening kickoff, and the Wolverines never recovered. The Buckeyes held the Wolverines to just 37 yards rushing on 30 attempts and 151

yards overall. A new twist installed by Hayes—a double tight-end formation for extra power blocking—helped his team rush for 242 yards on
that day. And when Ohio State running back Leo Hayden scored on a
four-yard pitch in the fourth quarter, it was over. The Buckeyes had a
20–9 victory and sweet revenge. When the final tick of the clock signaled the end of the game, Hayes fought through a mob of celebrating
fans with the game ball crammed into his armpit and tears in his eyes.[17]

"It was our biggest victory," Hayes said. "It was the biggest because
it makes up for what happened to us last year. The players were hurt.
They promised me all along they were going to play their greatest game
today—and they did. Going to the Rose Bowl wasn't the main thought
on their minds—it was avenging last year's loss."[18]

Indeed, the Buckeyes blew their shot at a national title for the second year in a row, with an upset defeat to Stanford in the Rose Bowl.
But the stage was set for annual clashes between the two teams that
became known as the Ten-Year War. Big Ten titles were always at stake
when the two teams met—Ohio State or Michigan won or tied for the
conference championship every year during that decade and shared it
five times.

Hayes and Schembechler took the rivalry to an extreme. Author
Greg Emmanuel explained the illogical and even absurd extent both
went to to gain an advantage in the game of psychological warfare in the
following excerpt from his book *The 100-Yard War*:

> The two coaches had raised the football drama from high art almost
> to high camp. Paranoia reached a level that would even make the
> era's Cold War participants shiver. Woody always whispered in the
> locker room when he visited Michigan Stadium because he was
> afraid Bo had the place bugged. Bo once saw a cameraman taking
> pictures of one of his team's practices, and he had the film confiscat-
> ed. He was afraid that pictures of UM formations would get back to
> Woody.
>
> Another year, Woody was watching a film of a Michigan game
> and noticed that the team up north was wearing a type of shoe he'd
> never seen before. Worried that Michigan might garner some kind of
> an edge on the field, Woody found exactly what kind of shoes they
> were wearing and got his team the exact same ones.
>
> Another time, he thought that Bo was trying to psych out his
> team, but not with shoes, with boobs. On a trip to Ann Arbor, Hayes

ordered all the waitresses to leave the dining area during the team's breakfast. He was sure that the comely servers had been hired by Bo to distract his team from the task at hand.[19]

Hayes had spoken about concentrating on opening-game foe Southern Methodist and worrying about the Wolverines later when he first arrived at Ohio State in 1951. But during the Schembechler era, his focus changed. He was obsessed with beating Michigan from spring practice forward every year.

"Woody would get ready [for Michigan] all year," said star running back Archie Griffin. "We used to say that Michigan was a separate season, a season in itself. . . . Spring practices we'd be getting ready for the Michigan defense. It was a constant preparation for *that* game—the whole season every Monday."[20]

There was no less passion on the Michigan campus, but perhaps it was more personal. The students there wore T-shirts that read "Crack Woody's Nuts," and Wolverines radio announcer Bob Ufer placed in his booth a miniature casket with a Hayes dummy inside.

Griffin, the only player in college football history to earn two Heisman Trophy awards, was a brilliant performer in the annual drama that was played out before 100,000 fans live and millions more on national television as American families prepared for Thanksgiving every year.

The 1973 clash in which he starred even extended beyond the playing field. Both teams entered the game undefeated. Griffin rushed for 59 yards in a first half that ended with Ohio State leading 10–0. And when Buckeyes defensive back Neal Colzie intercepted a pass in the end zone early in the third quarter, it appeared his team was destined to snag the undisputed Big Ten crown. But the Wolverines battled back. They boldly went for it on fourth down at the Ohio State 10-yard line and scored on a fake handoff and run by quarterback Dennis Franklin.

Griffin finished with 163 yards rushing, but the game ended in a 10–10 tie. Yet the fight for a Rose Bowl berth had just begun. A Big Ten rule had previously banned consecutive trips to the annual game, so back-to-back champions had been forced to stay home. But it had finally shed that rule and decided that the winner of the league title should represent the Big Ten in Pasadena. There was only one problem in 1973. The tie in Ann Arbor resulted in a tie for the title. The league athletic directors were forced to vote on that representative. Schembechler was confident they would give the nod to his Wolverines, who had, after all, dominated the game statistically. But the athletic directors had a different motivation. The Big Ten had lost the last three Rose Bowls, and they made their choice based on which team they believed had the best chance to win. And that team was Ohio State. The Wolverines, after all, had lost to Stanford in the New Year's Day game in 1972 to ruin their undefeated season and chance at an undisputed national championship.

Schembechler was livid. He learned of the snub before taping his weekly television show, left the assembled media, and walked into the studio to yell out some choice swear words and kick around some furniture. The Ohio State–Michigan rivalry had been ratcheted up a notch, but the rationale of the athletic directors proved to be justified. The Buckeyes thrashed Southern California in the Rose Bowl, 42–21, to bring honor back to the Big Ten.

Griffin was far less explosive in the next two clashes against the Wolverines. He was held scoreless the next season and managed just 46 yards rushing in 1975 but earned the Heisman Trophy in both those years, partly because the Buckeyes won both games. They used four field goals for a 12–10 win in 1974 and managed a 21–14 triumph in 1975. Little could Hayes have imagined that would be his last triumph over Michigan. The tide was about to turn in a direction that spelled doom for Hayes at Ohio State, his frustrations stemming from defeats to the Wolverines the next three years in which what had become his archaic "three yards and a cloud of dust" offense was held to nine points combined. The first two of those losses ruined undefeated seasons and played into an angry outburst that cost him his job.

It was December 29, 1978, a date that will live in infamy at Ohio State. A loss to the Wolverines had relegated his team to a berth in the Gator Bowl against Clemson, for which Hayes expressed no enthusiasm. The Buckeyes were trailing the Tigers, 17–15, in the final minutes of the game but were driving for what could have been the go-ahead or even winning score. All was lost, however, when a pass from quarterback Art Schlichter was intercepted by linebacker Charlie Bauman, who was tackled on the Ohio State sideline. Hayes snapped. He charged at Bauman and punched him underneath the chin as millions of national television viewers watched in stunned disbelief.

Given the option, Hayes refused to resign. He stated that that would be too easy for the university and said he would prefer to be fired. Hayes, who was indeed canned the day after the incident, never apologized to Bauman.

The Ten-Year War was over. The Ohio State–Michigan rivalry would never be the same. It would maintain the highest level of intensity but never again between the coaches. And that troubled Schembechler, who gave a psychological explanation as to why Hayes reacted violently to impending defeat in the Gator Bowl.

"I'm saddened by it," Schembechler told the media as his team prepared for the Rose Bowl. "I hate to see something like this happen. I was shocked . . . not shocked but disappointed. I hope you all look back over his career and all the good he's done . . . and not dwell so heavily on his indiscretions. . . . There's the pressure of coming to the end of a career. Things are slipping away from you and you're not winning enough. I just wish his career would have ended differently."[21]

The ignominious end of Hayes's career resulted in a boon to the career of one of his former assistants. Iowa State head coach Earle Bruce, who served as the Ohio State offensive line and defensive back coach in the late 1960s and early 1970s, infused new blood into what had become a staid and stale football program. He opened up the passing game, allowing the talented Schlichter to thrive. Schlichter, who was wildly erratic under Hayes in 1978 with four touchdowns and 21 interceptions, threw for 14 scores and just six picks under Bruce the following year. But he wasn't alone in his turnaround. The entire team performed better that season. They entered Michigan week undefeated and ranked second in the nation.

The showdown against the No. 13 Wolverines attracted an NCAA regular-season record crowd of 106,255 in Ann Arbor. The taut battle did not swing permanently in favor of Ohio State until senior linebacker Jim Laughlin charged in on a 10-man, all-out rush and blocked a punt early in the fourth quarter that was scooped up by defensive back Todd Bell and run into the end zone for the go-ahead touchdown.

Six weeks later, however, Bruce was plagued by the same malady that had befallen both Hayes and Schembechler throughout the 1970s. And that was the inability to win bowl games, including those with national championships hanging in the balance. The Buckeyes had risen to No. 1 in the country by the time they played Southern California in the Rose Bowl, but their 17–16 defeat doomed them to also-ran status. A loss the following year in the Liberty Bowl marked the eighth for the Buckeyes in nine bowl games from 1971 to 1980. Schembechler's teams lost all six they played during that same stretch. It has been speculated that the intensity and focus on the annual clash between the two teams resulted in bowl-game letdowns, as did the six weeks between the Michigan–Ohio State battles and New Year's Day games.

Meanwhile, the rest of the Big Ten was catching up. When unde-feated Illinois earned the Big Ten title in 1983, it marked the first time in 16 years that neither Ohio State nor Michigan tied or won the title since 1967. But the two teams staged a classic showdown in 1986 that reinvigorated the rivalry and sparked memories of a moment a genera-tion earlier that proved to be a watershed moment in the NFL.

It was the week leading up to Super Bowl III that Joe Namath of the heavy underdog New York Jets, which was housed in the upstart AFL, guaranteed a victory over the established and powerful Baltimore Colts of the NFL. The stunning Jets triumph helped set the stage for the merger between the two leagues. So, naturally, comparisons were made when cocky Michigan quarterback Jim Harbaugh told anyone within earshot in the week leading up to the 1986 game that his team would beat Ohio State and earn a Rose Bowl berth.

Then, like Namath, he made it happen. Harbaugh, whose father was a Wolverines assistant coach that raised him to be a Michigan fan, felt a sense of destiny. After all, his dad helped the team earn three Rose Bowl berths in the 1970s and he believed it was his right to guide his teammates to a trip to Pasadena.

His words angered and inspired the Buckeyes early and seemed to pressure Harbaugh, who threw two early interceptions. Ohio State jumped ahead, 14–3, but the Wolverines rebounded to take a 26–17 lead in the fourth quarter. But a touchdown pass from Jim Karsatos to future NFL Hall of Fame receiver Cris Carter cut the Buckeyes deficit to 26–24. And when Ohio State fell on a fumble with three minutes left, it appeared Harbaugh was not going to be remembered as the Nostrad-amus of sports prognosticators. The Buckeyes drove into field goal range, but placekicker Matt Frantz was wide left with his boot. Game over. The victory placed Michigan in a tie with Ohio State for the Big Ten championship.

Harbaugh was vindicated. But once again, Schembechler and his Wolverines were destined to lose in the Rose Bowl, this time to Arizona State. The bowl defeats were piling up and Schembechler was attracting criticism for it. But not as much as Bruce was in Columbus. Ohio State fans were accustomed to rooting for a national championship contender, but their team was simply not strong enough under Bruce in the 1980s.

The Buckeyes entered their game against Iowa in 1987 with a disappointing 5–3–1 record. They led, 27–22, with 30 seconds remaining. The Hawkeyes appeared doomed. They had fourth down, no timeouts, and only a 28-yard touchdown pass could save them. They needed a miracle—and they got one. Iowa tight end Marv Cook caught the ball at the 10-yard line, crashed through two Ohio State defenders, and scored the winning touchdown.

That play tipped the scales against Bruce. The assumption was that he would be fired after the season. But the powers that be at Ohio State could not wait. Hearing the rumors that Bruce's job was in jeopardy, Schembechler joked with respect and admiration that he should take over as athletic director at Michigan and hire Bruce as coach. But such words of kindness could not save Bruce. They canned him on Monday, five days before the annual showdown against Michigan.

There would be no interim coach. Bruce was a dead man walking as he prepared his team to face the Wolverines. The Buckeyes would have accepted a bowl bid had they beaten Iowa, but there was none offered now. The annual appreciation banquet thrown by the school was canceled. Defensive lineman Ray Holliman later lamented, "Maybe in years to come the wounds will be healed, but I'll always remember this and what they did to our senior year."[22]

The players banded together to support their departing coach. They wore "EARLE" headbands before the game. They fought back from a first half dominated by the team from that school up north at the home of the school up north, no less, to upset Michigan, 23–20. And in front of a national TV audience, they carried a beaming Bruce off the field. His last memory as an Ohio State coach was one of triumph and camaraderie.

Bruce was fired because he could not win the game, but he had just won one of the biggest of his career. Ironically, replacement John Cooper would fare far worse, particularly against Michigan. And

Schembechler? He too was bombarded with criticism over his failure to win even bigger games from a national perspective, those that could have earned him the NCAA Division I championship that eluded him throughout his career.

The writing was on the wall by that time for Schembechler. He underwent quadruple bypass surgery in December, nine months after Hayes died. He was absent when his team beat Alabama in the Hall of Fame Bowl two weeks later. He finished his college coaching career with a flourish, beating the Buckeyes in 1988 and 1989 for successive Big Ten titles before handing the job to assistant coach Gary Moeller. Nearly a century of combined Ohio State–Michigan football experience in which either Hayes or Schembechler strode the sidelines was over. And the conflict would never carry the same luster. The programs took turns dominating over the next three decades and significant show-downs were rare.

There were exceptions in the realms of upsets that destroyed the dreams of a rival seeking a national crown. There were also singular games and moments that reminded the nation that Ohio State–Michigan was still the most heated rivalry in the nation. An Ohio high school graduate who never considered becoming a Buckeye pro-vided one such moment in 1991. Wolverines wide receiver Desmond Howard told friends back home in Cleveland to pay special attention to him while watching the annual showdown. During the game Howard snagged a punt, bolted between two Buckeyes, broke a tackle, and sprinted down the sideline for a 93-yard touchdown. He ran into the end zone, stopped, bent his left leg, and stretched out his left arm as he clutched the football in his right, thereby creating the Heisman Trophy pose to the delight of the sellout crowd in Ann Arbor. Not only did the score aid in the 31–3 thrashing of the Buckeyes, but it also proved prophetic. Howard indeed became the first Michigan player since Tom Harmon in 1940 to win the coveted Heisman.

Cooper proved to be an adept recruiter at Ohio State, but his inabil-ity to defeat Michigan and seeming lack of appreciation for the intensity of the rivalry irked fans and eventually cost him his job. One such galling defeat occurred in 1995 after his team had achieved a 9–0 record and No. 2 ranking in the country. The Buckeyes had steamrolled over all in their path and had outscored their previous five opponents by a combined score of 216–62. They boasted such future NFL stars as running back Eddie George, who ran for nearly 2,000 yards on the season, wide receiver Terry Glenn, and defensive back Antoine Winfield. One would imagine a victory over the 18th-ranked Wolverines, who had already lost three times in league play under first-year coach Lloyd Carr, was a near certainty. But Ohio State fans knew better. Cooper already had a 1–5–1 record against Michigan.

Glenn was asked about the upcoming clash as it approached. He spoke about the journey through an unbeaten season and how his Buckeyes would not place the Wolverines on a pedestal. Then he uttered words that would haunt him and inspire their opponent throughout the week. He said, "Michigan's nothing."

Michigan was something that Saturday. The defensive backs were something, holding Glenn to a meager four receptions and, for the first time since the season opener, no touchdowns. But more something than anything was Wolverines battering-ram junior running back Tshimanga Biakabutuka, a Zaire native who set an Ohio State–Michigan game record by rushing for an absurd 313 yards. And when the final tick went off the clock to signal the end of a 31–23 defeat and hopes of a national championship, George spoke about the shattering of a dream. "We've got to live with this, and it's going to be something," he said with eyes swollen and red from crying. "I might not get over it. My life goes on. I imagine this loss will always be a part of it." [23]

A sense of déjà vu crept into Ohio Stadium the following year. The Buckeyes again entered the showdown unbeaten. Their defense had yielded more than 17 points just once in 10 games and had pitched three shutouts. They were ranked No. 2 in the country. The Wolverines were coming off back-to-back defeats to Purdue and Penn State to fall to No. 21 in the nation. A pep rally in Columbus attracted 20,000 Ohio State fans despite dreary, cold weather. But it seemed to be Cooper's destiny to lose to the Wolverines despite their usual inferiority.

It appeared that the gorilla was off his back when the Buckeyes trotted off the field at halftime with a 9–0 lead. Ohio State cornerback Shawn Springs, whose father, Ron, played at the school under Woody Hayes, crowed in the locker room that he had top wideout Tai Streets covered like a blanket. But in the third quarter, the Big Ten Defensive Player of the Year fell down covering Streets. The result was a 68-yard touchdown strike that shifted the momentum permanently. The Wolverines shut down the Buckeyes the rest of the way and added two field goals in a 13–9 victory. And all Springs could say sheepishly was that he learned trash-talking should be reserved for the postgame celebration.[24]

The triumph seemed to embolden Michigan, which used a 20–14 victory over Ohio State in Ann Arbor as a springboard to the 1997 national championship. It marked the first time since 1948 that the Wolverines won the crown with an unblemished record. Little could anyone have imagined that the most accomplished player on that team would be backup quarterback Tom Brady, who blossomed into a three-time Super Bowl winner and Hall of Famer with the NFL New England Patriots.

The powers that be at Ohio State could accept annual defeats to Michigan when their team was an annual national title contender. Cooper had already dropped to 1–8–1 against that school up north when the Wolverines were polishing off Washington State in the 1998 Rose Bowl to clinch the championship. Yet he maintained his job despite intensified calls for his ouster. But when he transformed the Buckeyes from potential champions to also-ran, he was doomed. The Buckeyes finished 6–6 in 1999 and placed a shocking eighth in the Big Ten, their worst standing since 1947. They lost four games in 2000, and that sealed his fate. Cooper was fired shortly after losing to unranked South Carolina in the Outback Bowl. His marks of 2–10–1 against Michigan and 3–7 in bowl games proved too much of a burden to carry. After his firing, he summed up the feelings of many Buckeyes fans who simply couldn't forgive him for his record against the Wolverines. "A lot of people are never going to like me," he lamented.[25]

Cooper was replaced by former Ohio State assistant Jim Tressel, who immediately expressed an appreciation for the rivalry that fans had waited in vain for more than a decade to hear from his predecessor. Tressel addressed a home crowd at halftime of a Buckeyes–Wolverines basketball game and announced his intention to beat Michigan on the gridiron. And that's just what he did. Tressel began in his first season a domination of the Wolverines that would last well into the next decade.

But it wasn't until his second year that the defeat of Michigan mattered from a national perspective. The surprising Buckeyes had rebounded from a three-game stretch in which they had lost 15 games for the first time since 1895 to 1897 and entered the showdown at 12–0 and ranked second in the nation behind the powerful University of Miami. The Wolverines were a stellar No. 12 coming into Columbus, but they couldn't control featured back Maurice Clarett, who rushed for 119 yards and set up the game-winning touchdown with a 26-yard catch and run to the Michigan 6. Ohio State emerged a 14–9 victory in front of a stadium-record crowd of 105,539 and six weeks later shocked the heavily favored Hurricanes in overtime in the Fiesta Bowl to clinch its first national championship since 1968.

The domination established by the Buckeyes in the Tressel era and comparative struggles of the Wolverines under Carr and the ill-fated regime of Rich Rodriguez that began in 2008, when Michigan suffered through its first nine-loss season in program history, was interrupted for just one memorable game. That showdown was forged by the brilliance of the Buckeyes and Wolverines, both of whom arrived in Columbus undefeated. Ohio State rested atop the national rankings, with Michigan right behind, when they clashed on November 18, 2006. It marked the first time since 1973 that the rivalry game was played between the two highest-rated teams in the country.

But the game was far more emotional for the Wolverines when kickoff rolled around. They were inspired by the death of Schembechler from a massive heart attack the day before. They yearned to win for the man that had brought Michigan football back to life two generations earlier. But Carr refused to take advantage of his passing to motivate his players. He believed that would show dishonor to his memory, so he simply told them to play in a way that would make him proud.[26]

Future NFL standouts peppered both rosters. Among them was Michigan quarterback Chad Henne, who continued to answer Ohio State touchdowns by leading scoring drives downfield. The Buckeyes led 28–14 at halftime. The Wolverines had surrendered more points in two quarters than they had in any game all season. But they battled back. They answered a 56-yard touchdown scamper by Ohio State's Antonio Pittman with the third touchdown of the game by fellow featured back Michael Hart. They answered a 13-yard touchdown catch by Brian Robiskie with a 16-yard scoring strike from Henne to Tyler Ecker with two minutes remaining in the game.

That score shrunk the Buckeyes' lead to 42–39. But Ohio State had never fallen behind in this game, and they never did. When the last had ticked off the clock, they were undisputed Big Ten champions. And the Wolverines were left to think about falling short for their departed coaching hero.

"It was definitely difficult for us," said Henne, whose 267-yard, two-touchdown effort paled in comparison to that of Buckeyes star quarterback Troy Smith, who threw for 316 yards and four scores. "Coach Carr loves [Schembechler] dearly and so do we. . . . It's sad to see him go. We dearly miss him. We tried to fight for him today."[27]

The Wolverines always tried to fight for Bo, just as the Buckeyes had always tried to fight for Woody until Woody tried to fight an opposing player. The Ohio State–Michigan rivalry didn't die along with Schembechler and Hayes. But the dominance of the Wolverines and then the Buckeyes from the late 1980s forward lost some of its luster. It took a classic showdown like the one in 2006 to remind one and all that the greatest rivalry in college football travels back and forth from Columbus to that state up north.

A reminder of that fact came in the 110th meeting of the two teams in 2013, two years after a host of NCAA violations had cost Tressel his job, eventually leading to former Florida coach Urban Meyer taking over the program. The unbeaten Buckeyes had won eight of the last nine against the Wolverines and were expected to run away and hide. But even after Ohio State quarterback Braxton Miller matched his career high with five touchdown passes and running back Carlos Hyde scored to give his team a 42–35 lead with two minutes remaining, it wasn't over. Michigan quarterback Devin Gardner drove his team downfield and tossed a scoring strike to Devin Funchess to close the gap to 42–41.

Wolverines coach Brady Hoke then took a turn for the dramatic. He disdained the extra point and an overtime shootout for the chance at a huge upset in regulation. But a two-point conversion pass from Gardner was intercepted by Tyvis Powell. Game over. The Buckeyes had survived in the first game in which the teams scored more than 40 points since 1987. One figured Hayes and Schembechler had to be rolling over in their graves.

"I have such a great respect for this rivalry," Meyer said. "Coach Hayes was from a different generation. He would have wanted a 10–9 game, but he would have wanted to see the two teams playing as hard as they can."

The Buckeyes and Wolverines have always done that. Hayes and Schembechler would have it no other way.[28]

Fact Box (through 2013)

Nickname: The Game

Trophy: None

Total meetings: 110

Series record: Michigan leads, 58–46–6

First meeting: 1897 (Michigan 36, Ohio State 0)

Largest margin of victory: Michigan, 1902 (Michigan 86, Ohio State 0)

Longest winning streak: Michigan, 9 (1901–1909)

Game Results (home team listed second unless at a neutral site)

1897: Ohio State 0, Michigan 36

1900: Ohio State 0, Michigan 0

1901: Michigan 21, Ohio State 0

1902: Ohio State 0, Michigan 86

1903: Ohio State 0, Michigan 36

1904: Michigan 31, Ohio State 6

1905: Ohio State 0, Michigan 40

1906: Michigan 6, Ohio State 0

1907: Ohio State 0, Michigan 22

1908: Michigan 10, Ohio State 6

1909: Ohio State 6, Michigan 33

1910: Michigan 3, Ohio State 3

1911: Ohio State 0, Michigan 19

1912: Michigan 14, Ohio State 0

1918: Michigan 14, Ohio State 0

1919: Ohio State 13, Michigan 3

1920: Michigan 7, Ohio State 14

1921: Ohio State 14, Michigan 0

1922: Michigan 19, Ohio State 0

1923: Ohio State 0, Michigan 23

1924: Michigan 16, Ohio State 6

1925: Ohio State 0, Michigan 10

1926: Michigan 17, Ohio State 16

1927: Ohio State 0, Michigan 21

1928: Michigan 7, Ohio State 19

1929: Ohio State 7, Michigan 0

1930: Michigan 13, Ohio State 0

1931: Ohio State 7, Michigan 0
1932: Michigan 14, Ohio State 10
1933: Ohio State 0, Michigan 13
1934: Michigan 0, Ohio State 34
1935: Ohio State 38, Michigan 0
1936: Michigan 0, Ohio State 21
1937: Ohio State 21, Michigan 0
1938: Michigan 18, Ohio State 0
1939: Ohio State 14, Michigan 21
1940: Michigan 40, Ohio State 0
1941: Ohio State 20, Michigan 20
1942: Michigan 7, Ohio State 21
1943: Ohio State 7, Michigan 45
1944: Michigan 14, Ohio State 18
1945: Ohio State 3, Michigan 7
1946: Michigan 58, Ohio State 6
1947: Ohio State 0, Michigan 21
1948: Michigan 13, Ohio State 3
1949: Ohio State 7, Michigan 7
1950: Michigan 9, Ohio State 3
1951: Ohio State 0, Michigan 7
1952: Michigan 7, Ohio State 27
1953: Ohio State 0, Michigan 20
1954: Michigan 7, Ohio State 21
1955: Ohio State 17, Michigan 0
1956: Michigan 19, Ohio State 0
1957: Ohio State 31, Michigan 14
1958: Michigan 14, Ohio State 20
1959: Ohio State 14, Michigan 23
1960: Michigan 0, Ohio State 7
1961: Ohio State 50, Michigan 20
1962: Michigan 0, Ohio State 28
1963: Ohio State 14, Michigan 10
1964: Michigan 10, Ohio State 0
1965: Ohio State 9, Michigan 7
1966: Michigan 17, Ohio State 3
1967: Ohio State 24, Michigan 14
1968: Michigan 14, Ohio State 50

1969: Ohio State 12, Michigan 24
1970: Michigan 9, Ohio State 20
1971: Ohio State 7, Michigan 10
1972: Michigan 11, Ohio State 14
1973: Ohio State 10, Michigan 10
1974: Michigan 10, Ohio State 12
1975: Ohio State 21, Michigan 14
1976: Michigan 22, Ohio State 0
1977: Ohio State 6, Michigan 14
1978: Michigan 14, Ohio State 3
1979: Ohio State 18, Michigan 15
1980: Michigan 9, Ohio State 3
1981: Ohio State 14, Michigan 9
1982: Michigan 14, Ohio State 24
1983: Ohio State 21, Michigan 24
1984: Michigan 6, Ohio State 21
1985: Ohio State 17, Michigan 27
1986: Michigan 26, Ohio State 24
1987: Ohio State 23, Michigan 20
1988: Michigan 34, Ohio State 31
1989: Ohio State 18, Michigan 28
1990: Michigan 16, Ohio State 13
1991: Ohio State 3, Michigan 31
1992: Michigan 13, Ohio State 13
1993: Ohio State 0, Michigan 28
1994: Michigan 6, Ohio State 22
1995: Ohio State 23, Michigan 31
1996: Michigan 13, Ohio State 9
1997: Ohio State 14, Michigan 20
1998: Michigan 16, Ohio State 31
1999: Ohio State 17, Michigan 24
2000: Michigan 38, Ohio State 26
2001: Ohio State 26, Michigan 20
2002: Michigan 9, Ohio State 14
2003: Ohio State 21, Michigan 35
2004: Michigan 21, Ohio State 37
2005: Ohio State 25, Michigan 21
2006: Michigan 39, Ohio State 42

2007: Ohio State 14, Michigan 3
2008: Michigan 7, Ohio State 42
2009: Ohio State 21, Michigan 10
2010: Michigan 7, Ohio State 37
2011: Ohio State 34, Michigan 40
2012: Michigan 21, Ohio State 26
2013: Ohio State 42, Michigan 41

Ohio State Bowl Game Appearances

1921 Rose Bowl: California 28, Ohio State 0
1950 Rose Bowl: Ohio State 17, California 14
1955 Rose Bowl: Ohio State 20, USC 7
1958 Rose Bowl: Ohio State 10, Oregon 7
1969 Rose Bowl: Ohio State 27, USC 16
1971 Rose Bowl: Stanford 27, Ohio State 17
1973 Rose Bowl: USC 42, Ohio State 17
1974 Rose Bowl: Ohio State 42, USC 21
1975 Rose Bowl: USC 18, Ohio State 17
1976 Rose Bowl: UCLA 23, Ohio State 10
1977 Orange Bowl: Ohio State 27, Colorado 10
1978 Sugar Bowl: Alabama 35, Ohio State 6
1978 Gator Bowl: Clemson 17, Ohio State 15
1980 Rose Bowl: USC 17, Ohio State 16
1981 Liberty Bowl: Ohio State 31, Navy 28
1982 Holiday Bowl: Ohio State 47, Brigham Young 17
1984 Fiesta Bowl: Ohio State 28, Pittsburgh 17
1985 Rose Bowl: USC 20, Ohio State 17
1985 Citrus Bowl: Ohio State 10, Brigham Young 7
1987 Cotton Bowl: Ohio State 28, Texas A&M 12
1990 Hall of Fame Bowl: Auburn 31, Ohio State 14
1992 Hall of Fame Bowl: Syracuse 24, Ohio State 17
1993 Citrus Bowl: Georgia 21, Ohio State 14
1993 Holiday Bowl: Ohio State 28, Brigham Young 21
1995 Citrus Bowl: Alabama 24, Ohio State 17
1996 Citrus Bowl: Tennessee 20, Ohio State 14
1997 Rose Bowl: Ohio State 20, Arizona 17
1998 Sugar Bowl: Florida State 31, Ohio State 14
1999 Sugar Bowl: Ohio State 24, Texas A&M 14

2001 Outback Bowl: South Carolina 24, Ohio State 7
2002 Outback Bowl: South Carolina 31, Ohio State 28
2003 Fiesta Bowl: Ohio State 31, Miami 24
2004 Fiesta Bowl: Ohio State 35, Kansas State 28
2004 Alamo Bowl: Ohio State 33, Oklahoma State 7
2006 Fiesta Bowl: Ohio State 34, Notre Dame 20
2007 BCS National Championship: Florida 41, Ohio State 14
2008 BCS National Championship: Louisiana State 38, Ohio State 4
2009 Fiesta Bowl: Texas 24, Ohio State 21
2010 Rose Bowl: Ohio State 26, Oregon 17
2011 Sugar Bowl: Ohio State 31, Alabama 26
2012 Gator Bowl: Florida 24, Ohio State 17
2014 Orange Bowl: Clemson 40, Ohio State 35

Michigan Bowl Game Appearances

1902 Rose Bowl: Michigan 49, Stanford 0
1948 Rose Bowl: Michigan 49, USC 0
1951 Rose Bowl: Michigan 14, California 6
1965 Rose Bowl: Michigan 34, Oregon State 7
1970 Rose Bowl: USC 10, Michigan 3
1972 Rose Bowl: Stanford 13, Michigan 12
1976 Orange Bowl: Oklahoma 14, Michigan 6
1977 Rose Bowl: USC 14, Michigan 6
1978 Rose Bowl: Washington 27, Michigan 20
1979 Rose Bowl: USC 17, Michigan 10
1979 Gator Bowl: North Carolina 17, Michigan 15
1981 Rose Bowl: Michigan 23, Washington 6
1981 Blue Bonnet Bowl: Michigan 33, UCLA 14
1983 Rose Bowl: UCLA 24, Michigan 14
1984 Sugar Bowl: Auburn 9, Michigan 7
1984 Holiday Bowl: Brigham Young 24, Michigan 17
1986 Fiesta Bowl: Michigan 27, Nebraska 23
1987 Rose Bowl: Arizona State 22, Michigan 15
1988 Hall of Fame Bowl: Michigan 28, Alabama 14
1989 Rose Bowl: Michigan 22, USC 14
1990 Rose Bowl: USC 17, Michigan 10
1991 Gator Bowl: Michigan 35, Mississippi 3
1992 Rose Bowl: Washington 34, Michigan 14

1993 Rose Bowl: Michigan 38, Washington 31

1994 Hall of Fame Bowl: Michigan 42, North Carolina State 7

1994 Holiday Bowl: Michigan 24, Colorado State 14

1995 Alamo Bowl: Texas A&M 22, Michigan 20

1997 Outback Bowl: Alabama 17, Michigan 14

1998 Rose Bowl: Michigan 21, Washington State 16

1999 Citrus Bowl: Michigan 45, Arkansas 31

2000 Orange Bowl: Michigan 35, Alabama 34

2001 Citrus Bowl: Michigan 31, Auburn 28

2002 Citrus Bowl: Tennessee 45, Michigan 17

2003 Outback Bowl: Michigan 38, Florida 30

2004 Rose Bowl: USC 28, Michigan 14

2005 Rose Bowl: Texas 38, Michigan 37

2005 Alamo Bowl: Nebraska 32, Michigan 28

2007 Rose Bowl: USC 32, Michigan 18

2008 Capital One Bowl: Michigan 41, Florida 35

2011 Gator Bowl: Mississippi State 52, Michigan 14

2012 Sugar Bowl: Michigan 23, Virginia Tech 20

2013 Outback Bowl: South Carolina 33, Michigan 23

2013 Buffalo Wild Wings Bowl: Kansas State 31, Michigan 14

2

ALABAMA VS. AUBURN: THE IRON BOWL

The game clock was still ticking. The players were still playing. The fans remained in the stands, though those rooting for Auburn were far quieter.

But the game was *over*. It had to be. Alabama led 16–3 with five minutes remaining in the game. And teams coached by the legendary Bear Bryant just didn't blow 16–3 leads in five minutes.

It was December 2, 1972. The Crimson Tide were undefeated and appeared destined to play for a national championship on New Year's Day. They were ranked second in the nation. Only one team—No. 10 Tennessee—had lost to them by fewer than 17 points. They were averaging 48.3 points in their previous four games and they boasted one of the premier defenses in the country.

The chances of Alabama losing the annual Iron Bowl at that point seemed as likely as Richard Nixon losing the presidential election to George McGovern a month earlier. That was a blowout, and the college football rivalry known as The Iron Bowl appeared destined for a similar conclusion.

But suddenly the Tide started to change. Alabama punter Greg Gantt lined up to boot the ball away. Auburn linebacker Bill Newton knew it might take defensive heroics to turn certain defeat into a miraculous victory. He had done his part already. He was en route to an amazing 21-tackle game. He had blocked a punt earlier in the year in the team's only defeat against Louisiana State and believed a repeat could get his team back into the game. He recalled that block when describing what happened next.

"We had on a similar type pass rush," Newton said. "I was rushing from the right side when I blocked the ball. I saw it bounce behind [Gantt]. [Defensive back David Langner] had broken through, but was pushed back to the outside on the right. The ball took a couple of bounces and it bounced up in his arms like a good bounce on the field in baseball. Thank goodness Langner was there; a lineman would have fallen on it and we still would never have scored. But he went into the end zone."[1]

Auburn had chopped its deficit to 16–10, but their archrivals still boasted a distinct advantage. The Tide needed just one or two first downs to ice the victory. That seemed quite likely considering their wishbone weaponry of all-world offensive lineman and future NFL standout John Hannah blocking for senior quarterback and Southeastern Conference Player of the Year Terry Davis. And even if they went three-and-out and punted, there would be precious little time for the Tigers to traverse the field for a touchdown. After all, they hadn't moved the ball past midfield on the stingy Alabama defense all afternoon. They had just seven first downs, 50 yards rushing, and 30 yards passing for the game. "We could have played all day and Auburn wouldn't have scored on our defense," offered Alabama linebacker Chuck Strickland.[2]

But when Auburn linebacker Mike Neel made a solo tackle on third down, the Tide was forced to punt again. The thought of another block, let alone one that resulted in a touchdown, could only creep into the fertile imaginations of Tigers fans hoping against hope. Even Newton believed that lightning striking twice was a virtual impossibility. He certainly didn't believe he could possibly play the role of hero again, even when Alabama lined up in the same blocking scheme it used for its punt earlier in the fourth quarter. Its protection collapsed on the first punt. Several Auburn rushers broke through; it was just that Newton made the block. Such a breakdown was wholly unlikely to happen twice. This was not the movie *Groundhog Day*.

"I did not ever feel I would have an opportunity to do it again," he admitted. "I figured to do my job and maybe somebody else could block it. This was not a Bill Newton pass rush."

Yeah, it was. Newton broke through again, stretched out his arms, and batted Gantt's boot. As if history repeated itself precisely, the ball again hopped into the eager hands of Langner, who sprinted into the end zone. The extra point gave Auburn a 17–16 lead.

"I did the same thing on both punts," explained Newton. "Instead of coming right at the tackle I lined up outside him and looped inside. Nobody touched me either time."[3]

The contrast in reactions was striking. Tigers coach Ralph Jordan leaped into the air on a jubilant sideline. The Tide stood in stunned silence. So did their home fans. The "Roll Tide Roll" cheer that had filled the air for two hours was nowhere to be heard.

Such a finish to an upset, which Newton clinched with an interception, would have been considered remarkable no matter the combatants. But that it was played between the two fiercest in-state rivals in the history of college football merely adds to the lore—never mind that Alabama recovered in 1973 to win the national championship. One must understand that there are no major professional sports teams in Alabama. College football is king. This is a rivalry that has motivated parents to skip their daughters' weddings to watch. This is an annual showdown that has been played during wakes and church services. This is a game that has been witnessed by women in labor in the hospital. The Iron Bowl is actually not a game. It is an event.

It is the Hatfields and McCoys of college football. And it all started on tiny Lakeview Baseball Park in Birmingham on the unlikely date of February 22, 1893. A crowd estimated between 4,000 and 5,000 arrived by train and other modes of transportation from throughout the state, forcing extra-ticket salesmen to spring into action. The media reported more about the buildup, excitement, and pageantry leading up to the gridiron clash than the game itself. Thanks to captain Tom Daniels, who scored two touchdowns, Auburn Agricultural and Mechanical College emerged with a sloppy 33–22 victory. And when it was over, a woman named Delma Wilson presented to Daniels a silver cup to commemorate the triumph.

"Gallant and victorious captain, in the name of the city of Birmingham I present you with this cup," she announced. "Drink from it and remember the victory that you have won this day. May you and your team live to see many more victories."[4]

Though the early games between the two teams were played with passion and intensity befitting rivals from the same state, they received little attention from fans or the media. The first era of Auburn–Alabama football was noteworthy only because the latter was coached by one John Heisman, for whom the most famous trophy in college football was named.

The Tigers, who have also been known as the War Eagles and Plainsmen, dominated the first meetings. In the four games between 1895 and 1902—they did not play from 1896 to 1899—Auburn emerged victorious in each by a combined score of 141–5. But the rivalry was not long for the college football world. What seemed like a small disagreement over how much to pay players for their services in an era well before the NCAA shut off all disbursements caused a long lull in the annual competition. The difference between what the two schools wanted to offer was a mere 50 cents per player, but that was enough to create a rift that would last four decades. The teams did not meet on the field again until 1948 despite the fact that both played in the same conference for well over a century.

Several attempts to revive the rivalry proved fruitless. Auburn president Dr. Spright Dowell offered that an Alabama–Auburn showdown would prove so meaningful that it would render meaningless the rest of the schedule. He was not alone in his lack of foresight. The potential of intense rivalries, geographic and otherwise, for bolstering the competitive spirit in college football could scarcely be imagined during Dowell's tenure in the 1920s.

One can only speculate as to the results of clashes between the two schools in particular seasons or periods. Suffice it to say that there would likely have been battles that would have gone down as classics. Both teams enjoyed immense success in various eras, including the one immediately following the breakdown of the series before World War I. Neither team suffered through a losing season from 1907 to 1917. The Tigers remained unbeaten in 1913 and 1914 to win successive Southern Intercollegiate Athletic Conference crowns and won a national title in the first of those years. The Crimson Tide snagged the title from 1924 to 1926 with a combined record of 27–1–1 under College Football Hall of Fame coach Wallace Wade and was generally accepted as the national champion in both of those seasons.

The Tigers had slid into mediocrity by that time. They rose and fell like a roller coaster as the Great Depression descended upon the nation. They compiled a shocking record of 6–29–2 from 1927 to 1930, won what was then known as the Southern Conference in 1930 with an unbeaten mark, continued to win for a short time, and then collapsed. Auburn managed no better than a 6–4–1 record from 1938 to 1949 and managed a 43–57–9 mark during that period.

Alabama, which steamrolled from 1904 to 1951 without a losing record, proved far more successful in the 1930s and 1940s under coach Frank Thomas, who followed Wade into the Hall of Fame. They captured national championships in 1934, 1941, and 1945. They earned conference titles in 1933, 1934, 1937, and 1945. Unlike Auburn, which earned lesser bowl bids in 1936 and 1937, the Crimson Tide were frequent postseason bowl participants. They won the Rose Bowl twice, as well as the Cotton Bowl and Orange Bowl from 1934 to 1942.

The fans of both teams lost opportunities to watch many of the premier standouts of the college game, particularly at quarterback and running back. College Football Hall of Famers at those positions, such as Johnny Mack Brown, Pooley Hubert, Riley Smith, Johnny Cain, Harry Gilmer, and Dixie Howell, peppered the Alabama roster, while stars like end Jimmy Hitchcock, running back Mark Gifford, and quarterback Travis Tidwell shone brightly for Auburn.

When the guns stopped firing and the bombs stopped dropping overseas in World War II, the fact that there were no battles fought between the Tigers and Crimson Tide seemed more senseless than ever. The first to reach out was Auburn, which suggested a continuation of the series in 1944. But they were shunned by the Alabama Board of Trustees, which claimed it feared too much emphasis on football at their school and added that such an intense rivalry would result in the loss of coaches emotionally damaged by the sting of such defeats.

The pressure to rekindle the annual clash became far too great to ignore by the end of the decade. The state legislature supported the Tide and the Tigers renewing their rivalry. That motivated a meeting between University of Alabama president John Gallalee and Auburn counterpart Ralph Draughon, during which it was indeed decided to shine up the rusty Iron Bowl and bring the annual battle back to life.

Trouble was feared from the student bodies on both sides leading up to the game scheduled for December 4, 1948. Notorious Birmingham

police commissioner Bull Connor, whose name later became synonymous with the racist, violent segregationist actions in his city during the
civil rights movement, summoned three students from both schools and
warned them against starting any fights or riots. But all the return of
The Iron Bowl would be remembered for was the most lopsided score
in its history—55–0—in favor of the Crimson Tide. It came as little
surprise considering the Tigers were muddling through a 1–8–1 season.

The spark that really rekindled the rivalry was lit stunningly the
following year. Alabama entered with a 6–2–1 record and Auburn was
1–4–3. But the Tigers had the All-American Tidwell, who had established scoring records that would remain in the annals of Auburn football history until Pat Sullivan shattered them in the late 1960s. It was
running back Bill Davis who played the role of hero, however, for the
Tigers. His 11-yard touchdown run in the fourth quarter proved to be
the winning score in a 14–13 upset. The Tide scored on their final
possession, but a missed extra point doomed them to defeat and made
Auburn coach Earl Brown a hero in Birmingham. "Brown would have
run for governor after that game," Tidwell remarked. "He was king of
the state."

Well, Brown would likely have received few votes in the Tuscaloosa
area, home of the Crimson Tide. And his popularity even in Birmingham proved quite fleeting. He was unceremoniously canned after a
winless 1951 season but would always be remembered despite his hor-
rible three-year record of 3–22–4 for coaching Auburn to a victory that
launched The Iron Bowl in earnest.

Legendary replacement Shug Jordan would emerge as the most successful coach in school history. The joke before Jordan arrived was that
"Auburn" stood for "Alabama Usually Beats Us 'Round November." He
immediately transformed the Tigers into national championship contenders in the 1950s, while Alabama suffered through the first dry spell
in the history of its program under coach Jennings B. Whitworth, who
guided the team to a stunning 0–10 record in 1955 and a 4–24–2 mark
from that year through 1957.

The contrast between the two programs in that year of Sputnik and
Elvis Presley was striking. Auburn raced to its first 10–0 record, winning the SEC and national championship behind a defense that yielded
just 28 points all season and pitched six shutouts. The impotent Crimson Tide were blanked five times. It raised nary an eyebrow when they

lost to the Tigers, 40–0. The axe was about to fall on Whitworth. Alabama soon began looking for a successor. A hopeful eye was cast on the son of a poor farmer from rural Arkansas who had played end at Alabama a generation earlier and had even suited up for one game in 1935 with a broken leg. His name was Paul "Bear" Bryant.

Bryant had earned a reputation as a strict disciplinarian during his short tenure, turning around what had been a terrible program at Texas A&M. During one summer practice upon his arrival there in 1954, he packed 48 players onto two buses and took them to Junction, Texas, for what amounted to a football boot camp. Bryant installed a "my way or the highway" mind-set among his players, 19 of whom did not take the highway back with the team. Bryant had weeded out those who could not handle what he considered a character-building process.

His strategy worked. He transformed the Aggies from one of the worst teams in the Southwestern Conference to the best in just three years. His team finished last in his first season and first in his third with a 9–0–1 record. After his fourth season, Alabama came calling. He met with outgoing athletic director Hank Crisp, his former assistant coach with the Crimson Tide, at a Houston hotel. Crisp assured Bryant he would replace him as athletic director and serve as the head football coach at Alabama. That was all Bryant needed to hear. He announced his departure from Texas A&M by telling his players, "Gentlemen, I've heard Mama calling, and now I'm going home." Bear Bryant was about to embark on arguably the most successful coaching tenure in the history of college football.[5]

The Alabama–Auburn rivalry would never be the same. The Crimson Tide won five games under Bryant in his first year—one more than their previous three seasons combined. After five consecutive defeats to the Tigers from 1954 to 1958, they won nine of the next 10. Alabama yielded 142 points in the five losses and zero in four consecutive victories that followed. Bryant had made a point of developing a tough and disciplined defense. Mission accomplished.

Bryant also thrived on recruiting players outside of Alabama, while Jordan maintained his focus in state. That gave the Crimson Tide a distinct advantage in the recruiting war. But one player Bryant landed from tiny Excel, a small town down the road from Mobile, proved to be arguably the finest in the history of the program. That was linebacker and center Lee Roy Jordan, whom Bryant considered the best talent he had ever coached. Jordan, who went on to a five-time Pro Bowl career with the Dallas Cowboys, led a 1961 defense that took Alabama football to new heights. The top-ranked unit in the nation yielded a mere 2.3 points a game and pitched six shutouts, including a 34–0 thrashing of Auburn that avenged a similar shutout by the Tigers four years earlier. A 10–3 victory over Arkansas in the Sugar Bowl clinched their first national championship since 1943 and first with an unbeaten record in 27 years. The Crimson Tide outscored their opponents 297–25 that season. The field goal they surrendered to the Razorbacks marked the first time they were scored upon in six weeks.

The greatness of both teams in the early 1960s heightened the intensity of the rivalry. The Tigers interrupted an era of Alabama dominance in the series in 1963 with a 10–8 victory that launched them ahead of the Tide in the national rankings and gave them an outside shot at the national championship that slipped away in an Orange Bowl loss to Nebraska. But Alabama got its revenge the following year behind a brash, missile-throwing quarterback named Joe Namath.

The 1964 Crimson Tide were not as dominant as their 1961 brethren. But they won all their close games during the regular season and entered with a 9–0 record against an Auburn team suffering through a down year. The Tigers gave the Tide a greater tussle than did fellow Southeastern Conference foes Florida, Louisiana State, and Georgia Tech, all of which were ranked in the top 10 in the nation when they played Alabama.

It was before that game that a moniker for the rivalry that accentuated the iron and steel industry in Birmingham first fell into widespread use. Jordan was speaking to his charges about bowl possibilities when one player chimed in that the only bowl his team was worried about was The Iron Bowl. Jordan liked the sound of it and began using the name on his television show. It soon spread throughout the state.

The Tigers were especially fired up to try to knock Alabama out of the unbeaten ranks in 1964. And the Crimson Tide understood that the Tigers stood in their way of another national crown. But Tucker Frederickson, an All-American back for Auburn who went on to a standout career with the New York Giants, explained that the passion against the Crimson Tide extended beyond the football field.

"We were always the little brother," Frederickson said. "They thought they were a step up socially from us. Auburn is a more agriculturally oriented college, and that was always thrown up at us. They looked down on us."[6]

They might have still been looking down on Auburn but with a bit more respect after the 1964 clash, which was the first in the series to be nationally televised. A sellout throng of 68,000 at Legion Field was split on both sides of the stadium between allegiances. The Tigers played the Tide tough throughout but could not overcome a kickoff return for a touchdown by Ray Ogden or a scoring strike from Namath to future Alabama coach Ray Perkins that gave their team a 21–7 lead in the fourth quarter. Final score: Alabama 21, Auburn 14.

The Crimson Tide was so strong that season that the victory clinched their second national title in four years despite an Orange Bowl match-up looming against Texas. Alabama lost that game, 21–17, to the Longhorns and were still deemed champions of the college football world. The Tide had emerged under Bryant as the most powerful program in the sport. The departure of Namath didn't prevent the Tide from overcoming an opening-game loss to Georgia in 1965 to go unbeaten the rest of the way. They clobbered Auburn, which somehow finished second in the SEC that season despite its first non-winning season since 1952, and knocked off Nebraska in the Orange Bowl to win its third crown in five years.

What became known as the Backyard Brawl was becoming an annual bashing by Alabama. And it continued in a 31–0 shutout in 1966, when Bryant had assembled perhaps his finest team. The Tide swept through the season undefeated and capped it with a 34–7 thrashing of Nebraska in the Sugar Bowl. But despite the immense talents of future NFL standout quarterback Ken Stabler, who had followed Namath behind center, as well as Perkins, stalwart center Cecil Dowdy, and defensive back Bobby Johns, a year that also featured other unbeaten teams relegated the Tide to third in the nation in the final national rankings behind Notre Dame and Michigan State.

That Alabama entered the season as a defending national champion, steamrolled through every opponent, and still finished third in the rankings was a slap in the face to some but a reflection of their segregationist policies to many voters who placed them behind the Fighting Irish and Spartans. Among those who believed that the Crimson Tide were cheated out of the national crown in 1966 was Bryant biographer Keith Dunnavant, who expressed his feelings in the following excerpt from his

2006 book, *The Missing Ring: How Bear Bryant and the 1966 Crimson Tide Were Denied College Football's Most Elusive Prize*:

> In the history of college football, no other team has ever won back-to-back national championships, finished undefeated and untied, and been denied the title. In the history of college football, no other team has ever been ranked No. 1 in the preseason poll, finished perfect, and then been denied the title. If the situation had been reversed, and Notre Dame was undefeated and bidding for a third consecutive title, the Fighting Irish most certainly would have been ranked No. 1.[7]

Though Bryant was making overtures at integrating his team by that time, Jordan beat him to the punch by adding a black player in 1969. It wasn't until the following year that Bryant integrated his team.

The frustration peaked for the Tigers after their 7–3 loss to Alabama in 1967, in which they dominated for three quarters only to lose it on a 47-yard touchdown pass by Stabler in the fourth. It marked their eighth loss in nine years—they would lose again to the Tide in 1968—and they had no answers. Jordan certainly didn't, and he expressed his exasperation following the game. "I really don't know what to say," Jordan told the *Birmingham News*. "I've been around long enough to know the only thing that counts is what you read on the scoreboard lights. . . . But I really don't think the best team won today."[8]

One significant difference between the two programs through most of the 1960s was that Alabama boasted two All-American quarterbacks in Namath and Stabler while Auburn struggled to move the ball through the air. The college game was changing and the Tigers had to change along with it to keep up with their archrivals. So Jordan recruited a quarterback from Banks High School in Birmingham named Pat Sullivan. The result was a dramatic turnabout in the fortunes of the Tigers and The Iron Bowl.

Jordan actually began opening up the offense with Loran Carter at quarterback in 1967 and 1968. Sullivan threw virtually the same number of passes in 1969 as Carter did the previous year. He just passed with far better accuracy and efficiency. Sullivan shattered school passing records from 1969 to 1971, during which time he threw for 6,530 yards and 54 touchdowns. His Tigers roared to a 26–7 record in those seasons and maintained a top-20 national ranking throughout. And in the process they ended The Iron Bowl dominance of their in-state rivals with victories in 1969 and 1970.

The turnaround was all too temporary for Auburn fans. Bear Bryant recruited some of the premier talent to ever grace a college football field in the early 1970s, and the result was a perennial national championship contender and Iron Bowl winner. The Crimson Tide forged a record of 109–13 from 1971 to 1980 and lost to the Tigers only in the "Punt, Bama, Punt" fiasco of 1972 during that stretch. They included future NFL Hall of Famers, such as tight end Ozzie Newsome and offensive linemen Dwight Stephenson and John Hannah. That trio, as well as such All-American stalwarts as running back Wilbur Jackson, cornerbacks Don McNeal and Jeremiah Castille, tackle Marty Lyons, and linebacker Barry Krauss helped Alabama win the Southeastern Conference championships in nine of those 11 years, including five straight from 1971 to 1975.

The Tide provided a portent of their dominance to come against Auburn in their Iron Bowl showdown of 1971, into which both teams entered unbeaten and untied and ranked in the top five in the nation. Sullivan had just learned that he had won the Heisman Trophy but didn't play like a trophy winner, as his team was held scoreless in the second half, turning a close game into a surprising 31–7 rout. Bryant had his team so inspired to avenge the 1972 loss to the Tigers that even usually staid All-American running back Jackson went "absolutely berserk" before the game, according to teammate Sylvester Croom.[9] Only a lopsided loss in the Orange Bowl prevented Alabama from winning yet another national championship.

A 28–0 loss to the Tide in 1975 proved to be the final game for Jordan, who retired after that season and handpicked offensive coordinator Doug Barfield as his replacement. Barfield's teams were not only clobbered five straight times by Alabama by a combined score of 179–80, but he could not maintain the consistent excellence forged by his predecessor. The Tigers slipped into mediocrity under Barfield, whose teams recorded an uncharacteristic 29–25 mark before he was replaced by Pat Dye. The Tide finished off their run of nine straight wins over Auburn in his first year. It was an annual torture for the Tigers and their fans. Alabama had become their Moby Dick. Among the tormented was former athletic director David Housel.

"Nine straight? Pure living hell," said Housel, whose wedding ring bears the words "BEAT BAMA." "Some people at Auburn were scarred forever because of that nine-year streak. Those people who were Auburn fans before 1981 and you mention the Alabama game, they would get tight, antsy and nervous." Adding off-the-field insult to on-the-field injury, Tide fans referred to Auburn as the "Cow College."[10]

Simply put, the Tigers needed talent. They were not only outcoached by Bryant and the Tide, particularly in the Barfield era, but they also didn't boast the weaponry to win the annual war. But while the legendary Bryant was readying for retirement in the early 1980s, Dye was setting out to recruit talent. And he attracted to his school the best skill position player in the history of The Iron Bowl and one of the greatest all-around athletes to ever grace a football field. His name was Bo Jackson.

Bryant saw enough of Jackson in his swan song of 1982. The freshman rushed for 114 yards and soared into the end zone for the winning touchdown in a 23–22 triumph that allowed the Tigers and their fans to regale for the first time since 1972. Dye exclaimed after the game that he heard Auburn alumni joke that they had grown accustomed to celebrating first downs against Alabama in lieu of any hope for a victory. But Jackson was changing the culture. He gave Bryant replacement and former Alabama standout Ray Perkins the opportunity to lament his immense talent in 1983 by single-handedly destroying the Crimson Tide to the tune of 256 yards rushing. The final score of 23–20 was achieved on a 71-yard Jackson touchdown run, which eclipsed by two yards his scoring jaunt earlier in the game. The victory clinched an undefeated league record and Southeastern Conference championship. The Tigers went on to beat Michigan in the Sugar Bowl and earn a No. 3 national ranking, their highest since the national championship season of 1957.

It seemed fitting that Bryant was not around to see his beloved Tide fall for a second straight season to their archrivals. One month after coaching Alabama to a Liberty Bowl victory in 1982 and retired, he died of a heart attack at age 69. One friend offered that he had nothing to live for if he wasn't coaching. His passing brought immense pressure on Perkins to live up to his memory. It was an impossible task.

"There was no way anybody could replace Bear Bryant or do anything that would have the fans view him the same way," said Van Tiffin, who served as placekicker for Perkins at Auburn in the mid-1980s. "The expectations were as if Bear Bryant were still coaching. That made it difficult. There was some rejection of coach Perkins, for the simple fact that he was not Bear Bryant."[11]

The diminutive Tiffin played Jekyll-Hyde in his quest to help Perkins. He missed two field goals in a downpour in 1983 to contribute mightily to the Alabama defeat. He sought to make up for it in 1985 if given the chance. Both teams had already lost twice, so there was no SEC or national title on the line. But this was The Iron Bowl. Everything was on the line. Alabama forged ahead 13–0 in the second quarter on a second Tiffin field goal. But Jackson, who was playing with two cracked ribs, scored a touchdown. A third Tiffin field goal followed, and the Tide led 16–10 at halftime.

A seesaw second half was on the verge of falling against Alabama when Auburn pulled ahead, 23–22, with 57 seconds remaining. The Crimson Tide took over on their own 20-yard line but promptly moved backward. On 3rd-and-18 from the 12, quarterback David Shula, son of legendary NFL coach Don Shula, threw a 16-yard pass, then Al Bell sprinted 20 yards on a fourth-down reverse. A Shula pass to Greg Richardson placed the ball on the Tigers' 35. On came Tiffin, who had booted one as long as 57 yards that season. But this 52-yard attempt was the greatest pressure kick of all. It was for one year of bragging rights in the state of Alabama. Tiffin booted the ball cleanly, and it dropped through the uprights. Game over. Alabama 25, Auburn 23. It was a moment he would never forget. And it really was a dream come true.

"I thought about making a big kick in that game," Tiffin said. "I thought about it a lot. When it comes down to the reality of the situation, though, you're not sure you want to be there. When you're dreaming about it, you don't ever think what would happen if you missed it." But Tiffin didn't miss it. And all Perkins could shout to him when it was over was, "I love you, Van Tiffin!"[12]

It would be the last time an Alabama coach would be celebrating a victory over Auburn until the following decade. Perkins bolted for the NFL Tampa Bay Buccaneers after a loss to the Tigers in 1986, and replacement Bill Curry was jettisoned after three straight Iron Bowl defeats. But they were far from alone in falling victim to the talented Auburn team of that era that lost all of two Southeastern Conference games from 1987 and 1989 in winning three consecutive league championships. The Tigers were loaded with talent but none greater than All-American defensive tackle Tracy Rocker, who became the first SEC player to win an Outland Trophy and Lombardi Award in the same season. Rocker earned Defensive Player of the Year honors in the conference in 1988.

The last victory in the four-year run in 1989 was particularly special because it was played in Auburn for the first time. The Iron Bowl had been in Birmingham from 1904 to 1988, with the schools switching off as home teams despite the fact that the city rests far closer to the Tide's Tuscaloosa home than the town of Auburn. But when Auburn expanded its Jordan–Hare Stadium to accommodate 87,000 fans, The Iron Bowl became a true home-and-home series. The Tigers celebrated playing on their own campus for the first time that year by extending their winning streak against Alabama to four with a 30–20 victory. In the process, they knocked the Tide from the ranks of the unbeaten and destroyed their national title hopes while forging a tie with them for a third straight SEC championship. Not bad for the first real Iron Bowl in Auburn's backyard. Dye referred to it as the most emotional day in school history.[13]

The emotions were quite the opposite in Tuscaloosa and for Alabama fans everywhere. The calls for Curry's job were raised to a fever pitch and the school accommodated by forcing him out despite the 10–0 start to the season and tie for the league crown. The position of head coach for arguably the most prestigious football program in America is a powerful lure—and it lured former Bear Bryant assistant Gene Stallings back to the school. Stallings had spent 25 years coaching in the NFL before returning to Alabama in 1990. His first year was a struggle, but while Dye was wearing out his welcome at Auburn with back-to-back five-win seasons in the early 1990s, Stallings was building one of the greatest teams in Crimson Tide history.

Alabama won 28 consecutive games from 1991 to 1993 behind a stalwart defense. The Tide peaked in 1992 with a 13–0 record highlighted by a 17–0 shutout of Auburn. The Iron Bowl was tied at halftime, but standout Alabama cornerback Antonio Langham intercepted a pass in the third quarter and ran it back 61 yards for a touchdown to provide all the scoring his team needed. The Tide followed with an SEC title-game victory over Florida and 34–13 domination of Miami that clinched their first undisputed national championship since 1979.

But the pendulum of temporary domination that had defined The Iron Bowl for generations stopped swinging for the rest of the decade. The enormous talent of future NFL Pro Bowl wide receiver Frank Sanders helped Auburn steamroll to a 13–0 record in 1993 and break its three-game losing streak to the Tide under new coach Terry Bowden. Bowden had replaced Dye, who was forced out under the weight of an NCAA investigation of player payments by boosters that grew so controversial it was featured on *60 Minutes*. But the teams traded triumphs into the next decade—Alabama managed the only two-game Iron Bowl winning streak in 1998 and 1999 during the next eight years.

One reason that neither dominated was that both fell into rare periods of mediocrity. The Tigers managed a national ranking higher than 14th just once from 1995 to 2003 and bottomed out at 3–8 under Bowden in 1998 in the first of two consecutive losing seasons. The Tide slide began in earnest in 1997. Three coaches and seven years later, they had a 51–46 record during that stretch, with marks of 4–7 (1997), 3–8 (2000), 4–9 (2003), and 6–6 (2004) behind them. Alabama fans hadn't experienced such a run of ordinary teams since the Jennings Whitworth period of the 1950s that ushered in the Bear Bryant era. Though winning The Iron Bowls of the late 1990s and early 2000s remained a source of pride, the fact that most often nothing but that pride was on the line caused the annual clash to lose some of its luster.

Yet even in seasons in which neither team had lived up to its glorious past, the loser of The Iron Bowl was forced to carry the burden for one year, during which its fans would prove to be a constant reminder that the following year had to be different. The players on both teams were either driven by their followers to exact revenge or maintain supremacy from the moment the final tick went off the clock in The Iron Bowl. Their fans wouldn't allow them to think any other way because they too were the subjects of ridicule when their team lost.

"If the players play hard and lose, they can at least walk off the field and live with themselves," Bowden said. "But that's not the way it is with the fans. In this state, it's the difference between being the brunt of jokes at the office all year and being the guy that tells them."[14]

Auburn and Alabama traded periods of greatness in the new century. The first to emerge from the doldrums suddenly and unexpectedly were the Tigers under coach Tommy Tuberville in 2004. His teams had lost at least four games every year since he arrived in 1999. But with prolific quarterback Jason Campbell, running back Cadillac Williams (who helped save Tuberville's job with a 204-yard explosion in a 2003 win over Alabama), and All-American defensive back Carlos Rogers leading the way, the Tigers buried foe after foe by an average of three touchdowns a game despite a schedule peppered by four nationally ranked teams.

The struggling Crimson Tide wasn't among them—they were on their way to a 6–6 season—but they showed their Iron Bowl pride by forging a 6–0 halftime lead over Auburn before the Tigers clawed back for a 21–13 victory. The Tigers' march to greatness concluded with an SEC title-game win over Tennessee and Sugar Bowl defeat of Virginia Tech that inched them up to No. 2 in the final national rankings.

Alabama could not seem to find a coach that could replicate the same consistency of greatness as Bryant and Stallings. Ray Perkins, Mike Dubose, Dennis Franchione, and Mike Shula all enjoyed occasional fine seasons, but Crimson Tide football had defined sustained college football prominence since Bryant took over in 1958. Six coaches had come and gone since Bryant retired in 1982, and only Stallings reached that level of success.

Soon Nick Saban would be added to the list. Shula was fired after a 2006 season in which the Tide managed their fifth non-winning record in the past 10 years. Alabama hired Saban away from the NFL Miami Dolphins. His career had been one long yo-yo ride from the college to pro ranks and back. But Saban found a home at Alabama as arguably its finest recruiter ever. He lured such premier skill position players as running backs Mark Ingram, Trent Richardson, and Eddie Lacy and wide receivers Julio Jones and Brandon Gibson to the school, as well as defensive standouts, such as linebacker Rolando McClain and tackle Marcell Dareus. Tide athletes recruited by Saban peppered the All-American teams and made immediate impacts on the NFL.

The result was the most significant long-term run of national contention for Alabama since the early 1990s. While their archrivals were struggling in 2009 following the resignation of Tuberville and hiring of first-year coach Gene Chizik, the Crimson Tide were embarking on one of their finest seasons. They manhandled such ranked teams as Virginia Tech, Mississippi, and South Carolina and reached Iron Bowl week unbeaten against an Auburn team that was destined for a fifth-place finish in the Southeastern Conference. But, as one might expect, the

Tigers gave the Tide their toughest tussle of the season. They bolted to a 14–0 lead and remained ahead 21–14 in the third quarter. Two Tide field goals chopped it to 21–20, but it took a late fourth-quarter drive and four-yard touchdown pass from Greg McElroy and Roy Upchurch with just over a minute remaining in the game, as well as a stout defensive stand in the closing minute, for Alabama to pull victory from the jaws of defeat and maintain their perfect season and national championship hopes.

It was the ideal Iron Bowl in which, as the old sports chestnut goes, the records could have been thrown out the window. Such maxims are often proven untrue, where the team with more talent most often emerges victorious. But the underdog always gives his all, and even the heaviest favorite must brace for a battle. Such was the case in 2009 and Chizik expressed no dissatisfaction to his players or to the media after the final tick of the game clock had doomed his team to defeat.

"I just told them that we're not walking out of here with our heads down," he said. "We're a family. We're a family when we win. We're a family when we lose. Everybody in that locker room that played did what we asked them to do. They fought for 60 minutes in that game. I'm not disappointed with anybody on our team. Nobody."[15]

Chizik and his Tigers would exact their revenge in 2010 after the Tide had secured their first national crown since 1992 with a 37–21 defeat of Texas in the BCS National Championship Game. Auburn rode two of the most overwhelming talents in the history of the college game to the same achievement. Dual-threat quarterback Cam Newton displayed his brilliance as a passer and runner with 2,854 yards through the air and 1,473 on the ground on the way to a Heisman Trophy, while defensive tackle Nick Fairley contributed a whopping 24 tackles for losses and 11½ sacks. It was no wonder that the Tigers climbed all season up the national rankings after starting at 22nd. Their victories were not taut struggles. They were slaughters. Opposing offenses simply could not keep up with Auburn, which averaged 41.7 points per game.

There were exceptions, games in which the Tigers were challenged. And, not surprisingly, the clash against the ninth-ranked Crimson Tide proved the toughest of all. History was made in 2010. No Auburn team had ever overcome a 24-point deficit to beat Alabama. But Newton and his Tigers did just that after the Tide washed over them with three touchdowns in the first quarter and a field goal midway through the second. Auburn appeared doomed, its national title hopes dashed as more than 100,000 fans in Tuscaloosa watched in disbelief. His team had been outgained by a ridiculous 314–2 count.

But Newton did not lead what could be described as a methodical comeback. While an oft-criticized Auburn defense stemmed the Tide, he fired salvos with touchdown passes of 36 and 70 yards, then scored on a one-yard run to cut the deficit to 24–21. The Tigers completed the rally with 12 minutes remaining in the game on a seven-yard scoring strike from Newton to Philip Lutzenkirchen, and the defense did the rest. Final score: Auburn 28, Alabama 27. It was among the most memorable Iron Bowls in the illustrious history of the annual event.

The Tide would roll back—they always have. They won national championships in 2011 and 2012, outscoring comparatively weak Auburn teams by a combined score of 91–14 in those two seasons. The Tigers, in fact, finished with a 3–9 record in 2012, their worst mark in 60 years. It was the most lopsided two-year stretch in the history of the rivalry. But Auburn rebounded for a fine 2013, which should surprise nobody. History tells us that neither the Tide nor the Tigers ever stay down long.

The battle that season proved to be epic. The undefeated and top-ranked Crimson Tide appeared destined to play yet again in the BCS Championship Game, but the once-beaten Tigers stood in their way. The game was tied at 28–28 when Saban called upon freshman place-kicker Adam Griffith to attempt a 57-yard bomb for the win. Auburn coach Gus Malzahn placed Chris Davis in the end zone just in case the ball traveled short. The only hope since the game clock had ticked off was a touchdown return. The odds against it were astronomical.

The kick indeed dropped just short of the goalpost. Davis caught it nine yards into the end zone and sprinted down the left sideline, then toward the middle of the field. His blocking was superb. The Tide was taken by surprise, as if they never believed a runback was possible. Davis ran 109 yards untouched for the score that knocked Alabama out and placed them into the title clash against Florida State.

There was much to celebrate for the Tigers. But that celebration was not just about the opportunity to play for a national championship, which they eventually lost. That is not what makes The Iron Bowl easily the greatest in-state rivalry in college football. Rather, it's the passion, the Alabama brother against Alabama brother. The words of short-lived Alabama coach Bill Curry explains it all. "When I first went to Alabama, I had some death threats because people from Alabama didn't want an Atlanta boy coaching their team," he said. "Our minister from back in Georgia was concerned and he called to see if we were okay. My wife said, 'Football is like religion here.' My minister said, 'It's more important.' He's right. It's more important than anything else in their lives."[16]

Only an Alabaman can truly understand.

Fact Box (through 2013)
   Nickname: The Iron Bowl
   Trophy: The Foy-ODK Sportsmanship Award
   Total meetings: 78
   Series record: Alabama leads, 42–35–1
   First meeting: 1893 (Auburn 32, Alabama 22)
   Largest margin of victory: Alabama, 1948 (Alabama 55, Auburn 0)
   Longest winning streak: Alabama, 9 (1973–1981)

Game Results (home team listed second unless at a neutral site)
   1893: Auburn 32, Alabama 22
   1893: Alabama 16, Auburn 40
   1894: Alabama 18, Auburn 0
   1895: Auburn 48, Alabama 0
   1900: Alabama 5, Auburn 53
   1901: Auburn 17, Alabama 0
   1902: Auburn 23, Alabama 0
   1903: Alabama 18, Auburn 6
   1904: Auburn 29, Alabama 5
   1905: Alabama 30, Auburn 0
   1906: Alabama 10, Auburn 0
   1907: Auburn 6, Alabama 6
   1948: Alabama 55, Auburn 0
   1949: Auburn 14, Alabama 13
   1950: Alabama 34, Auburn 0
   1951: Alabama 25, Auburn 7
   1952: Alabama 21, Auburn 0
   1953: Alabama 10, Auburn 7

1954: Auburn 28, Alabama 0
1955: Auburn 26, Alabama 0
1956: Auburn 34, Alabama 7
1957: Auburn 40, Alabama 0
1958: Auburn 14, Alabama 8
1959: Alabama 10, Auburn 0
1960: Alabama 3, Auburn 0
1961: Alabama 34, Auburn 0
1962: Alabama 38, Auburn 0
1963: Auburn 10, Alabama 8
1964: Alabama 21, Auburn 14
1965: Alabama 30, Auburn 3
1966: Alabama 31, Auburn 0
1967: Alabama 7, Auburn 3
1968: Alabama 24, Auburn 16
1969: Auburn 49, Alabama 26
1970: Auburn 33, Alabama 28
1971: Alabama 31, Auburn 7
1972: Auburn 17, Alabama 16
1973: Alabama 35, Auburn 0
1974: Alabama 17, Auburn 13
1975: Alabama 28, Auburn 0
1976: Alabama 38, Auburn 7
1977: Alabama 48, Auburn 21
1978: Alabama 34, Auburn 16
1979: Alabama 25, Auburn 18
1980: Alabama 34, Auburn 18
1981: Alabama 28, Auburn 17
1982: Auburn 23, Alabama 22
1983: Auburn 23, Alabama 20
1984: Alabama 17, Auburn 15
1985: Alabama 25, Auburn 23
1986: Auburn 21, Alabama 17
1987: Auburn 10, Alabama 0
1988: Auburn 15, Alabama 10
1989: Alabama 20, Auburn 30
1990: Alabama 16, Auburn 7
1991: Alabama 13, Auburn 6

1992: Alabama 17, Auburn 0
1993: Alabama 14, Auburn 22
1994: Alabama 21, Auburn 14
1995: Alabama 27, Auburn 31
1996: Alabama 24, Auburn 23
1997: Alabama 17, Auburn 18
1998: Alabama 31, Auburn 17
1999: Alabama 28, Auburn 17
2000: Auburn 9, Alabama 0
2001: Auburn 7, Alabama 31
2002: Auburn 17, Alabama 7
2003: Alabama 23, Auburn 28
2004: Auburn 21, Alabama 13
2005: Alabama 18, Auburn 28
2006: Auburn 22, Alabama 15
2007: Alabama 10, Auburn 17
2008: Auburn 0, Alabama 36
2009: Alabama 26, Auburn 21
2010: Auburn 28, Alabama 27
2011: Alabama 42, Auburn 14
2012: Auburn 0, Alabama 49
2013: Alabama 28, Auburn 34

Alabama Bowl Game Appearances

1926 Rose Bowl: Alabama 20, Washington 19
1927 Rose Bowl: Alabama 7, Stanford 7
1931 Rose Bowl: Alabama 24, Washington State 0
1935 Rose Bowl: Alabama 29, Stanford 13
1938 Rose Bowl: California 13, Alabama 0
1942 Cotton Bowl: Alabama 29, California 21
1943 Orange Bowl: Alabama 37, Boston College 21
1945 Sugar Bowl: Duke 29, Alabama 26
1946 Rose Bowl: Alabama 29, USC 26
1948 Sugar Bowl: Texas 27, Alabama 7
1953 Orange Bowl: Alabama 61, Syracuse 6
1954 Cotton Bowl: Rice 28, Alabama 6
1959 Liberty Bowl: Penn State 7, Alabama 0
1960 Bluebonnet Bowl: Texas 3, Alabama 3

1962 Sugar Bowl: Alabama 10, Arkansas 3
1963 Orange Bowl: Alabama 17, Oklahoma 0
1964 Sugar Bowl: Alabama 10, Mississippi 7
1965 Orange Bowl: Texas 21, Alabama 17
1966 Orange Bowl: Alabama 39, Nebraska 28
1967 Sugar Bowl: Alabama 34, Nebraska 7
1968 Cotton Bowl: Texas A&M 20, Alabama 16
1968 Gator Bowl: Missouri 35, Alabama 10
1969 Liberty Bowl: Colorado 47, Alabama 33
1970 Bluebonnet Bowl: Alabama 24, Oklahoma 24
1972 Orange Bowl: Nebraska 38, Alabama 6
1973 Cotton Bowl: Texas 17, Alabama 13
1973 Sugar Bowl: Notre Dame 24, Alabama 23
1975 Orange Bowl: Notre Dame 13, Alabama 11
1975 Sugar Bowl: Alabama 13, Penn State 6
1976 Liberty Bowl: Alabama 36, UCLA 6
1978 Sugar Bowl: Alabama 35, Ohio State 6
1979 Sugar Bowl: Alabama 14, Penn State 7
1980 Sugar Bowl: Alabama 24, Arkansas 9
1981 Cotton Bowl: Alabama 30, Baylor 2
1982 Cotton Bowl: Texas 14, Alabama 12
1982 Liberty Bowl: Alabama 21, Illinois 15
1983 Sun Bowl: Alabama 21, Southern Methodist 15
1985 Aloha Bowl: Alabama 24, USC 3
1986 Sun Bowl: Alabama 28, Washington 6
1988 Hall of Fame Bowl: Michigan 28, Alabama 24
1988 Sun Bowl: Alabama 29, Army 28
1990 Sugar Bowl: Miami 33, Alabama 25
1991 Fiesta Bowl: Louisville 34, Alabama 7
1991 Blockbuster Bowl: Alabama 30, Colorado 25
1993 Sugar Bowl: Alabama 34, Miami 13
1993 Gator Bowl: Alabama 24, North Carolina 10
1995 Citrus Bowl: Alabama 24, Ohio State 17
1997 Outback Bowl: Alabama 17, Michigan 14
1998 Music City Bowl: Virginia Tech 38, Alabama 7
2000 Orange Bowl: Michigan 35, Alabama 34
2001 Independence Bowl: Alabama 14, Iowa State 13
2004 Music City Bowl: Minnesota 20, Alabama 16

2006 Cotton Bowl: Alabama 13, Texas Tech 10 (vacated)
2006 Independence Bowl: Oklahoma 34, Alabama 31
2007 Independence Bowl: Alabama 30, Colorado 24
2009 Sugar Bowl: Utah 31, Alabama 17
2010 BCS Championship: Alabama 37, Texas 21
2011 Capital One Bowl: Alabama 49, Michigan State 7
2012 BCS Championship: Alabama 21, Louisiana State 0
2013 BCS Championship: Alabama 42, Notre Dame 14
2014 Sugar Bowl: Oklahoma 45, Alabama 31

Auburn Bowl Game Appearances

1937 Bacardi Bowl: Villanova 7, Auburn 7
1938 Orange Bowl: Auburn 6, Michigan State 0
1954 Gator Bowl (January): Texas Tech 35, Auburn 13
1954 Gator Bowl (December): Auburn 33, Baylor 13
1955 Gator Bowl: Vanderbilt 25, Auburn 13
1964 Orange Bowl: Nebraska 13, Auburn 7
1965 Liberty Bowl: Mississippi 13, Auburn 7
1968 Sun Bowl: Auburn 34, Arizona 10
1969 Astro-Bluebonnet Bowl: Houston 36, Auburn 7
1971 Gator Bowl: Auburn 35, Mississippi 28
1972 Sugar Bowl: Oklahoma 40, Auburn 22
1972 Gator Bowl: Auburn 24, Colorado 3
1973 Sun Bowl: Missouri 34, Auburn 17
1974 Gator Bowl: Auburn 27, Texas 3
1982 Tangerine Bowl: Auburn 33, Boston College 26
1984 Sugar Bowl: Auburn 9, Michigan 7
1984 Liberty Bowl: Auburn 21, Arkansas 15
1986 Cotton Bowl: Texas A&M 36, Auburn 16
1987 Citrus Bowl: Auburn 16, USC 7
1988 Sugar Bowl: Syracuse 16, Auburn 16
1989 Sugar Bowl: Florida State 13, Auburn 7
1990 Hall of Fame Bowl: Auburn 31, Ohio State 14
1990 Peach Bowl: Auburn 27, Indiana 23
1996 Outback Bowl: Penn State 43, Auburn 14
1996 Independence Bowl: Auburn 32, Army 29
1998 Peach Bowl: Auburn 21, Clemson 17
2001 Citrus Bowl: Michigan 31, Auburn 28

2001 Peach Bowl: North Carolina 16, Auburn 10
2003 Capital One Bowl: Auburn 13, Penn State 9
2003 Music City Bowl: Auburn 28, Wisconsin 14
2005 Sugar Bowl: Auburn 16, Virginia Tech 13
2006 Capital One Bowl: Wisconsin 24, Auburn 10
2007 Cotton Bowl: Auburn 17, Nebraska 14
2007 Chick-fil-A Bowl: Auburn 23, Clemson 20
2010 Outback Bowl: Auburn 38, Northwestern 35
2011 BCS Championship: Auburn 22, Oregon 19
2011 Chick-fil-A Bowl: Auburn 43, Virginia 24
2014 BCS Championship: Florida State 34, Auburn 31

3

ARMY VS. NAVY: WAR ON THE GRIDIRON

It has been generations since a large percentage of the premier high school football players in America opted to further their NFL ambitions at Army or Navy. Their annual clash draws little attention from the media. Neither team has even sniffed a national championship since the Kennedy administration.

But no college football rivalry in history boasts greater tradition and passion among its combatants than the one between the two service academies, which dates back to before the Spanish–American War.

The seeds of what eventually blossomed into an annual battle were planted in 1890 by a cadet named Dennis Michie. His academy didn't even have a football team, but he yearned to form one as a former prep high school player. He broached the possibility of an Army–Navy game with a friend in Annapolis. Michie understood the absurdity of such a

Figure 3.1.   Army–Navy football game, November 28, 1908. *Source: Library of Congress*

proposal. After all, Navy had begun its football program in 1879 and had fielded a team every year since 1881. Moreover, the Midshipmen had blossomed into a consistent winner. They had embarked in 1889 on a streak of 13 consecutive winning seasons.

That did not prevent Michie from seeking approval from the academy to form a football team. Piece of cake—the most powerful member on the academic board happened to be his father, Professor Peter Michie, of whom the cadets fondly referred to as "Old Pete." The elder Michie was skeptical of what seemed like a pie-in-the-sky idea from his son. After all, if you're going to start a football program, why not schedule a less imposing foe? But pop eventually gave in, and a team eventually known as the Army Black Wave was born.

The younger Michie faced an overwhelming task as coach, recruiter, and financial backer. Many of his fellow cadets knew nothing about football. But he ordered all whose weight exceeded 180 pounds to join the team. They were forced to run before reveille and practice on Saturday afternoons. There was little time to prepare for the game, which was played on a chilly, dark day in West Point on November 29, 1890. Despite the gloomy conditions, the lure of an Army–Navy battle on the gridiron attracted a sizeable crowd. And the fans watched what they expected to watch—a Navy team well versed in the sport dominating a slipshod Army group that didn't even appear to understand its rules. One Cadet defender grabbed a Midshipmen ball carrier but let him go when he believed the crowd was shouting its disapproval. The Navy player was as shocked as anyone in attendance when he was freed to cross the goal line for a touchdown. The Navy players added color and a military flavor to the game by barking out such signals as "Reef the topsail!" and "Stand by to clear anchor!"[1]

In the end, veteran Navy player Red Emerich had scored five touchdowns and his team had buried Army, 24–0. The following excerpt from one newspaper account made it look like the difference was far more substantial: "Navy's stalwarts, from the kick-off, were too much for the sadly ignorant cadets, and with charges around the ends and center rushes which the West Pointers tried to stop with might and main, succeeded in rolling rough shod over them."[2]

The thorough 24–0 victory for Navy set off a celebration back in Annapolis. A 24-gun salute to the team could be heard for miles as the Middies paraded through the streets blowing horns. Just one game had been played between the two Academies and already an intense rivalry had blossomed.

One reason for its interest at both academies is that one and all realized the similarities between football and the military strategy for which they were being trained. The parallels were indeed recognized from the start, as was explained in an article published in *Outing* magazine as the teams prepared for a rematch the following November. The following piece recounted the initial battle while making comparisons to the art of war:

> In 1890 a match was instituted between Annapolis and West Point and the enthusiasm provoked was remarkable. The West Point men had not enjoyed the same privileges as their more fortunate opponents in the way of previous outside matches, nor had they played the game in preceding years, as had the Annapolis men. In spite of these odds they put up a very plucky fight, and it is safe to say that if the game once obtains a foothold among these men its fascinations will make themselves felt so strongly as to perpetuate it wherever they go.
>
> These men are making a study of the art of war, and there is no sport known that in its very nature mimics that art as the game of football. The tactics, the formations, the strategies, the attack and defense, all belong equally to the military commander and the football captain.
>
> English and American commanders have both recognized the similarity of the football tactics to the tactics of war, and more than one has said that a good football player will make a good soldier.[3]

Michie had achieved his goal to launch a football program. The loss to Navy was the only game Army played that year, and they planned to expand their schedule and exact revenge on their military academy counterparts in 1891. Michie was overwhelmed by the task of running the program and coaching the team, so he sought out candidates to handle the latter responsibility. Since nobody with the requisite football knowledge and experience could be found on campus, he "hired" Yale graduate Harry Williams, a teacher who had played under renowned football instructor Walter Camp. Not a cent was paid to Williams, but he coached like a million bucks. He held practices twice a week and guided them to a 3–1–1 record leading into the rematch against Navy, this time in Annapolis on Thanksgiving weekend. The result was a smashing success for Army, as 3,000 fans expected a victory from a Navy team with a 5–1 record that was coached by former Princeton standout Edgar Allan Poe, a descendant of the legendary writer.

The battle was brutal. It was marred by bloodshed and two concussions as well as sprains and contusions. Army emerged with a 32–16 revenge victory that prompted a wild celebration at West Point as the Cadets marched around their post and fired an 11-gun salute—one for each member of the team. Back in Annapolis, despite the roughness of the game, the hosts invited their guests to a dance at the Navy boathouse in which the winners were toasted.

All seemed well with the budding rivalry, but its intensity, to borrow a nautical term, had gone a bit overboard during a showdown in Annapolis in 1893. The combatants not only battled on the field, but their fans also battled in the stands. A duel was proposed between a rear admiral and retired general at the Army–Navy Club in New York that could have ended in death but was narrowly avoided. An alarmed President Grover Cleveland called an emergency cabinet meeting in which it was decided to end the annual game due to an excess of violence. The teams did not play from 1894 to 1898, but their teams were far from dormant. Both established consistent winning programs despite revolving doors that had coaches coming and going after one-year stints. Army forged a 20–9–3 record as darkness descended upon its annual clash against Navy, while the Midshipmen were 29–8–2. Navy had peaked in the last two years of that run with a 15–2 record.

New American president Theodore Roosevelt understood that certain conditions must be met to forge a renewal of the rivalry. He listed them in an August 1897 directive to secretary of war Gen. Russell A. Alger. They included a strict ban on betting and a limit on practice time for the players. Mission accomplished—the Army–Navy clash returned on December 2, 1899, at Franklin Field in Philadelphia. The Cadets won that game and dominated the series for six years, winning five behind a defense that yielded a mere 5.7 points a game during that stretch. But they also boasted in 1901 a quarterback named Charlie Daly, whose experience in the sport included three varsity seasons at Harvard. Daly single-handedly destroyed Navy that year with a field goal and 100-yard kickoff return for a touchdown. The Midshipmen complained that Army was nothing without him. The Cadets claimed they could defeat Navy indeed, thereby alienating their best player, who quit playing and decided to help as coach. Army got edgy as the 1902 game approached and begged Daly to return to the field. That he did—and he played a major role in a 22–8 Army win in which seven Navy players were injured and taken off the field.

The violence that marred the Army–Navy rivalry was no different than what was occurring in other football fields on college campuses around the nation. A total of 23 players were killed in 1905, prompting some schools to ban the sport and motivating a meeting that included West Point captain Palmer Pierce in 1906 in which uniform rules for college football were drafted to reduce injuries. Included was legalizing the forward pass.

The Army–Navy rivalry continued unabated. The intensity of the battle was heightened in 1906 when the Midshipmen, perhaps inspired by the introduction of the song "Anchors Aweigh," pitched the first of two straight shutouts against a Cadet team that was embarking on an NCAA-record 32-year stretch of winning seasons. The early 20th century was marked by short stretches of dominance by both programs. Navy won three consecutive shutouts from 1910 to 1912. Army, which earned its first national championship in 1914 and added another undefeated season and crown in 1916, held Navy to 16 total points in four straight victories from 1913 to 1916. After World War I suspended the series for two years, the Midshipmen won three in a row, followed by eight Army victories interrupted by two ties in a 12-year period. Games scheduled in 1928 and 1929 were canceled due to a dispute over player eligibility.

That period proved particularly exasperating to Navy and its fans. The Midshipmen produced strong teams year after year but could not overcome their archrivals. Their frustration peaked in 1926, when only a 21–21 tie against Army in Chicago marred an undefeated season. The game is considered arguably the finest in the history of the series. It took a 65-yard touchdown drive for the Midshipmen to avoid defeat against the once-beaten Cadets. That score saved the season for Navy, which was declared the national champion by two of the many polls of that era.

The annual battle had gained such national interest that cities throughout the country competed for the right to host it. The game was played in such venues as Soldier Field in Chicago, Municipal Stadium in Baltimore, and the Polo Grounds in New York in front of sellout throngs. But the proximity of the two academies and the passion for the

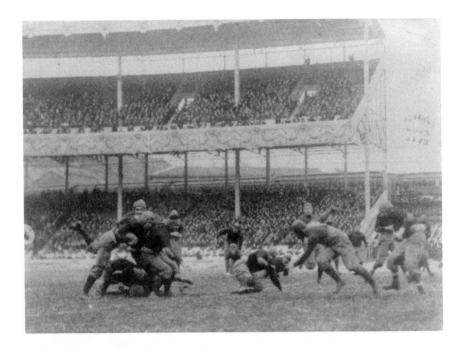

Figure 3.2.   Army–Navy game, Polo Grounds, New York, 1916. *Source: Library of Congress*

rivalry in Philadelphia resulted in that city's Franklin Field to become its permanent address in 1932. The game was moved in 1936 to new Municipal Stadium, which in 1982 became known as JFK Stadium. The Army–Navy rivalry had found an eternal home—and what more appropriate city than the birthplace of the nation? More than 100,000 fans would regularly attend games in an era in which such huge crowds were otherwise unheard of in college football. Even the Great Depression didn't prevent sellouts. It was no wonder that legendary sportswriter Grantland Rice dubbed the annual Army–Navy clash as "the biggest show in earth."[4]

The stars of both programs shined in the 1920s and 1930s. Navy boasted such future College Football Hall of Famers as halfbacks Tom Hamilton (1924–1926) and Buzz Borries (1932–1934) and offensive linemen Slade Cutter (1924–1926) and Frank Wickhorst (1924–1926). Army featured quarterback Chris Cable (1931–1934) and several premier linemen, including Ed Garbisch (1919–1921) and Harvey Jablonsky (1931–1933), all of whom were also voted into the Hall. But it was the 1940s that proved to be the golden era of Army–Navy football as the teams took turns dominating.

The decade did not start so promising for Army, which had suffered through its second straight losing season and worst year ever at 1–7–1 under embattled coach William Wood in 1940. Wood was dispatched in favor of Earl "Red" Blaik, a former end at the academy who had coached Dartmouth College into prominence. The cerebral and innovative Blaik surrounded himself with such assistants as future NFL Hall of Famers Sid Gillman and Vince Lombardi. Though he declined to get too close to his players, he proved inspirational to them. He once told Army running back Bob Anderson that he would be a key player in an upcoming victory over Navy. Anderson indeed played a role of hero in the defeat of the Midshipmen and declared after the game that he was "ready to run through a wall" for Blaik.[5]

Blaik wasted no time turning what was now referred to as the Black Knights around, but the dominance of Navy continued. Led by the talents of All-American tackle Don Whitmire, the Midshipmen had embarked on a five-game winning streak against their archrivals in 1939 in which they yielded just six points and pitched four shutouts. But Blaik was busily forming arguably the greatest college football teams ever assembled.

His Army teams blitzed all in their path from 1944 to 1946 in earning three consecutive national championships. The level of their dominance was unfathomable. In 1944, they outscored their opponents, 504–35, and ended their five-year losing streak to Navy with their closest win, 23–7. The Black Knights won by such ridiculous scores as 83–0, 76–0, and 69–7 behind the immense talents of running backs Doc (Mr. Inside) Blanchard and Glenn (Mr. Outside) Davis, who continued to destroy opposing defenses between and around the tackles through 1946.

Davis led the nation with 120 points scored that year, but he and his backfield mate were merely warming up. Davis averaged 11.5 yards per carry in 1945, an NCAA record that still stands. "Every time Davis touched the ball, it would be like an electric current going through the defending team," marveled Columbia standout Gene Rossides.[6]

But it was Blanchard, who also served as a linebacker, placekicker, and punter, who won the coveted Heisman Trophy that year, though he told the media selflessly that he would have voted for Davis. Blanchard drew praise from his fellow players, as well as coaches. "Have just seen Superman in the flesh," wired Notre Dame assistant coach Ed McKeever after watching Blanchard play. "He wears number 35 on his Army jersey. His name is Felix [Doc] Blanchard."[7]

A photo of Blanchard and Davis was splashed on the cover of *Time* magazine in 1945 as Army led the nation in both offense at 45.8 points per game and defense at an average of just 5.1 points allowed. They battered second-ranked Notre Dame, 48–0, which elevated Navy into that ranking, setting up what could have been an epic showdown against the Midshipmen. But it was no contest. Though Navy again gave Army its toughest tussle of the season, they were no match in a 32–13 blowout.

Only a tie against the second-ranked Fighting Irish marred another perfect season for the Black Knights in 1946, after which Davis indeed won his Heisman Trophy. Davis concluded his career with a career yards-per-carry average of 8.5 that remains an NCAA record. But the expected dismantling of a Navy team that had fallen to 1–7 heading into the game never happened. The Midshipmen nearly pulled off one of the most monumental upsets in the history of college football.

Army had beaten four nationally ranked teams in its first nine games, including No. 5 Pennsylvania the previous week. But quarterback Arnie Tucker was nursing an ankle injury, and Blanchard was sick and had lost 20 pounds. Blaik was wary that the bon voyage for Davis and Blanchard was going to be ruined.

"It would be just hell, I thought, to have this gang come this far with the effort they've made and then have the three-year record spoiled in the last game—and by the Navy," Blaik offered in a biography about him written by Tim Cohane titled *You Have to Pay the Price*. "We sure would never hear the end of that."[8]

His fears appeared unfounded despite the plucky play of the Midshipmen. A 52-yard touchdown blast over the middle by Blanchard and his 26-yard scoring reception from Davis gave Army a 21–6 lead. But Navy embarked on a 78-yard touchdown drive in the third quarter and added another touchdown early in the fourth. Only three missed extra points had prevented a tie game, but what the *New York Times* deemed to be the "upset of the ages" looked like a real possibility. And when Midshipmen star Lynn Chewning scampered 20 yards to the Army 3-

yard line for a first down with 90 seconds remaining, it appeared likely that the Black Knights were going to lose their first game since 1943. But a goal-line stand prevented Navy from scoring and clinched a third consecutive national title for Army.

Blaik's fears had been justified and nearly realized. He knew that the Midshipmen would be primed to play but was impressed by the level of their intensity. "That was the most inspired Navy team I ever saw," he said. "You can take a team that is supposed to be inferior and by a great spiritual lift do wonders."[9]

The championship era for Army did not slide by without its critics. Some scoffed that the competition was weakened by rosters decimated from the loss of players fighting overseas in World War II. They further contended that Army benefited from the influx of athletes who yearned to show their patriotism or even believed that playing for the team would allow them to battle on the gridiron rather than the front lines. But those who scoffed at the achievements of the Black Knights had no explanation for their continued excellence in 1946, more than a year after V-J Day officially ended American involvement in the war.

The near upset in 1946 would not be the first time a significantly inferior Navy team would scare Army or even slay the Knights. A sense of déjà vu washed over both programs two years later when All-American Army quarterback Arnold Galiffa led his unbeaten team into Philadelphia against the winless Midshipmen. The Knights had scouted their opponents 263–68, while Navy had not scored more than 14 points in any game and were coming off two straight shutouts.

Perhaps the outcome would have been different had the Cadets not been hit with a case of food poisoning the night before. But even such an occurrence couldn't explain Navy answering every Galiffa touchdown drive with one of its own. The Middies had not only tied the game at 21–21, but they also had possession late in the fourth quarter. So intriguing was the battle that the 50-man Secret Service crew charged with escorting President Harry Truman out of Municipal Stadium in Philadelphia couldn't convince him to leave. From the Navy sideline, he watched Midshipmen quarterback Bill Hawkins play the role of hero with two touchdowns and an interception that gave his team one last chance to score the winning points. The Black Knights held, but that was at best a moral victory. Navy had again ruined their perfect record, though they somehow maintained their No. 3 national ranking.

Lightning struck the same stadium again in 1950. The Black Knights steamrolled into their game against the Midshipmen undefeated behind such All-Americans as end Dan Foldberg and linebacker Elmer Stout. First-year Navy coach Eddie Erdelatz was beginning to turn around a program that had suffered through a 5–28–3 record the previous four years, but the Middies were not considered a threat to powerful Army, which was averaging more than 400 yards a game offensively. But a budding Erdelatz defense held the Black Knights to just 77 yards rushing, and quarterback Bob Zastrow engineered two touchdown drives in an improbable 14–2 victory that launched a permanent shift in the rivalry. Army would only once more win more than three games in a row.

Erdelatz finally brought stability to a football program that had never employed the same coach for more than five consecutive years. Meanwhile, an academic cheating scandal involving 37 Army players in 1951 destroyed its roster and nearly prompted Blaik to resign as coach. But after the first losing season since 1940, the Knights returned to form. Both teams were strong from 1953 to 1958, and their rivalry was embraced on a personal level by the two coaches. Erdelatz and Blaik did not like each other, according to longtime Navy scout Steve Belichick, whose son Bill coached the New England Patriots to three Super Bowl championships. "Eddie Erdelatz and Earl Blaik wouldn't give each other the time of day," said the elder Belichick.[10]

The relative evenness of the talent level and achievements of the two teams resulted in a rare period of balance. But it also produced some of the most memorable clashes because both teams were consistent winners. Neither contended for a national championship, but both spent time in the top 10, particularly in 1954. Navy soared to No. 6 in the nation that year on the strength of wins over ranked opponents Stanford and Duke. Army had risen to No. 5 after seven straight victories. Both teams boasted All-Americans in ends—Ron Beagle for Navy and Don Holleder for Army.

An intense, even battle was expected in Philadelphia, and the combatants did not disappoint. Erdelatz had dubbed his 1954 Midshipmen "The Team Named Desire," and they showed why after falling behind 20–14. They forged ahead on a six-yard touchdown run by quarterback George Welsh and stretched their lead to 27–20 on a five-yard score by Earle Smith. Navy preserved the win with a goal-line stand midway through the fourth quarter. The frustrated Black Knights ran out of time with the ball at midfield. And though the Middies went on to thrash Mississippi in the Sugar Bowl to finish the season as the fifth-ranked team in the nation, it was the win over Army that Beagle declared to be their most exciting achievement.

Navy had embarked on its finest four-year period in four decades. Its teams steamrolled to a mark of 29–6–4 from 1954 to 1957. The lone Army victory over the Midshipmen during that time came in 1955, when Holleder was switched from end to quarterback in a move critics derisively called "Blaik's Folly." But Holleder outplayed Welsh despite not completing one pass in a 14–6 victory. The Middies peaked in 1957 with an "emergency record" of 9–1–1 that featured wins over No. 5 Notre Dame, No. 10 Army, and No. 9 Rice in the Cotton Bowl. Only an upset defeat to North Carolina and loss to 16th-ranked Duke prevented the Middies from competing for a national championship. They held nine of their 11 opponents to seven points or fewer, including the Black Knights in a 14–0 shutout. Erdelatz credited that victory to Belichick, whose scouting report was so thorough that it allowed their team to blank an Army offense that led the nation in scoring and rushing yards.[11]

The Midshipmen were about to take charge of the rivalry on what would be considered a permanent basis if not for a 10-year run of Army dominance in the eighties and nineties. After 1958 Heisman Trophy winner and halfback Pete Dawkins led the Black Knights to an 8–0–1 record and 22–6 win over the Middies, two Heisman Trophy winners defined the early years of the following period for Navy. They were running back Joe Bellino and quarterback Roger Staubach.

Bellino, whose thick, muscular calves stood out on his five-foot-eight, 180-pound frame, boasted a combination of speed and power previously unseen at the academy. He arrived in 1957, the year before Blaik and Erdelatz both left their posts, the latter to replace Bear Bryant as head coach at Texas A&M. Bellino did not thrive in two years under Erdelatz, whose structured offense left him little freedom to show his wide range of ability. "[Erdelatz] was a very methodical guy," Bellino explained. "He didn't let me run wild. He wanted me to control how I ran across the field. Every play was designed for a touchdown. Every player had a certain thing to do, and if they all did it, we scored a touchdown."[12]

Bellino ran wild for replacement Wayne Hardin, who designed crea-
tive plays that put the ball in his star running back's hands with room to
roam. And his talent was never more evident than what he displayed in
a 1959 showdown against the Black Knights. He tied a series record by
scoring three touchdowns in a 43–12 thrashing of Army, which had
fallen to .500 for the first time in seven years under new coach Dale
Hall. Hardin understood how much it would mean for Bellino to break
the mark, so he called for him to run for an opportunity to score a
fourth touchdown, and when teammate Ron Brandquist got the ball
and scored, the coach was infuriated at quarterback Joe Tranchini and
threated to toss him out of the academy for not following orders. Tranchini, however, explained that Bellino refused to take the ball because
he wanted the hardworking Brandquist to taste the joy of scoring his
first touchdown of the season. Hardin found it difficult to complain
about such selflessness.

Bellino rushed for 564 yards in 1959 but was merely whetting the
appetites for those who yearned to watch him in full bloom. He blossomed into Heisman Trophy form in 1960 to lead the Midshipmen to a
9–2 record and Orange Bowl berth. Bellino racked up 1,114 yards of
rushing and receiving combined, ran for 5.0 yards per carry, and even
threw two touchdown passes in winning the award by a landslide. He
even intercepted a pass in the end zone on the final play to secure a
17–12 victory over Army.

The lowest point total scored by Navy during their five-year winning
streak over Army from 1959 to 1963 came in 1961, and it was no coincidence that was the only year they had neither Bellino nor Staubach.
The latter secured the starting quarterback job in the fourth game of his
sophomore season in 1962. He proved remarkably accurate in a time in
college football in which typical completion percentages paled in comparison to those of the modern era. Staubach hit on 68.4 percent of his
passes that year. He was virtually impossible to defend because of his
ability to hit receivers all over the field and propensity to gain ground
running the ball when flushed out of the pocket. Hardin created plays
in which the heady Staubach would roll out and decide whether to pass
or run. The Black Knights discovered to their frustration just how versatile Staubach was that year when he threw for two touchdowns and ran
for two more in a 34–14 victory. Not bad for a guy who considered
attending Notre Dame and a career as a priest.

Staubach peaked as a college quarterback as a junior in 1963. He passed for 1,474 yards, ran for 418 more, and was responsible for 16 touchdowns en route to winning a runaway voting for the Heisman Trophy. He guided the Midshipmen to the brink of a national championship, but it took a close victory in a classic showdown against Army to earn an Cotton Bowl berth against Texas.

The battle against the Black Knights was postponed for a week after the assassination of President John F. Kennedy. The devastation felt by the players and coaches surpassed that of the rest of the nation because Kennedy had been a Navy enlistee and had made no secret of his love for the academy and its football team. He had stopped by before the 1962 season to shake hands with every player and coach. The Midshipmen even marched in his 1961 inaugural parade. So when he was murdered, they were in no mood to play football. But when First Lady Jacqueline Kennedy expressed a desire for the game to be played, it was indeed held on December 7 in Philadelphia. "All I told the guys before the game is, 'Let's play a game worthy of a President.'" Hardin said. [13]

A strong Army team under second-year coach Paul Dietzel gave Navy all it could handle. The Black Knights forged ahead 7–0 before Middies fullback Pat Donnelly scored three touchdowns to give his team a 21–7 lead with 10 minutes remaining in the game. But an Army score and successful onside kick still had the outcome in doubt. The Cadets drove to the Navy 2-yard line, but confusion reigned and they failed to get a play off before the final tick of the game clock. One of the greatest games in Army–Navy history had ended without a crescendo.

So did what could have been a national championship season for Navy and two-Heisman career for Staubach. The second-ranked Midshipmen were clobbered by the Longhorns, 28–6, in the Cotton Bowl and collapsed in 1964 when injuries limited their quarterback. But their 1963 team is still considered their best ever.

The departure of Staubach in 1965 signaled the end of national recognition for both the Army and Navy football programs, perhaps not coincidentally as American involvement grew in the increasingly unpopular Vietnam War. Never again would either team contend for a national championship. And though both academies would still produce strong teams and talented players, the dominance of the Midshipmen, particularly since the turn of the century, has limited the competitiveness of the series.

The post-Staubach era didn't start out that way. After back-to-back losing seasons under Dietzel, the Black Knights recovered under new coach Tom Cahill for a short period of dominance over a Navy team that foundered throughout the Vietnam era. The Midshipmen managed just one winning season from 1965 to 1974 and really bottomed out in the last seven years of that stretch with a 20–55 record. Army embarked on a 23–7 run from 1966 to 1968 and was 6–2–1 against their archrivals from 1964 to 1972.

But though the eyes of the nation were no longer fixed on Philadelphia when the teams met in the final week of the regular season, the passion still remained in the hearts and minds of the players, coaches, alumni, and students at both academies. Huge crowds still converged on Philadelphia to watch the annual clash, perhaps more so because of its tradition and pageantry than for what became second-rate football talent compared to that of the Ohio States and Alabamas of the college football world. And the game has remained a nationally televised spectacle despite the relative mediocrity of the teams.

Army bottomed out at 0–10 in 1973 for its first winless season since it launched its program with a single defeat against Navy in 1890. The Black Knights became the personal punching bag for the Midshipmen for the next decade. Only in 1977 did they muster a victory over Navy during that time. The Middies, who were merely average in that period, were still far superior. In their nine defeats of Army from 1973 to 1983, they outscored their rivals, 293–49. They surrendered no more than 13 points in any of those games.

The later years of that era were highlighted by a Navy halfback deemed too small to thrive in the world of major college football. His name was Napoleon McCallum. Shunned by first-choice Michigan due to his size, the wannabe astronaut opted to play for the Midshipmen. Before he was done frustrating defenders with his quickness, shiftiness, and acceleration, he had rushed for 4,179 yards and set an NCAA Division I record with 7,122 all-purpose yards. Soon he had discarded his desire to become an astronaut and forged a career in the NFL.

McCallum was the last consensus All-American to play for either school through 2012. His departure signaled a temporary end to the control of the series imposed by Navy. Army enjoyed its final run of dominance from 1984 to 1996, during which time it won 10 of 13 games against the Midshipmen. But they did not win arguably the most memorable battle during that time.

It was December 9, 1989. Navy coach Elliot Uzelac had already been fired after a miserable three-year run in which his team compiled an 8–25 record and lost twice to Army. He was no more than a lame duck when the teams met, for a change, outside of Philadelphia. The academies had become open to playing in other venues by that time, including the Rose Bowl in Pasadena in 1983, and now it was the turn of Giants Stadium in New Jersey.

The Black Knights were no powerhouse, but they did boast a prolific running back in Mike Mayweather and were considered strong enough at 6–4 to be a likely candidate to overwhelm the weak sister from Annapolis, who sported a 2–8 mark and was averaging a mere 12.6 points a game. But Navy bolted to a 9–0 lead before two touchdown runs by Cal Cass put Army ahead, 14–9. The Black Knights maintained a 17–16 lead with five minutes remaining when the Middies embarked on a 63-yard drive to the Army 15-yard line with just 18 seconds left. That's when placekicker Frank Schenk booted a 32-yard field goal through the uprights for a 19–17 victory and gave Uzelac a fine going-away present.

Such dramatics in the Army–Navy rivalry disappeared soon after the Army run of the early and mid-1990s. After the Midshipmen bottomed out with a 1–20 record in the first two years of the new century, including the only 0–10 season in school history in 2001, new coach Paul Johnson turned the program around. His team managed just two wins in 2002, but he and replacement Ken Niumatalolo followed with eight straight winning seasons in which Navy qualified for lesser bowl games. The Black Knights, meanwhile, bottomed out at 0–13 in 2003 and managed just one winning season from 1997 to 2012 (7–6 in 2010), during which time they recorded a 47–139 mark. From 2002 to 2010, they lost every game to Navy by at least 12 points and were outscored, 322–91.

Despite their dominance, the Midshipmen continued to express a respect for their West Point counterparts, perhaps because their rivalry is unlike any other in college football. Navy linebacker Brye French, who knew something about the subject having been raised in the rivalry-crazed state of Alabama, spoke about those differences before the 2012 showdown against the Black Knights. "When you talk about the Alabama–Auburn rivalry in the Iron Bowl, yeah, that's a big rivalry, and there's hatred and a little history to it. But that's in-state. . . . When you

Figure 3.3.   Army vs. Navy, 2013. *Photo by Phil Hoffmann, used with permission*

talk about Army–Navy, you're talking about guys and gals serving our country around the world. If you watch it, you can see a difference. It's not based on hatred. The rivalry is based on the love of the game. We're not going to be signing contracts after the season to play in the NFL. We're playing because we love the game, and we're playing for our brothers."[14]

Indeed, the Black Knights and Midshipmen of the current generation can only read about the days of national championships and Heisman Trophy winners. But rivalries are not built and sustained on greatness. They are based on passion and mutual respect. And those qualities that define Army–Navy football are displayed on the gridiron every year.

Fact Box (through 2013)
   Nickname: None

Trophy: The Thompson Cup
Total meetings: 114
Series record: Navy leads, 58–49–7
First meeting: 1890 (Navy 24, Army 0)
Largest margin of victory: Navy, 1973 (Navy 51, Army 0)
Longest winning streak: Navy, 12 (2002–2013)

Game Results (home team listed second unless at a neutral site)
1890: Navy 24, Army 0
1891: Army 32, Navy 16
1892: Navy 12, Army 4
1893: Navy 6, Army 4
1899: Army 17, Navy 5
1900: Navy 11, Army 7
1901: Army 11, Navy 5
1902: Army 22, Navy 8
1903: Army 40, Navy 5
1904: Army 11, Navy 0
1905: Navy 6, Army 6
1906: Navy 10, Army 0
1907: Navy 6, Army 0
1908: Army 6, Navy 4
1910: Navy 3, Army 0
1911: Navy 3, Army 0
1912: Navy 6, Army 0
1913: Army 22, Navy 9
1914: Army 20, Navy 0
1915: Army 14, Navy 0
1916: Army 15, Navy 7
1919: Navy 6, Army 0
1920: Navy 7, Army 0
1921: Navy 7, Army 0
1922: Army 17, Navy 14
1923: Army 0, Navy 0
1924: Army 12, Navy 0
1925: Army 10, Navy 3
1926: Navy 21, Army 21
1927: Army 14, Navy 9

1930: Army 6, Navy 0
1931: Army 17, Navy 7
1932: Army 20, Navy 0
1933: Army 12, Navy 7
1934: Navy 3, Army 0
1935: Army 28, Navy 6
1936: Navy 7, Army 0
1937: Army 6, Navy 0
1938: Army 14, Navy 7
1939: Navy 10, Army 0
1940: Navy 14, Army 0
1941: Navy 14, Army 6
1942: Navy 14, Army 0
1943: Navy 13, Army 0
1944: Army 23, Navy 7
1945: Army 32, Navy 13
1946: Army 21, Navy 18
1947: Army 21, Navy 0
1948: Navy 21, Army 21
1949: Army 38, Navy 0
1950: Navy 14, Army 2
1951: Navy 42, Army 7
1952: Navy 7, Army 0
1953: Army 20, Navy 7
1954: Navy 27, Army 20
1955: Army 14, Navy 6
1956: Navy 6, Army 6
1957: Navy 14, Army 0
1958: Army 22, Navy 6
1959: Navy 43, Army 12
1960: Navy 17, Army 12
1961: Navy 13, Army 7
1962: Navy 34, Army 14
1963: Navy 21, Army 15
1964: Army 11, Navy 8
1965: Navy 7, Army 7
1966: Army 20, Navy 7
1967: Navy 19, Army 14

1968: Army 21, Navy 14
1969: Army 27, Navy 0
1970: Navy 11, Army 7
1971: Army 24, Navy 23
1972: Army 23, Navy 15
1973: Navy 51, Army 0
1974: Navy 19, Army 0
1975: Navy 30, Army 6
1976: Navy 38, Army 10
1977: Army 17, Navy 14
1978: Navy 28, Army 0
1979: Navy 31, Army 7
1980: Navy 33, Army 6
1981: Army 3, Navy 3
1982: Navy 24, Army 7
1983: Navy 42, Army 13
1984: Army 28, Navy 11
1985: Navy 17, Army 7
1986: Army 27, Navy 7
1987: Army 17, Navy 3
1988: Army 20, Navy 15
1989: Navy 19, Army 17
1990: Army 30, Navy 20
1991: Navy 24, Army 3
1992: Army 25, Navy 24
1993: Army 16, Navy 14
1994: Army 22, Navy 20
1995: Army 14, Navy 13
1996: Army 28, Navy 24
1997: Navy 39, Army 7
1998: Army 34, Navy 30
1999: Navy 19, Army 9
2000: Navy 30, Army 28
2001: Army 26, Navy 17
2002: Navy 58, Army 12
2003: Navy 34, Army 6
2004: Navy 42, Army 13
2005: Navy 42, Army 23

2006: Navy 26, Army 14
2007: Navy 38, Army 3
2008: Navy 34, Army 0
2009: Navy 17, Army 3
2010: Navy 31, Army 17
2011: Navy 27, Army 21
2012: Navy 17, Army 3
2013: Navy 34, Army 7

Army Bowl Game Appearances

1984 Cherry Bowl: Army 10, Michigan State 6
1985 Peach Bowl: Army 31, Illinois 29
1988 Sun Bowl: Alabama 29, Army 28
1996 Independence Bowl: Auburn 32, Army 29
2010 Armed Forces Bowl: Army 16, Southern Methodist 14

Navy Bowl Game Appearances

1924 Rose Bowl: Washington 14, Navy 14
1955 Sugar Bowl: Navy 21, Mississippi 0
1958 Cotton Bowl: Navy 20, Rice 7
1961 Orange Bowl: Missouri 24, Navy 14
1964 Cotton Bowl: Texas 28, Navy 6
1978 Holiday Bowl: Navy 23, Brigham Young 16
1980 Garden State Bowl: Houston 35, Navy 0
1981 Liberty Bowl: Ohio State 31, Navy 28
1996 Aloha Bowl: Navy 43, California 38
2003 Houston Bowl: Texas Tech 38, Navy 14
2004 Emerald Bowl: Navy 34, New Mexico 19
2005 Poinsettia Bowl: Navy 51, Colorado State 30
2006 Meineke Car Care Bowl: Boston College 25, Navy 24
2007 Poinsettia Bowl: Utah 35, Navy 32
2008 Eagle Bank Bowl: Wake Forest 29, Navy 19
2009 Texas Bowl: Navy 35, Missouri 13
2010 Poinsettia Bowl: San Diego State 35, Navy 14
2012 Kraft Fight Hunger Bowl: Arizona State 62, Navy 28
2013 Armed Forces Bowl: Navy 24, Middle Tennessee State 6

4

OKLAHOMA VS. TEXAS:
THE RED RIVER RIVALRY

The greatest team achievement in college football history was becoming a distant memory. It was October 12, 1963. Six years had passed since the Oklahoma football team ran its winning streak to 47 consecu-

Figure 4.1. Texas vs. Oklahoma. *Photograph used with permission from the University of Texas*

tive games to set an NCAA record. With every loss the reminiscences of that feat became weaker.

And there were many defeats that followed. The legend of Sooners coach Bud Wilkinson, who entered the 1960 season with an unfathomable record of 121–13–3 at the school, had been tarnished a bit. His team lost six games in 1960, more than it had in the previous six years combined. It managed a .500 record the following year before rebounding at 8–3 in 1962. Good for most coaches but not even ordinary for the great Bud Wilkinson.

Making matters direr on that fall afternoon in Dallas was that Oklahoma had lost their last five shootouts against archrival Texas and coach Darrell Royal, who played his college career under Wilkinson in the early 1940s. It was expected for pupil to beat teacher every so often, but this was getting ridiculous.

The Sooners, however, had reason for optimism. They had taken their momentum from the year before and run with it to the No. 1 ranking in the nation into the third week of the season. They had wrested that prestigious spot away from Southern California by beating the Trojans at their place in 110-degree heat the week before, 17–12. A victory over second-ranked Texas would cement their standing as the greatest team in America once again. Just like the 1950s.

The Longhorns had other ideas. They had not lost a regular-season game since 1961 and boasted a mark of 21–2–1 in their previous 24 games. Only a shocking tie against lowly Rice in 1962 prevented them from playing for the national championship that year. And they boasted perhaps the finest sophomore in the nation in future College Football Hall of Fame linebacker Tommy Nobis.

And it was his unit that dominated play. Nobis and fellow linebacker Scott Appleton, who racked up 18 tackles, shut down an Oklahoma offense that averaged 23.6 points that season to rank 11th in the nation. The die was cast when Texas quarterback Duke Carlisle, running the option offense to perfection, engineered three touchdown drives to stake his team to a 21–0 lead. The Texas fans among the 75,000 packing the Cotton Bowl began chanting, "We're number one! We're number one!" And soon it was true, courtesy of a 28–7 victory.

A battle between the top two teams in the country had just concluded, but Appleton spoke with reference, not about a showdown between two national powers, but about what was then known as The Red

River Shootout. It was a rivalry not just played for three hours on the gridiron. It was a war between the states. It was played out verbally as well as athletically. "It doesn't matter if they're number one in the nation or number 40," he explained. "It's not hard to be up for the Okies. But this time we felt something special. They had been saying for a year that they were going to beat us. Well, the time came today, and look what happened. . . . I don't mean to sound cocky, but this is something all of us felt very strongly about. Oklahoma wasn't really in the game. . . . Yeah, we're number one now. . . . We've been number one the last two years, but we let down. This year, we're not going to let down."[1]

Appleton was true to his word. The Longhorns were back at the Cotton Bowl on New Year's Day to beat second-ranked Navy and clinch their first undisputed national championship. It was the triumph over Oklahoma that launched them permanently into the No. 1 spot.

The term "friendly rivalry" has been tossed around in the world of sports for generations and it has never applied to Texas–Oklahoma. Former Sooner player and coach Gary Gibbs said simply that it's "based on hate."[2] And it has been since their first clash in 1900, when the Longhorns treated the Sooners with disrespect before the game and pushed them around like rag dolls between the lines.

Not that the Longhorns were unjustified in embracing the status of a bully in their early relationship with the Sooners. They were downright experienced in this football thing by the turn of the 20th century. Their program had only been in existence for two years longer, but Oklahoma had played a skeleton schedule since the birth of its team in 1895, with 10 games in five years. The Longhorns had not dipped their toes into the water. They had dived in with 45 games played and boasted a record of 36–8–1. And though the Oklahoma team, then known as the Rough Riders, were a fine 8–2, their lack of experience in the sport was scoffed by their neighbors to the south.

The reasoning behind launching such a rivalry was not limited to proximity. Many native Texans had moved to Oklahoma during the land rush of the 19th century. The two states, therefore, had something outside of geography in common.

It took about 16 hours for the Sooners to traverse the 400-mile journey to Austin by train, and they didn't arrive until nearly 7 a.m. on the morning of the game. They tried in vain to snag a little snooze time.

They arrived at the Varsity Athletic Field tired, yet enthusiastic. But the Longhorns were vindicated for their pregame boasting. They dominated all phases of their 28–2 victory, as star John DeLesdernier scored two touchdowns. So dominant was Texas that a headline in the *Austin Statesman* crowed that Oklahoma had given the team a "stiff practice game."[3]

The competition stiffened as the Sooners gained experience. Both teams continued to achieve winning records season after season, but Texas dominated the series with a defense that barely allowed its new rival to score. The Longhorns won six of the first seven games played between the two teams—five were played in Austin and the other two in Norman, Oklahoma—with the other ending in a tie. The Sooners were shut out only once but also scored more than six points only once during that stretch. They averaged just five points a game. They finally broke the losing streak with an offensively challenged 2–0 victory in 1905 before falling again to Texas the next two years.

By that time, however, new coach Bennie Owen had the offense heading in the right direction. He had learned his craft as an assistant under legendary University of Michigan head coach Fielding Yost, master of the prolific "point-a-minute" offense and stifling defense that was dominating the sport. By 1908, Owen's team was ready to avenge all its defeats to the Longhorns with one Texas-sized thumping.

It was Friday the 13th. It was also the coldest day in Norman in 10 years. Premier tackles Ralph Campbell and Willard Douglas dominated the line of scrimmage and teammate Charlie Wantland sprinted 90 yards on a punt return for a touchdown—the longest such gallop in Oklahoma history until future Texas coach Darrell Royal raced 95 with a punt return 40 years later. The game was a massacre. The fans were so thrilled at the Sooners' dominance that they embarked on a snake dance and threw their hats over the goal posts with their team leading 17–0 at *halftime*. Final score: Oklahoma 50, Texas 0. It would remain the most lopsided win in the rivalry until a 65–13 thrashing by the Sooners over the Longhorns 95 years later.

Among the witnesses at the 1908 game was Wantland's father, a rancher who was shocked at the violence inherent in the Texas–Oklahoma battle. He considered the fact that a new law had outlawed steer roping in rodeos and offered that lawmakers should have looked in a different direction for a ban in the world of local sports.

"This is the roughest thing I ever saw," he complained. "They ought to make them cut this out instead of steer roping."[4]

Some Oklahoma fans might have wished they had taken the elder Wantland up on that suggestion. Aside from a few short runs of success, including a 6–3 record from 1910 to 1919, the Sooners played the role of personal punching bags for the Longhorns until Wilkinson arrived in 1947. Texas shut down Oklahoma on nearly an annual basis with one of the finest defenses in the country. In 17 victories over the Sooners in 21 games from 1922 to 1947 (the rivalry was suspended from 1924 to 1928), the Longhorns held their rivals to 116 total points, an average of 6.4 per game, and recorded six shutouts. Texas enjoyed winning streaks of six and eight games during that two-decade run.

But despite the overall dominance of the team from the Lone Star State in the first half of the 20th century, the two programs staged many memorable showdowns. Among them was an epic battle in 1915, before which both teams had run roughshod over every foe in their paths. The Sooners had won all four games by shutout, including a 102–0 shellacking of Northwest Oklahoma. The Longhorns were coming off a 59–0 dismantling of Rice and were also unbeaten and unscored upon. It's no wonder that what was then a state-record 11,000 fans streamed into Gaston Park in Dallas to watch the clash between the two teams competing in what was sure to be the deciding game for the first-ever Southwest Intercollegiate Athletic Conference championship.

The Longhorns took control early on a fumble recovery and 10-yard touchdown run by Bert Walker to forge ahead, 7–0. But Oklahoma answered on a scoring strike from Frank McCain to Montford Johnson. In an era of college football when crashing through the lines by running backs was almost the exclusive mode of attack, the two teams fired 52 passes combined and racked up 700 total yards. The recklessness of the offenses resulted in 12 turnovers, including nine by the Longhorns. They somehow still snagged the lead in the third quarter on a five-yard touchdown run by Bob Simmons but missed the extra point, which proved crucial. The Sooners tied it on a second touchdown reception by Johnson and went ahead on the extra point by "Spot" Geyer. They held off a late Texas drive for a 14–13 victory.

News of the triumph prompted a wild celebration in the Panhandle State. The team made several train stops to allow the players and coaches to whoop it up with their football-crazed fans. The school band played the fight song for 4,000 people who stuffed the train depot in Norman to welcome back their gridiron heroes. Oklahoma took its momentum and ran with it to a 10–0 record and first SWC crown. Geyer was rewarded for his production by becoming the first player from that program to earn All-American status. Sooner fans were so grateful to Owen that they purchased and presented him with a new Hudson Super-Six automobile.

What could have been an intense rivalry over the next decade and beyond was halted due to a myriad of circumstances. World War I and a devastating Spanish flu epidemic prevented a battle of unbeatens in 1918 and ended the Sooners' season at 6–0. Their temporary switch to the Missouri Valley Conference in 1920 resulted in a two-year lull in the battle due to a league rule that banned teams from playing games at a neutral site. The Longhorns began their dominant stretch over the Sooners with victories in 1922 in Norman and 1923 in Dallas, but their desire to maintain a domination over their rivals from the north were frustrated from 1924 to 1928, when the rivalry was stopped again for various and sundry reasons.

The schools would remain in separate conferences until Texas finally left the SWC and joined the Big 12 in 1996. Oklahoma left the MVC in 1928 to join the Big Six, which eventually doubled in size, and has stayed there ever since. By the time the rivalry was renewed for good in 1929, both teams had different coaches. Owen had been replaced by Adrian Lindsey, who was replaced by Lewie Hardage, who was replaced by Lawrence Jones. All three failed to live up to the standards of on-field success established by their predecessor, as a long period of mediocrity settled upon Oklahoma football. New coach Clyde Littlefield enjoyed far more success with Texas, and it showed on the football field. The Longhorns extended the winning streak over the Sooners that began in 1922 and 1923 with triumphs every year from 1929 to 1932 in which their defenses dominated. A 9–0 loss to Oklahoma in 1933 could not stem the tide. The Longhorns surrendered just seven points to their rivals during another run of dominance from 1934 to 1936.

There was no secret to their success during that period. They simply boasted more talent. Among the best of the Longhorns was halfback and future College Football Hall of Fame inductee Harrison Stafford, an explosive runner and receiver and devastating blocker who was considered one of the toughest players of his generation. A mere walk-on who was ignored during the recruiting process, Stafford was three times an All-SWC selection and was chosen for several All-American teams.

That difference in talent widened in the 1940s, as did the scoring gap when the teams met on the field. After the Sooners stopped the bleeding from 1937 to 1939 with a tie and two victories over the Longhorns in Dallas, the latter resumed domination through World War II. Texas won every game from 1940 to 1947. They yielded just 21 total points in five consecutive victories from 1941 to 1945.

The stars of the era shone brightly for Texas, but none shone brighter than coach Dana X. Bible, who emerged as easily its finest to date. Despite the success of the program, no coach had remained in place for more than six years until Bible took over. He not only stuck around for nine years, but he also recruited many of the greatest players in Longhorn history. He inherited the team during the height of the Great Depression and managed a 3–14–1 record in his first two seasons. But his recruiting efforts began to pay dividends and he completed his run with seven straight winning seasons, three Cotton Bowl appearances in which his teams won twice and tied once, and an SWC title in 1941 as his team soared to fourth in the national rankings.

His most significant recruit of the era was quarterback Bobby Layne, who would blossom into a College Football and Pro Football Hall of Famer. Layne, considered a Major League Baseball pitching prospect upon his arrival at Texas, quickly ended that speculation with his exploits on the gridiron. He finished his career having completed 53 percent of his passes for a school-record 3,145 yards. Layne peaked in a 40–27 defeat of Missouri in the 1946 Cotton Bowl in which he accounted for every point with four touchdowns rushing, two more passing, and four extra points. His favorite target throughout his college career was fellow Hall of Famer Hub Bechtol, one of only two Texas football players to earn All-American honors three times. He caught nine passes for 138 yards in that victory over the Tigers.

Despite the lopsided nature of The Red River Shootout through most of the 1930s and 1940s, it had its exciting moments both on and off the field. Among them was the 1930 unveiling of Fair Park Stadium, which was renamed the Cotton Bowl in 1937 and provided the annual showdown with a permanent home with a seating capacity of 45,507. The place was only half-full when the first Texas–Oklahoma game was played there in 1930, but that still represented the largest crowd to date in the history of the game, which didn't experience its first sellout until 1945. The Great Depression and World War II played roles in keeping attendance down.

Everything changed in 1947. That's when Oklahoma coach Jim Tatum bolted to coach at Maryland and handed the reins to 31-year-old assistant Bud Wilkinson, whose only previous experience consisted of short stints as an assistant at Syracuse and Minnesota. Wilkinson changed the football culture at his school with a combination of tough discipline and fatherly understanding. He stressed to his players the importance of preparation. He insisted on holding his players to the highest academic and athletic standards. And he was as inspirational as any coach in school history. "You could feel like quitting school and joining the French Foreign Legion," offered 1950s Oklahoma fullback Billy Pricer. "Then you'd talk to him for 15 minutes and come out of his office singing 'Boomer Sooner,' thinking you owned half the university."[5]

Wilkinson installed the split-T offense, which his teams ran with the precision he demanded from every aspect and moment of its preparation and game execution. He posted practice schedules that broke down the activities nearly to the minute. But he was also an innovator. It was Wilkinson who invented the no-huddle offense that remains popular among college and NFL teams to this day. And he recruited not just the finest athletes but the smartest as well. He took pride in his belief that his teams could defeat athletically superior opponents with their intelligence on the field.

The arrival of Wilkinson signaled an end to Longhorn dominance in The Red River Shootout. Texas remained strong under coaches Blair Cherry and Edwin Price in the late 1940s and early 1950s before faltering in the middle of that decade, leading to the hiring of Royal and the heyday of the Oklahoma–Texas rivalry. Their teams were winners, but the Sooners quickly blossomed into national champions. They reached that lofty goal in 1950, a year after they blitzed through their season unbeaten, including a 35–0 thrashing of Louisiana State in the Sugar Bowl, only to place second behind Notre Dame in the voting for the national crown.

The 1950 Sooners were powered by sophomore running back Billy Vessels, who was on his way to rushing for 938 yards and an impressive 6.2 average that season, and senior quarterback Claude Arnold, who threw for 1,069 yards, 13 touchdowns, and just one interception all year. They were on a 23-game winning streak heading into their showdown against the undefeated Longhorns, who were decided underdogs despite boasting a team that would finish the season ranked No. 3 in the country.

The Sooners showed why they were heavy favorites from the start when Vessels scored the first touchdown with just four minutes ticked off the clock to give his team a 7–0 lead. But this new generation of Sooners had also grown accustomed to close battles with their archrivals despite their usual domination of other foes. It came as little surprise when Vessels counterpart Byron Thompson scampered 15 yards for a score in the second quarter to tie the game. The Longhorns appeared destined to forge ahead when they marched 66 yards to the Oklahoma half-yard line, but the Sooners rose up for a goal-line stand as time ran out in the first half.

Texas would regret that missed opportunity. A 50-yard interception return for a touchdown by Longhorn Bobby Dillon in the fourth quarter would have all but sealed the upset had they scored before intermission. And a missed extra point after the Dillon jaunt put Texas ahead only 13–7. A sense of disaster washed over Longhorn fans at the Cotton Bowl, and it happened with four minutes remaining in the game when punter Bill Porter, who had already blown the extra point, mishandled a low snap and was tackled on the Texas 11. Vessels steamrolled a Longhorns defender and careened into the end zone two plays later as Oklahoma secured a 14–13 lead. Soon it was over. Oklahoma fans stormed the field and tore down the goal posts to celebrate the first three-game winning streak over Texas since 1910 through 1912. The Sooners went on to extend their winning streak to 31 games and earn the first national championship.

Wilkinson and his Sooners, as well as their fans, attacked their rivals from every direction, including on the recruiting front. The young coach plucked some of his finest talent from the Lone Star State, including All-American tackle and placekicker Jim Weatherall, who played a key role in the 1950 triumph, as well as offensive linemen Jerry Tubbs and Ed Gray, whose 1956 squad shellacked Texas, 45–0. Wilkinson later specialized in recruiting premier running backs away from the Longhorns, including future NFL stars Joe Washington, Greg Pruitt, and Billy Sims.

Even the Oklahoma fans spooked the Longhorns on occasion. During a 49–20 dismantling of Texas in 1952, a group of Sooner supporters that called themselves the "Roughnecks" and sat behind the Longhorns bench fired blanks from double-barreled shotguns every time Oklahoma scored. The noise proved especially discomforting to Texas guard Harley Sewell, who had recently returned from action in the Korean War. After one particular shotgun volley, he was asked by Price if he was rested up enough to get back into the game. "Yeah, coach," he replied with a pained expression. "But this is worse than Korea."[6]

Wilkinson also took the lead in integrating his team. He recruited fullback Prentice Gautt in the mid-1950s, more than a decade before Texas provided a football scholarship to any African American player. Gautt spoke glowingly about the impact Wilkinson had on his life and his ability to handle the problems he faced in a period of racial hatred and discrimination, particularly in southern states such as Texas and Oklahoma. "If it hadn't been for Bud, there wouldn't have been any way that I'd have made it," Gautt said in a 1991 tribute to Wilkinson. "His talking and believing in me was probably the biggest things that helped me get over even the thought of being the first black."[7]

Yet despite the slights toward black players, the hiring of Royal flip-flopped the fortunes of the two teams in The Red River Shootout. Ironically, Royal had starred as a quarterback under Wilkinson at Oklahoma in 1949 and guided his team to two victories over Texas. Royal embarked on a coaching career immediately thereafter, landing his first head position at Mississippi State in 1953 before landing at Washington in 1956. He managed limited success in both jobs, but the powers that be at Texas showed their foresight by snagging Royal to replace Price, whose 1–9 mark in 1956 was the worst since the program began before the turn of the century.

Royal was like many coaches of his generation in disdaining the forward pass, citing the possibility of an incompletion or interception and even coining the oft-used warning, "Three things can happen when you pass and two of 'em are bad."[8] Like Wilkinson, he was a stickler for details in every facet of the game, even special teams. And he demanded that every player give his all on every play.

"He taught me how to compete," said center David McWilliams, who played under Royal in the early 1960s and later became head coach of the Longhorns. "Football is a contact sport, and he would not put up with any kind of dainty play. He was strict, and if in practice you stepped the wrong way, he'd get on you. If you loafed in the kicking game, you might not get back on the field. I loafed on the punt team once, and he ran it back 20 times the next week in films, asking me, 'What the hell are you doing?' I never loafed again."[9]

Royal arrived when the Sooners were putting the finishing touches on the greatest achievement in college football history—a 47-game winning streak that outdistanced the record that Wilkinson himself set earlier in his career by 16 games. Oklahoma launched its historic roll with a 19–14 defeat of Texas in 1953 and added four more victories over the Longhorns while running roughshod over the rest of their opponents and earning national championships in 1955 and 1956. Their final defeat of Texas during the streak was a 45–0 blanking in 1956 that proved to be Royal's last loss to Wilkinson. The turnaround was immediate and profound.

It began in 1958. Oklahoma had finally lost in an upset to Notre Dame the previous November, but it still maintained the No. 2 rank in the nation. Both teams entered the showdown undefeated, but the Sooners had already earned an impressive win with a 47–14 mashing of nationally ranked West Virginia. They were heavily favored to make it 10 of the last 11 over the Longhorns. And when they owned a 14–8 lead late in the game, it appeared the die was cast. After all, Texas had not scored more than seven points against Oklahoma in five years. But Royal inserted backup quarterback Vince Mathews to provide a spark. Mathews drove his Sooners downfield with time running out, then gave way to starter Bobby Lackey, who fired a 16-yard touchdown pass to Bob Bryant for the victory.

Oklahoma did not lose another game that season while Texas collapsed and lost three times in the last five games after reaching No. 4 in the national rankings. But the glory years of Sooner football were over, at least for another decade, while the Longhorns emerged as an annual national championship contender under Royal. The result was a long period of Texas dominance in The Red River Shootout.

The crown jewels of Royal recruiting efforts included running back James Saxton, whom Royal considered the quickest player in the nation. Saxton finished third in the 1961 Heisman trophy voting after leading the SWC in rushing with 846 yards and an average of eight yards per carry with nine touchdowns. Saxton helped the Longhorns soar to No. 1

in the country that season with his explosive speed and quickness that resulted in six runs of between 45 and 80 yards. Royal also landed San Antonio high school linebacker Tommy Nobis, whom *Sports Illustrated* in 1965 claimed to be the best defensive player in the college game.

Nobis, the only sophomore starter on the 1963 national championship team and a two-time All-American, was recruited heavily by Wilkinson, who sought to add him to his stable of premier players out of the Lone Star State. But what Nobis heard from his fellow Texans playing for the Sooners during his visit to Norman brought out his true loyalties and convinced him to reject Oklahoma. "They started talking about the state of Texas and what jerks the people were," Nobis recalled. "They were bad-mouthing the Longhorns and the state of Texas. I couldn't get out of that room fast enough."

The Longhorns took the momentum gained from the 1958 upset of Oklahoma and ran with it. They won their next seven games in the series, including the 1963 classic that knocked the Sooners off their top-ranked throne, with a stout defense that yielded an average of 6.7 points per game and no more than a touchdown in any Red River Shootout played from 1960 to 1965. Wilkinson had retired at the end of the 1963 season to pursue political and sports broadcasting ambitions. The Sooners managed a record of 15–15–1 in his absence until assistant coach Chuck Fairbanks was promoted to take over the program in 1967. His immediate success tied in with the brilliance of running back Steve Owens, a College Football Hall of Famer who rushed for 3,928 yards and 57 touchdowns in three seasons and proved to be the first in a long line of brilliant Oklahoma running backs.

By that time Royal had unleashed a new three-back set that took college football by storm. His wishbone offense, which he unveiled to start the 1968 season, highlighted the talents of running back Chris Gilbert, who rushed for 1,132 yards that year. It kept defenses guessing as to who would carry the ball. The result was a buzz saw ground game that keyed a 1969 national championship run in which the Longhorns scored nearly 40 points a game and clinched the title with victories over second-ranked Arkansas and ninth-ranked Notre Dame in the Cotton Bowl.

The Sooners figured what the Longhorns could do, they could do better. But it wasn't until 1971 that the Oklahoma wishbone was working at peak efficiency. It took backfield talent to pull it off—and the

Sooners had plenty. Quarterback Jack Mildren and speedy, shifty running back Greg Pruitt, who later starred in the NFL, combined for an obscene 3,049 yards and 38 touchdowns on the ground in 1971, during which Oklahoma led the nation with an average of 45.8 points a game. Whereas the Longhorns ran their wishbone as a power attack, the Sooners adjusted it to best utilize their burners around the edges. The same Oklahoma team that averaged less than seven points a game against Texas from 1958 to 1965 and had lost 12 of their previous 13 against their hated rivals exploded for a 48–27 victory in 1971. The blowout signaled another dramatic shift in The Red River Shootout.

But though only conference defeats to top-ranked Nebraska and ninth-ranked Colorado in the heyday of Big Eight football prevented Fairbanks from winning two consecutive national championships, he would not be around in 1973. A recruiting scandal forced the Sooners to forfeit nine victories earned in 1972 and also forced Fairbanks out in favor of assistant coach Barry Switzer. His rivalry against Royal was short lived—the latter remained at Texas only through 1976—but it included a classic clash in 1975 between two of the premier teams in college football.

The battle began not on the gridiron but in the media, which claimed that Oklahoma recruiters were using illegal enticements to lure top Texas high school talent to play for the Sooners. Royal joined the fray by working with the Southwest Conference to ram through an NCAA proposal that would limit the number of home visits allowed by a coaching staff. Royal believed that that would prevent Switzer from maximizing his ability to convince premier players from the Lone Star State to head north. Switzer was livid. He strongly denied offering Texas prep players money or gifts. In a grand exhibition of showmanship, he demanded that his coaches take a lie detector test to prove their innocence. He claimed that Texas players had agreed to play for the Sooners simply because of the greatness of the program. He added that his state simply didn't produce enough top high school talent, which necessitated forays into Texas. But one truth that nobody could deny was that Oklahoma had integrated its football team more than a decade before the Longhorns boasted their first African American player. There was no choice for black talent who might have otherwise weighed the two options.

Switzer kept his composure before the 1975 showdown. He kindly greeted Royal before the game, which blossomed into one of the greatest clashes in Red River Shootout history. The game was tied at 17–17 with eight minutes remaining when Oklahoma quarterback Steve Davis detected a defensive alignment that would stymie the play he called in the huddle. So he audibled for a runoff tackle in the now-famed wishbone offense to running back Horace Ivory, who rambled 33 yards for a touchdown.

The game was far from over. The Sooners had a 24–17 lead and the ball, but they were pinned back at their own 10-yard line with 2:25 remaining. At 3rd-and-8 a traditional punt appeared likely that would give the Longhorns a short field and a chance to embark on a game-tying drive. So offensive coordinator Galen Hall, who eschewed the passing game, called for a bit of trickery. Premier running back Joe Washington took a pitch then shocked one and all by kicking it. It bounced until it landed an amazing 76 yards from the line of scrimmage and pinned Texas back to its own 14. The Longhorns couldn't traverse that distance in such a short time and the Sooners had their fifth consecutive victory over their archrivals. Adding to the frustration for Texas fans everywhere was the fact that Washington was one of 16 of the top 44 Oklahoma players that had been plucked from the Lone Star State. And when it was over, Texas defensive tackle Brad Shearer expressed the feelings of every player involved in the game. "I just hate Okies, to put it bluntly," he said. "They hate me just as bad and that's what makes it a great game."[10]

An explosive Sooners offense was not the only ingredient to their success. They also boasted Oklahoma-bred Lee Roy and Dewey Selmon, the sons of farmers who followed sibling Lucious (who played through 1973) to the school. The Selmon brothers wreaked havoc on opposing offenses. Lee Roy, who anchored the defensive line, was the best of the bunch, recording 257 tackles and 28 sacks in 1974 and 1975 combined. He was a consensus All-American in both those seasons and earned the Outland Trophy as the premier lineman in college football as a senior before embarking on a brilliant NFL career that began when he was taken with the first selection of the 1976 draft by Tampa Bay and ended with a list of achievements that earned him induction into the Pro Football Hall of Fame.

While Lee Roy Selmon was arguably the greatest defensive player of his era in college football, the finest offensive talent wore a Texas uniform. That was running back Earl Campbell, perhaps the most explosive power back in the history of the sport. He was the target of an intense recruiting war between Switzer and Royal following a brilliant high school career in the small Texas town of Tyler. The former believed he had the right ammunition to land Campbell, but he was outgunned by the latter. "Earl should have been in my backfield," Switzer later lamented. "I thought we'd get him. He was the best high school player I've ever seen. I came back from seeing him play, and I told my staff that I had finally seen a high school player who could make an NFL team right out of high school. Mentally and physically, he was tough enough. And I stress how mentally tough he was." [11]

Campbell was a man among boys in some of his battles at the college level. He rushed for 928 yards as a mere freshman and 1,118 as a sophomore. Only a bad hamstring that knocked him out of four games in 1976 prevented him from taking a run at the Heisman Trophy that year, but he recovered in time to rack up 131 yards rushing and two touchdowns in a 27–12 triumph over Arkansas that gave Royal a royal sendoff after 20 years as Texas coach. Replacement Fred Akers shunned the wishbone in favor of the I-formation, from which Campbell thrived as a power back with stunning speed and elusiveness for his size. He rushed for 100 or more yards in 10 of 11 games en route to the 1977 Heisman and finished with 1,744 yards and 18 touchdowns on the ground. Among his efforts was a 124-yard, one-touchdown game against second-ranked Oklahoma that keyed a 13–6 victory and propelled the Longhorns into the No. 1 spot in the nation that they maintained until a loss to Notre Dame in the Cotton Bowl. Campbell also took the NFL by storm, leading that league in rushing in each of his first three years, and despite a spate of injuries that cut his career short, he joined his contemporary Selmon in the Pro Football Hall of Fame.

The Red River Shootout experienced a rare period of parity from the late 1970s into the early 1980s. Neither team won more than three consecutive games against the other from 1976 to 1984, though the Longhorns did manage to hold a 5–2–2 record during that period. Neither team suffered through a losing season throughout that period, so all the battles were highly anticipated. But none drew the attention of the 1984 clash, into which Texas sat atop the national rankings, with Oklahoma right behind.

The Longhorns were coming off an 11–1 season in which only a Cotton Bowl defeat knocked them out of national title consideration. They had already mashed No. 4 Penn State, 28–3, and beaten 11th-ranked Auburn as well. The Sooners lost four games in 1983 and entered the year ranked No. 16, but four straight victories, including one over nationally ranked Pittsburgh, had catapulted them to No. 2 in some polls.

A rainstorm soaked the Cotton Bowl field that night. The Longhorns seemed to justify their top ranking by securing a 10–0 halftime lead. But Oklahoma rallied to forge ahead, 15–12, with time running out. The Longhorns drove within field goal range, but a tie in this annual showdown was indeed akin to kissing your sister, so they eschewed the three-point attempt for one shot into the end zone. The pass from Texas quarterback Todd Dodge appeared to have been intercepted by Sooners defensive back Keith Stanberry, but the officials ruled it incomplete. That forced the Longhorns to accept a tie, which placekicker Jeff Ward assured with a boot as the last tick ran off the game clock. It was the fourth of five ties in the history of The Red River Shootout.

The programs then parted like the Red Sea. The Sooners continued their dominance of the Big Eight, winning three consecutive titles from 1985 to 1987 to run their total to 12 in 16 seasons under Switzer—they placed second in the other four. The Longhorns, meanwhile, drifted into mediocrity under Akers and McWilliams, who replaced him in 1987. Akers lost his job after coaching the team to its first losing season in 30 years, but McWilliams fared no better, with three losing seasons in his first five, including 1991, after which he was let go in favor of John Mackovic. It would not be until the turn of the century that the Longhorns regained their status as an annual title contender.

Such could not be claimed about the Sooners. Their 1985 edition overcame an early-season loss to the University of Miami to win eight straight games, including the thrashing of No. 2 Nebraska and a 25–10 upset of top-ranked Penn State in the Orange Bowl that secured a national crown. Oklahoma boasted an explosive offense behind emerging quarterback and future NFL Hall of Famer Troy Aikman and eventual All-Pro tight end Keith Jackson. But it was its stifling defense led by Vince Lombardi Trophy–winning tackle Tony Casillas and disruptive linebacker Brian Bosworth that made the Sooners the premier team in the country. The Sooners held opponents to 14 points or fewer in 11 of their 12 games.

Yet the superiority of the Oklahoma teams into the early 1990s was not reflected in The Red River Shootout. The Sooners did follow the 1984 tie with four straight wins, the last three of which they outscored the Longhorns by a combined total of 119–34. But in an unprecedented turn of events, Texas answered with four consecutive upsets from 1989 to 1992. The Sooners were nationally ranked and the Longhorns un-ranked entering each of those showdowns. Each proved devastating to Oklahoma, particularly when it boasted a 5–0 record before losing to Texas in 1990 and a 4–0 mark before falling in 1991.

By that time Switzer had been buried and dismissed under the weight of alleged recruiting violations and replaced by assistant coach and former Sooners linebacker Gary Gibbs. For the first time in the history of the program, both teams wallowed through a period of rela-tive struggles. Oklahoma finished no better than a tie for second in the SWC in six seasons under Gibbs, during which time it managed an uncharacteristic 44–26–2 record. The Longhorns compiled a 72–55–2 mark in 11 years under McWilliams and Mackovic, finishing out of the top 25 every year but one from 1987 to 1993. But the spoils in The Red River Shootout were earned by Texas, which lost just twice to Oklaho-ma and tied once from 1989 to 1999. Gibbs and embattled replacement John Blake, under whom the program bottomed out with a three-year record of 12–26, understood that the annual losses to the Longhorns sounded a death knell to their positions with the school. "Over time, the masses are going to grumble and grumble and declare you unfit," Gibbs said. "I don't think you have to be a head coach. You can be an assistant, but at some point you have to beat those guys, or you're going to be declared unfit."

Despite the team performances that had coaches on both banks of The Red River Shootout declared unfit, the era was not devoid of talent for either program. The best of the bunch was brilliant Texas running back Ricky Williams, who earned the nickname "Texas Tornado" by shattering the NCAA Division I-A career rushing record with 6,279 yards. He averaged at least 5.9 yards and rushed for more than 1,000 yards every year from 1995 to 1998, peaking as a senior with one of the greatest seasons in the history of college football. Williams exploded for nine touchdowns in his first two games, scored six more against Rice, rushed for 350 yards and five scores against Iowa State, and added 166 yards and two touchdowns in a 34–3 stomping of the Sooners. Williams finished his career with 601 total yards and five touchdowns in four games against Oklahoma. He rushed for 4,220 yards in his last two years with the Longhorns, capping his career by winning the Heisman Trophy.

That season was the third for Texas since joining Oklahoma in the Big 12 and first for its coach Mack Brown, who would eventually raise the program to traditional levels. He understood that it was Williams who allowed his debut season with the Longhorns to be a success at 9–3. "Having a back like Ricky opens up your entire playbook," Brown offered. "You know you can run and the other team knows you can run. It just opens everything up. Also, he never got hurt and he never missed practice. He was in such great shape and it always struck me how hard he worked. He was the first one on the field and the last one off of it and he always wanted to be on special teams. He was very tough and very competitive."[12]

The hiring of Brown at Texas and former University of Florida defensive coordinator Bob Stoops at Oklahoma sparked a renaissance in what in 2005 became known (due to antigun sentiment) as The Red River Rivalry. But it did result in immediate parity in their annual clash. Both teams were ranked at least in the top 11 in the nation every year they met from 2000 to 2004, but the Sooners dominated throughout. They won by at least 11 points in all five meetings, including maulings of 63–14 in 2000 and 65–13 in 2003. Their 2000 team was particularly impressive despite a lack of future NFL talent. They beat six national-ranked teams, including No. 2 Kansas State and No. 1 Nebraska in successive weeks to take over the top spot, then toppled third-ranked Florida State in the Orange Bowl to clinch the national championship. But they were no one-year wonder during those early years under Stoops, whose teams posted a 60–7 record during their run of dominance over the Longhorns.

The dam burst for the Sooners in 2005 as the Texans took out years of frustration. Brown had built a title contender of his own that season behind versatile quarterback Vince Young, who was on his way to exceeding 3,000 yards passing and 1,000 more rushing, as well as explosive running back and future NFL star Jamaal Charles, both of whom contributed mightily to an offense that averaged an absurd 50.2 points a game. Since the Sooners had finally come back to earth with two losses in their first four games, it appeared that the Longhorns were poised for revenge. And they got it. The die was cast in the first half when Charles bolted 80 yards for a touchdown and Young fired a 64-yard scoring strike to Bill Pittman. And when his team had completed a 45–12 victory, Young made sure he watched the forlorn Sooners trudge off the field. He understood their pain—and he was quite happy about it. "We wanted them to feel everything we were feeling," said Young, whose team rode the wave of that triumph to a national crown. "It was a great moment for all of us."[13]

That great feeling would likely have been achieved had Oklahoma budding superstar running back Adrian Peterson not sprained his ankle and been limited to three carries. But the game would undoubtedly have been closer. Peterson had exploded onto the scene as a freshman by leading the nation with 339 carries for 1,925 yards and 15 touchdowns. He exceeded 1,000 yards rushing in his next two seasons as well before joining the NFL Minnesota Vikings and emerging as one of the greatest backs in the history of the pro game.

Though neither team would win another national championship through 2013, the stars continued to shine on both sides of the Red River. The Sooners boasted four first-round picks in the 2010 draft, including quarterback and No. 1 selection Sam Bradford and three future Pro Bowlers—defensive tackle Gerald McCoy, offensive tackle Trent Williams, and tight end Jermaine Gresham. Texas players, such as tight end Jermichael Finley, defensive end Brian Orakpo, and safety Michael Griffin, blossomed into NFL Pro Bowlers as well.

Meanwhile, The Red River Rivalry went on. Both teams were ranked among the top 21 in the nation every time they met from 2006 through 2012. The Longhorns knocked the Sooners out of the No. 1 spot with a 45–36 victory in 2008.

The hatred continued. It was expressed in October 2013 with passion by a Texas fan known only as the Elusive Shadow, who wrote the following:

> I don't find any reason to hate a person simply because he went to OU, and when I hear fans physically hurting each other or otherwise losing their minds, I find it embarrassing that adults would stoop that low. It's only a game. But within that game, well, let's just say that I

smile when I see a dejected Stoops face or crying Oklahoma fans. . . .
I don't hate individual Sooners, but Oklahoma, the brand, the team,
the idea . . . I wish nothing more than humiliation and misery for
them. It's even better when we inflict it, of course. [14]

That same hatred has been felt by Sooners fans about Texas for more
than a century. That's what makes The Red River Rivalry as intense as
any in college football.

Fact Box (through 2013)
   Nickname: The Red River Rivalry
   Trophy: The Golden Hat
   Total meetings: 108
   Series record: Texas leads, 60–43–5
   First meeting: 1900 (Texas 28, Oklahoma 2)
   Largest margin of victory: Oklahoma, 2003 (Oklahoma 65, Texas
13)
   Longest winning streak: Texas, 8 (1940–1947, 1958–1965)

Game Results (home team listed second unless at a neutral site)
   1900: Oklahoma 2, Texas 28
   1901: Oklahoma 6, Texas 12
   1901: Texas 11, Oklahoma 0
   1902: Oklahoma 6, Texas 22
   1903: Oklahoma 6, Texas 6
   1903: Texas 11, Oklahoma 5
   1904: Oklahoma 10, Texas 40
   1905: Texas 0, Oklahoma 2
   1906: Texas 10, Oklahoma 9
   1907: Oklahoma 10, Texas 29
   1908: Texas 0, Oklahoma 50
   1909: Oklahoma 0, Texas 30
   1910: Oklahoma 3, Texas 0
   1911: Oklahoma 6, Texas 3
   1912: Oklahoma 21, Texas 6
   1913: Texas 14, Oklahoma 6
   1914: Texas 32, Oklahoma 7
   1915: Oklahoma 14, Texas 13
   1916: Texas 21, Oklahoma 7

1917: Oklahoma 14, Texas 0
1919: Oklahoma 12, Texas 7
1922: Texas 32, Oklahoma 7
1923: Oklahoma 14, Texas 26
1929: Texas 21, Oklahoma 0
1930: Texas 17, Oklahoma 7
1931: Texas 3, Oklahoma 0
1932: Texas 17, Oklahoma 10
1933: Oklahoma 9, Texas 0
1934: Texas 19, Oklahoma 0
1935: Texas 12, Oklahoma 7
1936: Texas 6, Oklahoma 0
1937: Oklahoma 7, Texas 7
1938: Oklahoma 13, Texas 0
1939: Oklahoma 24, Texas 12
1940: Texas 19, Oklahoma 16
1941: Texas 40, Oklahoma 7
1942: Texas 7, Oklahoma 0
1943: Texas 13, Oklahoma 7
1944: Texas 20, Oklahoma 0
1945: Texas 12, Oklahoma 7
1946: Texas 20, Oklahoma 13
1947: Texas 34, Oklahoma 14
1948: Oklahoma 20, Texas 14
1949: Oklahoma 20, Texas 14
1950: Oklahoma 14, Texas 13
1951: Texas 9, Oklahoma 7
1952: Oklahoma 49, Texas 20
1953: Oklahoma 19, Texas 14
1954: Oklahoma 14, Texas 7
1955: Oklahoma 20, Texas 0
1956: Oklahoma 45, Texas 0
1957: Oklahoma 21, Texas 7
1958: Texas 15, Oklahoma 14
1959: Texas 19, Oklahoma 12
1960: Texas 24, Oklahoma 0
1961: Texas 28, Oklahoma 7
1962: Texas 9, Oklahoma 6

1963: Texas 28, Oklahoma 7
1964: Texas 28, Oklahoma 7
1965: Texas 19, Oklahoma 0
1966: Oklahoma 18, Texas 9
1967: Texas 9, Oklahoma 7
1968: Texas 26, Oklahoma 20
1969: Texas 27, Oklahoma 17
1970: Texas 41, Oklahoma 9
1971: Oklahoma 48, Texas 27
1972: Oklahoma 27, Texas 0
1973: Oklahoma 52, Texas 13
1974: Oklahoma 16, Texas 13
1975: Oklahoma 24, Texas 17
1976: Texas 6, Oklahoma 6
1977: Texas 13, Oklahoma 6
1978: Oklahoma 31, Texas 10
1979: Texas 16, Oklahoma 7
1980: Texas 20, Oklahoma 13
1981: Texas 34, Oklahoma 14
1982: Oklahoma 26, Texas 22
1983: Texas 28, Oklahoma 16
1984: Oklahoma 15, Texas 15
1985: Oklahoma 14, Texas 7
1986: Oklahoma 47, Texas 12
1987: Oklahoma 44, Texas 9
1988: Oklahoma 28, Texas 13
1989: Texas 28, Oklahoma 24
1990: Texas 14, Oklahoma 13
1991: Texas 10, Oklahoma 7
1992: Texas 34, Oklahoma 24
1993: Oklahoma 38, Texas 17
1994: Texas 17, Oklahoma 10
1995: Oklahoma 24, Texas 24
1996: Oklahoma 30, Texas 27
1997: Texas 27, Oklahoma 24
1998: Texas 34, Oklahoma 3
1999: Texas 38, Oklahoma 28
2000: Oklahoma 63, Texas 14

2001: Oklahoma 14, Texas 3
2002: Oklahoma 35, Texas 24
2003: Oklahoma 65, Texas 13
2004: Oklahoma 12, Texas 0
2005: Texas 45, Oklahoma 12
2006: Texas 28, Oklahoma 10
2007: Oklahoma 28, Texas 21
2008: Texas 45, Oklahoma 36
2009: Texas 16, Oklahoma 13
2010: Oklahoma 28, Texas 20
2011: Oklahoma 55, Texas 17
2012: Oklahoma 63, Texas 21
2013: Texas 36, Oklahoma 20

Texas Bowl Game Appearances

1943 Cotton Bowl: Texas 14, Georgia Tech 12
1944 Cotton Bowl: Randolph Field 7, Texas 7
1946 Cotton Bowl: Texas 40, Missouri 27
1948 Sugar Bowl: Texas 27, Alabama 7
1949 Orange Bowl: Texas 41, Georgia 28
1951 Cotton Bowl: Tennessee 20, Texas 14
1953 Cotton Bowl: Texas 16, Tennessee 0
1958 Sugar Bowl: Mississippi 39, Texas 7
1960 Cotton Bowl: Syracuse 24, Texas 14
1960 Bluebonnet Bowl: Alabama 3, Texas 3
1962 Cotton Bowl: Texas 12, Mississippi 7
1962 Cotton Bowl: Louisiana State 13, Texas 0
1964 Cotton Bowl: Texas 28, Navy 6
1965 Orange Bowl: Texas 21, Alabama 17
1966 Bluebonnet Bowl: Texas 19, Mississippi 0
1969 Cotton Bowl: Texas 36, Tennessee 13
1970 Cotton Bowl: Texas 21, Notre Dame17
1971 Cotton Bowl: Notre Dame 24, Texas 11
1972 Cotton Bowl: Penn State 30, Texas 6
1973 Cotton Bowl: Texas 17, Alabama 13
1974 Cotton Bowl: Nebraska 19, Texas 3
1974 Gator Bowl: Auburn 27, Texas 3
1975 Bluebonnet Bowl: Texas 38, Colorado 21

1978 Cotton Bowl: Notre Dame 38, Texas 10
1978 Sun Bowl: Texas 42, Maryland 0
1979 Sun Bowl: Washington 14, Texas 7
1980 Bluebonnet Bowl: North Carolina 16, Texas 7
1982 Cotton Bowl: Texas 14, Alabama 12
1982 Sun Bowl: North Carolina 26, Texas 10
1984 Cotton Bowl: Georgia 10, Texas 9
1984 Freedom Bowl: Iowa 55, Texas 17
1985 Bluebonnet Bowl: Air Force 24, Texas 15
1987 Bluebonnet Bowl: Texas 32, Pittsburgh 27
1991 Cotton Bowl: Miami 46, Texas 3
1994 Sun Bowl: Texas 35, North Carolina 31
1995 Sugar Bowl: Virginia Tech 28, Texas 10
1997 Fiesta Bowl: Penn State 38, Texas 15
1999 Cotton Bowl: Texas 38, Mississippi State 11
2000 Cotton Bowl: Arkansas 27, Texas 6
2000 Holiday Bowl: Oregon 35, Texas 30
2001 Holiday Bowl: Texas 47, Washington 3
2003 Cotton Bowl: Texas 35, Louisiana State 20
2003 Holiday Bowl: Washington State 28, Texas 20
2005 Rose Bowl: Texas 38, Michigan 37
2006 Rose Bowl: Texas 41, USC 38
2006 Alamo Bowl: Texas 26, Iowa 24
2007 Holiday Bowl: Texas 52, Arizona 34
2009 Fiesta Bowl: Texas 24, Ohio State 21
2010 BCS Championship: Alabama 37, Texas 21
2011 Holiday Bowl: Texas 21, California 10
2012 Alamo Bowl: Texas 31, Oregon State 27
2013 Alamo Bowl: Oregon 30, Texas 7

Oklahoma Bowl Game Appearances

1939 Orange Bowl: Tennessee 17, Oklahoma 0
1947 Gator Bowl: Oklahoma 34, North Carolina State 13
1949 Sugar Bowl: Oklahoma 14, North Carolina 6
1950 Sugar Bowl: Oklahoma 35, Louisiana State 0
1951 Sugar Bowl: Kentucky 13, Oklahoma 7
1954 Orange Bowl: Oklahoma 7, Maryland 0
1956 Orange Bowl: Oklahoma 20, Maryland 6

1958 Orange Bowl: Oklahoma 48, Duke 21

1959 Orange Bowl: Oklahoma 21, Syracuse 6

1963 Orange Bowl: Alabama 17, Oklahoma 0

1965 Gator Bowl: Florida State 36, Oklahoma 19

1968 Orange Bowl: Oklahoma 26, Tennessee 24

1968 Bluebonnet Bowl: Southern Methodist 28, Oklahoma 27

1970 Bluebonnet Bowl: Alabama 24, Oklahoma 24

1972 Sugar Bowl: Oklahoma 40, Auburn 22

1972 Sugar Bowl: Oklahoma 14, Penn State 0

1976 Orange Bowl: Oklahoma 14, Michigan 6

1976 Fiesta Bowl: Oklahoma 41, Wyoming 7

1978 Orange Bowl: Arkansas 31, Oklahoma 6

1979 Orange Bowl: Oklahoma 31, Nebraska 24

1980 Orange Bowl: Oklahoma 21, Florida State 7

1981 Orange Bowl: Oklahoma 18, Florida State 17

1981 Sun Bowl: Oklahoma 40, Houston 14

1983 Fiesta Bowl: Arizona State 32, Oklahoma 21

1985 Orange Bowl: Washington 28, Oklahoma 17

1986 Orange Bowl: Oklahoma 25, Penn State 10

1987 Orange Bowl: Oklahoma 42, Arkansas 8

1988 Orange Bowl: Miami 20, Oklahoma 14

1989 Citrus Bowl: Clemson 13, Oklahoma 6

1991 Gator Bowl: Oklahoma 48, Virginia 14

1993 John Hancock Bowl: Oklahoma 41, Texas Tech 10

1994 Copper Bowl: Brigham Young 31, Oklahoma 6

1999 Independence Bowl: Mississippi 37, Oklahoma 23

2001 Orange Bowl: Oklahoma 13, Florida State 2

2002 Cotton Bowl: Oklahoma 10, Arkansas 3

2003 Rose Bowl: Oklahoma 34, Washington State 14

2004 Sugar Bowl: Louisiana State 21, Oklahoma 14

2005 Orange Bowl: USC 55, Oklahoma 19

2005 Holiday Bowl: Oklahoma 17, Oregon 14

2007 Fiesta Bowl: Boise State 43, Oklahoma 42

2008 Fiesta Bowl: West Virginia 48, Oklahoma 24

2009 BCS Championship: Florida 24, Oklahoma 14

2009 Sun Bowl: Oklahoma 31, Stanford 27

2011 Fiesta Bowl: Oklahoma 48, Connecticut 20

2011 Insight Bowl: Oklahoma 31, Iowa 14

2013 Cotton Bowl: Texas A&M 41, Oklahoma 13
2014 Sugar Bowl: Oklahoma 45, Alabama 31

5

NOTRE DAME VS. SOUTHERN CALIFORNIA: THE CROSS-COUNTRY CLASH

Knute Rockne was gone, but his spirit filled Notre Dame Stadium on November 21, 1931. The greatest coach that had ever graced a college football sideline had been killed in a plane crash eight months earlier. He even helped design the shiny new venue that had opened a year earlier.

The players, driven by his memory, were also driven to win a third straight national championship, but they had to overcome Southern California first. It was expected to be a blowout. Never mind that the Trojans were 6–1. Never mind that they had not lost since the season opener. Never mind that they had run roughshod over each of those foes by a combined score of 215–12. The Fighting Irish were two-time national champions. They had not lost since 1928. They were on a 26-game unbeaten streak. They had swept nine straight in 1929 on the road because the stadium was under construction. Even *Los Angeles Times* columnist T. A. D. Jones, whose brother Howard had been USC head coach since 1925, predicted that Notre Dame would win by two touchdowns. Nothing against his sibling—that was the general consensus.

Such a prognostication appeared to be justified most of the game, which was broadcast live nationally on radio. Touchdown runs by Fighting Irish fullback Steve Banas and teammate Marchy Schwartz, a future College Football Hall of Famer, gave their team a 14–0 lead heading into the fourth quarter. New Notre Dame coach Hunk Anderson went to fresh troops, benching his starters in favor of substitutes many considered as talented as any players in the nation. But the move served to wreck the momentum his team had gathered through the entire game. Trojans quarterback Gus Shaver, who had ignored a foot infection to play that day, scored on a one-yard run to slice the deficit to 14–6, but a blocked extra point appeared that it could prove fatal. Shaver scored again on the following possession to make it 14–13. That measly missed extra point indeed loomed large. But the USC defense was on a roll. It held Notre Dame once again and gave its offense the ball back with four minutes remaining. The Trojans thundered downfield, reaching the Irish 13-yard line with two minutes left. Placekicker Johnny Baker, whose blown point-after had him lined up to be the goat of the game, played the role of hero instead by booting a 23-yard field goal through the uprights. Soon it was over. Final score: USC 16, Notre Dame 14.

But there was no postgame party for the Trojans. Instead, they were escorted by Jones to the cemetery in which Rockne was buried, where they paid their respects. Their train caravan stopped off in Chicago, where they were all presented with derbies by a local hatmaker before making their way back to Los Angeles.

That's when the celebration began in earnest. The team was center stage for a ticker-tape parade through downtown attended by 300,000 delirious fans. The scene was described in the following passage from an article in the *Los Angeles Examiner*:

> A reception never before equaled from athletic stars turned downtown Los Angeles into a half holiday as the triumphant Trojans rode through the city at the head of a three-mile parade beneath a barrage of confetti and flowers. At the first cry of "Here they come" and the first notes of Harold Roberts' Trojan band, playing "Fight On!" men and women poured from every building. . . . Bankers and laborers . . . industrial kings and clerks . . . merchants and typists . . . for a day USC was the adopted alma mater of the city. Through the jammed lanes of humanity, the Trojan warriors who fought the battle of Notre Dame rode as heroes ride.[1]

The game had been filmed, narrated by local sportswriter Braven Dyer, and rushed into the Loews State Theater in Los Angeles, where moviegoers were thrilled to see what they had only heard. Not bad for a mere regular-season game—Southern Cal would win out to capture the Pacific Coast Conference crown and complete its run with a 21–12 triumph over Tulane in the Rose Bowl. They had wrested the national championship away from the Fighting Irish. Their fateful victory over Notre Dame is still considered the starting point for USC football greatness, but at the time it just gave its players a sense of retribution for stinging defeats the previous two years, during which two of their four losses were to that team from South Bend, Indiana.

"I've waited for two years for this day—but, boy, what revenge," crowed USC All-American running back Erny Pinckert.[2] Jones hailed his team as the greatest offensive machine he had ever coached. That was saying something. The victory over Notre Dame firmly recognized Jones at the time as the finest coach in USC history. But the Trojans had emerged as a team to be reckoned with from the start of their program in 1888. They launched their football program in style that year with a 16–0 victory over obscure Alliance and earned a 4–0 record in their first two years combined. They played between one and seven games every season, but their annual winning ways on the gridiron weren't established until Harvey Holmes became their first full-time coach in 1904. He was the first to last more than one season on the sideline—longevity that proved unmatched at USC until Gus Henderson coached the team from 1919 to 1924. But despite the lack of continuity, the Trojans suffered through just one losing season from 1903 to the end of the Henderson era.

The Fighting Irish enjoyed an even greater level of success in their early years. They managed their first "winning" season at 1–0 in 1889—two years after their program was launched—and didn't record a losing mark until 1933. They had earned a reputation as one of the finest teams in America well before Rockne took over as World War I was dying down in 1918. Notre Dame compiled a mark of 78–8–6 from 1906 to 1917 and embarked on unbeaten seasons in 1907, 1909, 1911, 1912, and 1913. That last season featured an All-American quarterback named Charles Dorais, whose favorite target was an end named Knute Rockne. The two teamed up that year to thrash Army with a heretofore little-known offensive weapon called the forward pass. Dorais later blossomed into a longtime college and NFL coach, but he learned his trade in 1919 as an assistant under Rockne at Notre Dame.

Rockne and Dorais took their playing talents to the professional ranks following their college careers. They played for the Akron Indians and Massillon Tigers before the former was hired as coach of the Fighting Irish in 1918. Arguably the most dominant era for one program in the history of college football was about to begin. His teams lost no more than two games just once in 13 seasons. They were the first Notre Dame teams to be recognized by the myriad of polls that determined national champions. The Irish earned titles recognized at least by some polls after unbeaten seasons in 1919, 1920, 1924, 1929, and 1930. His winning percentage of .881 remains the greatest in the history of the sport.

Their glory years were marked by the impact of the backfield quartet of quarterback Harry Stuhldreher, halfbacks Jim Crowley and Don Miller, and fullback Elmer Layden, all of whom ran wild over hapless defenders from 1922 to 1924. They were dubbed as the Four Horsemen by sports journalism giant Grantland Rice, whose description of their brilliance on the gridiron was published in the *New York Herald Tribune* in October 1924, after a Notre Dame defeat of Army in New York en route to a 10–0 record and national championship. "Outlined against a blue-gray October sky, the Four Horsemen rode again," he wrote. "In dramatic lore their names are Death, Destruction, Pestilence, and Famine. But those are aliases. Their real names are Stuhldreher, Crowley, Miller and Layden. They formed the crest of the South Bend cyclone before which another fighting Army team was swept over the precipice at the Polo Grounds this afternoon as 55,000 spectators peered down upon the bewildering panorama spread out upon the green plain below."[3]

The Four Horsemen never competed against USC. The seeds of the greatest rivalry in the history of Notre Dame football and arguably that of the Trojans as well was planted, oddly, by two female friends. Their involvement began when the Irish traveled to Nebraska in 1925. The result was plenty of hostility from Cornhuskers fans and a rare but thorough defeat that angered Rockne.

While the Irish had been the great explorers of college football in the early part of the 20th century, traveling all over to play in front of sellout throngs, the Trojans were homebodies. They had ventured out of California just eight times in the first 37 years of their program. But Gwynn Wilson, who served as the graduate manager of athletics at the

Figure 5.1. The Four Horsemen of Notre Dame. *Source: Library of Congress*

school, yearned for a matchup against powerful Notre Dame. He had been working feverishly and in vain to arrange a series of games against the Irish. He had finally gained permission to negotiate with Rockne by November 1925. He traveled by train to Lincoln to watch Notre Dame fall to Nebraska, after which an understandably crabby Rockne invited him and his newlywed wife Marion to sit with him and his wife Bonnie. But as the train rumbled on the tracks, Wilson failed to convince Rockne to schedule the Trojans. Perhaps still prickly over the fact that his team had just traversed half the country to get clobbered by the Cornhuskers, Rockne claimed that the Irish already traveled too much and trips to California would prove too taxing.

While Wilson was getting nowhere, however, his wife was bending the ear of Bonnie Rockne. The two women forged a friendship. Marion Wilson described to her the beauty of Southern California and the comforts of its warm climate. She spoke of the friendliness of its people and the goodness of its fresh fruit. Bonnie Rockne was convinced and soon she had succeeded in persuading her husband to launch a series against Southern California. Except for a break during World War II, the two teams would still be meeting annually nearly 90 years later.

The first clash, which was played in Los Angeles on December 4, 1926, proved to be more heated than anyone could have imagined. The passion for the rivalry had already been fueled when USC officials attempted in vain to hire Rockne away from Notre Dame. Newspaper accounts in Los Angeles tracked the four-day excursion as the Fighting Irish closed in on California. Rockne, who fancied himself rightfully as a marketing genius, promoted the game at each stop while scheduling workouts along the way. By the time kickoff rolled around, the entire nation had been made aware of the epic showdown between two teams that had been defeated just once that season. And, strangely, one of the least-known players on the field proved to be the hero in front of 74,378 fans that packed the Coliseum, the second-largest crowd in its history. Notre Dame backup quarterback Art Parisien keyed a 13–12 victory with a game-winning touchdown pass to halfback Johnny Niemiec with just two minutes remaining. Parisien had replaced star quarterback Charlie Riley just in time for his heroics. All in attendance but the crafty Rockne were shocked by the substitution. Included was *Los Angeles Times* reporter Braven Dyer, who wrote the following about Parisien:

> Few knew his name. Few had ever heard of him. But Rockne knew his worth, knew that this was the right time to use him. . . . It seemed suicidal to take Riley out. "Why remove the best player you have" was the wail. . . . Out came Riley and in came Parisien, a little insignificant chap, who got down behind All-American center (Art) Boeringer and reached for the pigskin.[4]

The rivalry was up and running. So impactful were the pregame publicity and competitiveness of the game in 1926 that 120,000 fans streamed into Soldier Field in Chicago the following year to witness the rematch, won again by one measly point by Notre Dame. The Fighting Irish, in fact, won three of the first four games against USC by that slimmest of margins. The last was a 13–12 squeaker in front of 112,000 at Soldier Field, a stunning turnout considering the game was played a mere three weeks after the stock market crash had ushered in the Great Depression. The only exception was a 27–14 Trojans victory in an undefeated 1928 season that motivated some pollsters to select them as the national champion.

The death of Rockne marked the death, albeit temporary, of Notre Dame gridiron dominance. The Irish fell to 3–5–1 in 1933, their first losing season since they managed a 1–2 mark in 1888, which barely counted since it was only the second year of the program's existence. Anderson was dispatched in favor of Layden, one of the Four Horsemen, who gained far greater success but failed to raise the program up to the championship standards set by the immortal Rockne. Layden coached his team to a 47–13–3 mark from 1934 to 1940 but lost at least one game every season.

Jones was faring no better during the height of the Depression than Layden. After peaking from 1931 to 1933 with a combined mark of 30–2–1 and winning two Rose Bowls, his Trojans stumbled upon hard times. They managed a record of 17–19–6 from 1934 to 1937. It was no wonder that the annual Notre Dame–USC clash took on less significance during that era. Not only were Americans far more concerned about where to procure their next meal, but also neither team was contending for national crowns.

That is, until 1938. The Trojans had finally emerged from their four-year morass and the Fighting Irish entered the early-December game unbeaten and top ranked nationally on the strength of several close victories and a defense that had yielded a mere 26 points in their first eight games and pitched four shutouts. But Notre Dame got off on the wrong foot late in the first half against USC and never righted itself. Quarterback Bob Saggau mysteriously called for a fake punt despite overwhelming odds of success with 22 yards needed for a first down. The Trojans took advantage of the mistake in judgment and execution to forge ahead on a 36-yard touchdown pass from Ollie Day to Al "Antelope" Krueger. That was all the points they needed in a 13–0 victory that destroyed the title hopes of their cross-country rival.

The Trojans should have savored that victory because soon defeats of the Irish were to become quite rare after former Notre Dame tackle Frank Leahy was lured away from his coaching job at Boston College to take over the Irish. It didn't take much persuading. Leahy was so desirous of accepting the offer that he worked feverishly to break his contract with Boston College. He had coached the Golden Eagles to an unbeaten season and Sugar Bowl victory in 1940, after which he signed a lucrative deal with the school. But when Notre Dame came calling, he wanted out, and he made no secret of it. He pleaded with school officials to let him go but to no avail. So he called a press conference and told the media the biggest lie he had ever uttered—that he had been freed of his contract with Boston College and was on the way to South Bend. That did the trick. Its vice president famously expressed his good riddance, calling him following the media session and stating, "Coach Leahy, you may go wherever you want, and whenever you want. Good-bye."[5]

The Eagles' loss was Notre Dame's gain. Leahy emerged as easily the greatest coach at that school since Knute Rockne. He coached and recruited future College Football Hall of Fame athletes, some with colorful nicknames, such as quarterbacks Johnny Lujack and Angelo (Springfield Rifle) Bertelli; ends Leon Hart, Jim (Jungle Jim) Martin, and Bob (Grandpappy) Dove; and halfbacks Rex (Six-Yard) Sitko and Creighton Miller. Those skill position players and an equally talented group of linemen, such as Hall of Fame tackle George Connor, formed the foundation of the 1940s Fighting Irish teams that dominated college football and their rivals from the Pacific.

Every team Leahy assembled from 1941 to 1949 finished the season ranked in the top 10, though his duties in World War II kept him sidelined in 1944 and 1945, which not coincidentally were the worst years for Notre Dame football during that decade. Leahy guided the Irish to a 60–2–5 record in his seven seasons in the 1940s. He captured national championships in 1943, 1946, 1947, and 1949, the last two of which his teams steamrolled through every opponent on their schedules.

It was no surprise that they dominated the Trojans during that era. Jones had been replaced in 1941 after compiling a 3–4–2 record, his fourth non-winning season in the last seven. After replacement Sam Berry coached USC to a 2–6–1 mark in 1941—which would remain the worst in the history of the program until 1957—former Trojans center Jeff Cravath became the first alumnus to serve as the school's head coach. He turned the program into a winner without the memorable talent that would grace its rosters in future generations. But they were no match for the Fighting Irish in the 1940s. In fact, they could barely score against the stingy Notre Dame defenses of that era. They were outscored 153–51 in seven games played between the two teams in the decade—the clashes from 1943 to 1945 were canceled due to the war.

Even when the Trojans were in the same class, they were outclassed on the field. Such was the case in 1947, when USC catapulted to No. 3 in the country on the strength of a 6–0–1 record and victories over nationally ranked California and UCLA. They hung around against the unbeaten Irish for one half, but a 76-yard touchdown run by Sitko after intermission began two quarters of Notre Dame dominance that didn't end until a 38–7 thrashing had been completed. Even Leahy, who was not one to pass out even the most warranted praise, gushed that he had never seen a better college football team than the one coached that day.

The Trojans had merely been another hapless victim of an Irish team that won all nine games by a combined score of 291–52. The Notre Dame juggernauts of the late 1940s were arguably the finest that ever graced a college football field. Only two ties, including one against USC in 1948, prevented them from forging a perfect record from 1946 to 1949. The knotted clash against the Trojans was all that kept the Irish from winning four consecutive national championships.

But as great a recruiting draw as Notre Dame was during that time, graduation is the great equalizer, and no program can maintain that level of dominance forever. The Fighting Irish returned from the stratosphere in the early 1950s, while new coach Jess Hill was improving the fortunes of USC. The team from South Bend plummeted to .500 in 1950 before working its way to back into national championship contention in its last two seasons under Leahy in 1952 and 1953. Hill guided his teams to six straight winning seasons, peaking at 10–1 in 1952. But the results on the field were the same when the two powerhouses clashed. The Irish maintained their superiority, beating their rival every year from 1951 to 1954 to give them a 10–1–1 record against the Trojans since 1940.

Most painful for the Trojans was a 9–0 blanking in snowy South Bend right after Thanksgiving in 1952 that prevented them from concluding an undefeated season and earning national championship consideration. The visitors from sunny Southern California were so unaccustomed to such frigid temperatures and icy conditions that they disdained a workout at Notre Dame Stadium in favor of their hotel ballroom. With no experience on how to handle the adverse weather behind them, they managed just 149 yards of total offense in the shutout defeat.

The end of the Leahy era in 1956 marked the temporary end of top-level competition between the two teams. The Trojans bottomed out at 1–9 under coach Don Clark in his first year as Hill's replacement and managed just one winning season after that until 1962. The Fighting Irish struggled under Terry Brennan, Joe Kuharich, and Hugh Devore, who combined on a wholly uncharacteristic 34–45 record from 1956 to 1963. Not even legendary quarterback Paul Hornung, who remains the only Heisman Trophy winner from a losing team and who later embarked on a Hall of Fame career with the NFL Green Bay Packers, could prevent Notre Dame from suffering through a 2–8 season in 1956.

Despite the relative parity of two foundering programs, the Fighting Irish maintained their dominance. They embarked on a five-game winning streak over their archrivals from 1957 to 1961 that raised their record to 15–3–1 in their last 19 meetings. Even strong Trojan teams fell victim to mediocre Notre Dame representatives. Southern Cal briefly rebounded in 1959 to rise to No. 7 in the nation and were expected to beat the unranked Irish, who nonetheless rose to the occasion in front of their own fans in South Bend for a 16–6 victory.

But new and powerful eras were on the horizon at both schools. The seeds were planted by the hiring of future College Football Hall of Fame coaches whose names would become synonymous with winning. The first to roam the sidelines was youthful John McKay, who served for one year as an assistant under Clark before landing the head coaching job at USC in 1960. He struggled with losing records in his first two years before his recruiting began to reap benefits. His Trojans blossomed in 1962 behind quarterbacks Pete Beathard and Bill Nelsen and All-American end Hal Bedsole, who averaged an amazing 25.1 yards per reception and scored 11 touchdowns. The innovative McKay installed the I-formation and utilized a toss play that required his offensive lineman to pull to one side of the field. The play proved key to their success in that fateful year. So did the respect of his players that did more than border on fear. It crossed that line. "John McKay was a dictator," said Trojans running back Willie Brown. "People were scared to hell out of him. . . . When he walked down the street you crossed to the other side. We were all afraid of him. But with that came a great deal of respect."[6]

An opening-week upset of nationally ranked Duke thrust the 1962 Trojans into the spotlight and they remained front and center the rest of the season. By the time they battled Notre Dame in Los Angeles to close the regular season, they were 9–0 and thirsting for revenge for five consecutive defeats. It was no contest. USC continued on its merry way with a 25–0 win, putting it away with two touchdowns in the fourth quarter and completing their third shutout of the year. They then clinched their first perfect season and national championship since 1932 with a wild 42–37 victory over second-ranked Wisconsin in the Rose Bowl.

The Fighting Irish stumbled along under Kuharich and Devore until 1964, when they turned to a Northwestern coach who had beaten Notre Dame in four consecutive meetings. His name was Ara Parseghian and his brilliance would jump-start the program into a new era of greatness and, in the process, elevate the national impact of the cross-country rivalry with USC.

Parseghian received a firsthand experience in the emotional roller coaster that players and coaches could experience before, during, and after battles between the Fighting Irish and Trojans in his first year. He guided his team into the most profound one-year turnaround in its history in 1964. An Irish band that had finished 2–7 the year before under Devore was 9–0 and ranked No. 1 in the nation behind the prolific All-American combination of Heisman Trophy–winning quarterback John Huarte, who passed for 2,000 yards, and end Jack Snow, who accounted for half that total, and a defense that had yielded just 6.3 points a game heading into the season finale against USC. The Trojans had risen to No. 2 in the country on the strength of a blowout defeat of Oklahoma, but three losses in five games sent them reeling and they were playing for nothing but pride when they welcomed the Fighting Irish. Southern Cal players sought to fire themselves up the day before the game by tearing down photos of Notre Dame standouts they had tacked to the walls of their lockers and performing strange dances on them while their teammates joyously urged them on.

Pride alone could not defeat Notre Dame and a 17–0 halftime deficit hurt Trojan pride. But running back Mike Garrett, who would follow Huarte as the Heisman Trophy recipient the following year, scored a touchdown on his team's first possession after intermission and suddenly the Irish were in a battle. Their lead had shrunk to 17–13 with just under two minutes remaining in the game when USC quarterback Craig Fertig hit halfback Rod Sherman on a 15-yard strike over the middle for a touchdown and the biggest upset of the college football season. For an Irish team needing one win to clinch a national championship, the dream was dead.

And when the final tick went off the game clock and the realization that their title hopes had been crushed hit them, they were despondent. Their reaction was described in the following passage by author Jim Dent in his book about that year in Irish football history titled *Resurrection: The Miracle Season That Saved Notre Dame*:

> The Fighting Irish lumbered off the field like an exhausted battle troop. Upon reaching the tunnel, they slowed to a funeral walk. They barely felt like putting one foot in front of the other. Inside the locker room, three players bounced their gold helmets off the concrete floor. A few others kicked the metal lockers. But for the most part, the fight was out of them. [Offensive tackle] Bob Meeker sat down on one side of the locker room and bawled into his hands.[7]

Meeker did the same on the bench after the defeat in a photograph that appeared in a December 11 issue of *Life* magazine. But though there was indeed much to mourn for the Fighting Irish that day, they also realized that their football program, which had reached its depths in the early 1960s, had been resurrected. And the very nature of an annual rivalry would at least allow the underclassmen to exact revenge in 1965.

Mission accomplished. The golden era of the rivalry continued that year with an Irish triumph over the fourth-ranked Trojans, but it was in 1966 that Notre Dame fully avenged their defeat of two years past. They rolled back into the Los Angeles Coliseum as the No. 1 team in the nation behind emerging quarterback Terry Hanratty and seven All-Americans, including future Minnesota Vikings star defensive end Carl Eller, who earned induction into both the College Football and Pro Football Halls of Fame. Their top ranking was criticized by some following a 10–10 tie against No. 2 Michigan State that is still considered by many the most ballyhooed college football game ever played. The Irish set out to prove they deserved the top spot. But first, they received some inspiration from Parseghian, who subtly, yet dramatically, reminded his players of the humiliation the team had suffered two years earlier in that same stadium. "Before that game, Ara came into the locker room and wasn't like himself," recalled premier Notre Dame tight end Jim Seymour. "Normally, he would leave the players completely alone, except maybe talk to the quarterback and receivers. But this time he came into the locker room and after we knelt down in prayer, he went over to the blackboard and wrote down '1964' and circled it and said, 'Let's go!'"[8]

Despite an injury that sidelined Hanratty, the Irish thoroughly dominated. Backup quarterback Coley O'Brien fired three touchdown passes and the defense returned two interceptions for scores for a 51–0 defeat of Southern Cal, the most loss in its storied history, after which McKay vowed never again to lose to Notre Dame. The victory clinched the first national championship for Parseghian.

McKay nearly made good on his promise, coaching his team to a 6–1–2 record against the Irish from 1967 to his retirement in 1975. His dominance during that era began in 1967 behind brilliant and eventually infamous running back O. J. Simpson, who as a mere junior that season rushed for 1,543 yards and 13 touchdowns to place second in the Heisman Trophy balloting. He ran behind holes opened up by Ron Yary, who is still considered one of the greatest linemen in football history. The Trojans steamrolled past Notre Dame, 24–7, that year on the strength of 150 yards and three touchdowns by Simpson, but fell out of the top national ranking with a stunning 3–0 loss to Oregon State. They needed a victory over new No. 1 and bitter rival UCLA to regain it and they did, knocking off the Bruins, 14–3, for the national title.

Southern Cal seemingly made the frustration of Parseghian and the Fighting Irish an annual event in the early seventies. Unranked Trojans teams knocked off No. 4 Notre Dame in 1970 and the sixth-ranked Irish the following year in South Bend. USC returned to form in 1972 behind explosive skill position players such as running back Anthony Davis and wide receiver Lynn Swann, who would later embark on a Hall of Fame career with the Pittsburgh Steelers, and buried Notre Dame, 45–23, on the way to an unbeaten record and another national championship. The Trojans finished that season with six victories over ranked opponents, including Ohio State in the Rose Bowl.

Seven years had passed since McKay asserted that he would never again fall to the Fighting Irish. Neither team had provided an inkling of what was in store in 1973, as both entered their late-October clash unbeaten. But Notre Dame boasted something USC did not—a stifling defense that surrendered a mere 20 points in five previous games combined. The Trojans entered on a 23-game unbeaten streak, but it ended that afternoon as the Irish held Davis, who had exploded for six touchdowns against them in 1972, to just 55 yards on 19 carries. Counterpart Eric Penick wrested the hero role away with an 85-yard touchdown run early in the third quarter that highlighted a 23–14 victory.

And when it was over, Penick expressed the difference between the showy Trojans and the staid, traditional Irish. When it was suggested after the game that he should have put an exclamation point on his touchdown run by sliding on his knees into the end zone, a dramatic flair Davis had incorporated into his scoring jaunts, Penick was quick and decisive in his reply. "On my knees?" he asked disgustedly. "I'm no hot dog. This is Notre Dame."[9] Soon Penick and his Irish were celebrating a second national championship in eight years under Parseghian.

Dramatic changes were about to take place at both schools, but the greatness of their teams and the intensity of their rivalry would not soon founder. The "Era of Ara" ended when he embarked on a career as a college football television analyst in 1975 and was replaced on the sideline by former Green Bay Packers coach Dan Devine. McKay left USC after the 1975 season to take over the expansion Tampa Bay Buccaneers of the NFL, but his team didn't miss a beat under John Robinson, who had served under McKay as an offensive coordinator from 1972 to 1974.

Robinson took the baton from McKay and ran with it in dominating the Fighting Irish. His teams won six of seven games against its archrival. Robinson had received a jolt in his first game as head coach in 1976 with a lopsided loss to unranked Missouri, but the Trojans spent the rest of that season making amends. They steamrolled past one and all on the strength of a battering ground game featuring future standout running backs Ricky Bell and Charles White. Notre Dame provided their stiffest competition in a run of blowouts, falling in Los Angeles, 17–13. Even second-ranked Michigan proved less of a test than the Irish in a 14–6 USC victory in the Rose Bowl that allowed the Trojans to wrest the No. 2 spot away.

The Devine era signaled the beginning of a decline for the Notre Dame football program that lasted until late the next decade. But that failure to live up to the tradition of gridiron greatness was interrupted in 1977, when the Irish embarked on a national championship season and temporarily halted a period of dominance in the rivalry behind Joe Montana, who began the season as the third-string quarterback and whose potential was not fully realized until he blossomed into arguably the finest ever to grace an NFL field.

Notre Dame spent nearly the entire year making up for a Week 2 loss to unranked Mississippi that nearly destroyed its title hopes. The first serious test came in South Bend against USC, whose only loss was by one point to rugged Alabama. The Trojans boasted some of the greatest talent ever assembled on a college football team, including offensive stars, such as White and tackle Anthony Munoz, who would later be considered the greatest offensive lineman in NFL history, and defensive standouts, such as linebacker Clay Matthews and cornerback Ronnie Lott.

But in a star-studded game, it was a little-known Irish senior cornerback and holder named Ted Burgmeier that would play the role of hero. With his team leading 13–7 late in the second quarter, he corralled a bad snap on an extra-point attempt, raced to his left, and lofted a pass into the end zone to halfback Tom Domin for a two-point conversion. Burgmeier, who doubled as a pole-vaulter for the Notre Dame track team, was merely warming up. A minute later he ran 21 yards on a fake field goal to set up a touchdown pass from Montana to All-American tight end Ken McAfee, who finished the game with eight catches, including two scores. Burgmeier later ran 38 yards with an interception and added four unassisted tackles to his effort. And after the 49–19 thrashing of USC had been completed, Burgmeier spoke with reporters that had found ample reason to ignore him. "I'm kind of tickled," he said. "I'm not usually the one in the sun."[10]

There would not be any more tickled players in the Devine era after battles against USC. The Irish, who completed their unlikely run to the 1977 national crown with a stunning blowout defeat of powerful Texas in the Cotton Bowl, managed three more winning records under Devine, whose swan song in 1980 was destroyed when USC defeated his second-ranked team in the last week of the regular season. They then stumbled well into the 1980s under Gerry Faust, whose brilliance as a perennial championship high school coach in Cincinnati did not translate into greatness at the college level. He coached the Irish to a

30–26–1 record in five seasons, but the Trojans fared no better after Robinson left in 1983 after two close-but-no-cigar runs at a national championship in 1978 and 1979 and was replaced by Ted Tollner, whose 4–6–1 mark in his first year was the worst USC had experienced since 1960.

The lone notable achievement for Faust was that he halted Irish subservience in the rivalry, which had lasted 16 years, during which time they had won just twice. Faust won his last three battles against Tollner and the Trojans, after which new Notre Dame coach Lou Holtz picked up the baton and ran with it to eight more consecutive defeats of USC, including five against nationally ranked teams. But his success extended far beyond annual triumphs over the Trojans. He cast both himself and his team as underdogs in the eyes of the nation to motivate his players. He used both toughness, such as scheduling off-season workouts at 6:15 a.m., and gentleness to extract maximum effort. "Look at me," he once told a sportswriter when asked his feelings about taking over the Fighting Irish. "I'm five foot ten, I weigh 150 pounds, I talk with a lisp, I look like I have scurvy, I'm not very smart, I was a terrible football player, and I graduated 234th in a high school class of 278. What do you think it feels like to be named head coach at Notre Dame?" [11]

Holtz guided the Irish to their last era of consistent greatness after he was hired away from the University of Minnesota in 1986. And none of his teams was greater than that of 1988 when, coincidentally and marvelously for college football fans, the Trojans had also risen to the status of national title contender. The Irish topped the rankings with fellow unbeaten USC on their heels when they clashed at the Coliseum on November 26 in what many consider the most significant showdown in the history of The Cross-Country Rivalry.

The nationally televised clash under the lights before 93,289 fans at the Coliseum—the largest crowd in the annual clash since 1955—didn't feature highly touted star players aside from USC All-American quarterback Rodney Peete. But it certainly pitted the two premier teams in the nation. The Trojans had exceeded 30 points seven times in securing a 10–0 record while the Irish had dethroned the University of Miami for the top ranking and had exceeded 40 points scored in four of their previous seven games. Holtz, ever the motivator, claimed in an effort to fire up his charges that his team had been disrespected. Never mind that it was ranked No. 1 in the country.

His strategy worked. The Irish forced four turnovers in the first half, battered Peete from beginning to end, bolted to a 14–0 lead in the first quarter, and cruised to a 27–10 win despite being outgained and managing just eight first downs to 21 for the Trojans. It wasn't a pretty win, but as Holtz emphasized after the game, "Our football team is prettier than I am, but that's about it. They don't play pretty all the time, but they sure play together as a team."[12]

The defeat of USC didn't clinch a national championship for the Fighting Irish, but a 34–21 victory over third-ranked West Virginia in the Fiesta Bowl six weeks later did. The last great era of Notre Dame football for a quarter century had been launched. While the Trojans were disintegrating under Robinson replacement Larry Smith, who followed two PAC-10 championships and second-place finish with a 3–8 mark in 1991, the team's worst in 34 years, Holtz and his Irish were establishing themselves as perennial national title contenders. Notre Dame finished in the top five in the country four times in six years from 1988 to 1993, placing second in 1989 and 1993, the season they ran their winning streak against USC to a rivalry-record 11 straight games. Only a revenge loss to Miami in 1989 and upset defeat to Boston College in 1993 prevented the Irish from winning national crowns in those years as well.

What followed was a rare period in which both teams fell out of the championship spotlight. The Trojans fired Smith with three years remaining on his contract and rehired Robinson, but he and replacement Paul Hackett failed from 1993 to 2000 to return USC football to its glory. Meanwhile, Notre Dame regressed into a period of comparative mediocrity under Holtz; Bob Davie; Tyrone Willingham; the first black coach in school history; and Charlie Weis, losing at least three games in every season from 1994 to 2009 and never completing a season ranked higher than 11th in the country.

The struggles were over far sooner for USC. Not so coincidentally, they ended upon the hiring of former NFL coach Pete Carroll in the capacity. Carroll set out to recruit the Trojans back into greatness. He coached Hackett's players to a 2–5 record to start the 2001 season, as frustrated and impatient fans called for his ouster. But Carroll coached quarterback Carson Palmer to a Heisman Trophy in 2002 and recruited

Matt Leinart, as well as high-powered running back Reggie Bush, to reinvigorate an offense that had lost the explosiveness for which it had been known for generations. Led by Leinart and 1,000-yard receivers Mike Williams and Keary Colbert, the Trojans averaged 41.1 points a game in 2003 and won their last nine straight, including a 45–14 thrashing of Notre Dame and Rose Bowl defeat of Michigan, to capture the national championship.

The comeback of a program from a decade of mediocrity was complete, but its dominance of Notre Dame and the college football world had just begun. The Trojans mashed the Irish, 41–10, in 2004 en route to a second consecutive national title and first unblemished record since 1972 on the strength of brilliant performances from Leinart, premier wideout Steve Smith, and backfield mates Bush and LenDale White, who combined to rush for more than 2,000 yards. It was no surprise that USC remained No. 1 in the nation from the first poll to the last, after a stunningly thorough 55–19 victory over Oklahoma in the Orange Bowl had many concluding that the 2004 Trojans ranked among the greatest teams to ever grace a college football field.

The Irish, meanwhile, were embarking on a brief rise from the ashes in the mid-2000s under Weis. The result was a classic clash against Southern Cal in 2005 that nearly had the home crowd in South Bend celebrating. The matchup of the unbeaten, top-ranked Trojans and 4–1 Irish, as well as prolific quarterbacks Leinart and Brady Quinn, who was in the process of throwing for 3,919 yards and 32 touchdowns that season, was highly anticipated. Weis left no stone unturned to inspire his team. He invited Montana and Rudy Ruettiger, a former undersized Fighting Irish wide receiver about whom Hollywood had made a popular film and who had forged a career as a motivational speaker, to speak to his players.

It seemed that the millions of fans of the rivalry deserved a thrill—each of its previous five games was decided by at least 11 points—and they got one. Neither team led by more than seven at any point in the game as they traded scores and displayed the talent befitting top-10 powers. The Trojans appeared ripe for an upset when Quinn barreled into the end zone to give Notre Dame a 31–28 lead with five minutes remaining. They looked doomed when an incompletion, sack, and short pass resulted in 4th-and-9. But with defeat one missed connection away, Leinart hit Dwayne Jarrett for a 61-yard gain to the Irish 13.

Three runs took it to the 1-yard line with time running out. Leinart lunged toward the goal line on the next play, but the officials ruled that he had been stopped short as he fumbled the ball out of bounds. Weis and his charges sprinted onto the field to celebrate a monumental, program-altering victory with delirious fans who had joined them.

Meanwhile, Carroll was claiming to the officials that the clock had continued to run after the fumble. They realized he was right and they ordered the field cleared for seven more seconds of play. This time Leinart left no doubt. He weaved into the end zone for the winning score. The Irish were distraught after defeat had been wrested from the jaws of victory. "The reaction of the fans on the field and then seeing how you kind of want it to come out, then seeing the exact opposite all in a matter of minutes," Quinn said. "People were shocked and pretty devastated."[13]

The relieved Trojans continued their apparent march to a national championship. They scored at least 50 points in every game but one the rest of the regular season behind the immense talents of Leinart, Bush, and White, who combined for an incredible 68 touchdowns for the season, while the two backs contributed 3,042 yards rushing between them. But, alas, a 41–38 loss to Texas in the BCS Championship Game at the Rose Bowl gave the Longhorns the title.

In the annals of college football history, those results proved meaningless. The Trojans were stripped of their 2004 crown and all their 2005 victories, as well as their two conference titles, due to NCAA violations revolving around Bush's amateur status. Bush was forced to forfeit his 2005 Heisman Trophy. His punishment and that of the program, which was banned from bowl games in 2010 and 2011 and lost 30 scholarships, was deemed by many harshest ever meted out by the ruling body of college sports.

Notre Dame, meanwhile, eventually reverted back to recent form after the excruciating loss to the Trojans in 2005. The Irish won 15 of their next 20 games but fell to 3–9 in 2007, their worst record in 44 years. They managed a 16–21 record in their final three seasons under Weis, who was replaced in 2010 by University of Cincinnati coach Brian Kelly. While the Trojans were falling under the weight of the sanctions that motivated Carroll to opt for a head coaching position with the NFL Seattle Seahawks in 2010, Kelly was fixing the Fighting Irish. He recruited well enough to launch them into contention for a national crown in 2012. Led by such All-Americans as tight end Tyler Eifert and cele-brated linebacker Manti Te'o, they bumped off nationally ranked Mich-igan State, Michigan, Stanford, and Oklahoma to soar from No. 22 in the country to the top spot, which was clinched with a 22–13 defeat of the struggling Trojans. Only a lopsided loss to No. 2 but heavily favored Alabama prevented Notre Dame from winning its first national cham-pionship since 1977.

Times were changing in the rivalry. The Fighting Irish won three of four meetings from 2010 to 2013 after losing eight straight. But the more times changed, the more they stayed the same. Notre Dame vs. USC had remained one of the greatest rivalries in college football near-ly nine decades after it was launched. "There's no hitting like the hitting in a USC–Notre Dame game," said Nick Pappas, who starred as a USC running back in the earliest years of the rivalry. "Any Trojan who ever played in a Notre Dame game remembers every tackle, every block, every play called in the huddle."[14]

Not even the 2,000 miles that separate the two schools could damp-en the spirits of the players, coaches, and millions of fans who still relish those memories.

Fact Box (through 2013)
Nickname: The Cross-Country Rivalry
Trophy: The Jeweled Shillelagh
Total meetings: 85
Series record: Notre Dame leads, 45–35–5
First meeting: 1926 (Notre Dame 13, USC 12)
Largest margin of victory: Notre Dame, 1966 (Notre Dame 51, USC 0)
Longest winning streak: Notre Dame, 11 (1983–1993)

Game Results (home team listed second unless at a neutral site)
1926: Notre Dame 13, USC 12
1927: USC 6, Notre Dame 7
1928: Notre Dame 14, USC 27
1929: USC 12, Notre Dame 13
1930: Notre Dame 27, USC 0
1931: USC 16, Notre Dame 14
1932: Notre Dame 0, USC 13

1933: USC 19, Notre Dame 0
1934: Notre Dame 14, USC 0
1935: USC 13, Notre Dame 20
1936: Notre Dame 13, USC 13
1937: USC 6, Notre Dame 13
1938: Notre Dame 0, USC 13
1939: USC 20, Notre Dame 12
1940: Notre Dame 10, USC 6
1941: USC 18, Notre Dame 20
1942: Notre Dame 13, USC 0
1946: USC 6, Notre Dame 26
1947: Notre Dame 38, USC 7
1948: Notre Dame 14, USC 14
1949: USC 0, Notre Dame 32
1950: Notre Dame 7, USC 9
1951: Notre Dame 19, USC 12
1952: USC 0, Notre Dame 9
1953: Notre Dame 48, USC 14
1954: USC 17, Notre Dame 23
1955: Notre Dame 20, USC 42
1956: Notre Dame 20, USC 28
1957: USC 12, Notre Dame 40
1958: Notre Dame 20, USC 13
1959: USC 6, Notre Dame 16
1960: Notre Dame 17, USC 0
1961: USC 0, Notre Dame 3
1962: Notre Dame 0, USC 25
1963: USC 14, Notre Dame 17
1964: Notre Dame 17, USC 20
1965: USC 7, Notre Dame 28
1966: Notre Dame 51, USC 0
1967: USC 24, Notre Dame 7
1968: Notre Dame 21, USC 21
1969: USC 14, Notre Dame 14
1970: Notre Dame 28, USC 38
1971: USC 28, Notre Dame 14
1972: Notre Dame 23, USC 45
1973: USC 14, Notre Dame 23

1974: Notre Dame 24, USC 55
1975: USC 24, Notre Dame 17
1976: Notre Dame 13, USC 17
1977: USC 19, Notre Dame 49
1978: Notre Dame 25, USC 27
1979: USC 42, Notre Dame 23
1980: Notre Dame 3, USC 20
1981: USC 14, Notre Dame 7
1982: Notre Dame 13, USC 17
1983: USC 6, Notre Dame 27
1984: Notre Dame 19, USC 7
1985: USC 3, Notre Dame 37
1986: Notre Dame 38, USC 37
1987: USC 15, Notre Dame 26
1988: Notre Dame 27, USC 10
1989: USC 24, Notre Dame 28
1990: Notre Dame 10, USC 6
1991: USC 20, Notre Dame 24
1992: Notre Dame 31, USC 23
1993: USC 13, Notre Dame 31
1994: Notre Dame 17, USC 17
1995: USC 10, Notre Dame 38
1996: Notre Dame 20, USC 27
1997: USC 20, Notre Dame 17
1998: Notre Dame 0, USC 10
1999: USC 24, Notre Dame 25
2000: Notre Dame 38, USC 21
2001: USC 16, Notre Dame 27
2002: Notre Dame 13, USC 44
2003: USC 45, Notre Dame 14
2004: Notre Dame 10, USC 41
2005: USC 34, Notre Dame 31
2006: Notre Dame 24, USC 44
2007: USC 38, Notre Dame 0
2008: Notre Dame 3, USC 38
2009: USC 34, Notre Dame 27
2010: Notre Dame 20, USC 16
2011: USC 31, Notre Dame 17

2012: Notre Dame 22, USC 13
2013: USC 10, Notre Dame 14

Notre Dame Bowl Game Appearances

1925 Rose Bowl: Notre Dame 27, Stanford 10
1970 Cotton Bowl: Texas 21, Notre Dame 17
1971 Cotton Bowl: Notre Dame 24, Texas 11
1973 Orange Bowl: Nebraska 40, Notre Dame 6
1973 Sugar Bowl: Notre Dame 24, Alabama 23
1975 Orange Bowl: Notre Dame 13, Alabama 11
1976 Gator Bowl: Notre Dame 20, Penn State 9
1978 Cotton Bowl: Notre Dame 38, Texas 10
1979 Cotton Bowl: Notre Dame 35, Houston 34
1981 Sugar Bowl: Georgia 17, Notre Dame 10
1983 Liberty Bowl: Notre Dame 19, Boston College 18
1984 Aloha Bowl: Southern Methodist 27, Notre Dame 20
1988 Cotton Bowl: Texas A&M 35, Notre Dame 10
1989 Fiesta Bowl: Notre Dame 34, West Virginia 21
1990 Orange Bowl: Notre Dame 21, Colorado 6
1991 Orange Bowl: Colorado 10, Notre Dame 9
1992 Sugar Bowl: Notre Dame 39, Florida 28
1993 Cotton Bowl: Notre Dame 28, Texas A&M 3
1994 Cotton Bowl: Notre Dame 24, Texas A&M 21
1995 Fiesta Bowl: Colorado 41, Notre Dame 21
1996 Orange Bowl: Florida State 31, Notre Dame 26
1997 Independence Bowl: Louisiana State 27, Notre Dame 9
1999 Gator Bowl: Georgia Tech 35, Notre Dame 28
2001 Fiesta Bowl: Oregon State 41, Notre Dame 9
2003 Gator Bowl: North Carolina State 28, Notre Dame 6
2004 Insight Bowl: Oregon State 38, Notre Dame 21
2006 Fiesta Bowl: Ohio State 34, Notre Dame 20
2007 Sugar Bowl: Louisiana State 41, Notre Dame 14
2008 Hawaii Bowl: Notre Dame 49, Hawaii 21
2010 Sun Bowl: Notre Dame 33, Miami 17
2011 Champs Sports Bowl: Florida State 18, Notre Dame 14
2013 BCS Championship: Alabama 42, Notre Dame 14
2013 Pinstripe Bowl: Notre Dame 29, Rutgers 16

USC Bowl Game Appearances

1923 Rose Bowl: USC 14, Penn State 3
1924 Christmas Festival: USC 20, Missouri 7
1930 Rose Bowl: USC 47, Pittsburgh 14
1932 Rose Bowl: USC 21, Tulane 12
1933 Rose Bowl: USC 35, Pittsburgh 0
1939 Rose Bowl: USC 7, Duke 3
1940 Rose Bowl: USC 14, Tennessee 0
1944 Rose Bowl: USC 39, Washington 0
1945 Rose Bowl: USC 25, Tennessee 0
1946 Rose Bowl: Alabama 34, USC 14
1948 Rose Bowl: Michigan 49, USC 0
1953 Rose Bowl: USC 7, Wisconsin 0
1955 Rose Bowl: Ohio State 20, USC 7
1963 Rose Bowl: USC 42, Wisconsin 37
1967 Rose Bowl: Purdue 14, USC 13
1968 Rose Bowl: USC 14, Indiana 3
1969 Rose Bowl: Ohio State 27, USC 16
1970 Rose Bowl: USC 10, Michigan 3
1973 Rose Bowl: USC 42, Ohio State 17
1974 Rose Bowl: Ohio State 42, USC 21
1975 Rose Bowl: USC 18, Ohio State 17
1975 Liberty Bowl: USC 20, Texas A&M 0
1977 Rose Bowl: USC 14, Michigan 6
1977 Bluebonnet Bowl: USC 47, Texas A&M 28
1979 Rose Bowl: USC 17, Michigan 10
1980 Rose Bowl: USC 17, Ohio State 16
1982 Fiesta Bowl: Penn State 26, USC 10
1985 Rose Bowl: USC 20, Ohio State 17
1985 Aloha Bowl: Alabama 24, USC 3
1987 Citrus Bowl: Auburn 16, USC 7
1988 Rose Bowl: USC 20, Michigan State 17
1989 Rose Bowl: Michigan 22, USC 14
1990 Rose Bowl: USC 17, Michigan 10
1990 John Hancock Bowl: Michigan State 17, USC 16
1992 Freedom Bowl: Fresno State 24, USC 7
1993 Freedom Bowl: USC 28, Utah 21
1995 Cotton Bowl: USC 55, Texas Tech 14

1996 Rose Bowl: USC 41, Northwestern 32
1998 Sun Bowl: Texas Christian 28, USC 19
2001 Las Vegas Bowl: Utah 10, USC 6
2003 Orange Bowl: USC 38, Iowa 17
2004 Rose Bowl: USC 28, Michigan 14
2005 Orange Bowl: USC 55, Oklahoma 19
2006 Rose Bowl: Texas 41, USC 38
2007 Rose Bowl: USC 32, Michigan 18
2008 Rose Bowl: USC 49, Illinois 17
2009 Rose Bowl: USC 38, Penn State 24
2009 Emerald Bowl: USC 24, Boston College 13
2012 Sun Bowl: Georgia Tech 21, USC 7
2013 Las Vegas Bowl: USC 45, Fresno State 20

6

HARVARD VS. YALE: THE GAME

Their football programs have been invisible for generations in the hierarchy of the college football elite. Their annual clashes receive little attention outside the Ivy League campuses in which their teams reside. Yet so legendary is the Harvard–Yale rivalry that their yearly battles are known simply as "The Game."

The relative obscurity in which they now play from a national perspective could not have been imagined in the late 1800s and early 1900s, when both teams were college football powers that combined for 18 national championships. The tradition of the rivalry still attracts sellout crowds in Cambridge and throngs for 50,000 to New Haven.

That tradition began in 1875, when Yale hosted the first clash. Competition between the schools was nothing new; they had already been battling in crew and baseball. Both football programs had been launched within the previous three years, which one might have believed would have resulted in parity during the early years of the rivalry. But after the Crimson won the initial battle, 4–0, the Bulldogs dominated, winning 14 of the next 16 meetings. That was a mean feat considering they had no coach from 1872 to 1887, during which time they achieved a stunning record of 79–5–8.

The hospitality shown by the Yale students before the rivalry kickoff clash in 1875, when about 150 Harvard fans were given a tour of the campus and fine housing, was not reciprocated following the game. A group of Crimson fans were arrested for loudly celebrating the victory in the streets of New Haven. But the rivalry eventually took on a more

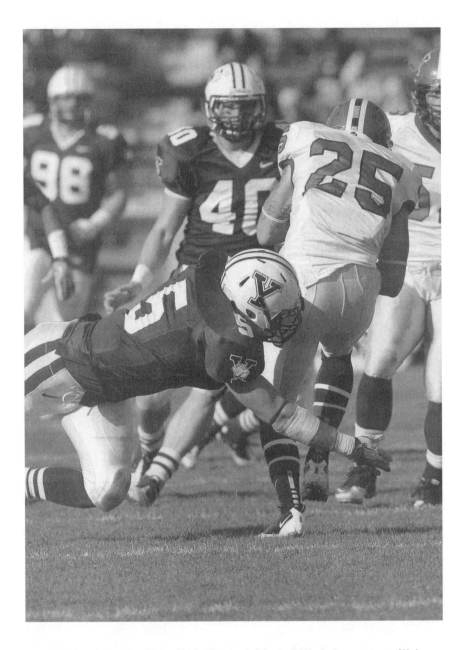

Figure 6.1.   Harvard at Yale, 2011. *Photograph by Jack Warhola, courtesy of Yale Athletics*

cordial nature that befitted the breeding and intellectualism of the players who were fortunate enough to have been accepted into those Ivy League institutions.

Walter Camp, whose name became synonymous with American youth football, was hired as the first Yale football coach in 1888. The dominance of the program reached a new level. He guided the Bulldogs to a 67–2 record in five seasons before handing the reins to William Rhodes, who lost just once in 27 games.

The late 1870s and 1880s proved frustrating to Harvard and its fans. The Crimson spent nearly every season clobbering all in their path until falling to perennial national champions Yale and Princeton. Harvard managed a record of 2–17–2 against those teams during that stretch. They lost only to Yale and Princeton five times from 1878 to 1889 before snagging their own national crown in 1890.

Such titles were more than mythical, even back before the turn of the 19th century. Several organizations picked champions and Yale was the most frequent winner with 19 in the 1800s, including seven undisputed. Future College Football Hall of Famers dotted their rosters of that era, such as legendary end Amos Alonzo Stagg, end Frank Hinkey, and a slew of linemen, including one colorfully nicknamed "Wild Bill" Hickok, but none proved more influential to team success than guard William "Pudge" Heffelfinger, who is considered by many the greatest player of his generation. The three-time All-American was credited for foiling the famed Princeton wedge blocking formation by hurtling himself into the Tigers and knocking them to the ground. So deadly was Heffelfinger that during the 1888 clash at the Polo Grounds in New York, Princeton player Hec Cowan screamed at him, "Cut that out or you'll kill somebody!"[1]

The Yale and Harvard players nearly killed each other six years later. The bloody 1894 battle was marred by one broken leg, one broken collarbone, and a brain contusion that landed a Yale player in the hospital, spurring rumors that he had been killed. Seven players in all were carried off the field during the Bulldogs' victory. Historian George Sullivan later wrote the following about the media reaction to what had become known as the Springfield Massacre:

> So savage was combat on a neutral Springfield gridiron . . . that newspapers printed a casualty summary similar to those listing vic-

tims of a disaster. The game's violence appalled the world and ignit-
ed a national uproar about football ferocity—outrange that threatened the sport's future.[2]

The violence of that clash, after which each team blamed the other,
prompted a cessation of hostilities for two years. Little had changed
upon its renewal in 1897. So important had the game become that it
was moved permanently to the end of the schedule a year later. But
after one victory and two ties to close the 1800s, the Crimson reestablished their place as the personal punching bags for their rival. They
simply boasted less talent well into the next century and the result was
Bulldog dominance. Harvard lost a mere 14 games from 1900 to 1910—
eight of them to Yale. Though the Crimson boasted such College Football Hall of Fame talent as quarterback Charles Dudley Dale and tackle
Hamilton Fish III during those years, the Bulldogs were loaded with
premier players, such as fullback Ted Coy, tackle James Hogan, quarterback Art Howe, and ends Tom Shevlin and John Kilpatrick. From
1903 to 1936, they boasted a whopping 36 All-Americans. What was
perplexing about their consistent greatness was their revolving door on
the sideline. Yale had no coach serving in successive seasons from 1899
to 1912 due to the unpaid nature of the position. But from 1900 to
1908, none lost more than one game and the team managed a combined
record of 90–4–5.

Despite the lopsided nature of the rivalry in its early years, the
passion displayed by its participants grew into legend. In 1908, Harvard
coach Percy Haughton purportedly choked a bulldog to death in front
of his players and tossed the dead carcass to the feet of his players to
inspire them. If the story is indeed true, it served a gruesome purpose,
as the Crimson broke a six-game losing streak (all of which were shutouts) to the live Bulldogs with a 4–0 victory. (Over the past decade,
several articles have busted the bulldog-choking myth; it appears that
Haughton did "choke" a paper mache bulldog and drag it around campus behind his car.)

By the second decade of the 20th century, the lack of continuity at
coach had finally begun to take a toll at Yale, and Haughton had transformed the Crimson into a perennial national championship contender.
Harvard was handed the crown in the majority of polls in 1910, 1912,
and 1913. It embarked on a 31-game winning streak from 1912 to the

middle of the 1915 season behind such talents as end Huntington
Hardwick, fullback Eddie Mahan, guard Stan Pennock, and halfback
Percy Wendell. The Crimson exacted revenge for the thrashings they
had received at the paws of the Bulldogs for more than a generation,
beating them four straight, including a 41–0 blanking in 1915.

Haughton was quite the innovator. He introduced such new ideas as
the unbalanced backfield, shifting defenses, the five-man defensive
line, defensive signals, and what was known as the "mousetrap play,"
which purposely allowed a defender to cross the line of scrimmage so
that he could be blocked on his side and cut down. The success of the
Crimson teams coached by Haughton was based on speed, timing, and
the proper execution of a comparatively thin playbook.

That 1912 defeat finally motivated Yale to hire a paid coach. Its
choice was Howard Jones, but it wasn't until his brother T. A. D. Jones
took over the position in 1916 that the Bulldogs regained their bark.
Jones proved as inspirational as Haughton without animal sacrifice, motivating his charges before their 1916 battle against Harvard by invoking

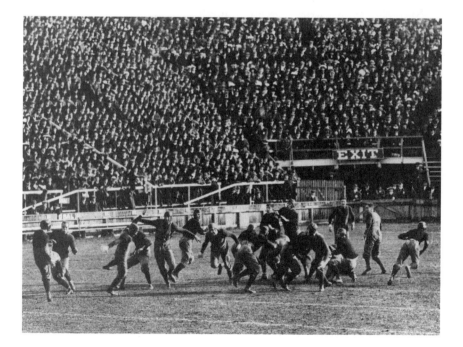

Figure 6.2. Harvard at the old Yale Field, 1912. *Courtesy of Yale Athletics*

the name of a fallen Yale football legend who had died less than a year earlier from pneumonia contracted while pacing the sideline during a Bulldogs game. "If any of you believe in the hereafter," he said, "you will know that Tom Shevlin is pacing up and down across the river, smoking that big black cigar and asking you boys to go out there and do it once again for papa."[3]

The fired-up Bulldogs ended their four-game losing streak to the Crimson that day with a 6–3 victory in which Joseph Neville scored the first Yale touchdown in the series since 1909, their last national title year. The game was played in front of an estimated 80,000 fans in New Haven.

World War I resulted in the suspension of the series the next two years. By that time, the dominance of future Ivy League teams in college football was over. Harvard, Yale, or Princeton had earned poll votes for every national championship from 1869 to 1913, but the emergence of college football powers in the Midwest early in the 20th century and the heightened competition on their own schedules spelled the end of supremacy for the Crimson and Bulldogs. Most of their All-Americans had long since ended their gridiron careers by the 1920s.

Not that both programs didn't field occasional powerhouses after hostilities in Europe ended. Now coached by Haughton disciple Robert T. Fisher, Harvard blitzed through its 1919 season unbeaten, knocking off Yale in the final regular season game before a 7–6 victory over Oregon in the Rose Bowl clinched a national championship. The star of that team was All-American halfback Eddie Casey, a future College Football Hall of Famer and Harvard coach. He snagged two key receptions in the only Crimson touchdown drive in the victory over the Ducks to win Most Valuable Player honors for the game.

Harvard followed with their last national title in 1920 and ran an unbeaten streak to 25 that included 18 shutouts the following year. The Crimson also maintained their mastery of Yale, winning their eighth of nine and fourth straight in the series in 1922. The Bulldogs were stumbling. They had assumed the role of Harvard through much of the early 20th century, winning most of their games before losing to Princeton in the annual rivalry showdown.

Then came 1923. That season had a different feel from the start. Not only were the Crimson struggling through their worst season since 1880 with a 4–3–1 record, but the Bulldogs also had emerged as a national power behind the All-American talents of fullback Bill Mallory and tackle Century Milstead. The power of the Bulldogs became evident in a midseason triumph in which they outscored powerful Army 24–0 in the second half to secure a 31–10 victory in front of 80,000 fans that had stuffed the Yale Bowl.

The Bulldogs then sought to avenge four consecutive defeats to the Crimson three weeks later. The game was played in a driving rainstorm in Cambridge. Jones sought to inspire his players before kickoff. "Gentlemen, you are now going to play football against Harvard," he said. "Never again in your whole life will you do anything so important."[4]

Particularly fired up, apparently, was Yale halfback Raymond Pond. He returned a fumble 63 yards for a touchdown through what legendary sportswriter Grantland Rice described in the *New York Herald Tribune* as "seventeen lakes, five quagmires and a water hazard."[5] The adventurous jaunt down the soaked, muddy field motivated Rice to nickname the halfback "Ducky" Pond, a moniker that would stick throughout his career as a player and coach, which ended in 1951. Pond's heroics proved crucial in a 13–0 victory, after which nearly 1,000 Bulldog supporters emerged from the Yale Club in New York City and marched to the Harvard Club to rub it in. They could not celebrate a national championship, however. A lack of strong competition aside from Army—Harvard and Princeton were both down that year—resulted in Yale being ignored in every poll despite its unbeaten record.

The defeat of the Crimson marked the beginning of an era of Bulldog dominance in the rivalry. Aside from a 1925 scoreless tie, Yale emerged victorious in every clash through 1927. Harvard managed to score just 13 points in those five games. But the retirement of Jones after a 14–0 defeat of the Crimson to put the finishing touches on a 7–1 season in 1927 and the hiring of successor Mal Stevens spelled the end of Yale greatness.

Gone forever were the days of national prominence for either team. But individual talent, such as Harvard quarterback Barry Wood and Yale counterpart Albie Booth, prevented the programs from falling into obscurity. In 1931 and 1932, Wood and tackle Irad Hardy became the last Division I All-Americans to wear Harvard uniforms (offensive linemen Dan Jiggetts and Michael Corbat would be so honored in Division I-AA in 1975 and 1982, respectively). Yale landed several players on All-

American teams after Booth in 1929 but would never return to national championship contention.

The Bulldogs did rise into the top 10 in the mid- to late 1930s behind the talents of back-to-back Heisman Trophy winners Larry Kelley and Clint Frank. Kelley, who became the first to be formally awarded the Heisman in 1936, caught 17 passes for 372 yards that season, quite a feat during an era of college football dominated by the ground game. Frank earned the Heisman in 1937. He was the team's most potent back, scoring four touchdowns against Princeton, and easily its best defender.

What he couldn't do was will his team to a victory over Harvard despite a sensational individual performance. Tickets for the showdown were being scalped for a then-unheard-of $25 apiece in the midst of the Great Depression. Former president Herbert Hoover was in attendance as the snow fell on the sellout crown in Cambridge. Frank played despite an injured knee and surgically repaired shoulder. And boy, did he play. He racked up an incredible total of 50 tackles in an attempt to keep the fifth-ranked Bulldogs unbeaten. The Crimson forged ahead 6–0 on a 25-yard touchdown pass from Frank Foley to Don Daughters. Frank engineered a third-quarter touchdown drive that gave his team the lead, but Foley scored on a nine-yard run to secure the upset. The score would undoubtedly have been more lopsided if not for the defensive heroics of Frank, whose perseverance and production despite worsening injury inspired game umpire Tom Thorp to exclaim, "He stuck it out when two iron men would have called it a day."[6] Despite his brilliance, the defeat haunted Frank. "I've thought about that game through a lot of sleepless nights," he later said. "I've been told to forget it, that perhaps it was the best thing that ever happened to me but I can't believe that."[7]

What he likely also could not believe was the collapse of his program after he left. After boasting a fine 24–8–1 record in his first four seasons as coach, Pond forged a 6–17–1 mark from 1938 to 1940, during which time future president Gerald Ford served as one of his assistants. Pond was replaced for one year by Spike Nelson, whose team also lost seven of eight games, before successor Howard Odell turned the Bulldogs around.

The Crimson beat Yale in four of five meetings from 1937 to 1941, but they weren't much better during that era. They managed an

18–18–5 mark from 1938 to 1942, bottoming out at 2–6–1 in that last of those seasons. The suspension of Harvard football over the next two years as World War II raged overseas served to allow the program to regroup and thrive quite temporarily in the late 1940s.

The Bulldogs continued to play during the war and enjoyed one last hurrah behind All-American end Paul Walker in 1944 when they inched their way into the national rankings at No. 20 by winning their first seven games before a season-ending tie against Virginia. That Yale could only squeeze into that ranking after steamrolling past its first seven foes indicates how far its program and that of other future members of the Ivy League had fallen in the eyes of the voters. Their schedules simply didn't measure up to the Alabamas, Oklahomas, and Ohio States of the college football world, nor could they recruit to anywhere near their levels. The academic standards of the Yales and Harvards, as well as the dreams of athletes to play at football factories that would prove to be stepping stones into the NFL, precluded those schools from competing for high-level talent.

Not that the universities cared all that much. Football greatness and national attention became low on the list of priorities at such schools. With nothing to play for but pride, the Harvard–Yale rivalry took on added importance emotionally for its combatants and fans. And when both happened to field strong teams, the annual battles gained significance in the hearts and minds of all involved.

One such clash occurred in 1946, when both teams entered The Game with one loss. A sellout crowd of 57,000 that packed Harvard Stadium were built up when their team raced to a 14–0 lead in the first quarter and deflated when the Bulldogs roared back to score 27 unanswered points behind running backs Ferdie "Bull" Nadherny and Levi Jackson, who was not only the first African American to play for Yale but was also named its captain in 1949.

That team was coached by colorful, rotund Herman Hickman, one of the greatest linemen in the history of college football at the University of Tennessee who had let himself go physically. Hickman earned a reputation as a bit of an oddball for his pregame speeches in which he attempted to link famous historical figures or eras with football. Before one game against Harvard, he used a Revolutionary War speech first delivered by Patrick Henry in an attempt to inspire his charges. He went back many centuries before another game to invoke the spirit of the Thracian gladiator Spartacus. "If we must fight, let us fight for ourselves," Hickman stressed to his players. "If we must slaughter, let us slaughter our oppressors! If we just die, let it be under the clear sky, by the bright waters, in noble, honorable battle!"[8]

Hickman proved to be a far superior orator than he was a coach. His teams managed a 16–17–1 record in four seasons before he was replaced by Jordan Olivar, who transformed the Bulldogs into a consistent winner despite spending his off-season running his insurance business in California. His assistant coaches took care of recruiting and when the school outlawed spring practices upon his arrival in 1952, he did not have to concern himself with that, either.

The Olivar era began with a bang. He guided a team that had dropped to 2–5–2 under Hickman the previous season to seven wins in nine games, including a 41–14 dismantling of Harvard in which quarterback Ed Molloy threw three scoring strikes to Ed Woodsum. But the humiliation of a 27-point shellacking was worsened for Harvard when Yale team manager Charlie Yeager, whom Olivar sent into the game, put the cherry on top by catching a two-point conversion after the final touchdown. But Yeager later claimed that the notion of shaming Harvard was not the motivating factor in seeking a brief claim to fame. "The idea certainly was not to embarrass Harvard," Yeager later said. "It really was kind of a Walter Mitty fantasy thing. . . . I doubt that Jordan had any idea of the huge impact, how Harvard would be outranged and consider it such an insult. I suspect he was kind of sorry afterward because of the repercussions.

"Yet the incident may have helped Harvard. Its football program had been going through tough times, and there was even talk of dropping the sport. But this so fired up everyone in Cambridge that it rallied them behind football. At least that's what I've been told by a number of Harvard people."[9]

Indeed, the Crimson had been struggling mightily. They suffered through a three-season stretch in which they won just five games before turning their program around with a four-game winning streak in 1952. They played The Game the next two years as if driven by thoughts of revenge and had become strong enough as a team to exact it. Harvard blanked Yale in 1953 and followed with another triumph a year later.

By that time the de-emphasis of sports at Harvard, Yale, and other schools that would eventually make up the Ivy League had been completed. Athletic scholarships were no longer offered. Postseason bowl invitations were outlawed. Spring practices were a thing of the past. And since their schedules were dominated by like-minded institutions, the schools decided to form the Ivy League in 1956. No longer were Harvard and Yale independent. The motivation of playing for a conference championship, which was sometimes on the line when they clashed to close the season, added to the luster of the matchup despite the shrinking interest on a national level.

The Ivy League was launched at just the right time for the Bulldogs, who were on a roll under Olivar. They swept through their conference schedule unbeaten to win its first crown, capping the feat with a 42–14 victory over the slipping Crimson and scoring at least 40 points in each of their last three games. That defeat was the last straw for Harvard coach Lloyd Jordan, whose records had worsened every year since 1952, leading to his ouster in favor of an unknown staid tactician named John Yovicsin, who became the longest-tenured and one of the most successful coaches in school history. His teams generally rose to the occasion in The Game, forging an 8–5–1 record against Yale from 1957 to 1970.

Yovicsin was far from inspirational. He depended on others to do their jobs mentally, emotionally, and physically. "He was a business-like leader who would delegate a lot to his coordinators," explained wide receiver Pete Varney, who played under Yovicsin in the late 1960s. "He was very low-key. At the type of school we attended, there was a lot of self-motivation from the players. We were playing because we loved it, not because we had a scholarship."[10]

The battles during that era were among the best and most significant the rivalry had ever experienced. Harvard outscored Yale, 63–6, in successive thrashings in 1958 and 1959, the second of which completed a late-season collapse that wiped out a 5–0 start that had Yale soaring to No. 13 in the nation. But there would be no collapse in 1960 as the Bulldogs finished the season undefeated and ranked No. 14 after they easily knocked Princeton from the unbeaten ranks and avenged the two defeats to Harvard with a 39–6 victory. Olivar considered the 1960 team the best in school history.

He might have retracted that statement later in that decade. Yale coach Carmen Cozza had taken over the program in 1965 and transformed it into an Ivy League power. He certainly got help from two of the finest skill position players in conference history—quarterback Brian Dowling and running back Calvin Hill. In 1968, the former shattered season and career school records for touchdowns and passing yards. The latter rejected scholarship offers in favor of a Yale education and a chance to play quarterback, thereby breaking an unspoken color barrier like his hero, Jackie Robinson. The presence of the prolific Dowling, who was also lured in as a member of Cozza's first recruiting class, forced the coach to move Hill to halfback early in his freshman year. Hill was upset but didn't allow it to affect his play. He developed a tremendous chemistry with Dowling, with whom he would sometimes invent plays on the fly. "It wasn't a symphony, it was jazz," said Hill, who also starred on the track team. "There was a lot of improvisation. Brian was a John Coltrane. It was fun. Football was fun. If you thought you could beat a guy, you just invented something."[11]

The pair proved instrumental in the blossoming of the Bulldogs in 1967 and 1968, when they won 16 consecutive games. And in one of those once-in-a-lifetime scenarios, the Crimson also emerged as a power in 1968. Both teams entered The Game with 8–0 records. And it proved worthy of the hype, as well as a needed respite from the virulent antiwar protests that had rocked the Harvard campus in that most violent year in American history.

The clash pitted a Yale offense that ranked sixth in the nation with an average of 35.2 points a game against a Harvard defense that was leading the country by yielding a meager average of 7.6 points. But Dowling threw for two touchdowns, including one that made Hill the all-time leading scorer at the school, and ran for another as the Bulldogs bolted to a 22–0 lead in the second quarter. The Crimson appeared doomed, especially when Yovicsin benched starting quarterback George Lalich in favor of junior Frank Champi, who began the year as the fourth string. Champi responded with a touchdown pass of his own to cut the deficit to 22–6 at halftime.

Lalich was again benched after a three-and-out after intermission. Champi led a scoring drive that closed the gap to 22–13, but Dowling answered with a touchdown run to stretch the Yale lead to 29–13 with 10:44 remaining in the game. And when Dowling marched his team downfield yet again with four minutes left, the only mystery that seemingly remained was the final score. Yale's sixth fumble of the game appeared meaningless, especially when Champi also lost the ball on the next possession. But Harvard tackle Fritz Reed scooped it up and ran 25 yards to the Bulldogs 15. Champi then tossed his second touchdown pass to Bruce Freeman to cut the deficit to 29–19. Harvard needed a two-point conversion to stay alive and got one after a pass interference call provided a second chance. It was 29–21 with 42 seconds remaining.

The Crimson would still need a miracle. And when Bill Kelly recovered an onside kick, it seemed destiny was on their side. Dowling was so desperate that he asked Cozza if he could join the defense on the field—after all, he had recorded 32 interceptions in high school. The request was denied. A 14-yard run by Champi and a penalty moved Harvard to the Yale 20 with 32 seconds left. After two incompletions, the Crimson shocked everyone in the stadium by calling a draw play that netted 14 yards. Harvard called time-out with 14 seconds remaining. The tension reached a fever pitch when Champi was sacked at the 8-yard line, which forced the Crimson to burn their final time-out with three seconds left.

The next play seemed to take an eternity. Champi dropped back to pass, pump-faked twice, ran forward, faked two more throws, scrambled back to the 16, looked right, turned left, and spotted running back Vic Gatto getting open in the end zone. Champi heaved the ball in his general direction as he was getting hit by the Yale defender. Touchdown. "I thought someone was breathing down my neck," Champi explained. "I scrambled. I threw off my wrong foot. Gatto was open for a moment. After that, I remember feeling a sense of inevitability. I thought, 'We've come this far.' I was very confident. It was inevitable."[12]

Harvard had scored two touchdowns in 42 seconds, but there was the small matter of another two-point conversion to secure a tie. There was also the small matter of clearing off the Crimson fans that had stormed the field. What happened next seemed like a fait accompli. Champi rolled right and hit a slanting Pete Varney in the middle of the end zone to complete one of the most miraculous comebacks in college football history. So thrilling was the accomplishment that the memorable headline in the Harvard student newspaper screamed, "Harvard beats Yale, 29–29."[13] Cozza, on the other hand, was both dumbfounded and distressed. "It was almost like a nightmare, really," he said. "I don't know how else to explain it. We feel like we lost it, even though we didn't. Something like that won't happen again in 1,000 years."[14]

It didn't happen in 1974, but the result was equally painful for the Bulldogs, which entered The Game that season undefeated and ranked No. 1 in the nation defensively with an average of 5.7 points yielded per game behind future NFL standout defensive back Gary Fencik. Meanwhile, host Harvard had lost just once in the conference and was playing for a share of its title. But that defeat had occurred the week before against Ivy League weakling Brown. Fans wondered if the Crimson could recover from the blow.

Both teams had remained forces in the Ivy League since the epic 1968 showdown. Cozza was in the midst of a 31-year run at Yale, while Joe Restic had replaced Yovicsin at Harvard in 1971 and would remain there through 1993. Cozza was already established as one of the finest coaches in Bulldog history, while his counterpart was in the process of doing the same with the Crimson. It was no wonder that Harvard Stadium was jammed when the combatants took the field in 1974. And it was no wonder that there were many groans emanating from the stands when the first quarter led to two Yale touchdowns. But those groans turned to cheers when Crimson prolific southpaw quarterback Mike Holt, who doubled as a top baseball pitcher, answered with scoring strikes to future All-Pro punter Pat McInally and Peter Curtin, the second of which occurred with nine seconds remaining in the first half and gave Harvard a 14–13 lead.

The second half was dominated by defense. Yale forged ahead on a field goal and maintained its lead with five minutes remaining in the game. Harvard was pinned back on its own 5-yard line. The Hawaiian-born Holt sought to bring calm to his teammates in the huddle. "This is great, isn't it?" he exclaimed. [15] It was far from great for Holt, who was playing with a concussion. But he engineered a drive to the Yale 1-yard line with 19 seconds left. Holt then sprinted left, saw that McInally was double covered, and crossed the goal line for the score that knocked the Bulldogs from the ranks of the unbeaten and gave Harvard a piece of the Ivy League crown.

Even a tie against a Cozza-coached team of that era seemed like a triumph for the Crimson, who were generally .500 or better, but not at the level of the perennial conference champion Bulldogs, who had embarked on an era of dominance. They won six titles from 1974 to 1981, achieving a record of 60–11–3 during that stretch, and they would have won a seventh had they not lost to Harvard in 1975. They achieved greatness through a consistent offense and stalwart defense that never allowed opponents an average of more than 12.4 points a game from 1975 to 1980. Their 1976 unit yielded a mere 8.6 points a game, which ranked third in the nation.

They did not, however, dominate Harvard. The Crimson indeed beat Cozza and his Bulldogs in 1974, 1975, and 1979 and lost by just one touchdown in 1978. One major reason for their success was the innovative Restic, who brought the "Multiflex" offense to his program. He changed formations and sent several men in motion before every snap, thereby causing confusion and uncertainty for opposing defenses. He believed it was most effective against premier defenders who reacted instinctively to what they saw because what they saw and reacted to was not the play the Crimson ended up running. "The ball's coming, they don't know where," Restic explained. "You're running the football, they're running for coverage. We set in motion, we change the set, they're running, they're scrambling." Cozza knew all about it. "When we play Harvard," he said, "we have to be ready to defend the United States."[16]

The mediocrity that descended on both programs began when they were moved to Division I-AA in 1982. Yale hit a tailspin from which it would not emerge until Cozza had been replaced by Jack Siedlecki in 1997. The Bulldogs dropped from 9–1 in 1981 to 1–9 in 1983 and never recovered under Cozza. They managed just five winning seasons from 1982 to 1996 and won no Ivy League crowns, though they shared one with Princeton in 1989. Harvard fared much better for a while, earning shares of the conference title in 1983 and 1984 and winning it outright in 1987 before a monumental collapse. The Crimson managed a mark of 34–57–1 from 1986 to 1996 as Restic gave way to Timothy L. Murphy.

The struggles of both teams brought parity in the rivalry. Neither team won more than two consecutive meetings from 1979 to 1994. The Murphy era, however, changed everything. He transformed the Crimson into an Ivy League power and the dominant team in the series. Siedlecki managed to turn the Bulldogs into a perennial conference title contender, but they were frustrated on nearly an annual basis by Harvard. The only interruption from the dominance was a three-game Yale winning streak from 1998 to 2000. The Crimson won 15 of the other 16 games played between the two teams from 1995 to 2013.

The first incarnation of Harvard greatness under Murphy was in 1997, when only a loss to Bucknell prevented an unbeaten season. The Crimson steamrolled past every Ivy League foe on their way to their first unshared conference crown in 10 years. The heroes of that season were quarterback Rich Linden, who passed for 2,099 yards and 16 touchdowns, and running back Chris Menick, who rushed for 1,267 yards and 13 scores.

Murphy and his charges were just getting rolling. After three mediocre seasons, they embarked on one of the greatest runs in program history. The Crimson won all nine games in 2001 for their first unbeaten, untied season in 88 years. They achieved the feat through virtually mistake-free football, committing just nine turnovers the entire year, and the talent of wide receiver Carl Morris, who caught 71 passes for 943 yards and 12 touchdowns. The 2004 Crimson matched that success with a 10–0 record behind future NFL standout quarterback Ryan Fitzpatrick, who accounted for 2,432 yards and 18 touchdowns through the air and on the ground to win Ivy League Most Valuable Player honors.

Fitzpatrick was not the first sensational quarterback of the era to grace the field when the two combatants met. That distinction would be achieved by Yale signal caller Joe Walland, who led his team to a 9–1 record in 1999, its finest in 18 years, and capped his brilliant season with a 24–21 victory over Harvard in which he overcame the flu to toss the game-winning touchdown pass to Eric Johnson, who scooped the ball up inches off the ground with just 29 seconds remaining in the fourth quarter. The play capped off the most prolific passing performance in Yale history. Walland completed 42 of 67 passes (attempting an astounding 51 in the second half alone) for 437 yards. Johnson became only the third player in the history of Division I-AA football to catch 21 passes or more. And when it was over, Murphy heaped praise on his quarterback. "Eric Johnson is a hell of a football player, but Joe Walland is special," he said. "Walland is one of those quarterbacks who wills things to happen. He should have legendary status in this neck of the woods now."[17] Walland finished his career with nine Yale career records, including passing yards with 4,832 and touchdowns with 46.

But neither Walland nor Fitzpatrick was involved in the most epic Harvard–Yale clash of the era in 2005. Neither team was of championship caliber that season, but the rivalry had long since abandoned the notion that it was about winning titles or earning its way into the national consciousness.

The Crimson entered on a three-game winning streak and was certainly a superior team, but the Bulldogs roared to a 14–3 lead that motivated Murphy to blast his players in the locker room. He was shocked when they responded by yielding a 65-yard touchdown drive to start the second half that put them behind, 21–3. But staring doom in the eye, the Crimson finally came to life behind premier halfback Clifton Dawson, who rushed for 128 yards in the game but closed the gap to 21–10 on a 16-yard touchdown reception from quarterback Liam O'Hagan. Then it was the turn of Harvard cornerback Steven Williams to play the role of hero with a pick-six that made it 21–16 early in the fourth quarter. After a Yale field goal, O'Hagan tied it at 24–24 on a scoring strike to Alex Breaux and two-point conversion on a quarterback draw. The comeback was complete, but it took the first three-overtime game in Ivy League history to decide the outcome. Dawson, who later earned a short stint in the NFL, clinched the victory with an eight-yard touchdown run to give Harvard its largest comeback victory ever in the series. "For weeks and weeks people said it was the greatest game they had ever seen," Murphy later exclaimed. "Not just the greatest Harvard–Yale game but the greatest game. For a coach, you don't think about that until you get exposed to people who have seen a lot of those games. There are a lot of people out there who have seen 50 of them."[18]

The victory marked the fifth straight for Harvard over Yale. The Bulldogs ended that run in 2006, but the Crimson continued their dominance with a seven-game winning streak from 2007 to 2013, the longest in the history of the rivalry since Yale won eight in a row in the 1880s. But that rivalry was kept alive not by the outcome of its annual clashes, but by the passion of its participants, including the fans. In 2004, a group of students claiming to be the Harvard Pep Squad distributed 1,800 red and white pieces of heavy construction paper to Harvard fans, to whom they explained that if they flashed their sheets simultaneously, they would spell out "GO HARVARD!" But the "Harvard Pep Squad" was actually a group of mischievous Yale students. And when the Harvard fans held up their papers for their entire home stadium to see, it read, "WE SUCK."

Indeed, only the Bulldogs sucked that day. The Crimson emerged with a 35–3 victory. But the prank showed the college football world that the spirit of the rivalry was alive and well decades after it had faded from the national spotlight.

Fact Box (through 2013)
    Nickname: The Game
    Trophy: None
    Total meetings: 130
    Series record: Yale leads, 65–57–8
    First meeting: 1875 (Harvard 4, Yale 0)
    Largest margin of victory: Yale, 1957 (Yale 54, Harvard 0)
    Longest winning streak: Yale, 8 (1880–1889)

Game Results (home team listed second unless at a neutral site)
    1875: Harvard 4, Yale 0
    1876: Harvard 1, Yale 2
    1878: Yale 1, Harvard 0
    1879: Harvard 0, Yale 0
    1880: Yale 1, Harvard 0
    1881: Harvard 0, Yale 4
    1882: Yale 1, Harvard 0
    1883: Yale 23, Harvard 2
    1884: Harvard 0, Yale 52
    1886: Yale 29, Harvard 4
    1887: Yale 17, Harvard 8
    1889: Yale 6, Harvard 0
    1890: Yale 6, Harvard 12
    1891: Yale 10, Harvard 0
    1892: Yale 6, Harvard 0
    1893: Yale 6, Harvard 0
    1894: Yale 12, Harvard 4
    1897: Yale 0, Harvard 0
    1898: Harvard 17, Yale 0
    1899: Yale 0, Harvard 0
    1900: Harvard 0, Yale 28
    1901: Yale 0, Harvard 22
    1902: Harvard 0, Yale 23
    1903: Yale 16, Harvard 0
    1904: Harvard 0, Yale 12

1905: Yale 6, Harvard 0
1906: Harvard 0, Yale 6
1907: Yale 12, Harvard 0
1908: Harvard 4, Yale 0
1909: Yale 8, Harvard 0
1910: Harvard 0, Yale 0
1911: Yale 0, Harvard 0
1912: Harvard 20, Yale 0
1913: Yale 5, Harvard 15
1914: Harvard 15, Yale 5
1915: Yale 0, Harvard 41
1916: Harvard 3, Yale 6
1919: Yale 3, Harvard 10
1920: Harvard 9, Yale 0
1921: Yale 3, Harvard 10
1922: Harvard 10, Yale 3
1923: Yale 13, Harvard 0
1924: Harvard 6, Yale 19
1925: Yale 0, Harvard 0
1926: Harvard 7, Yale 12
1927: Yale 14, Harvard 0
1928: Harvard 17, Yale 0
1929: Yale 6, Harvard 10
1930: Harvard 13, Yale 0
1931: Yale 3, Harvard 0
1932: Harvard 0, Yale 19
1933: Yale 6, Harvard 19
1934: Harvard 0, Yale 14
1935: Yale 14, Harvard 7
1936: Harvard 13, Yale 14
1937: Yale 6, Harvard 13
1938: Harvard 7, Yale 0
1939: Yale 20, Harvard 7
1940: Harvard 28, Yale 0
1941: Yale 0, Harvard 14
1942: Harvard 3, Yale 7
1945: Harvard 0, Yale 28
1946: Yale 27, Harvard 14

1947: Harvard 21, Yale 31
1948: Yale 7, Harvard 20
1949: Harvard 6, Yale 29
1950: Yale 14, Harvard 6
1951: Harvard 21, Yale 21
1952: Yale 41, Harvard 14
1953: Harvard 13, Yale 0
1954: Yale 9, Harvard 13
1955: Harvard 7, Yale 21
1956: Yale 42, Harvard 14
1957: Harvard 0, Yale 54
1958: Yale 0, Harvard 28
1959: Harvard 35, Yale 6
1960: Yale 39, Harvard 6
1961: Harvard 27, Yale 0
1962: Yale 6, Harvard 14
1963: Harvard 6, Yale 20
1964: Yale 14, Harvard 18
1965: Harvard 23, Yale 0
1966: Yale 0, Harvard 17
1967: Harvard 20, Yale 24
1968: Yale 29, Harvard 29
1969: Harvard 0, Yale 7
1970: Yale 12, Harvard 14
1971: Harvard 35, Yale 16
1972: Yale 28, Harvard 17
1973: Harvard 0, Yale 35
1974: Yale 16, Harvard 21
1975: Harvard 10, Yale 7
1976: Yale 21, Harvard 7
1977: Harvard 7, Yale 24
1978: Yale 35, Harvard 28
1979: Harvard 22, Yale 7
1980: Yale 14, Harvard 0
1981: Harvard 0, Yale 28
1982: Yale 7, Harvard 45
1983: Harvard 16, Yale 7
1984: Yale 30, Harvard 27

1985: Harvard 6, Yale 17
1986: Yale 17, Harvard 24
1987: Harvard 14, Yale 10
1988: Yale 26, Harvard 17
1989: Harvard 37, Yale 20
1990: Yale 34, Harvard 19
1991: Harvard 13, Yale 23
1992: Yale 0, Harvard 14
1993: Harvard 31, Yale 33
1994: Yale 32, Harvard 13
1995: Harvard 22, Yale 21
1996: Yale 21, Harvard 26
1997: Harvard 17, Yale 7
1998: Yale 9, Harvard 7
1999: Harvard 21, Yale 24
2000: Yale 34, Harvard 24
2001: Harvard 35, Yale 23
2002: Yale 13, Harvard 20
2003: Harvard 37, Yale 19
2004: Yale 3, Harvard 35
2005: Harvard 30, Yale 24
2006: Yale 34, Harvard 13
2007: Harvard 37, Yale 6
2008: Yale 0, Harvard 10
2009: Harvard 14, Yale 10
2010: Yale 21, Harvard 28
2011: Harvard 45, Yale 7
2012: Yale 24, Harvard 34
2013: Harvard 34, Yale 7

Harvard Bowl Game Appearance

1920 Rose Bowl: Harvard 7, Oregon 6

7

GEORGIA VS. FLORIDA: THE WORLD'S LARGEST OUTDOOR COCKTAIL PARTY

Florida Times-Union sportswriter Bill Kastelz was taking a stroll near the Gator Bowl in Jacksonville, home of the annual Florida–Georgia clash, sometime before a game in the 1950s. His memory had deserted him by the time he told the story to his paper in October 2000. But he remembered one incident quite clearly. He recalled a drunken fan stumbling up to a cop and offering him a drink.

The odd sight seemed to represent the spirit of the rivalry. He also noticed that fans were using binocular cases to place a flask in and that many were guzzling beer and sipping mixed drinks quite openly while authorities simply ignored them. So when Kastelz expressed that thought while banging away on his typewriter, he emerged with a nickname for the annual affair. He called it "The World's Largest Outdoor Cocktail Party."[1]

The moniker stuck. It stuck after Gators fans stormed the field and ripped down the goalposts after a 27–0 thumping of Georgia in 1984. It stuck after Bulldogs fans did the same following a 24–3 upset of top-ranked Florida in 1985 in a near riot that resulted in 65 arrests. It stuck after the Jacksonville City Council decided it would simply award the goalposts to the winning school, which never happened because neither Florida nor Georgia wanted them. It stuck after several efforts by both universities to disassociate themselves from the nickname. It stuck because it *is* The World's Largest Outdoor Cocktail Party.

The partisan tailgating is legendary—and it begins well before Saturday. Those seeking hotel rooms in Jacksonville during rivalry week can forget it—they've been booked for months. The parking areas outside what is now known as EverBank Field become small towns days before kickoff. Motor homes and RVs begin to fill the areas with flags and other accoutrements proudly displaying their owners' allegiances. Some boast the blue and orange colors of the Gators. Others show off the red and black of the Bulldogs. Areas inhabited by Florida fans feature signs proclaiming it to be "Alligator Alley." Others hosting Georgia fans boldly announce that they are on "Bulldog Boulevard." The barbecue smoke wafting through the air can be smelled a football field away. And, as usual, the fans on both sides are washing down their burgers, chicken, and ribs with rivers of beer and booze. They are cordial with each other until Saturday. Then they are as virulent of enemies as their gridiron combatants on the field.

Yet despite the heated nature of the rivalry and the fierce competition on game day, the hatred that has been the theme of other annual battles across America does not infiltrate either camp at Georgia or Florida. Their conflict is based on respect and a sense of fair play. The players, coaches, and fans understand that superiority is decided on the field and no harsh words or hard feelings can change that. There is a feeling of Old South geniality that permeates the environment before, during, and after the event. "It's a relatively sportsmanlike rivalry," explained Terry Hoage, who starred for Georgia as an All-American safety in the early 1980s. "There's no name calling or calling each other out before the game. It's a true athletic contest. We're going to see who's the best. The atmosphere in the stands is one of excitement and enthusiasm, not one of animosity."[2]

Now if they can only figure out when the rivalry began. The debate rages. Georgia claims its kickoff was its 52–0 stomping of Florida in 1904. Florida claims it didn't even have a football program until 1906. That claim is not based on shame over the result two years later. That school claims its first game against Georgia was in 1915, when the Bulldogs emerged victorious by an almost equally lopsided score of 37–0. Speculation is that the Georgia triumph in 1904 was actually against Florida Agricultural College, whose name change to the University of Florida in 1903 wasn't recognized by the state until 1906.

In the overall history of the rivalry, it doesn't matter. The irreversible fact is that if parity is a necessary ingredient in a rivalry, there was no rivalry until the early 1950s, before which Georgia made a victory over Florida nearly an annual event. In fact, The World's Largest Outdoor Cocktail Party has been marked by periods of dominance by both teams. Georgia has enjoyed four winning streaks of five games or more. Florida has embarked on four winning streaks of four games or more, including one of seven games and another of six in a 13–1 run from 1990 to 2003.

Not that the Gators were pushovers in their early years. They were unbeaten in the first year of their claimed existence in 1911 and forged winning records in each of their first five seasons. But after eight years of mediocrity under various coaches beginning in 1902, new coach Alex Cunningham transformed the Bulldogs into a national power by the second decade of the 20th century. All-Americans, such as halfback Bob McWhorter and quarterback David Paddock, led the team to its first era of dominance. Georgia managed a mark of 25–6–6 from 1910 to 1913 before setting out to make a mockery of its annual battles against Florida starting in 1915. The Bulldogs laid the groundwork for a trend that year with a 37–0 triumph in Macon, Georgia. They not only battered the Gators every year through 1920, but they also didn't allow a point. They beat Florida four straight times (with two years off due to World War I) by a stunning combined score of 130–0.

The Gators cried "uncle" after a 56–0 thrashing in 1920 as the annual clash, which was really no rivalry at all at the time, laid dormant for five years. By the time it was renewed, both teams were members of the Southern Conference. Florida had emerged as a regional power, compiling a record of 27–7–4 from 1922 to 1925. But wouldn't you know it—the Gators collapsed in 1926, just in time to play the Bulldogs again. The result was a 32–9 defeat in which they finally scored their first points against Georgia, followed by 28–0 loss in 1927 to a loaded Bulldogs team that finished the season with a 9–1 mark behind All-American ends Tom A. Nash and Chick Shiver.

In 1928, however, new coach Charlie Bachman pieced together the finest Florida teams since the program was launched. The Gators boasted the most explosive offense in the nation behind such talent as halfback Clyde Crabtree and Dale Van Sickel and a stalwart offensive line. Their 26–6 defeat of host Georgia that year kept them unbeaten and in the hunt for a national championship, but a season-ending defeat to Tennessee dashed their hopes. But their rise to prominence was brief. The Gators again defeated the Bulldogs in 1929, when they won eight games for the second consecutive season. But they then fell into a prolonged period of mediocrity marked by a revolving door in the coaching ranks, a distinct lack of talent (they had no All-Americans from 1931 to 1951), and what seemed like annual defeats to Georgia. None of their five coaches from 1927 to 1949 remained in place for more than five years. Florida won no more than six games in any season from 1930 to 1951, during which time Florida was within two wins or losses of .500 every year but one. The permanent move of the rivalry game in 1933 to Jacksonville, where it gained the mystique of being played at night, did nothing to halt Georgia dominance.

The Bulldogs lost just three games to the Gators in that stretch. Unlike their rivals to the south, they thrived through stability on the sideline—Harry Mehre was the head coach from 1928 to 1937 and Wallace Butts had the reins from 1939 to 1959—and a steady influx of premier players. Skill position standouts, such as halfbacks Vernon "Catfish" Smith, John Bond, and Frank Sinkwich and fullback Bill Hartman, kept the Bulldogs winning in the 1930s. Sinkwich was a unanimous All-American who also earned the first Heisman Trophy in Georgia history in 1942.

That season marked the most humiliating pounding ever experienced by the Gators at the hands of the Bulldogs. Florida had been decimated by the loss of players to the fight overseas in World War II. Georgia managed to keep its sensational team intact thanks to an ROTC program that kept its players eligible. Gators fan and blogger Ryan Ferguson gave his rather biased outlook on the discrepancies between the two programs that year in a 2006 article for AOLNews. He wrote the following:

> In '42, with World War II in full swing, most universities had sent their strongest and most able-bodied men to fight Hitler's advance through Europe. The University of Florida's football team roster was decimated by the righteous cause; as a result, most of the Gators on that '42 team were freshmen or physical rejects from the armed forces. Somehow, though, despite the world-changing events taking place overseas, Georgia had managed to keep an All-American quality squad together, thanks in part to their ROTC program. Instead of

fighting for America, Georgia's boys were dating girls, eating week-end feasts with their families, sleeping in warm, safe beds, and piling points on teams which could barely line up correctly. The first-string Gator players who would have worn orange and blue through those years, representing Florida with pride, answered a higher calling. They bravely fought and died in places like North Africa, Egypt, and Guadalcanal. They were fighter pilots. They were infantrymen. They were tank commanders. Georgia's football team, meanwhile, was running scrimmages, putting on football clinics and destroying all those who came before them. When Georgia coach Wally Butts faced the Gators that year, he ran the score up to 75–0—all the way through the fourth quarter. It was the single worst loss Florida ever suffered at the hands of Georgia. Think about that. 75–0 against a bunch of skinny freshmen who couldn't qualify for the military. Now that's class. That's the true Georgia Bulldogs.[3]

What Ferguson saw as the true Bulldogs also finished 9–1–1 in 1941, a season in which every game aside from the Orange Bowl victory over Texas Christian was played before the Japanese bombing of Pearl Harbor prompted American involvement in the war. And Georgia wasn't the only school to maintain a strong football program in the early 1940s. Included among the stalwarts was Auburn, whose 1942 victory over the top-ranked Bulldogs prevented them from remaining unbeaten and competing for their first national championship.

Not every Bulldog avoided military service overseas. Among those that showed flashes of brilliance before leaving to engage in battle was halfback Charley Trippi, who is still considered one of the finest players in the history of the school. Trippi gave a glimpse of his talent by rushing for 130 yards in the 1943 Rose Bowl victory over UCLA, then returned from the war in 1946 to display the form that made him a consensus All-American. Trippi led what became known as the Southeastern Conference in 1933 in points with 84 and racked up 1,366 yards of total offense. He earned the Maxwell Trophy as the most valuable player in college football and placed second in the Heisman Trophy balloting.

Trippi helped the Bulldogs steamroll past every opponent on the schedule, including North Carolina in the Sugar Bowl. But despite the fact that a scoreless tie that year between Army and Notre Dame left those teams with a blemish on their records, they earned nearly all the first-place votes as national champion by various polls. The unbeaten Bulldogs were left to ponder their ranking of third in the country.

Meanwhile, the Gators and their fans were left to ponder why they had remained Georgia's personal punching bag for so many years. New governor and University of Florida graduate Fuller Warren decided to take action in 1949. He spoke with passion about turning the program around. Soon coach Raymond Wolf was dispatched in favor of Bob Woodruff, who was lured away from Baylor for what was then an astounding $17,000 a year, the highest salary ever provided a state employee. Money alone wasn't enough to convince Woodruff to sign on the dotted line. He wanted Florida football to soar to a level to which its competitors had long before reached in various aspects of their programs. He demanded that the capacity of Florida Field be raised to 40,000, as well as increased pay for assistant coaches and autonomy for the entire athletic program away from university control. Woodruff got all he asked for and took over the reins in 1950.

The results were not what Fuller dreamed about when he vowed to put a nationally recognized football team on the field. But Woodruff did recruit players that began to make All-American lists and Gator squads that inched their way into the lower realms of the national rankings. He also became the first Florida coach to turn the rivalry against Georgia around. Never mind that the transformation was due partly to the lean years experienced by the Bulldogs in the mid-1950s. Gator fans starving for victories against them weren't about to complain that they were achieved against weaker competition.

The Florida teams of that era finally boasted talent that could compete against the Bulldogs. Woodruff understood the need to build from the inside out, so he attracted such All-American linemen in the 1950s as Charlie LaPradd, Joe D'Agostino, John Barrow, and Vel Heckman. He also lured a quarterback named Doug Dickey, who combined with fullback Rick Casares to batter the Bulldogs, 30–0, in 1952. Casares did the dirty work with 108 yards rushing and a touchdown to set in motion the first period of Gator dominance in the history of the series. Florida won 10 of 12 meetings between 1952 and 1963, though it was Woodruff replacement Ray Graves that coached them into national prominence.

What the rivalry lacked, however, was greatness. The Gators never boasted a championship contender during the years of Georgia dominance. And the Bulldogs were down when Florida began its run of victories. Their only flash under Butts after 1948 was a 10–1 season in 1959 that featured the heroics of All-American guard and eventual Auburn coach Pat Dye, as well as future NFL star quarterback Fran Tarkenton. But even Tarkenton couldn't guide his team to better than a 6–4 mark in 1960 despite leading the SEC in passing with 1,189 yards.

It was not until 1966 that a truly meaningful game from a national perspective was played as a capper to The World's Largest Outdoor Cocktail Party. The unbeaten Gators had finally groomed a superstar in quarterback Steve Spurrier, who was in the midst of a Heisman Trophy season in which he completed 61.5 percent of his passes for 2,012 yards, 16 touchdowns, and just eight interceptions. They had yielded seven points or fewer in four of their previous six games to soar into the national rankings and reach No. 7—the highest in program history—by the time they faced Georgia. The surprising Bulldogs were finally flourishing again under third-year coach Vince Dooley. They too would have been undefeated if not for a one-point loss to Miami of Florida. They boasted a ball-control ground game and one of the most aggressive and effective defenses in the nation, one that had yielded seven or fewer points in five of their first seven games behind such All-Americans as safety and future NFL standout Jake Scott and defensive tackle George Patton (who was indeed named after the legendary general).

The stage was set for the most important Georgia–Florida showdown in history. The Bulldogs unleashed their blitz against Spurrier, who responded in the first quarter by guiding his team 86 yards downfield for a touchdown. But the aggressive strategy began reaping dividends for Georgia, which trailed just 10–3 at halftime.

The Bulldogs showed they had more bite than bark in the second half. Their running backs churned up yards and their blitzers put Spurrier on his back. They tied the game on a 65-yard drive in which they threw nary a pass. And after defensive back Lynn Hughes intercepted a Spurrier pass and raced in for a touchdown, the Bulldogs took the momentum and ran with it. By the time the teams had finished churning up the Gator Bowl turf, the Bulldogs were celebrating a 27–10 victory. Flush with confidence, they finished their season with victories over fifth-ranked Georgia Tech and No. 10 Southern Methodist in the Cotton Bowl to earn the No. 4 ranking in the nation. But it was the defeat of Florida—their first ranked opponent of the season—that gave them the impetus to achieve greatness. And after that game, as Spurrier trudged off the field, a Bulldogs fan rubbed a bit of salt in his wounds. "There he goes, Mr. Quarterback," the man snickered. "Some quarterback."[4]

Parity had been realized for the first time in the history of the rivalry, as Dooley waged individual battles with Graves and Doug Dickey, who succeeded him in 1970. Neither Florida nor Georgia won more than two consecutive meetings from 1962 to 1975. The Bulldogs suffered through no losing seasons from 1964 to 1974. The Gators had just one from 1962 to 1977. They had begun to change the landscape of college football. The Southeast had been dominated in years past by Alabama and Georgia Tech. The Crimson Tide remained a force, but the Yellow Jackets had peaked in the 1950s and were crashing back to mediocrity. Meanwhile, the Gators and Bulldogs were earning national ranking recognition. Georgia reached No. 4 in the country every year from 1965 to 1968 and No. 6 in 1969 and 1971. Florida peaked between fourth and 14th in the nation 11 times between 1964 and 1977. And though both teams most often stumbled out of the top 20 by season's end, they had planted the seeds for the dominance that would come in later years and an era in the rivalry that was marked by top talent and important battles.

Among the top talent involved in an important battle was Florida consensus All-American defensive end Jack Youngblood, who dominated at the college level before launching a Hall of Fame career with the Los Angeles Rams. Led by Youngblood and prolific sophomore quarterback John Reaves, the 1969 Gators had peaked at No. 7 in the country before a stunningly lopsided loss to Auburn. They had a chance to recover against a Georgia team that was in the midst of its own late-season collapse but managed a 13–13 tie at the Gator Bowl. The Bulldogs, who had reached No. 6 at midseason, managed a record of 0–4–1 in their last five games to fall to .500. They made up for it in 1971 with their finest season in a quarter century. Only a late-season loss to Auburn prevented them from achieving their first perfect record since 1946. They yielded just 28 points and pitched four shutouts during an eight-game stretch before the dam broke defensively in the 35–20 defeat to the Tigers.

But it was Florida that cornered the market on frustration in the mid-1970s—and it was Georgia that turned the screws every year. Led by such skill position brilliance of running back Jimmy DuBose and fleet wideout Wes Chandler, who would forge a standout career with the San Diego Chargers, the Gators appeared on the verge of capturing an SEC title every year from 1974 to 1976. They were ranked sixth in the nation and coming off an upset of No. 5 Auburn when they were beaten 17–16 by unranked Georgia in 1974. They were unbeaten in conference play heading into The World's Largest Outdoor Cocktail Party the following year but left Jacksonville with a 10–7 defeat to the Bulldogs.

Those losses would seem like minor setbacks compared to 1976. The Gators were riding a six-game winning streak heading into the annual showdown against Georgia, which was ranked No. 7 in the country and would have been unbeaten if not for an upset loss to SEC rival Mississippi. It was the most anticipated Florida–Georgia game since 1966 and it appeared that the Gators were going to run away and hide after they scored 27 points in the first half against a vaunted Bulldogs defense that had pitched three shutouts in their first six games. Flushed with overconfidence after securing a two-touchdown halftime lead, Florida players began talking in the locker room about ring sizes. The SEC title was in the bag.

Far from it. The Gators collapsed in the second half. Dickey shut down the passing attack that had forged the advantage in favor of a ball-control game and clock management. The result was catastrophic. It allowed the Bulldogs to stage a comeback against a Florida defense that was ranked last in the conference. Quarterback Ray Goff used his arm and his legs to lead Georgia to four second-half touchdowns. And when Dickey, whose conservatism might have cost his team a victory, decided to play the role of riverboat gambler and go for a first down on 4th-and-1 at his own 30-yard line, the Gators were doomed. Running back Earl Carr was stopped dead in his tracks and the Bulldogs had all but clinched a 41–27 win. A Jacksonville newspaper published a story the next day about the game headlined "Fourth and Dumb." And Carr contributed a notable quote: "When I was running the play," he said, "I was asking myself why in the world we were running the play." Dickey was asking the same question after the game about several plays. He took the blame for the defeat. "[Our coaching staff] did a miserable job in the second half," he said. "I made some dumb calls."[5]

Dooley and his Bulldogs didn't need dumb calls from any opponent to embark in the early 1980s on the greatest run in program history.

They just needed the finest talent it had ever produced. All-Americans, such as placekicker Rex Robinson, cornerback Scott Woerner, safety Terry Hoage, defensive tackle Jimmy Payne, and defensive end Freddie Gilbert, peppered their rosters of that era. But it was one of the most dominant players in college football history that made the biggest impact and transformed the Bulldogs from contender to national champion. And that was running back Herschel Walker.

Walker could very well have been the only player in history to win three Heisman Trophies, placing second in the voting in 1980 and third in 1981 before securing it in 1982. He established an NCAA rushing record for freshmen in 1980 with 1,616 yards and by the time he had finished his brilliant career had set 10 NCAA rushing records and 15 SEC marks before earning greatness in the NFL. He also led his team to four consecutive defeats of Florida, including a 44–0 stomping in 1982 that was the most lopsided Bulldog defeat of the Gators in 14 years.

It remained to be seen if Walker would even be placed on the field in 1980 by Dooley, who had gained a reputation for not using freshmen. But when Walker rushed for 84 yards and two touchdowns in a comeback defeat of Tennessee in the season opener, Dooley knew he could not maintain that policy any longer. Walker ran wild as the Bulldogs raced to an 8–0 start and reached No. 2 in the nation, their highest ranking in 38 years, heading into their annual clash against a 6–1 Gators team that had staged a remarkable comeback from a devastating winless season in 1979 under first-year head coach Charley Pell. What followed was one of the most memorable games in the history of the rivalry.

Florida not only had a chance to avenge the 1970s defeats to Georgia that wiped out its SEC title hopes by turning the tables, but it could also forge a first-place tie with the Bulldogs with a victory. The Gators appeared on the verge of doing just that when they led 21–20 and had Georgia pinned back at its own 7-yard line with a mere 80 seconds left to tick off the game clock. Walker had already rushed for 228 yards, but he would not play the role of hero. Instead, it was quarterback Buck Belue and speedy wide receiver Lindsay Scott, who anchored the school's 440-meter relay team and was merely the secondary receiver on the play. Belue rolled out and eventually found Scott, who snagged the ball, reversed his field, and sprinted down the sideline for a shocking 93-yard touchdown and a 26–21 triumph. The moment became known in Bulldog lore as "Run, Lindsay, run."

That heroism brought redemption to Scott, whose athletic scholarship for the fall semester had been stripped the previous spring after he engaged in a verbal altercation with his girlfriend, whom he had invited into his dorm room. He got into a shoving match with his academic counselor, who had demanded that his girlfriend leave, which caused Dooley to give him the choice of sitting out the season or paying his own tuition. Scott chose the latter, a move that saved the season for the Bulldogs. "I'm really pleased for Lindsay because of all the things that have happened to him," Dooley said after the game. "I'm probably the worst thing that's happened to him. I've been very hard on him. That last pass today was just supposed to be a first-down play but Lindsay turned it into a game-winner for us. So I'm not going to sit here and act like the great coach. But if you're going to be undefeated, you've got to win some this way, too."[6]

The dramatic defeat of Florida not only catapulted Georgia to No. 1 in the nation, but it also served as a launching pad for the greatest season in its football history. The Bulldogs concluded the run to their only undisputed national championship with a 17–10 defeat of seventh-ranked Notre Dame in the Sugar Bowl. They couldn't repeat that success behind Walker and a slew of fellow All-Americans the next two years—their top-ranked team in 1982 blew the national title with a Sugar Bowl loss to Penn State—but they did win the SEC crown in each of those seasons and even managed a 10–1–1 record after Walker left in 1983. The Bulldogs had clawed their way to a 43–4–1 record in four years and had beaten Florida in each of them.

The Gators were experiencing problems aside from their annual defeat to their archrivals. Pell had fallen victim to a recruiting scandal and other violations investigated by the NCAA and was forced out in favor of assistant coach Galen Hall. The program lost 15 scholarships in each of the next three years and lost bowl game privileges in 1984 and 1985. Hall, who had been at Florida for less than a year, wasn't particularly in tune with The World's Largest Outdoor Cocktail Party, but he knew how to run an offense. Sensational linebacker Wilber Marshall had graduated in 1983, but the Gators still managed their best back-to-back seasons in 1984 and 1985 since the late 1920s. They steamrolled past all eight foes upon Hall's promotion in 1984 to finally win their first

SEC crown (though they were forced by the NCAA to vacate it), blanked Georgia along the way to break a six-game losing streak, and finished third in the nation.

The Gators took their momentum and ran with it in 1985 behind senior quarterback Kerwin Bell, future NFL running back Neal Anderson, and premier linebacker Alfonzo Johnson. They were unbeaten in eight games and ranked No. 1 in the nation for the first time in the history of the program before meeting Georgia, which had fallen back to earth after their incredible run to begin the decade.

It has been speculated that the excitement that the top ranking brought the Gators weakened their focus on the task at hand that week. Bell spoke later about a conversation with Hall two days before the game in which both admitted fear that the team was not ready to play. And those fears were realized. A Florida team coming off a defeat of No. 6 Auburn laid an ostrich-sized egg against the Bulldogs. They yielded 100-plus yards rushing to both Keith Henderson and freshman Tim Worley, as well as sack after sack, in a 24–3 defeat. It was their smallest single-game point total since their 1982 shutout loss to Georgia.

The Bulldogs made it 15 of 19 over the Gators with victories from 1987 to 1989. Even brilliant Florida running back and all-time NFL leading rusher Emmitt Smith, who ran for 3,928 yards and 36 touchdowns in three college seasons, couldn't stem the tide. But the end of the Dooley years marked the end of Georgia dominance. A new era in the rivalry began in the new decade with two former quarterbacks—Spurrier at Florida and Goff at Georgia—having taken over the coaching reins at their respective schools by 1990. The result was the longest period of Florida supremacy in the history of the annual clash.

Spurrier transformed the Gators from an occasional national contender into perennially one of the most powerful programs in the country. He coached an incredible 33 All-Americans in the 1990s, including such consensus picks as defensive linemen Brad Culpepper (1991) and Kevin Carter (1994); wide receivers Jack Jackson (1994), Reidel Anthony (1996), Ike Hilliard (1996), and Jacquez Green (1997); quarterback Danny Wuerffel (1996); offensive lineman Jason Odom (1995); and defensive back Fred Weary (1997). Spurrier simply landed more superior talent than Goff, though the latter did recruit superstar running back Garrison Hearst, who finished third in the 1992 Heisman Trophy balloting. Goff managed just two seasons of six or more wins and finished his seven-year run at Georgia with an uncharacteristic 46–34–1 record. It was no wonder that Florida won every rivalry game from 1990 to 1996, marking the longest winning streak in the series since the Bulldogs took seven straight in the 1940s. The Gators won those games by a combined score of 293–108 and five of them by at least 31 points.

There are two exceptions—and it was among the greatest games in Georgia–Florida history. The 1993 Bulldogs had recovered from a 1–4 start to win three straight heading into the showdown against the 5–1 Gators, whose dream of their first-ever undefeated season had been dashed by Auburn the week before. Georgia was no contender but did boast two premier skill position players in quarterback Eric Zeier and running back Terrell Davis, who later thrived as an All-Pro with the Denver Broncos.

A torrential downpour had soaked the field. The freshman Wuerffel, who was in the process of throwing for 2,230 yards and 22 touchdowns that season, lost his accuracy with the slippery football and was replaced by backup Terry Dean after his team fell behind 17–13. Dean justified the move by leading the Gators to a field goal and touchdown for a 23–20 halftime lead. They remained ahead, 33–26, when Zeier marched the Bulldogs to the Florida 12-yard line with five seconds remaining. Georgia fans erupted when Zeier fired a touchdown pass, but the officials ruled that Florida defensive back Anthone Lott had called time-out before the snap because he realized his team had just 10 players on the field. Lott was whistled for pass interference on the next play, giving Georgia one last shot at the 2-yard line to tie or win the game. But, alas, Zeier threw incomplete as the final seconds ticked off the clock. His 386 yards and two touchdowns through the air had been wasted.

The frustration of losing to Florida again boiled over for the Bulldogs. "I've never wanted to win more in my life," Davis said following the defeat. "Right now I'm not willing to accept that we've let Florida beat us four years in a row. It's degrading. . . . I want to go out and line up right now. This is our biggest rivalry, so it's probably the worst loss I've ever had in my life."[7]

The Georgia Bulldogs would be forced to become accustomed to the feeling. They lost the next three games to Florida by a rather disturbing combined score of 151–38. The only novel aspect of the first two of those games was that they were played at the campus stadiums rather than the Gator Bowl, which was in the process of a renovation. But the Bulldogs could take solace in the knowledge that they were far from the only victims of a Gator stomp during those seasons. Florida reached No. 1 nationally at some point in each of those three years behind their tremendous array of offensive talent. The Gators finished fourth in the nation in scoring in 1994, second in 1995, and first in 1996 at 47 points per game. It was in that last of those three seasons that they finally realized their dream of winning a national championship. They avenged a loss to Florida State by clobbering the top-ranked Seminoles in the Sugar Bowl to clinch the crown. And Wuerffel was rewarded for his efforts with a Heisman Trophy.

By that time Goff had been dispatched. His last three teams had combined for a 17–16–1 record and had experienced annual bashings by the Gators, which led to the hiring of Jim Donnan. Donnan pushed the program in the right direction. He plucked a gem by recruiting consensus All-American cornerback Champ Bailey, who even contributed greatly as a wide receiver. Donnan not only guided his team to a 10–2 record in 1997 but also to a stunning upset of the sixth-ranked Gators that season. Florida entered as a 19-point favorite, which seemed justified when Georgia quarterback Mike Bobo threw three early interceptions, but the Bulldogs came alive with four picks of their own and tailback Robert Edwards ran for 124 yards and four scores to secure the rare 37–17 win.

But though the Bulldogs performed consistently better under Donnan than they did under Goff, winning at least eight games every year from 1997 to 2000 and finishing in the top 20 nationally in each of those seasons, they could not solve the Gators, who followed the 1997 defeat with six more wins in a row to give them a 13–1 record against the Bulldogs from 1990 to 2003. Even the 2001 resignation of Spurrier after an incredible 12 consecutive years of 11 victories didn't stop the onslaught. Replacement Ron Zook managed comparatively awful 8–5 records in his first two seasons but still managed successive triumphs over Georgia.

The 2002 defeat proved monumentally disappointing to the Bulldogs. Second-year head coach Mark Richt, who had taken over after serving as offensive coordinator and quarterbacks coach at Florida State, had constructed their finest team since the early 1980s. They had soared to No. 5 in the nation on the strength of an 8–0 record, victories over nationally ranked Alabama and Tennessee, a traditionally stingy defense led by consensus All-American end David Pollack that finished the year ranked fourth in the nation, and an offense that had scored 100 points in their previous two games combined.

The Gators, on the other hand, were slipping. They entered the battle on their first two-game losing streak since 1999 despite an explosive offensive triumvirate of quarterback Rex Grossman, running back Earnest Graham, and wide receiver Taylor Jacobs, all of whom would forge NFL careers. But Jacobs left early in the game with a knee injury, weakening the Florida offense.

The Bulldogs still owned a 13–12 lead early in the fourth quarter, when Grossman, who proved to be the star of the game with 339 yards passing, guided his team on an 89-yard drive he deemed to be the finest of his season. He capped it with a 10-yard touchdown pass to tight end Ben Troupe, whose heroics were made tougher to take for Bulldogs fans since he had been recruited out of their home state. But the 20–13 loss was far more difficult to accept for the Georgia players themselves, particularly the seniors who had never experienced a victory over their archrivals. "It's real unbearable," said tearful All-American senior tackle Jon Stinchcomb, whose brother Matt had starred with the Bulldogs in the late 1990s. "For the rest of our lives, all the seniors will know that they never beat Florida. . . . That's a pretty tough pill to swallow."[8]

The victory highlighted Zook's short tenure at Florida. The Gators failed to reach the standards set by Spurrier and they replaced Zook with Urban Meyer, who had stunningly transformed Utah into a national power and undefeated Bowl Championship Series (BCS) participant. By 2006, his Florida recruits were beginning to bear fruit and he had embarked on one of the most dominant runs in college football history.

The Gators rode the talents of such consensus All-Americans and future NFL standouts as quarterback Tim Tebow, defensive backs Reggie Nelson and Joe Haden, wide receiver Percy Harvin, linebacker Brandon Spikes, and center Maurkice Pouncey to three 13–1 seasons in the next four years and national championships in 2006 and 2008. Only a loss to second-ranked Alabama in the 2009 SEC title game, which for the Crimson Tide avenged a 2008 defeat in the same title clash, prevented the Gators from winning a third crown.

And only a 2007 loss to Georgia in an inexplicable down year for Florida prevented a third six-game winning streak in the series since 1990. Richt had established himself as the most successful Bulldogs coach since Dooley, but he could not match his predecessor's penchant for beating the Gators, though it must be cited that that latter never had to battle teams with the talent boasted by Meyer. Georgia managed a mark of 74–18 under Richt from 2002 to 2008, but five of those defeats were to Florida.

The last was not as frustrating nor as important at the first, but it was more humiliating. The Bulldogs had entered the 2008 season as the top-ranked team in the country. They boasted such future NFL super-stars as quarterback Matthew Stafford, running back Knowshon Moreno, and wide receiver A. J. Green. A loss to Auburn all but ended their national championship dreams, but they had matched Florida with one-loss records heading into the annual showdown.

The contest was no contest. Stafford threw three interceptions after intermission and the Gators scored five unanswered touchdowns in the second half to cruise to a 49–10 victory, their most lopsided defeat of Georgia in the history of the series. Meyer rubbed salt in Bulldog wounds by using two remaining time-outs with less than a minute remaining in the game to give his players additional time to celebrate. The move was a response to Richt ordering his players to absorb an excessive celebration penalty after scoring a first-quarter touchdown the year before. Meyer admitted after the 2008 blowout that the memory of that Bulldogs end-zone party fueled a feeling of revenge that his team certainly exacted that night.

The best news for the Bulldogs was received when Meyer, whom many had deemed a mercenary, hightailed it to Ohio State in 2011 and was replaced by Will Muschamp. It seemed no coincidence that his departure marked the beginning of the first three-game winning streak for Georgia in the series since 1987 to 1989. The Bulldogs, who had dropped to 6–7 in 2010 for their first losing season in 14 years, rebounded to go 10–4 in 2011 and 12–2 in 2012.

The Georgia–Florida battle that year had rare national championship implications for both teams. The 6–1 Bulldogs featured perhaps the premier linebacker ever to grace their uniform in junior Jarvis Jones, who the following year led the nation in tackles for losses for 24½ and sacks with 14½. The Gators, who boasted consensus All-American safety Matt Elam, entered unbeaten and ranked third in the nation.

They were undefeated no more after the final tick went off the clock. Georgia held Florida to three field goals by future NFL standout Caleb Sturgis, and secured a 17–9 lead on a 45-yard touchdown pass from quarterback Aaron Murray to Malcolm Mitchell; and the defense, which Bulldogs senior defensive back Shawn Williams publicly accused earlier in the week for being too soft, continued to limit the explosive Gators to their lowest point total of the season to clinch the victory. The hero was Jones, who rose to the occasion with 13 tackles, three sacks, and two forced fumbles. He spoke after the game about taking Williams's words to heart. "Shawn challenged us and we took it personal," he said. "As men, when another man challenges you, it will be personal. The guys stepped up to the challenge."[9]

Perhaps the Bulldogs had begun a long period of domination in the series when they extended their winning streak over the Gators to three in 2013. Perhaps not. Only time and talent will dictate the course of the future. But one thing seems certain. The World's Largest Outdoor Cocktail Party will remain a happening and significant football event for generations to come.

Fact Box (through 2013)

Nickname: The World's Largest Outdoor Cocktail Party
Trophy: The Okefenokee Oar
Total meetings: 91
Series record: Georgia leads, 49–40–2
First meeting: 1915 (Georgia 37, Florida 0)
Largest margin of victory: Georgia, 1942 (Georgia 75, Florida 0)
Longest winning streak: Florida, 7 (1990–1996); Georgia, 7 (1941–1948)

Game Results (home team listed second unless at a neutral site)

1915: Georgia 37, Florida 0
1916: Georgia 21, Florida 0
1919: Georgia 16, Florida 0
1920: Florida 0, Georgia 56
1926: Florida 9, Georgia 32
1927: Georgia 28, Florida 0

1928: Florida 26, Georgia 6
1929: Florida 18, Georgia 6
1930: Florida 0, Georgia 0
1931: Georgia 33, Florida 3
1932: Florida 12, Georgia 33
1933: Georgia 14, Florida 0
1934: Georgia 14, Florida 0
1935: Georgia 7, Florida 0
1936: Georgia 26, Florida 8
1937: Florida 6, Georgia 0
1938: Georgia 19, Florida 6
1939: Georgia 6, Florida 2
1940: Florida 18, Georgia 13
1941: Georgia 19, Florida 3
1942: Georgia 75, Florida 0
1944: Georgia 38, Florida 12
1945: Georgia 34, Florida 0
1946: Georgia 33, Florida 14
1947: Georgia 34, Florida 6
1948: Georgia 20, Florida 12
1949: Florida 28, Georgia 7
1950: Georgia 6, Florida 0
1951: Georgia 7, Florida 6
1952: Florida 30, Georgia 0
1953: Florida 21, Georgia 7
1954: Georgia 14, Florida 13
1955: Florida 19, Georgia 13
1956: Florida 28, Georgia 0
1957: Florida 22, Georgia 0
1958: Florida 7, Georgia 6
1959: Georgia 21, Florida 10
1960: Florida 22, Georgia 14
1961: Florida 21, Georgia 14
1962: Florida 23, Georgia 15
1963: Florida 21, Georgia 14
1964: Georgia 14, Florida 7
1965: Florida 14, Georgia 10
1966: Georgia 27, Florida 10

1967: Florida 17, Georgia 16
1968: Georgia 51, Florida 0
1969: Florida 13, Georgia 13
1970: Florida 24, Georgia 17
1971: Georgia 49, Florida 7
1972: Georgia 10, Florida 7
1973: Florida 11, Georgia 10
1974: Georgia 17, Florida 16
1975: Georgia 10, Florida 7
1976: Georgia 41, Florida 27
1977: Florida 22, Georgia 17
1978: Georgia 24, Florida 22
1979: Georgia 33, Florida 10
1980: Georgia 26, Florida 21
1981: Georgia 26, Florida 21
1982: Georgia 44, Florida 0
1983: Georgia 10, Florida 9
1984: Florida 27, Georgia 0
1985: Georgia 24, Florida 3
1986: Florida 31, Georgia 19
1987: Georgia 23, Florida 10
1988: Georgia 26, Florida 3
1989: Georgia 17, Florida 10
1990: Florida 38, Georgia 7
1991: Florida 45, Georgia 13
1992: Florida 26, Georgia 24
1993: Florida 33, Georgia 26
1994: Florida 52, Georgia 14
1995: Florida 52, Georgia 17
1996: Florida 47, Georgia 7
1997: Georgia 37, Florida 17
1998: Florida 38, Georgia 7
1999: Florida 30, Georgia 14
2000: Florida 34, Georgia 23
2001: Florida 24, Georgia 10
2002: Florida 20, Georgia 13
2003: Florida 16, Georgia 13
2004: Georgia 31, Florida 24

2005: Florida 14, Georgia 10
2006: Florida 21, Georgia 14
2007: Georgia 42, Florida 30
2008: Florida 49, Georgia 10
2009: Florida 41, Georgia 17
2010: Florida 34, Georgia 31
2011: Georgia 24, Florida 20
2012: Georgia 17, Florida 9
2013: Georgia 23, Florida 20

Georgia Bowl Game Appearances

1942 Orange Bowl: Georgia 40, TCU 26
1949 Rose Bowl: Georgia 9, UCLA 0
1946 Oil Bowl: Georgia 20, Tulsa 6
1947 Sugar Bowl: Georgia 20, North Carolina 10
1948 Gator Bowl: Maryland 20, Georgia 20
1949 Orange Bowl: Texas 48, Georgia 21
1950 Presidential Cup: Texas A&M 40, Georgia 20
1960 Orange Bowl: Georgia 14, Missouri 0
1964 Sun Bowl: Georgia 7, Texas 0
1966 Cotton Bowl: Georgia 24, Southern Methodist 9
1967 Liberty Bowl: North Carolina State 14, Georgia 7
1968 Sugar Bowl: Arkansas 20, Georgia 16
1969 Sun Bowl: Nebraska 45, Georgia 6
1971 Gator Bowl: Georgia 7, North Carolina 3
1973 Peach Bowl: Georgia 17, Maryland 16
1974 Tangerine Bowl: Miami of Ohio 21, Georgia 10
1976 Cotton Bowl: Arkansas 31, Georgia 10
1977 Sugar Bowl: Pittsburgh 27, Georgia 3
1978 Bluebonnet Bowl: Stanford 25, Georgia 22
1981 Sugar Bowl: Georgia 17, Notre Dame 10
1982 Sugar Bowl: Pittsburgh 24, Georgia 20
1983 Sugar Bowl: Penn State 27, Georgia 23
1984 Cotton Bowl: Georgia 10, Texas 9
1984 Citrus Bowl: Georgia 17, Florida State 17
1985 Sun Bowl: Arizona 13, Georgia 13
1986 Hall of Fame Bowl: Boston College 27, Georgia 24
1987 Liberty Bowl: Georgia 20, Arkansas 17

1989 Gator Bowl: Georgia 34, Michigan State 27
1989 Peach Bowl: Syracuse 19, Georgia 18
1991 Independence Bowl: Georgia 24, Arkansas 15
1993 Citrus Bowl: Georgia 21, Ohio State 14
1995 Peach Bowl: Virginia 34, Georgia 27
1998 Outback Bowl: Georgia 33, Wisconsin 6
1998 Peach Bowl: Georgia 35, Virginia 33
2000 Outback Bowl: Georgia 28, Purdue 25
2000 Oahu Bowl: Georgia 37, Virginia 14
2001 Music City Bowl: Boston College 20, Georgia 16
2003 Sugar Bowl: Georgia 26, Florida State 13
2004 Capital One Bowl: Georgia 34, Purdue 27
2005 Outback Bowl: Georgia 24, Wisconsin 21
2006 Sugar Bowl: West Virginia 38, Georgia 35
2006 Chick-fil-A Bowl: Georgia 31, Virginia Tech 24
2008 Sugar Bowl: Georgia 41, Hawaii 10
2009 Capital One Bowl: Georgia 24, Michigan 12
2009 Independence Bowl: Georgia 44, Texas A&M 20
2010 Liberty Bowl: University of Central Florida 10, Georgia 6
2012 Outback Bowl: Michigan State 33, Georgia 30
2013 Capital One Bowl: Georgia 45, Nebraska 31
2014 Gator Bowl: Nebraska 24, Georgia 19

Florida Game Bowl Appearances
1953 Gator Bowl: Florida 14, Tulsa 13
1958 Gator Bowl: Mississippi 7, Florida 3
1960 Gator Bowl: Florida 13, Baylor 12
1962 Gator Bowl: Florida 17, Michigan State 7
1966 Sugar Bowl: Missouri 20, Florida 18
1967 Orange Bowl: Florida 27, Georgia Tech 12
1969 Gator Bowl: Florida 14, Tennessee 13
1973 Tangerine Bowl: Miami of Ohio 16, Florida 7
1974 Sugar Bowl: Nebraska 13, Florida 10
1975 Gator Bowl: Maryland 13, Florida 0
1977 Sun Bowl: Texas A&M 37, Florida 14
1980 Tangerine Bowl: Florida 35, Maryland 20
1981 Peach Bowl: West Virginia 26, Florida 6
1982 Bluebonnet Bowl: Arkansas 28, Florida 24

1983 Gator Bowl: Florida 14, Iowa 6
1987 Aloha Bowl: UCLA 20, Florida 16
1988 All-American Bowl: Florida 14, Illinois 10
1989 Freedom Bowl: Washington 34, Florida 7
1992 Sugar Bowl: Notre Dame 39, Florida 28
1992 Gator Bowl: Florida 27, North Carolina State 10
1994 Sugar Bowl: Florida 41, West Virginia 7
1995 Sugar Bowl: Florida State 23, Florida 17
1996 Fiesta Bowl: Nebraska 62, Florida 24
1997 Sugar Bowl: Florida 52, Florida State 20
1998 Citrus Bowl: Florida 21, Penn State 6
1999 Orange Bowl: Florida 31, Syracuse 10
2000 Citrus Bowl: Michigan State 37, Florida 34
2001 Sugar Bowl: Miami 37, Florida 20
2002 Orange Bowl: Florida 56, Maryland 23
2003 Outback Bowl: Michigan 38, Florida 30
2004 Outback Bowl: Iowa 37, Florida 17
2004 Peach Bowl: Miami 27, Florida 10
2006 Outback Bowl: Florida 31, Iowa 24
2007 BCS Championship: Florida 41, Ohio State 14
2008 Capital One Bowl: Michigan 41, Florida 35
2009 BCS Championship: Florida 24, Oklahoma 14
2010 Sugar Bowl: Florida 51, Cincinnati 24
2011 Outback Bowl: Florida 37, Penn State 24
2012 Gator Bowl: Florida 24, Ohio State 17
2013 Sugar Bowl: Louisville 33, Florida 23

8

LAFAYETTE VS. LEHIGH: THE FIRST RIVALRY

It was November 12, 1884. A recount of votes in New York State was confirming the election of Grover Cleveland as the first president to serve two nonconsecutive terms. Bare-knuckled boxer John L. Sullivan was preparing to pummel opponent Alf Greenfield so viciously that he would be arrested in the ring. And fledgling football programs from Pennsylvania schools Lafayette and Lehigh were launching one of the most storied rivalries in the history of the sport.

Only the Leopards (known then as the Maroons for their team color) boasted any experience with the newfangled sport. They learned it from a former Princeton player named Theodore L. Welles—and they certainly played it badly. Lafayette had only won twice in two seasons. But they were far more adept than the Mountain Hawks (known then as the Engineers), who were embarking on their first-ever football game with just three undergraduates who had ever played the game. Their teammates had a mere three weeks to learn it.

The result was predictable. The Leopards clawed their visitors from beginning to end for a 50–0 victory. Lehigh captain Richard Harding Davis, who later toiled as a journalist, author, and playwright, had arranged for the game to be played and even covered it for the student newspaper. In recalling the clash, which attracted just 250 fans who shelled out a quarter apiece, it seemed he regretted organizing the event but not because of the final score. "My chief recollections of that first game consist of my personal encounters with the spectators and

Figure 8.1.   The first Lafayette–Lehigh football game, 1884. *Courtesy of Lafayette College*

Easton policemen, who had an instinctive prejudice to Lehigh men that was expressed by kicking them in the head when one of them went under the ropes for the ball," Davis said.[1]

The Leopards fell back to earth the following week against a Princeton team that was to Lehigh in football what Leonardo da Vinci was to a four-year-old child in art. They lost to the Tigers by an embarrassing 140–0 score, but they knew that a second game against the Mountain Hawks would prevent them from sliding through the rest of the season winless. Lehigh, which followed its first loss to Lafayette with a 61–0 defeat to Rutgers, finally scored the first touchdown in program history in their rematch against the Leopards but still lost by a lopsided 34–4 score.

Little could anyone have imagined that those two Keystone State schools situated a mere 16 miles apart had begun a rivalry that would still be going 130 years later. But one sensed a competitiveness growing as early as their second meeting of 1886, when quite fortuitously for the

Leopards the referee was their team manager, H. L. Forceman, who called the game with the objectivity of a boxer officiating his own match. In the second half of a scoreless game, a Lafayette player picked up the ball and ran it to the Lehigh 3-yard line during a time-out. Forceman allowed the play to stand, which motivated the Mountain Hawks to leave the field. A Lafayette player then picked up the ball with no defense to stop him and ran it into the end zone for what his team claimed to be a 4–0 victory that Lehigh maintains to this day was a scoreless tie. "It was indeed a most lamentable state of affairs when two colleges like Lehigh and Lafayette, situated so near each other, and whose relations ought to be of the most intimate kind cannot play a friendly game of football without causing so much ill feeling on both sides," decried an editorial in a local newspaper the next day.[2]

What the columnist did not understand was that there was no such thing as a friendly game of football. The rivalry sparked a passion in the players and fans on both sides that often resulted in violence. Pitched battles often marred activities on and off the field. Camaraderie was unheard of among heated rivals, such as what the Leopards and Mountain Hawks were becoming.

What they were not becoming was comparable rivals. After securing their first two defeats of Lafayette in successive weeks in 1888, a season in which they blossomed with a 10–2 record, the Hawks began a period of domination in which they would forge an 11–1–1 record against their Pennsylvania neighbors while playing them twice or even three times in a year through 1893. That domination peaked with a 66–6 thrashing of the Leopards in 1890.

Soon, however, Lafayette turned the tables, forging an 18–4 record against the Mountain Hawks from 1895 to 1911. Ironically, it was in 1896, the year in which the series was suspended due to an eligibility dispute, that the Leopards won their first of three national championships with an 11–0–1 record behind tackle and future legendary University of Michigan coach Fielding Yost and All-American guard Charles Rinehart. Their 6–4 victory over the University of Pennsylvania was among the most publicized games of the era and one of just two games in which they did not shut out their opponent.

The player whose questioned eligibility will be forever known as interrupting the most played rivalry in college football history was prolific running back George Barclay, who had scored eight touchdowns in the previous two seasons and whom Lehigh pointed out had spent time the previous summer in semipro baseball. But Barclay would be better remembered for creating the first football helmet, which he and some of his teammates used in the defeat of Penn.

The lopsided nature of the rivalry in which the teams traded periods of superiority, as well as the geographic proximity of the schools, spurred competitive fervor among the fans. One tradition that was launched on both campuses was a pregame bonfire. That annual event began in 1888 after a Mountain Hawks upset of the Leopards when a group of overzealous Lehigh freshmen tore down the bleachers for a spur-of-the-moment celebration on their home field and set them on fire. Students from both schools would thereafter pile up wooden boxes and crates before games that they intended to light after their team had secured victory. They would also attempt to sneak onto the other campus and light their bonfire prematurely. A Lehigh student once devised an airplane that he attempted in vain to send into a Lafayette bonfire and spark it. Lafayette students answered by sending flaming arrows into a Lehigh bonfire, but that attempt was quelled by sand and blankets placed on the fire by Lehigh students. Lafayette has since forced a discontinuation of the tradition, while Lehigh officials have allowed it only as a pregame ceremony.

The turn of the 20th century was marked by what Lafayette players and fans considered a show of disloyalty that would go down in the school's football annals as perhaps its most fiendish act. That was when coach S. B. Newton, who had guided the Leopards to a brilliant 30–6 record from 1899 to 1901, jumped ship to take over their hated rivals. Newton immediately transformed a Lehigh team that had ended the 1901 season on an eight-game losing streak into winners—though only temporarily. The Mountain Hawks not only forged a 16–5–2 record the next two years but also ended a six-game losing streak to the Leopards with two consecutive victories. Their resurgence, however, was short lived. Lehigh plummeted to 1–8 in 1904 and finished its 1905 season on a four-game losing streak that included a 53–0 shellacking at the hands of Lafayette. By that time, the rivals had limited their annual clashes to one.

Lafayette control of the series was absolute. Not only did the Leopards beat the Mountain Hawks on nearly an annual basis, but they also most often pitched a shutout. Lafayette forged a 19–5 record in The

Rivalry from 1894 to 1911 and prevented Lehigh from scoring in 14 of those games, including six in a row from 1899 to 1901. Even the advent of the forward pass early in the 20th century didn't help the Mountain Hawks—it was Lafayette tackle Aaron Crane who threw the first touchdown pass in the series in 1909 to help his team to a 21–0 victory.

Not that the Mountain Hawks were pushovers. They finished .500 or better every year under coach Byron Dixon from 1906 to 1909. But while they were winning a bit more than they were losing, the Leopards were maintaining annual greatness behind such Walter Camp All-Americans as fullbacks David Cure and George McCaa, center Walter Bachman, and guard Frank Kelly. From 1899 to 1911 they forged a record of 103–25–6, generally losing only to such powers of the era as Pennsylvania and Princeton.

The Leopards finally fell back to earth before and during World War I, and the Mountain Hawks swooped down upon them, winning six of seven meetings from 1912 to 1918. The most memorable was a 78–0 mauling in 1917, the most lopsided in series history, in which Lehigh halfback Raymond B. "Snooks" Dowd embarked on an adventure that is considered perhaps the most memorable play ever in The Rivalry. Dowd actually ran the wrong way with the ball, circled his own goalposts, and then traversed the field to score a touchdown in which it was estimated he ran 115 yards. It can be assumed that he always ran down the first-base line and not the third-base line after hitting the ball as a major league infielder in the 1920s.

The sweet taste of success turned sour again for the Mountain Hawks, who lost 10 consecutive games to the Leopards from 1919 to 1928. Lafayette coach John B. Sutherland took over in 1919 and immediately ended the program's short bout with mediocrity. He transformed his team into national champions in 1921, spurred by the talent of guard Frank Schwab, the first-ever Leopards player to earn first-team All-American status. Lafayette swept through its season undefeated, avenging five consecutive losses to Pennsylvania along the way and burying Lehigh, 28–6 to close out the year (The Rivalry was moved to the season finale in 1916 and has remained there).

The annual dominance of Lafayette had some critics of the series calling for its end. Others yearned to move it to the beginning of the season, when the outcome wouldn't seem like a foregone conclusion. Some Leopards followers had grown far more interested in a rumored annual showdown against powerful Notre Dame than maintaining a rivalry against a team that had become a personal punching bag.

Sutherland had bolted for the University of Pittsburgh and given way to Herbert McCracken when Lafayette won its second national title in six years in 1926, which it concluded with a 35–0 blanking of Lehigh for its third consecutive shutout. A new group of All-Americans, such as running backs George Wilson and Frank Kirkleski and tackle Bill Cothran, guided that team to a perfect record. Wilson led the nation with 20 touchdowns and later became one of four Lafayette players inducted into the College Football Hall of Fame.

By that time the calls for an end to the annual battles between the Leopards and Mountain Hawks had escalated into shouts. It would take a Lehigh victory to soften the screams and it finally happened in 1929, not as a result of soaring Hawks but rather a drop to mediocrity from their neighbors. The Leopards had lost four of their last five games heading into the battle that year against second-year Lehigh coach Austin Tate and his team, and it took a blocked kick as time expired by Mountain Hawks substitute center Tommy Ayre to secure their first victory over Lafayette since World War I was drawing to a close in 1918. The victory was trumpeted to the skies in the Lehigh student newspaper, which indicated that the years of Leopard dominance in the series was over. "[Austin] pointed for the Lafayette game and was rewarded by victory," it read. "The team pointed for it, too, and a harder fighting Lehigh team cannot be found in our local football annals. Our hats are off to the 1929 team and its gallant leader, 'Tubby' Miller. They have not only won from Lafayette, breaking the long string of defeats, but they have set a fashion which the teams of the years to come will emulate. When the slogan of 'Beat Lafayette' is uttered next year, it will not be a half-hearted hope that inspires the utterance but a full-bodied confidence in sure achievement. 'Lafayette, we are here'—to stay!"[3]

That proclamation was, to say the least, premature. The Leopards failed to revert to their early 1920s greatness, but they were strong enough to embark on a four-game winning streak against their archrivals after the 1929 defeat. It was nothing to brag about. The Mountain Hawks sunk from mediocrity in the immediate post–World War I era to abysmal in the late 1920s and beyond. They suffered through one miserable season after another under coaches Perry Wendell and Tate from 1925 to 1933, compiling a record of 23–55–5 during that stretch and managing the only winning season in 1929. A brief rise during the height of the Great Depression resulted in .500-or-above marks and defeats of miserable Lafayette teams from 1934 to 1936, but the Leopards resumed their dominance and maintained it for a long period thereafter.

The Mountain Hawks simply didn't have the talent to compete in most of the years. But they quite often rose to the occasion against vastly superior foes. The most notable example was played on November 20, 1937, when a Lafayette team that had finished with the worst record in its history at 1–8 the previous year was attempting to complete an undefeated season. Led by a stifling defense and halfback Tony Cavallo, the first Associated Press All-American in program history, the Leopards had yielded just six points all year (to Rutgers) and pitched six shutouts in seven games heading into their showdown against Lehigh.

The Mountain Hawks? They had taken the opposite path. They had soared in 1936 to 6–2, their finest mark since 1917, but had suffered a precipitous drop to 1–7 as they prepared to play Lafayette. What was expected was a massacre. What fans got was a taut defensive struggle. Only a fortunate call by an official saved the Leopards from a momentous upset and the loss of their unbeaten season. Lehigh standout George Ellstrom, who later became the first Lehigh graduate to be killed in World War II, ran 36 yards for an apparent touchdown but was ruled to have stepped out of bounds.[4] The Leopards held on for a 6–0 victory.

Many wondered if Lehigh would ever rise to the level of its neighbor on the gridiron. The Leopards lost nary a game in the next 15 played between the two teams—only a 7–7 tie in 1942 prevented them from forging a perfect mark against the Mountain Hawks during that period. They doubled up their dominance of Lehigh in 1943 and 1944 as the teams clashed twice each year because of wartime travel restrictions. The Leopards won those four games by a combined score of 205–7.

Not that Lafayette was a world-beater during the prewar-to-postwar years. Its records varied wildly from season to season. The Leopards went 4–5 in 1939 and 9–0 in 1940 behind All-American halfbacks James Farrell and George Mayer. They finished 6–1 in 1944 and 1–7–1 in 1945, their lone triumph achieved against Lehigh. They lost nine of 11 games in 1946 and early 1947, then rebounded to win 13 of 16. But they were strong enough to beat the Mountain Hawks, who compiled a

17–55–7 mark from 1937 to 1946. Lehigh was particularly devastated by the loss of players during the war, losing 11 consecutive games in 1943 and 1944 and experiencing six consecutive shutout defeats to the Leopards during the last three years of the conflict.

The Rivalry was only a rivalry in name and spirit. One such show of passion for the annual battle occurred in 1936, when Lehigh students, buoyed by a rare two-game winning streak by their charges over the Leopards, sneaked into Fisher Field in the dead of night with the intention of painting "Beat Lafayette" on the turf. They were caught after completing "Beat Laf," but the deed could not be undone. The incomplete sentence remained for all to see when the battle commenced the following day.

The pranks eventually turned into a game of "Can You Top This?" Lehigh students once stole the sword from a statue of General Lafayette. Lafayette counterparts then painted the Lehigh statues maroon and white. The shenanigans added spice to a rivalry that has over the years been dulled a bit by the domination of one program or the other.

That domination finally swung in the favor of the Mountain Hawks in 1950. The shift was the result of both the deterioration of the Lafayette program and the rise of Lehigh. The former can be traced back to 1948. Popular coach Ivan Williamson had guided his charges to a 7–2 record, including an as-usual defeat of Lehigh to conclude the regular season. The team was honored to be invited to a Sun Bowl clash on New Year's Day against the Texas College of Mines. It was the first time Lafayette had received a bowl invitation in 25 years. But when school president Ralph Cooper Hutchinson informed the president of that school that the Leopards had a black player named David Showell on their roster, the invitation was revoked. Texas law prohibited black players on the same field as whites on a state-owned field.

Showell reportedly told his teammates to go without him. He was accustomed to racism from his time in the segregated U.S. Army. Despite the injustices, he completed flight school and served with the Tuskegee Airmen during World War II. His fellow players reluctantly agreed to play, but the faculty forced the athletic committee to decline the invitation without explanation.

The result was mayhem. Lafayette students marched to Hutchinson's home and demanded to know why their team would not be playing in the Sun Bowl. Hutchinson informed them of the truth, setting off a firestorm of protest. The students demanded that Hutchinson wire the chairman of the bowl committee asking to reconsider and allow Showell to play. That request was turned down.

The students were incensed. About 1,000 of them passed a formal resolution the next morning. It read: "We protest the racial discrimination against one of our fellow students and declare without equivocation our firm resolve that all Americans have equal rights under the law."[5] Several TCM players expressed the same sentiment. Tri-captain Jake Rhodes spoke about fighting alongside blacks in the war and his acceptance of competing against them on the gridiron.

The game selection committee issued a statement that such a law prohibiting blacks from competing in the Sun Bowl didn't exist, but Hutchinson insisted that was what he was told. The result was that the Leopards were replaced by Virginia and the 1949 Sun Bowl became forever known at Lafayette as "The Greatest Game Never Played."

Williamson bolted for the University of Wisconsin after that season, and perhaps not so coincidentally, the program collapsed. Despite the continued presence of top quarterback Frank Downing, the Leopards dropped to 2–6 in 1949, though they did complete their 15-year unbeaten streak against Lehigh with a 21–12 victory to end the season.

That it was considered a major upset was a reflection of the opposite directions in which the programs were headed. The Leopards had slipped into a period of futility from which they would not fully emerge until 1955. They managed just one winning season from 1949 to 1954, recording a 13–39 mark during that stretch and bottoming out at 0–9 in 1952. The Mountain Hawks finally found success under coach Bill Leckonby, with six straight winning seasons from 1947 through 1953, including a 9–0 record in 1950 that featured major contributions from such first-team All-Americans as running back Dick Doyne and guard/linebacker Bill Ciarvino.

That season marked the beginning of an about-face in The Rivalry. Lehigh, which overwhelmed its opponents in 1950 by a combined score of 301–77 and ended the year with back-to-back shutouts, took out years of frustration with a 38–0 thumping of Lafayette, its most lopsided triumph over its archrival in 15 years.

The perfect season was more remarkable when considering that 1949 All-American Dick Gabriel, who had exceeded 1,000 yards rushing that year, spent most of it sidelined with injuries. But Doyne picked up the slack with 994 yards, averaging 110.4 per game, fifth best in school history. Doyne later recalled the one-game-at-a-time perspective that allowed his team to steamroll through the 1950 season unbeaten. "None of us ever spoke about going undefeated," said Doyne, who was taken by the Chicago Cardinals in the fourth round of the NFL draft that year. "Even after we beat a great Dartmouth team, we just kept going one game at a time and it really wasn't until after the Lafayette game that going unbeaten was mentioned."[6]

Gabriel, who was drafted both by the Detroit Lions and into the U. S. Army in 1950, was statistically more impressive. He averaged 6.6 yards per rushing attempt in his career, including 8.1 in 1949, both of which remain school records. He exploded for a 97-yard run against Franklin & Marshall in 1948 and ran one punt return 88 yards for a touchdown and one kickoff return 95 yards for a score.

The duo could have brought national attention had the 1950 group voted to accept offers to play in the Tangerine Bowl or Sun Bowl. But many of them rejected the notion of five weeks' extra practice. They considered the regular-season schedule far more important than any postseason game, which they deemed meaningless. Those that did want to make the trip, however, were disappointed when school president Martin Whitaker cast the deciding vote against it with the thought that it would cut into study time for upcoming exams.

What they did not deem meaningless was the blanking of Lafayette to put the cherry on top of what remains the only undefeated season in school history. They had served as personal punching bags for the Leopards for generations. Lafayette had boasted a record of 47–14–1 against Lehigh since 1895.

And though it would take another decade before the pendulum swung forcefully in the Mountain Hawks' direction—the Leopards won three straight meetings from 1953 to 1955 by a combined score of 127–6—the turnaround would take hold in the late 1950s and Lehigh would remain the dominant team thereafter.

The lopsided nature of The Rivalry from generation to generation has been a reflection of one program experiencing a period of strength and the other an era of weakness. There have indeed been many blow-outs in the series. But on occasion, even when one team was a regional power and the other a doormat, battles have been spirited and close. One such example occurred when the winless Leopards took the 7–2

Mountain Hawks down to the wire in 1952. It took a 23-yard touchdown pass from diminutive Lehigh reserve sophomore quarterback John Conti and three goal-line stands by his defense to wrest victory from the jaws of defeat. A similar scenario created a sense of déjà vu in 1961, when a Lafayette team that finished the season with a record of 2–6–1 nearly toppled a Lehigh bunch with the opposite mark. The Mountain Hawks needed a 20-yard field goal from Andy Larko to secure a 17–14 triumph that year. That boot provided a fine departing gift for Leckonby, who left the post after 16 seasons and had proven instrumental in transforming the program into one of the best in the region.

The 1950s marked the height of pranking, which became quite imaginative. Lafayette students began driving to the Bethlehem train station following vacation breaks and offering to drive Lehigh peers home with the claim that they were school representatives on a mission to get as many of them back to their campus homes as quickly as possible. They offered the Lehigh students food and drink. The unsuspecting students were "kidnapped" and had their heads shaven to the skull. Despite warnings to such pranksters from their school administration, Lafayette students would also embark on trips to Bethlehem to give unwanted haircuts to any Lehigh students they could grab after Mountain Hawks fans attempted to set the Lafayette bonfire alight prematurely during rivalry week.

The departure of Leckonby ushered in a period of ineptitude at Lehigh that coincided with equally abysmal Lafayette teams. The Mountain Hawks dropped to 3–6 in 1962 under new coach Mike Cooley and continued on a free fall for the rest of the decade after replacing him with Fred Dunlap in 1965. They suffered through nine consecutive losing seasons from 1962 to 1970, including a 0–9 disaster in 1966. They bottomed out from 1963 to 1966, during which time they owned a 3–32–1 mark.

Two of those three victories were achieved against Lafayette, which indicates the struggles its program was experiencing in the 1960s. The Leopards boasted losing records every year from 1961 through 1967, with a seven-year mark of 16–45–3. But some might cite 1968 as the year the domination of Lehigh in The Rivalry that continued well into the next century began.

Led by All-American split end Mike Miller and fullback Tom Triolo, Lafayette entered the showdown at 7–2, the best it had achieved after nine games since 1948. After a season-opening loss to Rutgers, they had yielded just 44 points in eight games. The Mountain Hawks boasted quite the opposite capability on defense, surrendering 28 or more points in seven of the previous eight games. But Lehigh emerged with a 21–6 victory.

There would be no need for upsets of Lafayette in the 1970s. Lehigh was finally rewarded for its patience with Dunlap, who transformed the program into a Division II power before turning it over in 1976 to assistant coach John Whitehead, who took the momentum and ran with it. The Mountain Hawks not only won eight of nine meetings against the Leopards from 1971 to 1979, but they also compiled an overall record of 76–27–3 from 1973 to 1981. They attracted such first-team All-Americans as offensive linemen Dave Melone and John Hill, future Atlanta Falcons quarterback Kim McQuilken, and wide receiver Steve Kreider, who also embarked on a fine NFL career after peaking with Lafayette as a junior with 1,181 yards receiving, an incredible 22.3 per-catch average and 12 touchdowns. The respect Dunlap earned from his players translated into success on the field far better in the 1970s than it had in the previous decade.

The seeds of that heretofore rare period of gridiron success were planted in the living room of the McQuilken family when Dunlap convinced the high school quarterback to enroll at his school despite a comparatively unheralded football program and the inability to offer an athletic scholarship. McQuilken was more intrigued by the potential scholarly pursuits and benefits offered by Lehigh than competing on its gridiron, which he explained in the following passage from his book, *The Road to Athletic Scholarship*:

> Lehigh had not had a winning football season in ten years. I liked the academic challenge at Lehigh but I wasn't sure about the football part of the equation. Fortunately, Lehigh had a very persuasive coach in Fred Dunlap. Coach Dunlap convinced me that all his team needed was a pass-oriented quarterback to lead to the promised land of Division II football. My parents and I were also pretty convinced that he and his assistant Walt King were not leaving our living room until I signed.[7]

McQuilken indeed signed and emerged as easily the most productive quarterback in Lehigh history. He shattered every school passing record, leaving with 6,996 yards and 37 touchdowns through the air. He also showed grit that critics believed to be lacking among players competing at universities far better known for their academics than their football programs. One example occurred in 1972, when his Mountain Hawks were prime for an upset against Lafayette. They led just 14–6 in the fourth quarter when McQuilken sustained a concussion. Though he knew he had been concussed, he refused to come out of the game. He later admitted he had no idea what he was doing on the field, but he executed the plays well enough to keep his team ahead until the final tick of the clock.

The era of greatness at Lehigh was launched the following year. The team won four straight games, including a 45–13 dismantling of its archrival, earning its first postseason berth in its history. The Mountain Hawks lost to Western Kentucky in the first round of the Division II playoffs but still won the coveted Lambert Cup, which was presented to the best small-division team in the East.

McQuilken's career was over, but Lehigh dominance had just begun. The team won 12 of 13 games during one stretch in 1974 and 1975 and captured another Lambert Cup in the latter year despite being eliminated in the first round of the playoffs again, this time by New Hampshire in the final game of Dunlap's 11-year coaching career at the school.

It was Whitehead, however, who would eventually send the Mountain Hawks soaring to the top. Whitehead boasted quite a different personality than his predecessor. He was a tough, tobacco-chewing offspring of Pennsylvania coal miners who proved inspiration to his players. But his first season was marked by mediocrity and a rare defeat to Lafayette. Lehigh had clinched nothing more than a better-than-even record heading into The Rivalry game, while the Leopards had blossomed around midseason to enter on a three-game winning streak. They were thoroughly outplayed by the Mountain Hawks, which outgained them by 210 yards and racked up 16 more first downs, but they finished the right side of a 21–17.

But just as rare Lehigh victories of a bygone era were followed by defeat after defeat, the same fate befell the Leopards in generations beyond. They were thoroughly outclassed by the Mountain Hawks in the next four meetings, losing all of them by a combined score of 116–35 and tallying just three total points in the last two.

They weren't alone in their misery. Propelled offensively by the combination of Kreider and All-American quarterback Mike Rieker, Lehigh blossomed in 1977. The Mountain Hawks hit their stride around midseason, averaging 37 points in steamrolling past their last eight opponents, including Massachusetts and California–Davis to earn a berth against Jacksonville (Alabama) State in the Pioneer Bowl in Wichita Falls, Kansas, with a Division II championship on the line. The Mountain Hawks were the leading passing team in the nation while using an archaic wing-T formation that befuddled the Gamecocks in the title clash. Rieker scored on a one-yard plunge and hooked up with Kreider on touchdown passes of nine and seven yards. Meanwhile, the defense was pitching its third shutout of the season and pouncing on four fumbles to secure a 33–0 victory and the national crown. "They were baffled by the Wing-T. I couldn't believe it," crowed Rieker as his team celebrated. "They didn't see it all day. We have never run our people like we did today."[8]

They ran their people quite well into the next decade before Whitehead and his program ran out of steam and descended into mediocrity with a 4–6 record in 1982, its worst in 12 years. The 1980s were marked by a rare period of parity between Lehigh and Lafayette, which stocked its program during that decade with Division I-AA first-team All-Americans, such as linebacker Joe Skladany (1981), guard Tony Green (1982), and quarterback Frank Baur (1988). The difference maker was coach Bill Russo, who arrived after a 3–7 season in 1981 and immediately turned the program around. "He was a winner," said late-1980s Lafayette running back Tom Costello. "He wouldn't accept anything less and wasn't afraid to speak his mind to make sure we understood what his feelings were at any given time. He was a black-and-white guy. There was no gray area with him."[9]

His impact was instant and dramatic. The 1981 Leopards raced to a 5–0 record and finished 9–2, its finest mark in 41 years. An offense that had scored six or fewer points in eight of 10 games the year before averaged 27.3 that season. But the Mountain Hawks were putting the finishing touches on their era of greatness. Only a loss to Eastern Kentucky prevented them from winning a second national championship in three years in 1979. Their first-round defeat in 1980 kept them from continuing what could have been their first undefeated season since 1950. They were still a powerhouse in 1981. Breaking away from the typical scenario in a rivalry peppered with games between teams on opposite ends of the talent spectrum, the one that season between Lafayette and Lehigh was a comparative Clash of the Titans.

Both teams arrived in Bethlehem that day with just two losses. The game was televised locally for the first time. A rivalry record crowd of 19,414 packed Taylor Stadium. And despite the prolific offenses boasted by both teams—Lehigh had averaged 37.5 points in its previous four games—the defenses ruled the day. The score stood at 3–3 in the fourth quarter when the Leopards, who had come away empty on several forays deep into Mountain Hawks territory, finally broke through on a game-winning touchdown run by halfback Rodger Shepko with nine minutes remaining. The Lafayette defense held a Lehigh offense that ranked No. 1 nationally in Division I-AA with 443 yards per game down to a mere 153. The defeat destroyed any hope for the Mountain Hawks to embark on a third consecutive playoff run.

The trading of triumphs in 1980 and 1981 marked the beginning of the only extended period of parity in the history of The Rivalry. Neither team beat the other more than twice in a row until Lehigh snagged its third straight in 1997. By that time, both teams were in the Patriot League, first known as the Colonial League, which was formed as a football-only conference in 1986 before changing its name and becoming a full-fledged athletic entity in 1990.

Both programs became entrenched in mediocrity during that period, which explains the evenness of the series. They fielded fine teams only on rare occasions, such as in 1988, when Baur and his Leopards clawed their way to an 8–2–1 record and 5–0 in the Colonial League to win the title, which they clinched with a defeat of the Mountain Hawks.

That game proved to be one of the most memorable in the history of The Rivalry. The final score was indicative of the athletic prowess boasted by both teams. Lehigh arrived with the top-ranked offense in the nation with Lafayette right on its heels. Baur and Mountain Hawks counterpart Jim Harris rushed their teams downfield. The latter completed 23 of 29 passes for 372 yards in the first half alone and a 35–30 halftime lead as his offense tallied touchdowns in each of its five possessions. Meanwhile, Costello—a mere freshman—was shredding the Lehigh defense en route to a 216-yard rushing performance. The Leopards finally took control by scoring 17 unanswered points in the second half for a 52–38 lead. A late Mountain Hawks score only served to close the gap in a 52–45 shootout in which the teams combined for a whopping 1,257 total yards.

Like McQuilken at Lehigh a generation earlier, Baur had blossomed into the greatest quarterback ever to grace the gridiron at his school. He garnered national attention in that junior season in which he broke school records in passing yards (2,621) and touchdowns (23) while pacing the nation with a 171.1 quarterback rating. He was featured on the cover of *Sports Illustrated* not only as a Heisman Trophy candidate but also as a sensitive and interesting individual beset by a stuttering problem and gifted as a pianist. His size and power impressed NFL scouts, but a perceived lack of arm strength kept NFL teams from calling on draft day. He hooked up as a free agent with the New York Giants, but a series of injuries prevented him from maximizing his potential as a professional quarterback.

The Leopards would never again match that level of success under Russo, who departed in 2000 as the most successful coach in school history after 19 years as the helm. But they did win the Patriot League title in 1992 behind a stunning performance by sophomore running back Erik Marsh, who piled up 1,365 yards and 10 touchdowns on the ground and peaked in a 32–29 victory over Lehigh in which he exploded for a school-record 251 yards and put the cherry on top with the game-winning score. Marsh specialized in steamrolling the Mountain Hawks. He rushed for 249 yards and a touchdown against them in 1993 and added 214 yards and three scores in a 39–14 dismantling a year later en route to earning Patriot League Most Valuable Player honors and helping his team overcome a 0–6 start to take the conference championship.

Meanwhile, Whitehead was replaced in 1986 by Hank Small but coached Lehigh to just one memorable season. His 1991 team, led by wide receivers Horace Hamm and Jason Cristino, finished 9–2 and capped the year with a 36–18 victory over Lafayette. But their second era of dominance would have to wait until Small was replaced by Kevin Higgins, who took over in 1994. Higgins guided the Mountain Hawks to three consecutive Patriot League championships from 1998 to 2000 before replacement Pete Lembo added a fourth in 2001, posting a seventh consecutive defeat of the Leopards along the way.

Those four Lehigh teams, which combined for a 45–5 record, were easily the best in school history. They featured such first-team All-

Americans as defensive end Nick Martucci, offensive lineman Brian McDonald, running back Ronald Jean, defensive back Abdul Byron, linebacker Ian Eason, and wide receiver Josh Snyder. But a national championship continued to elude them. They fell in either the first or second round in each of those four seasons.

Their domination of Lafayette, however, was thorough. The era of parity had come to a screeching halt. Though the Leopards played the Mountain Hawks tough more often than not, their 10-game losing streak from 1995 to 2001 remains the longest in the history of The Rivalry.

That era of futility ended in 2002 under new coach Frank Tavani. They managed four victories in five years against Lehigh early in the new century, which brought with it an era of top-level competition between the teams in what had become the most played series in college football. They shared Patriot League titles in 2004 and 2006, but it was the clash in 2005 with a playoff berth on the line that proved most memorable during that period. The Leopards had their backs against the wall, trailing 19–17 with a mere 46 seconds remaining and the ball on the Lehigh 37. Tavani considered a long field goal on 4th-and-10 but opted to try for the first down. Lafayette did better than that. Quarterback Jason Davis, who was only in the game because starter Brad Maurer had sustained a shoulder separation on the team's first possession of the game, found running back Jonathan Hurt streaking down the right sideline. Davis launched a perfect pass to Hurt for the game-winning touchdown.

Lafayette had gained control of the series. Their exciting 21–17 defeat of Lehigh in 2007 made it four straight, their longest winning streak against the Mountain Hawks since the late 1940s. Their teams of that period boasted several first-team All-Americans, including tailback Joe McCourt, linebacker Maurice Bennett, and tackles Mike Saint Germain and Jesse Padilla. But what the Leopards could not achieve that their archrivals had a penchant for doing was advance past the first round of the playoffs. They were bounced in the first round by a combined 46 points in 2004, 2005, and 2006.

They might have had another chance in 2009 after winning eight of their first nine games, but a 27–21 upset loss in overtime to the Mountain Hawks seemed to reverse course of The Rivalry. It jump-started a Lehigh program that had foundered since the arrival of coach Andy

Coen in 2006. Powered by All-American and future NFL offensive lineman Will Rackley, Coen's crew split its first four games in 2010, then ran off eight consecutive victories, including a 20–13 triumph over a stubborn Lafayette team that had fallen to 2–10 and a first-round playoff defeat of Northern Iowa before falling in the semifinals. The season marked the first of two consecutive Patriot League championships for the Mountain Hawks, who again reached the Division I-AA semifinals in 2011, this time behind the aerial combination of quarterback Chris Lum and future NFL wide receiver Ryan Spadola, before being eliminated. Lehigh made it five in a row over Lafayette in 2012, but the Leopards turned the tables in 2013 with a 50–28 triumph that clinched their fourth Patriot League championship since 2004.

The nation paid little attention, as it had to the annual clash for generations. Lehigh–Lafayette paled in comparison to Ohio State–Michigan or Auburn–Alabama. But the Mountain Hawks and Leopards, as well as their fans, were already thinking about the 150th meeting between the Keystone State neighbors in 2014. In some corners of the college football world, tradition and supremacy even among the most insignificant programs means a lot. Such is the case with what is still known simply as The Rivalry.

Fact Box (through 2013)
  Nickname: The Rivalry
  Trophy: None
  Total meetings: 149
  Series record: Lafayette leads, 77–67–5
  First meeting: 1884 (Lafayette 50, Lehigh 0)
  Largest margin of victory: Lehigh, 1917 (Lehigh 78, Lafayette 0)
  Longest winning streak: Lafayette, 10 (1919–1928)

Game Results
  1884: Lafayette 50, Lehigh 0
  1884: Lafayette 34, Lehigh 4
  1885: Lafayette 6, Lehigh 0
  1885: Lehigh 6, Lafayette 6
  1886: Lafayette 12, Lehigh 0
  1886: Lafayette 0, Lehigh 0
  1887: Lehigh 10, Lafayette 4

Figure 8.2.   Lafayette vs. Lehigh, 2013. *Courtesy of Lafayette College*

1887: Lafayette 6, Lehigh 0
1888: Lehigh 6, Lafayette 4
1888: Lehigh 16, Lafayette 0
1889: Lehigh 17, Lafayette 10
1889: Lehigh 6, Lafayette 6
1890: Lehigh 30, Lafayette 0
1890: Lehigh 66, Lafayette 6
1891: Lehigh 22, Lafayette 4
1891: Lehigh 6, Lafayette 2
1891: Lehigh 16, Lafayette 2
1892: Lafayette 47, Lehigh 0
1892: Lehigh 15, Lafayette 6
1893: Lehigh 22, Lafayette 6
1893: Lehigh 10, Lafayette 0
1894: Lafayette 28, Lehigh 0
1894: Lehigh 11, Lafayette 8
1895: Lafayette 22, Lehigh 12
1895: Lafayette 14, Lehigh 6
1897: Lafayette 34, Lehigh 0

1897: Lafayette 22, Lehigh 0
1898: Lafayette 22, Lehigh 0
1898: Lehigh 11, Lafayette 5
1899: Lafayette 17, Lehigh 0
1899: Lafayette 35, Lehigh 0
1900: Lafayette 35, Lehigh 0
1900: Lafayette 18, Lehigh 0
1901: Lafayette 29, Lehigh 0
1901: Lafayette 41, Lehigh 0
1902: Lehigh 6, Lafayette 0
1903: Lehigh 12, Lafayette 6
1904: Lafayette 40, Lehigh 6
1905: Lafayette 53, Lehigh 0
1906: Lafayette 33, Lehigh 0
1907: Lafayette 22, Lehigh 5
1908: Lehigh 11, Lafayette 5
1909: Lafayette 21, Lehigh 0
1910: Lafayette 14, Lehigh 0
1911: Lafayette 11, Lehigh 0
1912: Lehigh 10, Lafayette 0
1913: Lehigh 7, Lafayette 0
1914: Lehigh 17, Lafayette 7
1915: Lafayette 35, Lehigh 6
1916: Lehigh 17, Lafayette 0
1917: Lehigh 78, Lafayette 0
1918: Lehigh 17, Lafayette 0
1919: Lafayette 10, Lehigh 6
1920: Lafayette 27, Lehigh 7
1921: Lafayette 28, Lehigh 6
1922: Lafayette 3, Lehigh 0
1923: Lafayette 13, Lehigh 3
1924: Lafayette 7, Lehigh 0
1925: Lafayette 14, Lehigh 0
1926: Lafayette 35, Lehigh 0
1927: Lafayette 43, Lehigh 0
1928: Lafayette 37, Lehigh 14
1929: Lehigh 13, Lafayette 12
1930: Lafayette 16, Lehigh 6

1931: Lafayette 13, Lehigh 7
1932: Lafayette 25, Lehigh 6
1933: Lafayette 54, Lehigh 12
1934: Lehigh 13, Lafayette 7
1935: Lehigh 48, Lafayette 0
1936: Lehigh 18, Lafayette 0
1937: Lafayette 6, Lehigh 0
1938: Lafayette 6, Lehigh 0
1939: Lafayette 29, Lehigh 13
1940: Lafayette 46, Lehigh 0
1941: Lafayette 47, Lehigh 7
1942: Lehigh 7, Lafayette 7
1943: Lafayette 39, Lehigh 7
1943: Lafayette 58, Lehigh 0
1944: Lafayette 44, Lehigh 0
1944: Lafayette 64, Lehigh 0
1945: Lafayette 7, Lehigh 0
1946: Lafayette 13, Lehigh 0
1947: Lafayette 7, Lehigh 0
1948: Lafayette 23, Lehigh 13
1949: Lafayette 21, Lehigh 12
1950: Lehigh 38, Lafayette 0
1951: Lehigh 32, Lafayette 0
1952: Lehigh 14, Lafayette 7
1953: Lafayette 46, Lehigh 0
1954: Lafayette 46, Lehigh 0
1955: Lafayette 35, Lehigh 6
1956: Lehigh 27, Lafayette 10
1957: Lehigh 26, Lafayette 13
1958: Lafayette 14, Lehigh 14
1959: Lafayette 28, Lehigh 6
1960: Lehigh 26, Lafayette 3
1961: Lehigh 17, Lafayette 14
1962: Lehigh 13, Lafayette 6
1963: Lehigh 15, Lafayette 8
1964: Lafayette 6, Lehigh 6
1965: Lehigh 20, Lafayette 14
1966: Lafayette 16, Lehigh 0

1967: Lafayette 6, Lehigh 0
1968: Lehigh 21, Lafayette 6
1969: Lehigh 36, Lafayette 19
1970: Lafayette 31, Lehigh 28
1971: Lehigh 48, Lafayette 19
1972: Lehigh 14, Lafayette 6
1973: Lehigh 45, Lafayette 13
1974: Lehigh 57, Lafayette 7
1975: Lehigh 40, Lafayette 14
1976: Lafayette 21, Lehigh 17
1977: Lehigh 35, Lafayette 17
1978: Lehigh 25, Lafayette 15
1979: Lehigh 24, Lafayette 3
1980: Lehigh 32, Lafayette 0
1981: Lafayette 10, Lehigh 3
1982: Lafayette 34, Lehigh 6
1983: Lehigh 22, Lafayette 14
1984: Lafayette 28, Lehigh 7
1985: Lehigh 24, Lafayette 19
1986: Lafayette 28, Lehigh 23
1987: Lehigh 17, Lafayette 10
1988: Lafayette 52, Lehigh 45
1989: Lafayette 36, Lehigh 21
1990: Lehigh 35, Lafayette 14
1991: Lehigh 36, Lafayette 18
1992: Lafayette 32, Lehigh 29
1993: Lehigh 39, Lafayette 14
1994: Lafayette 54, Lehigh 20
1995: Lehigh 30, Lafayette 27
1996: Lehigh 23, Lafayette 19
1997: Lehigh 43, Lafayette 31
1998: Lehigh 31, Lafayette 7
1999: Lehigh 14, Lafayette 12
2000: Lehigh 31, Lafayette 17
2001: Lehigh 41, Lafayette 6
2002: Lafayette 14, Lehigh 7
2003: Lehigh 30, Lafayette 10
2004: Lafayette 24, Lehigh 10

2005: Lafayette 23, Lehigh 19
2006: Lafayette 49, Lehigh 27
2007: Lafayette 21, Lehigh 17
2008: Lehigh 31, Lafayette 15
2009: Lehigh 27, Lafayette 21
2010: Lehigh 20, Lafayette 13
2011: Lehigh 37, Lafayette 13
2012: Lehigh 38, Lafayette 21
2013: Lafayette 50, Lehigh 28

9

CALIFORNIA VS. STANFORD:
THE BIG GAME

Forget what the Tin Man lugged around in *The Wizard of Oz*. The Stanford Axe is the most famous in the world.

OK, it's not really an axe. It's known as the Axe Trophy and it's the coveted spoils for the winner of the annual gridiron clash between Stanford and California known with reverence as The Big Game. And it's not just coveted by those intended to covet it.

In 1946, a group of Cal students donned aviator overalls and goggles, strolled into the Tressider Union on the Stanford campus, unbolted the Axe display case, and absconded with it.

Two years later, the Axe Trophy was stolen from Cal's Stephen's Union and placed appropriately against a tree near the Stanford golf course.

In 1953, Stanford pranksters smashed through a Cal trophy case and ripped off the Axe but thoughtfully left five bucks to pay for the broken glass. The Cal rally committee paid for a phony Axe Trophy, claiming it was the real one and that the thieves had the replica. Soon the real Axe was returned.

Silly, mindless pranks, one and all. One might argue they were unbecoming of students representing two of the finest academic institutions in the nation. But they served as a diversion for a student body challenged by the rigors of tough coursework, just as football has been used by players on both sides as an escape from the same intense studies. Most of those that suit up on Saturdays for Stanford and California,

Figure 9.1.   California vs. Stanford, 2003. *Source: Michael Pimentel/GoldenBear-Sports.com*

even among the elite talents, haven't prioritized football over academ-ics. The combatants boast a respect and even kindness for one another that some might construe as a lack of passion. They are all in the same boat playing for schools that truly value scholarship over athletics. "The thing I appreciated about Stanford was that you were truly a student-athlete from the day you walked in," recalled Duncan McColl, who earned All-American honors at that school as a defensive lineman in the mid-1970s. "They said, 'Studies come first.'"[1]

The result has been more stringent admission standards that have limited the talent level at both schools. The Cardinal and Golden Bears have boasted national championship contenders but not with the same consistency of their in-state brethren, such as Southern California, or such perennial powers as Ohio State and Alabama. But within such restrictions, they have produced many of the greatest players and teams in the history of college football. And they have played some of its most memorable games.

The most extraordinary of all was played at California Memorial Stadium on November 20, 1982. Senior John Elway, perhaps the finest quarterback to ever grace a college football field, had just assumed the role of hero. He had converted a 29-yard pass over the middle to Emile Harry to set up a Mark Harmon field goal that gave their team a 20–19 lead with just four seconds remaining in the game. It was over. Elway was destined to win the Heisman Trophy and the Cardinal were headed to the Hall of Fame Bowl.

It seemed the only disastrous scenario would be a return for a touchdown, so Harmon squibbed the ensuing kickoff to ensure that no return specialist would get his hands on the ball, which was then sent from one Golden Bear to another on a series of laterals. As if using sleight of hand to keep the play alive, they managed to continue tossing the ball back without fumbling it away or getting tackled. It was tossed from defensive back Richard Rodgers into the eager hands of secondary mate Kevin Moen with nary a Cardinal in front of him. There was, however, one impediment on the way to the end zone. And that was the Stanford band, which in anticipation of victory had already begun marching onto the field. Moen weaved his way through the oncoming instrumentalists before bowling over and trampling trombonist Gary Tyrrell in the end zone. Arguably the most improbable touchdown ever scored had given his team the victory. And the call by Cal radio announcer Joe Starkey would be immortalized forever. "The ball is still loose as they get it to Rodgers!" he began. "They get it back now to the 30, they're down to the 20. . . . Oh, the band is out on the field! He's gonna go into the end zone! He's gone into the end zone! . . . And the Bears, the Bears have won! The Bears have won! Oh, my God! The most amazing, sensational, dramatic, heart-rending, exciting, thrilling finish in the history of college football! California has won the Big Game!"[2]

Understandably overwhelmed and frustrated Stanford coach Paul Wiggin summed up the commotion and emotion with all the clarity he could muster. "What could I see?" he asked rhetorically. "I saw the band, I saw our team, I saw a lateral, I saw a flag go down, I saw a guy pick up a flag, I saw all kinds of things. It was basically a 10-second nightmare."[3]

The seeds of the rivalry were not planted until a decade after Cal launched its football program in 1882. The team played more of a variation of rugby than football and their competition was San Francis-

co–area club teams with such colorful nicknames as the Posens, Mer-
lons, Onions, and Wasps. They generally provided little competition for
the Cal college boys, who steamrolled to a 28–4–3 record and four
unbeaten seasons through 1890. They clearly needed stronger competition from teams representing fellow universities, and Stanford graduate
John Whittemore took the first step in making that a reality in 1891. He
formed a team at that school and was invited to play Cal, but he declined with the understandable thought that his green charges would
get their clocks cleaned.

Whittemore deemed his Stanford team ready the following spring,
and the battle was scheduled for March 19 at the Haight Street
Grounds in San Francisco. The clash was enthusiastically received. Various reports claim between 10,000 and 20,000 fans jammed the field to
witness history. So poorly was the event planned and so surprising was
the turnout that Stanford manager Herbert Hoover, who later occupied
the White House and fumbled the economy, was forced to scramble to
find anything in which to place admission fees. Worse, the teams had
forgotten to bring one significant item to the proceedings—a football.
The game was delayed for an hour before sporting goods store proprie-
tor David Goulcher rode by horseback to his place of business to procure the necessary pigskin.

Despite its head start in building a football program and holding a
distinct size advantage, Cal did anything but dominate the kickoff to the
rivalry. The quicker Cardinal were considered a distinct underdog, but
two touchdowns by Carl Clemens and another by Whittemore secured
it a 14–0 lead (touchdowns were worth just four points at the time) and
they hung on in the second half for a 14–10 victory.

The rousing success of the first Stanford–Cal clash, which brought in
tremendous revenue, motivated the teams to schedule another that
year (which ended in a tie) and a series of Thanksgiving Day battles.
The games were highly anticipated, not just because of the natural
geographic rivalry and the relative evenness between the two teams, but
also due to the lack of college football programs in the area. Their
expanding schedules in the 1890s included almost exclusively high
schools and clubs—both played nobody but Reliance Club teams of San
Francisco and San Jose in 1897 until concluding their schedules with
their annual meeting. It was not until 1899, when both teams shut out

Nevada and Cal blanked Oregon, that they began to play other college teams.

By that time, one of the most legendary and influential coaches in college football history had come and gone at Stanford. Walter Camp took over the program in 1892, left for one year, then returned for the 1894 and 1895 seasons. Camp, who had already restructured the sport back east to resemble modern football rather than rugby, guided the Cardinal to an 11–3–2 record during his tenure, including a 2–0–3 mark against Cal. Among the triumphs against the Golden Bears for the man known as "The Father of American Football" was a controversial 6–0 victory in 1894 in which the officials disallowed a second-half Cal touchdown, causing great consternation. An editorial in the *Berkeleyan* followed not with the insinuation that the referees were rooting for Stanford, but rather that they could not recognize a touchdown when they witnessed one.

The spirit of The Big Game was growing as the 20th century approached. Cal brought to the Haight Street Grounds in 1896 a live bear cub as a tribute to the bear that had been a state symbol since 1846. The animal was removed at halftime, marking the first of several vain attempts to use such a beast as a mascot. The football team eventually followed the lead of the school's track team, which in 1895 traveled to the East Coast to compete against some of the premier competition in the nation under a blue banner featuring a large golden bear in the center. They won the track meet and hailed the bear flag as its lucky charm. The football program adopted the flag as well but continued to bring live bear cubs to games. The animal would inevitably grow increasingly scared of the large crowd and would have to be removed. But it would bring a sense of pride to the home crowd. The California rooting sections of the early 1900s could be heard reciting the following "Oski Yell" during games: " *Oski wow wow! . . . Whiskey wee wee! . . . Olee! Muckie-eye! . . . Olee! Berkeley-eye! . . . California! Wow!*"

The cheer and the inability to make a live mascot work in the 1930s inspired Cal to utilize the talents of one William Rockwell, a Long Beach Junior College transfer who had donned a Viking costume and led cheers at football games at that school. Rockwell, whose shyness was transformed into effervescence inside the outfit, wore a homemade bear head, baggy pants, large letter sweater, oversized shoes, and white gloves for his 1941 debut. He would walk on the crossbar between goalposts and attempt to wrest the football out of the hands of referees. He led cheers, waved to children, and flirted with coeds. Oski the Mascot was born.

The birth of The Big Game was followed by spirited and top-level competition. Both teams dominated the high school, club, and fledgling college programs from 1898 well into the early 1900s. Three Stanford victories and a tie against Cal from 1894 to 1897 were answered by four wins in five years by the Golden Bears. The Cardinal steamrolled to a combined 39–7–7 record from 1900 and 1905, but that paled in comparison to the 52–6–10 mark compiled by their archrivals from 1898 to 1905, which included undefeated seasons in 1898, 1901, and 1902. So dominant was the Golden Bears defense that they gave up a total of 79 points in 68 games and pitched 57 shutouts during that eight-year stretch. Yet three of their six defeats were to Stanford.

That era was highlighted not only by spirited competition between the rivals but also by the first appearance of the Axe, which would remain the symbol of gridiron superiority for well over a century. Strangely, however, it was first seen during a baseball game played between the two schools on April 14, 1899. Stanford yell leader Billy Erb, who purchased an axe with a 15-inch blade, used it to decapitate a stuffed bear donning Cal blue and gold.

Drunk with power, Erb and his fellow Cardinal fans began to chop up every symbol of the Golden Bears in sight, including blue and gold ribbons, thereby inciting the wrath of Cal supporters, who charged the Stanford stands, wrested the Axe away, and had it taken to a San Francisco butcher shop. The thief had the handle chopped off, hid the blade underneath the shirt, and transported it across the San Francisco Bay into Oakland. The mission was accomplished despite security efforts launched by Stanford fans who tipped off the law of the possibility that the Axe could be on the way to the Cal campus. And there it remained—one law professor from each school ruled that it rightfully belonged to Cal and suggested that it be used as a symbol of the gridiron rivalry.

The Big Game was pretty much the only game of consequence for the two schools in the early years. There was an exception, however, in 1902, when national powerhouse Michigan, which had outscored its opponents that season 501–0, accepted an invitation to play Stanford in the first Rose Bowl. The game was the brainchild of those running the

annual Tournament of Roses Parade, which sought to increase attendance in its event by staging a football game on New Year's Day. The
battle against the Wolverines proved disastrous and embarrassing. So
dominant was Michigan in a 49–0 shellacking that the game was called
after three quarters. Adding to the humiliation was the fact that the
Wolverines were coached by Fielding Yost, who had bolted Stanford
after guiding it to a 7–2–1 mark in 1900.

The Cardinal recovered quite well, however, losing only to Cal the
following year and embarking on undefeated seasons in 1903 and 1905.
But both the Cal and Stanford programs soon became victims of the
justified antifootball hysteria that gripped the nation in the earliest
years of the 20th century. The *Chicago Tribune* in 1904 reported that
18 players had been killed and 159 seriously injured playing the sport in
that year alone. It was decided by the presidents of the two schools that
football be replaced by rugby, which, granted, was no Saturday afternoon picnic.

The parity that marked the first two decades of the football rivalry
was maintained after the switch to rugby in 1906. Three Stanford victories to begin the rugby rivalry were matched by Cal, which in the 1880s
and beyond blossomed into a perennial national champion. But that
school reinstated its football program in 1915, followed by Stanford
three years later. Much had changed in the world of West Coast college
football by then. Both schools were able to fill their schedules with
opponents representing other universities. The competition was stiff
enough to prevent Stanford from capturing the dominant form it displayed before shelving its football program.

But the same could not be said about the football program of the
Golden Bears, who emerged from hibernation to develop one of the
finest college teams ever assembled under coach Andy Smith. Cal not
only won the newly formed Pacific Coast Conference five times in
seven years from 1918 to 1924, but it also went unbeaten in the last five
of the those seasons, compiling a record of 44–0–4 and sweeping four
straight from Stanford by a combined score of 117–7. The Cardinal
were not alone in their inability to score against the Golden Bears, who
were scored upon in only 10 of 38 games from 1920 to 1923 and gave
up just seven points in 1923. Several of their stars of the era wound up
in the College Football Hall of Fame, including end Brick Muller and

linemen Stan Barnes, Walter Gordon, Babe Horrell, and Dan McMillan.

Though the national crown was purely mythical in that era as a hodgepodge of polls all made their own determinations, Cal was deemed the champion by more than any other school in the nation in 1920 and 1921 and given the title by at least one after each of the next two seasons as well.

A sixth consecutive defeat of Stanford appeared likely in 1924, but the Cardinal had landed that year a legendary coach of their own in Glenn Scobey Warner, more popularly known as Pop Warner, after which the most significant youth football program was later named. Warner had already established himself as far back as the late 1800s as a brilliant tactician and the genius at the Carlisle Indian Industrial School in Pennsylvania who had transformed an unknown named Jim Thorpe into arguably the greatest football player of the first half of the 20th century. Warner brought some of his innovations, such as the screen pass and the single-wing and double-wing formations, to Stanford, and the results were immediate and tremendous. His Cardinal stood at 6–0 heading into their showdown against the Golden Bears, whose record had been blemished only by a tie against Washington. He also boasted fullback Ernie Nevers, who had spent his college career shredding opposing defenses and later not only forged a Hall of Fame career in the NFL but also pitched briefly in the major leagues.

At six foot one and 205 pounds, Nevers was considered a giant of the era at his position. The man nicknamed "Big Swede" and "Big Dog" by his teammates was as versatile and talented as any player in the college game. He was known for playing fearlessly and with reckless abandon, on occasion shedding his helmet and throwing himself back into action without one. It was no wonder that Warner considered him a superior player to anyone he had ever coached—even Thorpe. "I consider Nevers the better player because he gave everything he had in every game," Warner said. Warner added the following in his autobiography: "In an era of great ones—Red Grange of Illinois, George Gipp and the Four Horsemen from Notre Dame, Elmer Oliphant and Chris Cagle of Army, or even Jim Thorpe of Carlisle—Nevers always stood a bit taller when trying to compare others to him."[4]

There was just one problem when the Clash of the Titans rolled around on November 22, 1924: Nevers was sidelined with a broken ankle. So when the Cardinal fell behind 20–6 with less than six minutes remaining in the game before 77,000 fans at Cal's Memorial Stadium and 20,000 more peering in from nearby Tightwad Hill, they appeared doomed. But Stanford backup quarterback Ed Walker responded with a 20-yard touchdown pass to Ted Shipkey and 34-yard scoring strike to Murray Cuddeback to cap an 81-yard drive in the final seconds to forge a 20–20 tie and secure a trip for the Cardinal to the Rose Bowl.

That clash against Knute Rockne's Notre Dame Fighting Irish and their legendary Four Horsemen proved to be Nevers's finest hour. He remained on crutches until two days before the showdown but shed them in favor of braces made from inner tubes that were wrapped so tightly he could barely feel his legs. Even Warner, who admired Nevers for his toughness, doubted he could thrive under such restrictions. But it was always never-say-never for Nevers. He played all 60 minutes and outgained the all four of the Horsemen combined. He finished with 117 yards on 34 carries and not only handled the ball on every snap but also intercepted a pass and contributed to 80 of his team's tackles on defense. Not even a 27–10 defeat could diminish the brilliance of his performance.

Nor could it halt the momentum Stanford had built under Warner, who coached the team to nine consecutive winning seasons and an overall record of 71–7–8 before leaving in 1933. With All-American end Shipkey leading the way, he peaked in 1926 by guiding the Cardinal to their first of two national championships as only a Rose Bowl tie against Alabama marred a perfect year. And in what was developing as a teeter-totter series against Cal in which both teams would take turns dominating for several years, Warner had begun to put Stanford on top. The Cardinal claimed a 5–1–3 advantage over the Golden Bears during his tenure.

In the process, they handed Cal its only loss and killed their Rose Bowl chances in 1929, which proved quite disappointing to its team captain, Roy Riegels, a premier center and linebacker who would always be linked to one of the most embarrassing moments in college football history, for which he would have liked to have made amends. In a 1929 Rose Bowl defeat to Georgia Tech, he picked up a fumble and bolted for the Georgia Tech end zone before reversing course and sprinting toward his own goal line, thereby forever earning the nickname "Wrong Way Riegels." Teammate Ben Lom tracked him down and tackled him on the 1-yard line, but a subsequent blocked punt resulted in a two-point safety. And since the Golden Bears lost by just one point, the infamous jaunt cost them the game.

Warner quit to coach Temple in 1933, but he left replacement C. E. Thornhill with several presents. They were five recruits who would blossom into All-Americans—linemen Bill Corbus, Bones Hamilton, and Bob Reynolds; end Monk Moscrip; and brilliant fullback Bobby Grayson. The star-studded cast helped Thornhill pick up where Warner left off. He coached the Cardinal to a 25–4–2 record from 1933 to 1935, and only a Rose Bowl defeat to Alabama prevented an unbeaten season and national championship consideration in the second of those years. Their 13–0 victory in The Big Game in 1935 knocked the Pacific Coast Conference champion Golden Bears out of the undefeated ranks. It marked the 19th of 20 shutouts registered by their defense during the three-year run.

But the teeter-totter was about to switch again. New Cal coach Leonard Allison, who was about to emerge as their finest coach since Smith manned the sidelines, recruited the finest athletes that had ever graced a Golden Bears uniform. Future College Football Hall of Famers, such as halfbacks Sam Chapman and Vic Bottari and center Bob Herwig dotted the roster, as did such as All-Americans quarterback John Meek, end Perry Schwartz, and guard Vard Stockton. While the bloom had fallen off the rose for Thornhill, whose Stanford teams collapsed in the late 1930s, Cal blossomed into a national power. The Golden Bears not only pitched three straight shutouts of Stanford in winning four in a row from 1936 to 1939, they also recorded a 20–1–1 mark in 1937 and 1938, won league titles in both those seasons, and finished the first one ranked second in the nation. They capped 1937 with a 13–0 defeat of fourth-ranked Alabama in the Rose Bowl.

Figure 9.2.   A California–Stanford football game in Berkeley, California, Novem-ber 22, 1930. *Source: Library of Congress*

The Cardinal, however, would enjoy one more flight before World War II beckoned players from both programs and shut down Stanford football for three years. The seeds of that success were planted with the hiring of coach Clark Shaughnessy away from the University of Chicago after a 1939 season in which they finished 1–7–1, the worst full-season record in their history. Shaughnessy installed the T-formation, considered at the time as archaic but being revived with great success by Chicago Bears coach George Halas and quarterback Sid Luckman. Shaughnessy moved Frankie Albert from tailback to quarterback, and the Cardinal took off in 1940. They not only more than tripled their point total from the previous year, but they also yielded just 9.5 points a game in steamrolling through the season undefeated. Included was a 13–7 defeat of Cal to end the regular season and a 21–13 win over Nebraska in the Rose Bowl to secure the No. 2 ranking in the country behind Minnesota.

The move of Albert to quarterback proved brilliant. He was not only a consensus All-American in 1940 and 1941, but he also later embarked on a Pro Bowl career in the NFL. His ability to deceive defenses was his greatest asset. Shaughnessy called him "a magician with the ball" and later marveled at his abilities despite his lack of speed or strength. "His talents were primarily those of a faker," he added.[5]

Albert joined the Navy during the war, as did many of his Stanford teammates. So complete was the devastation to the roster that the school suspended its football program from 1943 to 1945. Cal was also hindered by defections overseas but continued to play. The mediocrity that had permeated its program continued through the war. The same Golden Bears that had won 20 of 21 games under Allison in the late 1930s managed a record of 29–47–2 from 1939 to 1946, two years after he had departed. The school scrambled to find a sideline success, hiring new coaches in 1945, 1946, and 1947 before landing Lynn "Pappy" Waldorf, who had enjoyed limited success at Northwestern. Waldorf transformed Cal into a perennial Pacific Coast Conference contender and one of the premier teams in the country.

Waldorf endeared himself to his players through his concern for them beyond the gridiron. His nickname was a reflection of the admiration his players felt for him as a paternal figure. "He was, to me, like God," offered quarterback Joe Kapp, who played under Waldorf in

1956. "He had the deepest voice and was a big man. Everything was big about him, his voice, his leadership, his command."[6]

Waldorf coached a sleuth of Golden Bears that had finished 2–7 a year earlier to a 9–1 mark in 1947. The star of that team was junior running back Jackie Jensen, who later starred as a slugger with the American League Boston Red Sox. A slaughter was expected when Cal, which had soared to No. 10 in the national rankings, prepared to play a Stanford team that was on the verge of its first winless season and had scored a mere 26 points in its previous six games combined. But one of the greatest upsets in college football history seemed likely when the Cardinal led 18–14 with three minutes remaining and the Golden Bears 80 yards from an end zone they needed to reach to win. There would be no methodical drive. Quarterback Paul Keckley heroically entered after missing the last two games with a shoulder injury and fired an 80-yard touchdown pass to Jensen for the victory.

The Golden Bears were merely warming up. They won the Pacific Coast Conference championship in each of the next three years, establishing themselves as mainstays in the top 10 throughout behind such future College Football Hall of Famers as Jensen and guards Rod Franz and ferocious Les Richter, who doubled as a middle linebacker and later embarked on an NFL Hall of Fame career with the Los Angeles Rams. Cal swept through each of those regular seasons unbeaten, but national championship consideration fell by the wayside in Rose Bowl defeats to Northwestern, Ohio State, and Michigan. Stanford provided the only other blemish from 1948 to 1950 with a 7–7 tie to end the regular season and send the Golden Bears reeling into their loss to the Wolverines.

That tie seemed to have a tonic effect on the Cardinal, who enjoyed a brief turnaround, peaking in 1951 by winning their first nine games behind the talents of consensus All-American end Bill McColl and catapulting to No. 3 in the national rankings. The Stanford surge made The Big Game more intriguing. After all, the Golden Bears had not lost it since 1946. But Cal, which had finally reached the top spot nationally at midseason for the first time ever before losing to USC, used 98 yards rushing and two touchdowns from premier running back John Pappa to topple Stanford from the ranks of the unbeaten. Pappa had risen to the occasion after boldly predicting a Cal victory in media interviews during the week leading up to the game. The reeling Cardinal were then clobbered, 40–7, by Illinois in the Rose Bowl.

Stanford soon slipped back into mediocrity, but it did plant the seeds for a well-earned reputation of attracting the finest high school quarterbacks with the recruiting of Bobby Garrett in the early 1950s. Such illustrious and future NFL signal callers as John Brodie, Jim Plunkett, John Elway, and Andrew Luck graced Cardinal uniforms on the way to professional greatness.

Garrett, whose stuttering problem resulted in difficulty calling plays and who did not achieve success in the NFL after being selected by the Cleveland Browns with the first overall pick in the 1954 draft, was a consensus All-American in 1953. But that was the season Stanford began its slide from which it would not fully recover for another 55 years. The Cardinal enjoyed occasional strong seasons in every decade through the 1990s but could not ride their often-brilliant quarterbacks to national championship contention until well into the 21st century.

The same held true with Cal, which collapsed in the mid-1950s, falling to 1–9 in 1957, their worst record in 60 years. The Golden Bears continued to fail in the early 1960s under three different coaches, including future NFL Hall of Fame coach Marv Levy, reeling to a 13–44–3 mark from 1959 to 1964. They won no more than seven games in any season from 1952 to 1974.

The Big Game, however, survived as a viable rivalry through generations of uninspiring performances. The teams traded victories every year from 1954 to 1958, the year in which Cal said good-bye to brilliant senior quarterback Joe Kapp and began its last three-game winning streak until the turn of the century. Most notable about that run was the 1959 performance of Golden Bears quarterback Dick Norman, who threw for what was then an NCAA record 401 yards in a 20–17 victory.

Despite its relative mediocrity, the Cardinal boasted enough firepower in the 1960s and beyond under coaches Jack Curtice and John Ralston to dominate the Golden Bears. They beat Cal six straight for the first time in the history of the series from 1961 to 1966, then won eight of 11 from 1968 to 1978. They rose briefly to national prominence from 1968 to 1970 behind Plunkett, who became their first Heisman Trophy winner his senior year. Plunkett led his team to a 29–28 defeat of their archrivals in 1969 with a scintillating performance in which he threw for 381 yards and two touchdowns to cap a 7–2–1 season.

The Cardinal took their momentum and ran with it into 1970, during which Plunkett threw for 2,980 yards and 19 scores. They entered The Big Game with an 8–2 mark and a Rose Bowl bid secured and were expected to beat a Cal team with its usual .500 record with ease. But Plunkett was outplayed by Golden Bears counterpart David Penhall, who guided his team to a 22–14 victory. Stanford recovered to stun favored Ohio State on New Year's Day, but one was left to wonder what had happened late in the season to a team that had at one point soared to No. 3 in the national rankings.

Those who believed the Cardinal underachieved that season with fine skill position talent, which included diminutive wide receiver Randy Vataha, who followed Plunkett to the New England Patriots, would have felt the same about the Cal teams of the mid-1970s. The Golden Bears boasted a beast of a back in Chuck Muncie, All-American quarterbacks Steve Bartkowski and Joe Roth, and explosive wide receiver Wesley Walker. Muncie, Bartkowski, and Walker went on to forge fine NFL careers and only tragedy that befell Roth prevented him from following the same path. Yet Cal lost at least three games in every season in which any of them played under coach Mike White and beat Stanford only twice during that run.

Its finest run came in 1975 after two losses to open the season. With Muncie and Walker blossoming for their most productive seasons and Roth taking over for Bartkowski without missing a beat, the Golden Bears won eight straight, including successive victories over nationally ranked USC, Washington, and Air Force, the second of which occurred before a sellout home crowd and national TV audience as Muncie rushed for 143 yards. The Trojans were ranked fourth in the country coming in before losing to the Golden Bears for only the second time since 1958. Armed with momentum, Cal took out years of frustration on Stanford in a 48–15 thrashing in which Muncie rushed for four touchdowns and tossed another to Walker.

It seemed inevitable that Roth would follow Bartkowski as a No. 1 pick in the NFL draft. He had thrown for 1,880 yards and 14 touchdowns in 1975. He endeared himself to his teammates and coaches with his studiousness, modesty, and introspective nature. But his performance suffered the following year. His touchdown-to-interception ratio flip-flopped. What he didn't tell anyone was that the melanoma cancer that he had battled as a junior college student had reappeared. Roth died after that season. His number was retired during halftime of a 1977 game against USC in which his inspired teammates stunned 10th-ranked USC.

Among the most ironic and surprising developments in the history of the rivalry was that Cal halted its long period of losing during the era after a strapping gunslinger named Elway had arrived on the Stanford campus. The Golden Bears defeated the Cardinal in three of four meetings from 1979 to 1982 despite an overall record of 19–26 during that period. Even the 1980 Cal team that entered the showdown with a 2–8 mark and a four-game losing streak in which it scored 39 total points managed to upend Elway and his Cardinal. The hero that day was a Golden Bears walk-on quarterback with the curious name of J Torchio, who scored the winning touchdown on a bootleg around left end. Meanwhile, his defensive teammates had harried the sophomore Elway into completing fewer than half his pass attempts in a 28–23 upset.

And though Elway blossomed into arguably the greatest quarterback in college football history, throwing for 8,805 yards and 71 touchdowns in his three seasons as the full-time starter before being selected No. 1 in the 1983 draft, his teams enjoyed limited success. Stanford managed a mark of just 21–22–1 during his four years at the school.

The 1982 Cal triumph forever known as The Play heightened the frustration for the Cardinal and threatened to reverse the course of the rivalry. But Stanford rebounded to recapture the dominance it had pretty much maintained over its northern Golden State rival since 1961. It captured the coveted Axe seven times from 1984 to 1992, losing just once during that period, then embarked on a seven-game winning streak in The Big Game from 1995 to 2001. By the time the final tick went off the game clock in the last of those years, the Cardinal owned a 31–18–2 record against the Golden Bears in the last 51 meetings.

That second tie proved to be among the most memorable, if not important, showdowns between the two teams. Neither team boasted a winning record heading into the game, which appeared destined to be won by the Golden Bears when they drove to the Stanford 3-yard line with four seconds remaining and the score tied at 19–19. After all, future All-American placekicker Robbie Keen was not about to miss a chip shot. But Cardinal redshirt freshman Tuan Van Le sprinted in and blocked the kick to keep the score deadlocked and, since his team had won The Big Game the year before, keep the Axe in Stanford hands.

Cal frustration reached a fever pitch in 1990. The Golden Bears had already won seven games, a total they had not surpassed since 1977, while the Cardinal entered with a 4–6 record. Stanford coach Denny Green boldly called for a two-point conversion try after quarterback Jason Palumbis cut the deficit to 25–24 on a touchdown pass to future Denver Broncos standout receiver Ed McCaffrey with seconds remaining. Cal supporters stormed the field when the attempt failed, but the clock had not run out. Their team was penalized 15 yards for delay of game, after which Stanford recovered an onside kick. Golden Bears fans again believed they had won when Palumbis misfired on a pass to McCaffrey, but a roughing-the-quarterback call gave the Cardinal another chance and moved them into field goal range. Placekicker John Hopkins booted a 39-yarder as time expired to give Stanford an unlikely 27–25 victory that avenged its even more bizarre defeat eight years earlier.

The teams then embarked on trading success stories—Cal in 1991 and Stanford in 1992 under coach Bill Walsh, who had guided the team in the late 1970s before transforming the NFL San Francisco 49ers into NFL juggernauts. The success of the Golden Bears in their glory year seemed to come out of nowhere and left just as quickly and unexpectedly. They had only won one of their last four regular-season games in 1990 but opened the 1991 season with five consecutive wins and rested at 9–1 heading into The Big Game. Led by All-American and future standout NFL wideout Sean Dawkins, the Golden Bears were ranked sixth in the nation when they traveled to Stanford.

So confident was Cal wide receiver Brian Treggs of a victory that he boldly and publicly exclaimed that he would move to Palo Alto if his team was defeated. Thus inspired, the Cardinal used their punishing ground game to bury the Golden Bears. Bullish running back "Touchdown" Tommy Vardell spent much of the day pounding out yards behind 300-pound All-American Bob Whitfield. Vardell finished with 182 yards and three scores on a workmanlike 39 carries against a Cal defense that stuffed the box and dared him to run.

The result was a 38–21 victory for Stanford. And when it was over, Cardinal cornerback Darrien Gordon stopped Treggs trudging off the field and let him know that he could share his place in Palo Alto if he was indeed going to make good on his promise. "He kind of laughed about it, but I don't think he'll be coming," Gordon said. Treggs was good-naturedly embarrassed by his boast-gone-wrong. "Unfortunately, it didn't work out the way I planned," he said. "I think I'm going to go out right now and start looking for an apartment."[7]

The Golden Bears had little chance for revenge the next year. Walsh had taken a strong Green team that ended the 1991 regular season on a seven-game winning streak and made it even stronger while Cal was in the process of losing six of its last seven games. They had already beaten nationally ranked Notre Dame, UCLA, USC, and Washington State, so their 41–21 triumph in The Big Game came as no surprise as they finished the season at No. 13 in the nation.

Walsh could not maintain the same level of success in his last two years at Stanford, winning just seven games in 1993 and 1994 combined and losing twice to Cal. But the rivalry quickly reverted to form as the Golden Bears suffered through a miserable era in the mid- to late 1990s despite the talents of such All-Americans and future NFL stars as tight end Tony Gonzalez, linebacker Scott Fujita, cornerbacks Deltha O'Neal and Nnamdi Asomugha, and defensive end Andre Carter. Cal managed a combined mark of 25–64 from 1994 to 2001, bottoming out in 2001 at 1–10. And for the first time in the history of The Big Game, the Golden Bears lost seven in a row to their archrival despite the fact that Cal was generally mediocre throughout that era.

It seemed nearly impossible that Stanford could dominate the series for so long. Fate and new Cal coach Jeff Tedford finally stepped in as the new century picked up a head of steam. The former Canadian Football League quarterback was given his first head-coaching position by the school in 2002 after he had served as the offensive coordinator at fellow PAC-10 school Oregon. Tedford immediately transformed the Golden Bears into winners behind such brilliant players as Asomugha, future NFL standout quarterbacks Kyle Boller and Aaron Rodgers, and tailback J. J. Arrington.

The improvement was dramatic. Their 1–10 season in 2001 was followed by a 7–5 mark in the first year under Tedford, including a three-game winning streak and defeat of nationally ranked Michigan State to open the season. Cal wasted no time wresting away control of The Big Game, blasting Stanford 30–7 to conclude its best year since 1993. That wasn't much of a test, however. The Cardinal finished that season with five consecutive losses and with a 2–9 mark, their worst in 19 years.

But that final-game triumph would be no one-hit wonder. Tedford and his Golden Bears were about to take their turn as the dominant program in the rivalry. The 2002 victory kicked off a run of five straight and seven of eight over Stanford—and all of them until 2009 were blowouts. The Cardinal lost by at least nine points in every game from 2002 to 2006 and in 2008. The outcomes were a reflection of the direction both teams had taken. Cal forged winning records under Tedford every season from 2002 to 2009, peaking with a 10–2 record, seven-game winning streak, and Holiday Bowl berth in 2004 and PAC-10 cochampionship two years later. Stanford suffered through losing seasons every year from 2002 to 2008 before recovering under new coach Jim Harbaugh.

Just as Tedford made an impact on the Golden Bears earlier in the decade, the former gritty NFL standout quarterback did the same for the Cardinal. The 2007 Harbaugh hiring, however, took longer to reap rewards. But his recruiting began paying benefits in 2009. Quarterback Andrew Luck and running back Toby Gerhart emerged as All-American talent, cornerback Richard Sherman displayed skills that translated into NFL greatness, and Stanford catapulted to No. 14 in the country with a stunningly lopsided 55–21 defeat of USC leading up to the clash against the Golden Bears.

That battle featured a showdown between Gerhart and Cal featured back Shane Vereen. Gerhart rushed for 136 yards and four touchdowns, outperforming his counterpart. Vereen required more than twice as many carries to total 193 yards and three scores. But the Golden Bears defense stifled Luck from beginning to end and keyed a 34–28 victory. They clinched their seventh Big Game defeat in eight years when linebacker Michael Mohamed intercepted a Luck pass at the Cal 3-yard line with less than two minutes remaining.

The pendulum, however, was about to swing in the opposite direction. A golden era of Stanford football was about to begin under Harbaugh and continue after he bolted to coach the San Francisco 49ers and handed the reins to offensive coordinator David Shaw in 2010. Harbaugh and Shaw recruited such All-American talent as Luck, tight ends Coby Fleener and Zach Ertz, and offensive linemen Jonathan Martin and David DeCastro in developing offensive juggernauts and dominant teams in the second decade of the 2000s. But their hopes for a national championship were dashed by an untimely defeat every year.

The Cardinal averaged 40.3 points per game in 2010, when only a loss to fourth-ranked Oregon prevented them from competing for a national championship, and Luck earned his first of two second-place finishes in the Heisman Trophy voting. They soared to No. 4 in the country in 2011 behind an offense that scored 43.2 points a game, but another defeat to the Ducks doomed them in their quest for a crown. They vaulted from No. 21 to No. 8 in the nation with a 2012 upset of second-ranked USC and upset the No. 1 Ducks, but a loss to unranked Washington again killed their dreams of a national title. And their ascension to No. 5 in the country was rendered meaningless by a stunning defeat to unranked Utah.

But though their loftiest ambitions had been squelched in each of those four seasons, they had again become annual owners of the Axe as the Golden Bears had fallen on hard times, going 15–22 in their last three seasons under Tedford and plummeting to 1–11 under first-year coach Sonny Dykes in 2013. It was in that year the 10th-ranked Cardinal shattered a Big Game record for points scored and margin of victory with a 63–13 dismantling of their archrival in which wide receiver Ty Montgomery scored five touchdowns.

And when it was over, the Cardinal learned that an Oregon loss ensured their participation in a PAC-12 North Division championship and the right to play for a Rose Bowl berth, which they later earned. But Shaw expressed the priority of his players and every participant in The Big Game throughout its history. "Once they made the announcement [about the Oregon defeat] in the stadium, that's why I love coaching at Stanford, that's why I love our guys. Our guys said, 'We don't care about the game, we have to keep the axe.'"[8]

The Axe thieves of generations past would have been mighty proud to have heard those words. But they would not have been surprised.

Fact Box (through 2013)
   Nickname: The Big Game
   Trophy: The Stanford Axe
   Total meetings: 116
   Series record: Stanford leads, 59–46–11
   First meeting: 1892 (Stanford 14, California 10)
   Largest margin of victory: Stanford, 2013 (Stanford 63, California 13)

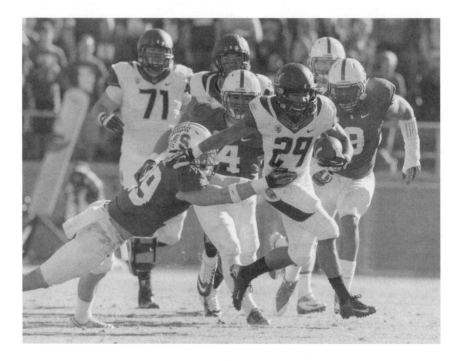

Figure 9.3.   California vs. Stanford. *Source: Michael Pimentel/GoldenBear-Sports.com*

Longest winning streak: Stanford, 7 (1995–2001)

Game Results (home team listed second unless at a neutral site)
    1892: Stanford 14, California 10
    1892: California 10, Stanford 10
   ·1893: Stanford 6, California 6
    1894: California 0, Stanford 6
    1895: Stanford 6, California 6
    1896: California 0, Stanford 20
    1897: Stanford 28, California 0
    1898: Stanford 0, California 22
    1899: California 30, Stanford 0
    1900: California 0, Stanford 5
    1901: Stanford 0, California 2
    1902: California 16, Stanford 0
    1903: Stanford 6, California 6

1904: California 0, Stanford 18
1905: Stanford 12, California 5
1906: California 3, Stanford 6 (Rugby)
1907: Stanford 21, California 11 (Rugby)
1908: California 3, Stanford 12 (Rugby)
1909: Stanford 13, California 19 (Rugby)
1910: California 25, Stanford 6 (Rugby)
1911: Stanford 3, California 21 (Rugby)
1912: California 3, Stanford 3 (Rugby)
1913: Stanford 13, California 8 (Rugby)
1914: California 8, Stanford 36 (Rugby)
1919: California 14, Stanford 10
1920: Stanford 0, California 38
1921: California 42, Stanford 7
1922: California 28, Stanford 0
1923: Stanford 0, California 9
1924: Stanford 20, California 20
1925: California 14, Stanford 27
1926: Stanford 41, California 6
1927: California 6, Stanford 13
1928: Stanford 13, California 13
1929: California 6, Stanford 21
1930: Stanford 41, California 0
1931: California 6, Stanford 0
1932: Stanford 0, California 0
1933: California 3, Stanford 7
1934: Stanford 9, California 7
1935: California 0, Stanford 13
1936: Stanford 0, California 20
1937: California 13, Stanford 0
1938: Stanford 0, California 6
1939: California 32, Stanford 14
1940: Stanford 13, California 7
1941: Stanford 0, California 16
1942: California 7, Stanford 26
1946: Stanford 25, California 6
1947: California 21, Stanford 18
1948: Stanford 6, California 7

1949: California 33, Stanford 13
1950: Stanford 7, California 7
1951: California 20, Stanford 7
1952: Stanford 0, California 26
1953: California 21, Stanford 21
1954: Stanford 20, California 28
1955: California 0, Stanford 19
1956: Stanford 18, California 20
1957: California 12, Stanford 14
1958: Stanford 15, California 16
1959: California 20, Stanford 17
1960: Stanford 10, California 21
1961: California 7, Stanford 20
1962: Stanford 30, California 13
1963: California 17, Stanford 28
1964: Stanford 21, California 3
1965: California 7, Stanford 9
1966: Stanford 13, California 7
1967: California 26, Stanford 3
1968: Stanford 20, California 0
1969: California 28, Stanford 29
1970: Stanford 14, California 22
1971: California 0, Stanford 14
1972: Stanford 22, California 24
1973: California 17, Stanford 26
1974: Stanford 22, California 20
1975: California 48, Stanford 15
1976: Stanford 27, California 24
1977: California 3, Stanford 21
1978: Stanford 30, California 10
1979: California 21, Stanford 14
1980: Stanford 23, California 28
1981: California 21, Stanford 42
1982: Stanford 20, California 25
1983: California 27, Stanford 18
1984: Stanford 27, California 10
1985: California 22, Stanford 24
1986: Stanford 11, California 17

1987: California 7, Stanford 31
1988: Stanford 19, California 19
1989: California 14, Stanford 24
1990: Stanford 27, California 25
1991: California 21, Stanford 38
1992: Stanford 41, California 21
1993: California 46, Stanford 17
1994: Stanford 23, California 24
1995: California 24, Stanford 29
1996: Stanford 42, California 21
1997: California 20, Stanford 21
1998: Stanford 10, California 3
1999: California 13, Stanford 31
2000: Stanford 36, California 30
2001: California 28, Stanford 35
2002: Stanford 7, California 30
2003: California 28, Stanford 16
2004: Stanford 6, California 41
2005: California 27, Stanford 3
2006: Stanford 17, California 26
2007: California 13, Stanford 20
2008: Stanford 16, California 37
2009: California 34, Stanford 28
2010: Stanford 48, California 14
2011: California 28, Stanford 31
2012: Stanford 21, California 3
2013: California 13, Stanford 63

Stanford Bowl Game Appearances

1902 Rose Bowl: Michigan 49, Stanford 0
1925 Rose Bowl: Notre Dame 27, Stanford 10
1927 Rose Bowl: Stanford 7, Alabama 7
1928 Rose Bowl: Stanford 7, Pittsburgh 6
1934 Rose Bowl: Columbia 7, Stanford 0
1935 Rose Bowl: Alabama 29, Stanford 13
1936 Rose Bowl: Stanford 7, Southern Methodist 0
1941 Rose Bowl: Stanford 21, Nebraska 13
1952 Rose Bowl: Illinois 40, Stanford 7

1971 Rose Bowl: Stanford 27, Ohio State 17
1972 Rose Bowl: Stanford 13, Michigan 12
1977 Sun Bowl: Stanford 24, Louisiana State 14
1978 Bluebonnet Bowl: Stanford 25, Georgia 22
1986 Gator Bowl: Clemson 27, Stanford 21
1991 Aloha Bowl: Georgia Tech 18, Stanford 17
1993 Blockbuster Bowl: Stanford 24, Penn State 3
1995 Liberty Bowl: East Carolina 19, Stanford 13
1996 Sun Bowl: Stanford 38, Michigan State 0
2000 Rose Bowl: Wisconsin 17, Stanford 9
2001 Seattle Bowl: Georgia Tech 24, Stanford 14
2009 Sun Bowl: Oklahoma 31, Stanford 27
2011 Orange Bowl: Stanford 40, Virginia Tech 12
2012 Fiesta Bowl: Oklahoma State 41, Stanford 38
2013 Rose Bowl: Stanford 20, Wisconsin 14
2014 Rose Bowl: Michigan State 24, Stanford 20

California Bowl Game Appearances

1921 Rose Bowl: California 28, Ohio State 0
1922 Rose Bowl: Washington & Jefferson 0, California 0
1929 Rose Bowl: Georgia Tech 8, California 7
1938 Rose Bowl: California 13, Alabama 0
1949 Rose Bowl: Northwestern 20, California 14
1950 Rose Bowl: Ohio State 17, California 14
1951 Rose Bowl: Michigan 14, California 6
1959 Rose Bowl: Iowa 38, California 12
1979 Garden State Bowl: Temple 28, California 17
1990 Copper Bowl: California 17, Wyoming 15
1992 Citrus Bowl: California 37, Clemson 13
1993 Alamo Bowl: California 37, Iowa 3
1996 Aloha Bowl: Navy 42, California 38
2003 Insight Bowl: Virginia Tech 52, California 49
2004 Holiday Bowl: Texas Tech 45, California 31
2005 Las Vegas Bowl: California 35, Brigham Young 28
2006 Holiday Bowl: California 45, Texas A&M 10
2007 Armed Forces Bowl: California 42, Air Force 36
2008 Emerald Bowl: California 24, Miami 17
2009 Poinsettia Bowl: Utah 37, California 27

2011 Holiday Bowl: Texas 21, California 10

10

FLORIDA STATE VS. MIAMI: THE GAME WITHOUT A NAME

The bowl season started early in 1991. Granted, the November 16 tussle in Tallahassee between Miami and Florida State was technically an independent game between two teams from separate leagues. The Hurricanes had just joined the Big East, while the Seminoles were

Figure 10.1.   Miami vs. Florida State, 1993. *Source: JC Ridley/Caneshooter.com*

newcomers to the Atlantic Coast Conference. But make no mistake about it. This was a bowl battle in disguise.

Indeed, it was more than that. It was the national championship game before the official national championship game. Florida State was undefeated and ranked first in the nation. Miami was undefeated and ranked second in the nation. Such titanic struggles were common during that era between those Gator State greats. But none had arrived with greater anticipation. Some were calling it with justification the Game of the Century.

Both teams had used a different formula to dominate. The Hurricanes did it with the finest defense in the country, one that had yielded just 7.2 points a game heading into the showdown behind such stalwarts as linebackers Darrin Smith and Jessie Armstead and defensive back Darryl Williams. The Seminoles had ridden an explosive, deep offense led by quarterback Casey Weldon to 10 consecutive victories, including a stunningly thorough 51–31 mauling of third-ranked Michigan. Their defensive strength was a ball-hawking secondary led by cornerback Terrell Buckley, who would lead the nation with 12 interceptions that season.

The stage was set for a fight to the finish. But when Florida State placekicker Gerry Thomas slammed his third field goal of the game through the uprights in the fourth quarter, such dramatics appeared unlikely. The Seminoles led 16–7. Their offense had doubled the average points per game Miami had previously allowed that season. And their defense had been harassing and hurrying Hurricanes quarterback Gino Torretta from the outset. Even a 45-yard field goal by Miami placekicker Carlos Huerta didn't change expectations. After all, his team had proven unable to score a touchdown since its first possession of the game.

Seven minutes remained. Seven minutes before the hopes of a national championship would be dashed for the Hurricanes. "Dig deep in your hearts," Torretta pleaded to his offensive teammates in the huddle.[1] They responded by yielding their sixth sack. But that merely served to strengthen his resolve. He began to drive his team downfield. He hit tight end Coleman Bell for 22 yards. Successive runs by Stephen McGuire netted 25. Another pass to Copeland put the Hurricanes on the shadow of the goal line, and fullback Larry Jones took it in from there. Miami 17, Florida State 16.

Despondent Seminole fans stopped their "Scalp 'em!" tomahawk chops and cheers, but they knew there was still hope. There was plenty of time to drive into scoring position, and indeed their offense did just that. They marched to the Miami 17 for what appeared to be a chip-shot, game-winning 34-yard attempt. Heck, Thomas had already nailed three that day. But, alas, his try faded to the right of the upright. It was over. Thomas returned to the sideline, squatted, and stared into space. Weldon paced near the bench and repeated the only two words that came to mind: "Oh God . . . Oh God . . . Oh God." And as his team lamented the defeat in a despondent locker room, Florida State coach Bobby Bowden spoke about how one play—you pick it—proved the difference between victory and defeat.[2]

Such was a familiar scene after games pitting the Hurricanes against the Seminoles during that era. This was not merely a rivalry embraced geographically. It had grown into a battle with national implications. The eyes of the college football world were focused on Miami or Talla-hassee when those two teams clashed. Not only have their games prov-en crucially important to the landscape of the sport, but their athletes also were annually and justifiably touted as some of the finest in the game.

It wasn't always that way. Both schools got a late jump into football. The University of Miami wasn't even founded until 1926. Florida State didn't admit men until 1947, the year it launched its program. The former wasted no time joining the fray in college football and a fresh-man team did so with great aplomb, winning all eight of its games that season and yielding a mere 13 points along the way. Sadly, but appro-priately, a hurricane delayed the beginning of that season. It ripped through the area in mid-September, killing more than 130 people and postponing plans to build a 50,000-seat stadium on campus. The varsity team did not take the field until 1927 and managed a 3–4–1 record under coach Howard Buck. The early Hurricanes played close to .500 football in their first decade but were not exactly competing against the juggernauts Florida, Georgia, and North Carolina, which began to dot their schedule in the late 1930s. Among their first stars was running back Eddie Dunn, who scored all three touchdowns in a 1938 defeat of the Gators and finished his playing career with a slew of school rushing and scoring records before serving as its coach for two years during World War II.

The Hurricanes celebrated the end of hostilities overseas with its finest season to date in 1945 under coach Jack Harding, who had worked in that capacity for six seasons before joining the navy for two years. He returned to a mess—Miami had plummeted to 1–7–1 under Dunn in 1944. But the return of talented players from the service bolstered the roster the following year. The Hurricanes recovered from an early loss to Georgia to go unbeaten in their last eight games, including triumphs over such established college football powers as Florida, Michigan State, and Auburn. They then earned the biggest win in school history, securing an Orange Bowl defeat of Holy Cross on an 89-yard interception return by Al Hudson on the last play of the game.

The Harding era ended with a thud, however, when they lost their last five games in 1947 to finish 2–7–1, prompting his ouster in favor of Andy Gustafson, who had previously served as backfield coach at Army and would emerge as the most successful coach at Miami until the 1980s. More eventful in 1947 was the launching of the Florida State program. New coach Ed Williamson faced a daunting task. He accepted the job just a few weeks before his charges played their first game. He was neither paid nor given any scholarship players with which to work. That his Seminoles managed to remain within eight points of three of their five goes that season is a credit to his performance.

The school took a similar scheduling tack as its future archrival. Florida State took advantage of lesser lights in regional college football to win 24 of 26 games under coach Don Veller from 1948 to 1950. The inclusion thereafter of larger and stronger competition in the early 1950s resulted in mediocrity. Among those more established and talented opponents was Miami, which shared the field with the Seminoles for the first time on October 5, 1951, at the Orange Bowl. Florida State boasted a 13-game winning streak heading into the clash, but Veller was under no illusions. His school was a member of the short-lived Dixie Conference, which disallowed subsidization of athletics by its members. Miami football was far better funded. "I have no thoughts of being able to defeat them," Veller said before the game. "Under present policies, we're not strong enough to compete with them."[3] His crystal ball was sharp. Final score: Miami 35, Florida State 13.

The score was not merely a reflection of the differences in policy. The Hurricanes emerged as a national power for the first time under Gustafson. They forged a mark of 9–1–1 in 1950, which they concluded as the 15th-ranked team in the nation, and followed with an 8–3 record a year later. Defensive tackle Al Carapella; halfback Jim Dooley, who became the first first-round draft pick in school history; guard Nick Chickillo; and end Frank McDonald all earned All-American status for Miami in the early 1950s.

Florida State left the Dixie Conference after the 1951 season to forge an independent schedule, which it maintained in football until hooking up with the Atlantic Coast Conference in 1992. But the Seminoles fared no better as gridiron nomads. They enjoyed a one-year resurgence under coach Tom Nugent in 1954, winning eight of their last nine regular-season games before falling in the Sun Bowl. But they won between four and seven games every year thereafter through 1963 and lost eight of nine games to their archnemesis from 1951 to 1962, including such embarrassments as 27–0 in 1953, 34–0 in 1955, and 40–13 in 1957.

It took the retirement of Gustafson and several years under new coach Bill Peterson for the Seminoles to reverse the course of the rivalry. The colorful Peterson was the Dizzy Dean of college football, making a mockery of the English language. His butchery of proper grammar became known as "Petersonisms." He once said that a tentative receiver "hears footprints" and that an appreciative crowd "gave me a standing observation." He once told his players to "pair off in groups of threes" and warned that one shouldn't "kill the goose that lays the deviled egg."[4] But he certainly could coach.

Peterson, who had no experience at the college level before his arrival, hired offensive guru and future Seminoles coach Bobby Bowden as an assistant and recruited first Florida State superstar Fred Biletnikoff to the school. Biletnikoff had shown only glimpses of brilliance as a junior in 1963, when his 99-yard interception return for a touchdown helped his team beat Miami for only the second time in 10 meetings. But he blossomed the following year to catch 57 passes and lead the nation with 1,189 yards receiving. Florida State soared to No. 10 in the country on the strength of five straight victories to start the season, including a shutout of Miami; dropped out of the national poll after a loss to unranked Virginia Tech; then went unbeaten the rest of the way. They not only beat Florida for the first time, but they put the cherry on top with a 36–19 defeat of Oklahoma in the Gator Bowl, in which Biletnikoff scored four touchdowns to give him 15 for the season. He became the first consensus All-American in school history and was soon forging a Hall of Fame career in the NFL.

The ascension of the Seminoles coincided with the demise of the Hurricanes, which lasted until the early 1980s despite the influx of brilliant talent, such as quarterback George Mira, who earned Heisman Trophy consideration after leading the nation in total offense with 2,318 yards as a senior; three-time All-American defensive end Ted (the Stork) Hendricks; and future Minnesota Vikings star running back Chuck Foreman. One coach after another tried in vain to halt the slide that began in earnest in 1968, the year after Charlie Tate had guided the team to its second straight bowl berth behind the disruptive Hendricks. Five more coaches, including two-time American Football League champion Lou Saban, attempted to turn around the program to no avail.

Peterson not only launched the Seminoles into the national consciousness, but he also flip-flopped the rivalry in his team's favor. Florida State won the last five games against Miami during his tenure, which lasted from 1960 to 1970. His departure proved disastrous. Those he recruited performed well for two years under replacement Larry Jones, winning their first five games in 1971 and earning a Fiesta Bowl berth, then streaking to a 6–1 start the following season. But they were outscored 331–98 in 1973 and lost to Miami for the first time in 11 years. Florida State would play the role of personal punching bag for the Hurricanes over the next generation. Miami won 13 of the next 20 meetings and lost two in a row to the Seminoles just once through 1994. The Hurricanes won four of five from 1973 to 1977 despite their own monumental struggles. After all, Miami's 6–5 marks in 1974 and 1978 was the best it could muster from 1968 to 1979.

Among the greatest upsets in the history of the rivalry occurred on September 24, 1977. It was that season in which Bowden had transformed Florida State into a national power, a status it would maintain through 2013. Miami was on its way to accruing what had become a typical 3–8 record, but it emerged from the showdown with a 23–17 victory. The defeat seemed to kick-start the Seminoles, who embarked on a six-game winning streak and never looked back. Their sustained greatness as a program began that year and they had Bowden to thank for it. He was respected and admired for his unpretentiousness not only by his players but also by his peers. Wake Forest coach Jim Grobe had the following to say:

> Bobby was a humble leader. . . . When you would see him at a meeting you would think, "there's the great Bobby Bowden." But Bobby never acted like a big shot. You'd never know Bobby Bowden was Bobby Bowden. If you ever beat his team, which was rare, he was always gracious to you and never blamed his team or coaches. If you lost to him, he would always tell the press what a good team you had and offer high praise.
>
> At one point we beat Florida State a couple of times. After one of those games, I met Bobby at midfield and he said, "Jim, you ought to be ashamed of yourself." I thought, "Oh, no! What have I done to offend this legend?" Then he laughed and said, "Beating an old man like me."
>
> He was a man of principle and character and had his priorities straight for himself, staff and players. He always wanted to set a good example and lived his faith in front of the world and never backed off from his beliefs. There aren't many out there like him.[5]

Bowden guided the 1977 Seminoles to their first bowl victory in 13 years. His team took a small step back the following year before blossoming into a national championship contender in 1979 behind such talent as All-American defensive lineman Ron Simmons, who later forged a career as a professional wrestler. Florida State steamrolled through the regular season unbeaten and was ranked fourth in the nation, but a lopsided defeat to No. 5 Oklahoma in the Orange Bowl ended all national title consideration.

All was not well at Miami, however. Annual mediocrity had turned off the fans, who were staying away in droves. Saban proved to be a keen recruiter, attracting such talent as future NFL Hall of Fame quarterback Jim Kelly, who started all four years for the Hurricanes and finished his college career with 5,228 yards passing. But Saban's two-year run in 1977 and 1978 was marred by tragedy and controversy. His wife committed suicide and he underwent heart bypass surgery before he coached a single game for Miami. He returned in time for the season opener, but his team finished the 1977 season with a lowly 3–8 mark. The Hurricanes rebounded to finish 6–5 a year later. All seemed well until two of his players tossed a Jewish student into a lake. Saban claimed it to be a harmless prank, but it was later proven to be anti-

Semitic bullying and the media jumped all over it. Though Saban was never charged with harboring hatred toward any racial or religious group, the school administration were angered that he didn't take a strong enough stand. He left the school after two seasons. It remains unknown whether that incident or his disenchantment with the lack of money provided the football program motivated his departure.

Whatever the case, replacement Howard Schnellenberger took the momentum gained on the field in 1978 and ran with it. Schnellenberger, who had coached in the NFL since 1966 and was coming off a four-year stint as Miami Dolphins offensive coordinator, transformed the Hurricanes into a national power and the Miami–Florida State rivalry into one of the greatest and most significant in the history of college football. The brilliance of both teams in the 1980s and beyond resulted in memorable matchups with national implications.

With just one exception, the Hurricanes and Seminoles were ranked among the top 20 teams in the country for every rivalry game from 1981 to 1994. Schnellenberger and Jimmy Johnson, who took over in 1984, and Bowden convinced the finest high school players in the nation to take their talents to sunny Florida (the Gators didn't enjoy similar success until the 1990s). The schools had emerged as football factories and their annual battles became legendary.

Clash-of-the-Titans games had been a rarity until that era, which was officially launched at the Orange Bowl in 1980. Both teams arrived at 3–0 as more than 50,000 fans provided the largest crowd at the stadium since 1971. And though Schnellenberger admitted that 40,000 of them were rooting for the Seminoles, the blossoming of the Hurricanes had brought some excitement to his campus as well. Miami gained the first break in a titanic defensive struggle when a pass interference call near the end of the first half set up the first touchdown of the game. The Hurricanes maintained a 10–3 lead until Florida State crossed the goal line late in the fourth quarter to chop the deficit to 10–9. The always-aggressive Bowden eschewed the extra-point attempt for a two-point conversion and the win, but Miami nose tackle and future NFL standout Jim Burt blasted through the line to block a pass from Seminoles quarterback Rick Stockstill and clinch the victory.

The teams played classic after classic. The Schnellenberger era peaked with a national championship in 1983 behind the immense talents of future Cleveland Browns star quarterback Bernie Kosar and eventual All-American wide receiver Eddie Brown, who went on to star with the Cincinnati Bengals. That crown would not have been earned without a scintillating comeback victory over the Seminoles in the final week of the regular season. The Hurricanes had rebounded from an opening-game loss to Florida to win nine in a row heading into the showdown. They had held their opponents to just 62 points combined during that stretch. But they found themselves down to Florida State, 16–7, in the third quarter. Kosar sliced the deficit to 16–14 on a touchdown pass to Brown.

When the Hurricanes drove into field goal range late in the fourth quarter, it gave placekicker and Confederacy president namesake Jefferson Davis a chance for vindication. Davis had blown a chip shot against Maryland in 1982, costing his team an Aloha Bowl berth. "After that game, he was downtrodden," Schnellenberger recalled. "I put my arm around him and said, 'You'll get another chance to hit a big one.'" And when that opportunity arrived that night against the Seminoles, Davis gave assurance to Schnellenberger, who had continued to show faith in him. "This one's for you, coach," he said.[6] Sure enough, he booted the ball through the uprights to secure a 17–16 win and Orange Bowl matchup against No. 1 Nebraska.

The Cornhuskers were a powerhouse. They had remained the top-ranked team in the country throughout the season. They led the nation in scoring at an absurd 50.3 points a game. They had won games by such ridiculous scores as 84–13, 63–7, 69–19, 72–29, and 67–13. But they could not beat the Hurricanes, who bolted to a 17–0 lead and held on for a 31–30 victory and their first national championship. The upset was clinched when Miami safety Ken Calhoun tipped a two-point conversion attempt that would have given Nebraska the lead. It was a moment he would never forget. After all, he had not only given his school the title. He had also given the state of Florida its first national crown. "We were the Cinderella team, and it fired us up," Calhoun said. "Being a Cinderella to such a powerhouse was something everyone on the team got up for."[7]

That triumph was a hard act to follow, especially since Schnellenberger bolted to coach a Miami team in the United States Football League that never materialized because the owner decided it could not compete with the Dolphins. The result was that the University of Miami lured an unproven Oklahoma State coach named Jimmy Johnson to take over. After one season of adjustment, he turned the program into one of the most dominant in college football history. Johnson molded or recruited such All-American talent as defensive tackles Jerome Brown and Russell Maryland, quarterbacks Vinny Testaverde and Steve Walsh, wide receiver Michael Irvin, and defensive back Bennie Blades. It was no wonder that his teams forged a record of 44–4 from 1985 to 1988, peaking at No. 2 in the rankings in the first of those seasons, reaching the top spot in each of the last three, and clinching a second national championship in 1987 with an Orange Bowl defeat of top-ranked Oklahoma that concluded an unbeaten season.

Most satisfying for fans of the rivalry that year was that Bowden had also nurtured his Seminoles into the ranks of national power. They had lost at least three games every year from 1982 to 1986 but blossomed in 1987 behind an offense that ranked second in the country at 40.2 points a game and a defense anchored by brash, flamboyant cornerback Deion Sanders, who proved to be one of the finest athletes ever to grace a football field, both at the college and professional levels.

The Miami–Florida State clash that season proved as epic as anticipated. The fourth-ranked Seminoles appeared in control with a 19–3 lead in the third quarter before Walsh came to life. He tossed touchdown passes to Melvin Bratton and Irvin, who would later star for Johnson again with the Super Bowl champion Dallas Cowboys. Walsh and Irvin assumed the hero mantles again with 2:22 remaining in the game with a 73-yard scoring strike that gave their team a 26–19 lead.

The Seminoles responded with a quick drive downfield that struck pay dirt when quarterback Danny McManus fired a touchdown pass to Ronald Lewis. But Bowden proved again his belief that a tie was as satisfying as kissing one's sister. He went for the two-point conversion with 48 seconds left in the game. A McManus pass was batted down, preserving not only Miami's third consecutive defeat of Florida State but also its national title dreams that eventually turned into reality.

The pain had yet to subside from that defeat for the Seminoles when they took an even more agonizing sock to the gut from the Hurricanes in 1988. Florida State had recovered from the 1987 defeat to win the rest of their games, defeat Nebraska in the Fiesta Bowl, and finish third in the national rankings. They were sitting at No. 1 when they visited Miami to open the following season. Little did they know that the Hurricanes had in the off-season adopted the revolutionary and highly effective "46" defense run that coach Buddy Ryan and his Chicago Bears had ridden to the Super Bowl championship. Ryan had visited the school on a scouting mission and imparted words of wisdom along the way. The Hurricanes unveiled their new defense against the Seminoles with mind-boggling results. They forced five interceptions and one fumble, held Heisman Trophy hopeful Sammie Smith to just six yards in 10 carries, and walked off the field with a 31–0 victory, the first shutout forged against Florida State in 12 years. And that, ironically, was achieved by Miami in the second game of Bowden's tenure in 1976.

So thorough was the lambasting that Hurricanes defensive end Willis Peguese was taken aback at the ineptitude of the Florida State offense. "They must've had a lot of busted plays," he said after the game. "I mean, they can't be that bad. It was ridiculous. Too ridiculous. I just stopped and said, 'What is this?'"[8]

The Seminoles recovered to steamroll through the rest of the regular season undefeated and cap another dominant year with a defeat of Auburn in the Sugar Bowl to finish third in the national rankings. A loss to Notre Dame bumped the Hurricanes out of the top spot, but they victimized the rest of their foes as well, including Nebraska in the Orange Bowl, to secure the No. 2 ranking at season's end.

That would be the last college football game Johnson would ever coach. The Dallas Cowboys beckoned after the 1988 season, so Miami lured Dennis Erickson away from the head coaching position at Washington State. Not even the loss of Johnson could derail the runaway train that was Hurricanes football in the late 1980s and early 1990s. Erickson snagged the baton and kept the program running at full speed.

His first team boasted the premier defense in the nation at a mere 10.6 points a game. Anchored by All-American linemen Greg Mark and future NFL standout Cortez Kennedy, the unit yielded 10 points or less to eight of 12 opponents. Among the exceptions was Florida State, which took advantage of the absence of Miami starting quarterback Craig Erickson (no relation to his coach) to hand its rival its only loss. Replacement Gino Torretta, a mere redshirt freshman who captured the Heisman Trophy three years later, was unprepared to cope with a defense that featured such All-Americans as linebacker Odell Haggins and safety LeRoy Butler, an eventual All-Pro with the Green Bay Packers. On the first play from scrimmage, Butler intercepted Torretta, who remained overwhelmed in a 24–10 defeat that broke the Hurricanes' four-game winning streak against the Seminoles.

The nationally televised battle again proved that the toughest opponent for both teams was its archrival. Miami won its next four regular-season games by at least 17 points, including a 27–10 revenge defeat of top-ranked Notre Dame, and clinched its third national championship in seven years with a 33–25 victory over Alabama in the Sugar Bowl. Florida State, meanwhile, ended the season on an 11-game winning streak and catapulted to No. 3 in the country with a 41–17 pounding of Nebraska in the Fiesta Bowl.

The dominance of the Hurricanes in the series—they won their seventh of eight in 1992—left the Seminoles frustrated in their quest for their first national championship. They had finished in the top five in the final ranking six years in a row from 1987 to 1992 but lost five times to Miami (which joined the Big East Conference in 1991) during that stretch, representing more than half of their total number of defeats.

Revenge was inevitable, and it finally arrived in 1993. Bowden had assembled one of the most balanced teams in the annals of college

Figure 10.2.   Miami vs. Florida State, 1993. *Source: JC Ridley/Caneshooter.com*

football. His offense ranked first in the country at 41.2 points a game, while his defense also stood atop the nation at 9.9 points a game. Quarterback Charlie Ward tossed 27 touchdowns and just four interceptions in earning the Heisman Trophy before embarking on a career as a guard in the NBA. Linebacker Derrick Brooks was named ACC Defensive Player of the Year. Cornerback Corey Sawyer was a consensus All-American. And when the Hurricanes arrived on the schedule, they were all ready. Final score: Florida State 28, Miami 10. It was finally time to celebrate. "Total adrenaline, total elation," exclaimed Florida State linebacker Ken Alexander. "Three years of frustration are gone. I can't describe the feeling."[9] The Seminoles remained No. 1 in the rankings in all but one week of the season, clinching their first national title when placekicker Scott Bentley booted a 22-yard field goal with 21 seconds remaining to clinch an 18–16 triumph over second-ranked Nebraska in the Orange Bowl.

They had wrested the mantle of college football's most dominant program away from the Hurricanes. The seeds of Miami's temporary struggles were planted in March 1994, seven months before their last defeat of Florida State until the turn of the century, when academic advisor Tony Russell pleaded guilty to aiding in the falsification of grant applications for 85 student-athletes and landed in jail. NCAA investigators also looked into claims of drug abuse, sexual assault, ill treatment of campus police, and a relaxed attitude toward the behavior of athletes by coach Erickson. The result was three years of probation and a severe cut to scholarships. Erickson bolted after the 1994 season for greener pastures with the Seattle Seahawks and was replaced by Dallas Cowboys defensive coordinator Butch Davis. The restrictions placed on the program filtered down to performance on the field. The Hurricanes ended a 10-year run in which they steamrolled to a 107–13 record and three national championships with five consecutive seasons with three or more defeats. Included was a 5–6 record in 1997, their first losing mark since 1979.

The Seminoles took full advantage of their struggles, winning every clash from 1995 to 1999 by a combined score of 179–68. Among the lopsided results was a 47–0 thrashing in 1997. Such dominance was expected from Florida State, which continued its incredible run into Bowden's third decade at the helm in the late 1990s. Bowden recruited star after star to Tallahassee, such as defensive ends Peter Boulware and Andre Wadsworth, wide receivers Peter Warrick and Anquan Boldin, linebacker Sam Cowart, nose tackle Corey Simon, and placekicker Sebastian Janikowski, whose leg was so powerful and accurate that he was actually snagged in the first round of the NFL draft. The Seminoles of that era peaked in 1999 by not only winning their ninth consecutive Atlantic Coast Conference title but completing their first undefeated season since 1950 and clinching its second national championship with a 46–29 stomping of Virginia Tech in the Sugar Bowl.

Florida State finished one of the most remarkable eras of dominance in the history of college football with its 11–2 record in 2000. It had not lost more than two games in a span of 14 seasons, during which it boasted a stunning mark of 152–19–1 against strong competition. Most remarkable is that it finished all of those seasons ranked among the top four teams in the nation. But it wasn't until the Seminoles ran the table in 1999 that Bowden felt fulfilled. "I never had an undefeated team up until 1999," he said. "So I never had a team picture hanging in my office. I used to keep an empty picture frame in there and tell the squads that I wanted to fill that thing with a perfect team one day. After we beat Virginia Tech in the Sugar Bowl to become the first wire-to-wire AP national championship team, our athletic director had a picture frame with him in the locker room. It took us a while, but we finally filled that frame."[10]

The Hurricanes, meanwhile, wasted no time rebounding from the crippling NCAA sanctions of the mid-1990s under Davis, who left to coach the NFL Cleveland Browns in 2001, with replacement Larry Coker. The former recruited some of the finest high school talent in the country in the late 1990s, including linebacker Dan Morgan, wide receivers Santana Moss and Andre Johnson, running back Clinton Portis, offensive tackle Bryant McKinnie, tight ends Jeremy Shockey and Kellen Winslow Jr., safety Ed Reed, linebacker Jonathan Vilma, and defensive tackle Vince Wilfork. All would go on to star in the NFL. The result was not only a run of success that rivaled that of the late 1980s and early 1990s but also the wresting away of dominance in the rivalry. Miami achieved its first six-game winning streak over Florida State from 2000 to 2004. Included was a sweep in the only season in which the teams met twice. The Hurricanes won twice in 2004, including a 16–14 win in the Orange Bowl that vaulted them to No. 5 in the national rankings.

That triumph caused only a minor celebration in comparison to 2001. The Hurricanes entered that season on a 10-game winning streak, courtesy of the 2000 edition, which shook off all remnants of the sanction era and beat Florida in the Sugar Bowl to finish the season at No. 2 in the country. The 2001 team, playing for Coker in his first year at the helm, was loaded on both sides of the ball. The three-headed backfield monster of Portis, who rushed for 1,200 yards; Willis McGahee; and Frank Gore would all emerge as NFL Pro Bowlers. Quarterback Ken Dorsey threw for 2,652 yards and 23 touchdowns, which was no surprise considering he boasted such targets as Johnson and Shockey. It was also no wonder that the offense ranked third in the country in scoring at 42.7 points a game. What was hard to believe was that the defense was even better. Reed, who intercepted nine passes, Vilma, and Wilfork anchored a unit that led the nation in points allowed at 9.8 per game. Miami yielded seven or fewer points in eight of their 12 games. Its leakiest performance was in a 49–27 thumping of the Seminoles.

The 2001 Hurricanes were among the most dominant and talented college football teams of all time. They won 10 of their 12 games by 22 points or more. They steamrolled past every opponent and clinched their fifth national championship in 19 years with a 37–14 stomping of Nebraska in the Rose Bowl. Their path to the title was strewn with five nationally ranked opponents, including Syracuse and Washington, whom they defeated by a combined score of 124–7.

What was frightening to foes was that the Hurricanes returned many of their stars in 2002. They had run their winning streak to 28 games when they clashed against Florida State on October 12. They were expected to win easily—the Seminoles had lost four games the year before and had already fallen to Louisville two weeks earlier. But when Miami fell behind 27–14 in the fourth quarter, it appeared its magic had run out. Dorsey, however, had only lost once in his college career and wasn't about to double that total without a heroic effort. He hit Kevin Beard on a 2-yard touchdown pass midway through the quarter, then set up another score on a screen pass to McGahee, who sprinted 68 yards to the Florida State 11. Running back Jason Geathers took it in from there to give his team a 28–27 lead. The Seminoles responded with a drive to the Miami 26, but as had happened several times before, they missed a game-winning field goal. The Hurricanes had escaped.

And they extended their winning streak to 34 before losing a controversial and epic overtime Fiesta Bowl battle against Ohio State.

Thus ended the last era of Miami greatness for at least the next decade. The Hurricanes lost at least three games every season through 2013, though just once dropping under .500. The Seminoles fared little better as the new century progressed—neither team was ranked higher than 13th for their annual meetings from 2006 to 2012. The result was a balance of power for several years until Florida State embarked on a four-game winning streak in 2010. By the last two of those years, the Seminoles had emerged again as a national power behind such All-Americans as defensive end Bjoern Werner, center Bryan Stork, and most significantly quarterback and freshman Heisman Trophy winner Jameis Winston, who threw for 4,057 yards and 40 touchdowns in 2013, replacing fellow standout E. J. Manuel at that position.

The 2013 Seminoles opened the season ranked modestly at No. 11 in the nation, but a 51–14 thrashing of third-ranked Clemson vaulted them into that spot. They proved overwhelming on offense, scoring at least 41 points in each of their first 11 games, including 63 in a shutout of nationally ranked Maryland and a whopping against hapless Idaho. They won their fourth straight against Miami, 41–14; clobbered Duke in the Atlantic Coast Conference Championship Game; then met second-ranked Auburn in the BCS Championship Game. It resulted in a classic confrontation. A Florida State victory and first national championship since 1999 were earned when Winston tossed a game-winning touchdown pass to 1,000-yard receiver Kelvin Benjamin with a mere 13 seconds remaining.

The Seminoles were back, but a rivalry that had been defined by the greatness of both programs had yet to make a full recovery. Based on decades of dominance, it seemed only a matter of time before the Hurricanes joined them at the elite level.

Fact Box (through 2013)
> **Nickname:** None
> **Trophy:** The Florida Cup (annual round-robin including University of Florida)
> **Total meetings:** 58
> **Series record:** Miami leads, 31–27
> **First meeting:** 1951 (Miami 35, Florida State 13)

Largest margin of victory: Miami, 1976 (Miami 47, Florida State 0); Florida State 1997 (Florida State 47, Miami 0)

Longest winning streak: Florida State, 7 (1963–1972)

Game Results (home team listed second unless at a neutral site)
1951: Florida State 13, Miami 35
1953: Florida State 0, Miami 27
1955: Florida State 0, Miami 34
1956: Florida State 7, Miami 20
1957: Miami 40, Florida State 13
1958: Florida State 17, Miami 6
1959: Miami 7, Florida State 6
1960: Florida State 7, Miami 25
1962: Florida State 6, Miami 7
1963: Florida State 24, Miami 0
1964: Florida State 14, Miami 0
1966: Florida State 23, Miami 20
1969: Florida State 16, Miami 14
1970: Florida State 27, Miami 3
1971: Florida State 20, Miami 17
1972: Florida State 37, Miami 14
1973: Miami 14, Florida State 10
1974: Florida State 21, Miami 14
1975: Miami 24, Florida State 22
1976: Florida State 0, Miami 47
1977: Miami 23, Florida State 17
1978: Florida State 31, Miami 21
1979: Miami 23, Florida State 40
1980: Florida State 9, Miami 10
1981: Miami 27, Florida State 19
1982: Florida State 24, Miami 7
1983: Miami 17, Florida State 16
1984: Florida State 38, Miami 3
1985: Miami 35, Florida State 27
1986: Florida State 23, Miami 41
1987: Miami 26, Florida State 25
1988: Florida State 0, Miami 31
1989: Miami 10, Florida State 24

1990: Florida State 22, Miami 31
1991: Miami 17, Florida State 16
1992: Florida State 16, Miami 19
1993: Florida State 28, Miami 10
1994: Florida State 20, Miami 34
1995: Miami 17, Florida State 41
1996: Florida State 34, Miami 16
1997: Miami 0, Florida State 47
1998: Florida State 26, Miami 14
1999: Miami 21, Florida State 31
2000: Florida State 24, Miami 27
2001: Miami 49, Florida State 27
2002: Florida State 27, Miami 28
2003: Miami 22, Florida State 14
2004: Miami 16, Florida State 14 (Orange Bowl)
2004: Florida State 10, Miami 16
2005: Miami 7, Florida State 10
2006: Florida State 13, Miami 10
2007: Miami 37, Florida State 29
2008: Florida State 41, Miami 39
2009: Miami 38, Florida State 34
2010: Florida State 45, Miami 17
2011: Miami 19, Florida State 23
2012: Florida State 33, Miami 20
2013: Miami 14, Florida State 41

Miami Bowl Game Appearances
1935 Orange Bowl: Bucknell 26, Miami 0
1946 Orange Bowl: Miami 13, Holy Cross 6
1951 Orange Bowl: Clemson 15, Miami 14
1952 Gator Bowl: Miami 14, Clemson 0
1961 Liberty Bowl: Syracuse 15, Miami 14
1962 Gotham Bowl: Nebraska 36, Miami 34
1966 Liberty Bowl: Miami 14, Virginia Tech 7
1967 Bluebonnet Bowl: Colorado 31, Miami 21
1981 Peach Bowl: Miami 20, Virginia Tech 10
1984 Orange Bowl: Miami 31, Nebraska 30
1985 Fiesta Bowl: UCLA 39, Miami 37

1986 Sugar Bowl: Tennessee 35, Miami 7

1987 Fiesta Bowl: Penn State 14, Miami 10

1988 Orange Bowl: Miami 20, Oklahoma 14

1989 Orange Bowl: Miami 23, Nebraska 3

1990 Sugar Bowl: Miami 33, Alabama 25

1991 Cotton Bowl: Miami 46, Texas 3

1992 Orange Bowl: Miami 22, Nebraska 0

1993 Sugar Bowl: Alabama 34, Miami 13

1994 Fiesta Bowl: Arizona 29, Miami 0

1995 Orange Bowl: Nebraska 24, Miami 17

1996 Carquest Bowl: Miami 31, Virginia 21

1998 Micron PC Bowl: Miami 46, North Carolina State 23

2000 Gator Bowl: Miami 28, Georgia Tech 13

2001 Sugar Bowl: Miami 37, Florida 20

2002 Rose Bowl: Miami 37, Nebraska 14 (BCS National Championship)

2003 Fiesta Bowl: Ohio State 31, Miami 24 (BCS National Championship)

2004 Orange Bowl: Miami 16, Florida State 14

2004 Peach Bowl: Miami 27, Florida 10

2005 Peach Bowl: LSU 40, Miami 3

2006 MPC Computers Bowl: Miami 21, Nevada 20

2008 Emerald Bowl: California 24, Miami 17

2009 Champs Sports Bowl: Wisconsin 20, Miami 14

2010 Sun Bowl: Notre Dame 33, Miami 17

2013 Russell Athletic Bowl: Louisville 36, Miami 9

Florida State Bowl Game Appearances

1950 Cigar Bowl: Florida State 19, Wofford 6

1955 Sun Bowl: Western 47, Florida State 20

1958 Bluegrass Bowl: Oklahoma State 15, Florida State 6

1965 Gator Bowl: Florida State 36, Oklahoma 19

1966 Sun Bowl: Wyoming 28, Florida State 20

1967 Gator Bowl: Florida State 17, Penn State 17

1968 Peach Bowl: Louisiana State 31, Florida State 21

1971 Fiesta Bowl: Arizona State 45, Florida State 38

1977 Tangerine Bowl: Florida State 40, Texas Tech 17

1980 Orange Bowl: Oklahoma 24, Florida State 7

1981 Orange Bowl: Oklahoma 18, Florida State 17
1982 Gator Bowl: Florida State 31, West Virginia 12
1983 Peach Bowl: Florida State 28, North Carolina 3
1984 Citrus Bowl: Florida State 17, Georgia 17
1985 Gator Bowl: Florida State 34, Oklahoma State 23
1986 All-American Bowl: Florida State 27, Indiana 13
1988 Fiesta Bowl: Florida State 31, Nebraska 28
1989 Sugar Bowl: Florida State 13, Auburn 7
1990 Fiesta Bowl: Florida State 41, Nebraska 17
1990 Blockbuster Bowl: Florida State 24, Penn State 17
1992 Cotton Bowl: Florida State 10, Texas A&M 2
1993 Orange Bowl: Florida State 27, Nebraska 14
1994 Orange Bowl: Florida State 18, Nebraska 16
1995 Sugar Bowl: Florida State 23, Florida 17
1996 Orange Bowl: Florida State 31, Notre Dame 26
1997 Sugar Bowl: Florida 52, Florida State 20
1998 Sugar Bowl: Florida State 31, Ohio State 14
1999 Fiesta Bowl: Tennessee 23, Florida State 16
2000 Sugar Bowl: Florida State 46, Virginia Tech 29
2001 Orange Bowl: Oklahoma 13, Florida State 2
2002 Gator Bowl: Florida State 30, Virginia Tech 7
2003 Sugar Bowl: Georgia 26, Florida State 13
2004 Orange Bowl: Miami 16, Florida State 14
2005 Gator Bowl: Florida State 30, West Virginia 18
2006 Orange Bowl: Penn State 26, Florida State 23
2006 Emerald Bowl: Florida State 44, UCLA 27
2007 Music City Bowl: Kentucky 35, Florida State 28
2008 Champs Sports Bowl: Florida State 42, Wisconsin 13
2010 Gator Bowl: Florida State 33, West Virginia 31
2010 Chick-fil-A Bowl: Florida State 26, South Carolina 17
2011 Champs Sports Bowl: Florida State 18, Notre Dame 14
2013 Orange Bowl: Florida State 31, Northern Illinois 10
2014 BCS National Championship: Florida State 34, Auburn 31

11

GRAMBLING STATE VS. SOUTHERN: THE BAYOU CLASSIC

It's not just a game. It's not just football. It's a show of empowerment and pride for historically black colleges and African American athletes. It's a festival.

Figure 11.1. Grambling State vs. Southern. *Courtesy of Southern University Athletics*

It's The Bayou Classic. It doesn't kick off with the kickoff and end with the final tick of the game clock. And it doesn't involve only the players representing the Louisiana universities of Grambling State and Southern.

There is an economic development summit. There is a Thanksgiving Day parade. There is a golf tournament. There is a Friday night Greek Show, followed by a clash between "The World Famed" Tigers marching band and a Southern outfit known as "The Human Jukebox." There is a beauty pageant pitting coeds from both schools. There is a night-before formal party. There is the River Jam, the Celebrity Bash, and the Gospel Lunch.

And, oh yes, there is a game between two of the premier black football programs in the nation. Grambling State and Southern have both developed dozens of NFL standouts and several of the finest players in the history of the sport. The former gained particular renown under legendary coach Eddie Robinson, who set an NCAA record with 408 victories that stood until Penn State coach Joe Paterno broke it in 2009. The latter program blossomed under Arnett William "Ace" Mumford, whose quarter century was highlighted by 11 Southwestern Athletic Conference titles and five Black College National Championships. The only shame is that Robinson–Mumford battles were rare—the rivalry did not begin on an annual basis until 1959, three years before Mumford died.

Robinson was the son of a cotton sharecropper who began coaching at what was then known as the Louisiana Negro Normal and Industrial Institute at age 22 in 1941. The school was too poor to furnish housing, so he lived with school president Dr. Ralph Jones and gave a night watchman at the school named Jessie Applewhite football tickets to perform the duties of equipment manager. Robinson not only toiled on the gridiron but also as the baseball, men's basketball, and women's basketball coaches. He even placed the yard lines on the football field, washed uniforms, and drove the team bus.

Football was his passion, however, and he yearned to turn a program around that had struggled under five previous coaches. Other schools, such as Southern, Wiley College in Texas, the famed Tuskegee Institute in Alabama, and Florida A&M, had already established winning traditions and planted the seeds for future black college football success in generations to follow. And since Southern was a potential state rival, he sought to place his program on the same level.

But a more powerful motivation emerged. Southern had been considered academically superior to Grambling for generations. Southern had been birthed by an act of the Louisiana state legislature in the 1880s and established on the banks of the Mississippi River in Baton Rouge for nearly three decades before Robinson arrived on the Grambling campus. Grambling was founded in 1901 and attracted many students that could not meet the rigorous academic standards of its rival. It was not even a four-year college until the 1940s. Those differences led to a condescending attitude at Southern from an intellectual standpoint that filtered down to the football programs. "Southern used to treat Grambling like the little brother," Robinson said. "There were times when Southern was not interested in playing us. They'd play Wiley, Prairie View, stop over and play us a practice game a day or two before their big game, and work the plays. They'd beat us, of course."[1]

The Jaguars had begun their habit of beating the Tigers before Robinson began making his profound impact. They pitched three shutouts against Grambling in the 1930s by a combined score of 93–0. By that time Mumford had begun to transform Southern into a powerhouse. A University of Southern California graduate, he had already coached at three small colleges before landing at Southern. He guided his Jaguars to Southwestern Athletic Conference crowns in 1937, 1938, and 1940, the second of which he achieved his only unbeaten record.

Mumford was a pioneer of the man-in-motion offense but gained virtually no recognition for his efforts as a black coach in a Jim Crow South that remained segregated throughout his coaching tenure. The media gave the football programs at black schools little attention until the integration of the NFL in the late 1940s and beyond created interest. But those who knew and were influenced by Mumford understood the impact he made on his players and college football. "I've never met a man that I thought as much of," said All-American Leonard Barnes, who played under Mumford before working his way to become chancellor of Southern University, Shreveport. "This man was a football genius, a person who was committed to excellence on and off the field. You didn't play for the old man unless you took care of your studies. He was a stern academician."[2]

Southern proved to be a breeding ground for black coaches, including several at Grambling, such as Emory Hines, who preceded Robinson. But the first clash between Mumford and Robinson would have to wait until after 1946, during which the Grambling program was suspended for two years. Robinson, whose team was making rapid progress, was coming off a 10–2 season in 1945, but Mumford was in the process of coaching his team to the first of five consecutive conference championships and first postseason triumph, a 64–7 thrashing of Tuskegee in the Yam Bowl. The Jaguars beat the Tigers easily that year, but their feeling of superiority would end the following year.

It was 1947. The integration of Major League Baseball by Jackie Robinson had brought a sense of pride to Robinson, who also yearned to do something special. Grambling fullback Paul "Tank" Younger, who became the first player from a predominantly black college to join the NFL and emerged as a star with the Los Angeles Rams, had helped transform his team into a power. He overwhelmed the Jaguars, despite tremendous defensive attention, with help from backfield mate Roy Givens, who sprinted 43 yards for a touchdown that clinched a 21–6 victory. But it was an incident after fine Southern back Snow Taylor tallied its lone score that Robinson recalled years later with clarity in the following passage of his autobiography:

> When [Snow] crossed the goal line, he slammed the ball down and tried to stare down John Christophe, our defensive back. Snow told John, "I'm so good that I don't even run like I'm human." John was startled, since Grambling's guys just didn't act like that.
>
> The next time Snow carried the ball, Tank, Christophe, and some of our other guys tackled him hard, causing some bleeding. Tank turned to John—but so Snow could hear him—and said, "Funny, he sure bleeds like a human."[3]

The animosity between the teams grew. Tensions boiled over in 1948 when a brief scuffle broke out after a hard hit delivered by a Grambling lineman on a Southern back. Some shoving followed, but players on both sides quickly quelled the confrontation. Mumford blamed the Tigers and cut off the rivalry, which remained dormant for 11 years. The incident also prevented Grambling from joining the SWAC, forcing it into the Midwest Conference instead until the invitation into the former was finally extended in 1959.

Grambling broke into the Midwest Conference in style with one of the most dominant teams in its storied history. The Tigers used an explosive offense and stifling defense that yielded no more than seven points in nine of their first 10 games to finish the season undefeated and earn their first National Black College Championship. The only exception was final foe Florida A&M, which fell 28–21 in a game dominated by Grambling lineman Willie Davis, a dean's list student who went on not only to an NFL Hall of Fame career with the legendary Green Bay Packers teams of the 1950s and 1960s but also to earn his master's degree during his playing career despite enormous odds in an America that still created obstacles to prevent black academic achievement.

The Tigers entered the Southwestern Athletic Conference at an inopportune time. Not only did they field their first losing team in eight years, but Mumford also was in the process of earning his last two league titles and, in 1960, his fifth Black College National Championship. Driven by the talents of future NFL players, such as wide receiver Donnie Davis and tackles Charlie Granger and George McGee, the Jaguars renewed the rivalry with three consecutive victories over the Tigers, including one that proved to be their only defeat in 1960 and forced the sharing of the league crown.

The passing of Mumford in 1962 forced former Jaguars basketball coach Robert Henry Lee to serve as his replacement for two seasons, starting a revolving door at the top that did not stop spinning for three decades. Southern hired 10 different coaches from 1962 to 1992 (including Marino Casem twice), none of whom lasted more than five years. They managed to win just two conference titles during that time and earned no major bowl berths.

Meanwhile, Robinson was becoming a legend. His Tigers not only won every Southwestern Athletic Conference crown from 1965 to 1969, but they also won the National Black College Championship in 1968 and began peppering the AFL and NFL with future stars. The flood began in earnest in 1963 when defensive tackle and future NFL Hall of Famer Buck Buchanan became the first Grambling player to be plucked in the first round of a pro draft, going No. 19 overall to the Kansas City Chiefs. But wide receiver Clifton McNeil and defensive tackle Ernie Ladd had already forged their noteworthy careers, followed by such luminaries as defensive back Willie Brown, running back Essex Johnson, wide receiver Charlie Joiner, and quarterback James

Harris, who gained notoriety as the first black full-time starting quarter-back in the NFL.

Equally noteworthy was the integration of the Grambling team by Robinson. In 1968, Californian and quarterback Jim Gregory became his first white player, though he never started a game. The story of their relationship was told in a 1981 made-for-TV movie titled *Grambling's White Tiger*. Olympic champion Bruce Jenner played Gregory with actor and singer Harry Belafonte assuming the role of Robinson. What Gregory endured was real life and a bit harrowing, but he was more accepted by his teammates, coaches, and Grambling student body. "When I first arrived, I had a lot more trouble with the white community than the black community," said Gregory, who went on to serve as a high school football coach and art teacher in his home state. "But a lot changed during my years there. Bear Bryant got his first black player at Alabama in 1970."[4]

Other white players would eventually follow at both schools. Southern boasted a white starting quarterback named Marcus Jacoby in the late 1990s. Even in those more enlightened years, his status created controversy. Early in his college career, a Southern student offered his view to the school newspaper that black universities should recruit "their own" for such positions as quarterback and that the scholarship should have been given to a black athlete. That raised the ire of Southern graduate and *Baton Rouge Advocate* writer Edward Pratt, who claimed he had heard such feelings expressed by Jaguars fans and others. Pratt responded with the following rebuttal:

> I think it's racist and wrong-headed. Had a white columnist said that about LSU's African-American quarterback Herb Tyler, that person certainly would have been branded a racist. The NAACP and other civil rights organizations would have been quick to retaliate.
>
> To the writer and his supporters, here is some food for thought. What if major college and professional programs still held their racist positions that black athletes were not smart enough to play positions that require quick decision-making like quarterback? Or center? Or middle linebacker? . . . Meanwhile, Jacoby's success or failure as quarterback should be measured by his physical and mental ability and whether he gets the job done. Nothing else.[5]

The Jaguars continued to play the Tigers tough in the 1960s. They forged a tie for the SWAC championship in 1966 with a 41–13 victory and utilized the talents of future NFL Hall of Fame defensive back Mel Blount, secondary mate and future Pro Bowler Ken Ellis, and eventual Philadelphia Eagles four-time Pro Bowl receiver Harold Carmichael to eke out one of the most thrilling and certainly debated battles in the history of the rivalry before an overflow crowd at Grambling in 1969. The controversy began when Grambling fullback William O'Neill launched himself into the end zone just before halftime. But the official ruled that he fumbled before crossing the plane. The lost six points cost the Tigers dearly in a 21–17 defeat.

The game crammed a rivalry-record 27,000 fans into a stadium that seated 18,000. Fans, including the governor of Louisiana, jammed the embankment looking over the field. The seeds for the increased interest in the rivalry and in Grambling football were planted by the showing of a made-for-television documentary titled *One Hundred Yards to Glory*, which spotlighted Robinson and the penchant of a coach from a pre-dominantly black college to produce NFL talent.

Just as Neil Armstrong was taking one giant leap for mankind, the rivalry was about to take one giant leap for college football. The throng in 1969 proved that the respective campus venues were far too small to accommodate the growing interest in the annual Grambling–Southern clashes. Fans at both sites ripped down fences to catch a glimpse of sold-out games. Robinson admonished the powers that be in 1973 to move the game to a larger neutral site. The battle that year was played before 40,000 at Shreveport, and that still wasn't big enough. So it was shifted to the Louisiana Superdome the following year and officially earned the title of Bayou Classic. A packed house of 76,753 watched a Grambling team—featuring such future NFL Pro Bowlers as defensive lineman Gary Johnson and wide receiver Sammy White and on the path to an 11–1 record and National Black College Championship—blank the Jaguars, 21–0.

The crowds that besieged the Superdome opened many eyes, as did the growing dominance of the Tigers against their archrivals. Their winning streak in The Bayou Classic reached nine games in a 28–15 defeat of Southern in 1978 behind quarterback Doug Williams, who would blossom into an NFL starter and, as a member of the Washington Redskins, the first black quarterback to win a Super Bowl. Williams was a phenomenon with the Tigers. He led all of college football in 1977 with 3,286 yards passing and 38 touchdowns. He eventually replaced Robinson as Grambling coach in 1998.

Many believe Robinson should have departed earlier for a career promotion, but neither major programs at predominantly white universities nor NFL teams were ready to hire a black coach. Los Angeles Rams owner Carroll Rosenbloom flew him to the coast for discussions in 1977 but offered only an assistant head coaching position, which an insulted Robinson promptly rejected.

The growing acceptance and recruitment of premier black athletes, particularly in the south, eventually weakened the talent base at both Grambling and Southern. Though top black high school players could still maintain their dreams of playing in the NFL while performing at either school, they understood that earning a scholarship at such football factories as Alabama or Louisiana State would result in stronger competition and greater attention from pro scouts and the media. Cable television and lucrative network contracts were changing the landscape of college football, and neither Grambling nor Southern were featured on national broadcasts. The problem became more acute in the early 1980s, when a Supreme Court ruling broke the NCAA monopoly on televised college football, which motivated the networks to maximize viewership by showing games that would create the most regional and national interest. The result was devastating to such programs as Grambling and Southern. Even the usually upbeat Robinson criticized the ruling. "I hate to sound negative, but the truth is I can't see much good coming out of it [the Supreme Court decision] for small schools," he said in 1985. "It's tough enough now for us to compete with colleges that have 30 to 40,000 students. A TV appearance might bring us as much as $350,000 and that's money we simply can't do without if we're going to continue at the level to which our fans and alumni have become accustomed to.

"We finance a lot of other sports with that money, and so do a lot of other schools our size. Obviously we can't compete for national attention with Alabama, Notre Dame, and Penn State [and] unless the NCAA can regroup and get all the major colleges to agree on a plan that's equitable for everyone, I'm afraid it's going to be a drastic case of the rich getting much richer."[6]

The rich indeed got richer, but The Bayou Classic grew more competitive. The Jaguars broke their nine-game losing streak to the Tigers with a 14–7 victory in 1979. Robinson rebounded with a 10–2 record, National Black College Championship, victory over Southern, and NCAA I-AA playoff berth in 1980. But the days of Grambling dominance were over. Southern responded by taking two straight from its archrival for the first time since 1960 and 1961. The Tigers lost at least three games every year from 1981 to 1991. They suffered their first losing season in 28 years in 1987. And though they tamed the Jaguars in seven of 10 meetings from 1983 to 1992, their dominance was over.

Despite its struggles comparative to its glory years, Grambling continued to produce NFL talent. The school produced 15 NFL draftees from 1981 to 1991, including Pro Bowl defensive backs Albert Lewis and Everson Walls. Southern also nurtured significant talent during that period, the best of which was future NFL All-Pro defensive back Aeneas Williams.

Yet the Jaguars were a picture of instability at the top. The school continued to lose or fire coaches after short stints until the arrival of Pete Richardson, who boasted no experience beyond five years at tiny Winston-Salem State. Richardson emerged as the most successful coach in school history not named Ace Mumford. Southern suffered through three consecutive losing seasons before Richardson began his tenure in 1993 and proceeded to achieve a record of 11–1 and shut out South Carolina State in the Heritage Bowl. He not only coached his team to three Black College National Championships in his first five seasons and four SWAC crowns in his first seven years, but he also brought a serious approach to his job and expected his players to do the same. "He got the maximum out of his kids," said Jabbar Juluke, a senior on the 1993 team. "It wasn't just being a coach but being a father figure to tell when you were wrong, to tell you that you need to go to class and try to prepare you for life. It was more than just football. . . . He came in with a different philosophy. He was hard but fair, the best way I can put it. He was a players' coach, and we bought in right away. He did it his way."[7]

The Richardson era also signaled the beginning of the first period of domination by Southern in The Bayou Classic and, coincidentally, an unheard-of stretch of struggles for Grambling. The Jaguars won eight straight from their archrivals from 1993 to 2000. Included was a 30–7 thrashing in 1997 that proved to be a sad swan song for Robinson, whose last three teams compiled a combined record of 11–20. The domination continued in the first three years after Williams took over the Tigers, but the 1999 and 2000 meetings lived up to the billing.

It appeared in the first half of the 1999 clash that Grambling would not only end its losing streak but also do it in a rout. Quarterback Lionel Hayes fired three touchdown passes, including two to wide receiver Randy Hymes, and ran for another to give his team a 31–10 halftime lead. And when Southern quarterback Troy Williams left the game with a dislocated hip, victory seemed all but assured. After all, what could Jaguars backup quarterback Terrance Levy do to erase a 21-point deficit?

Plenty. Levy ran for a seven-yard score in the third quarter before leading a 74-yard touchdown drive to chop the deficit to 31–24. Levy then took advantage of a Grambling fumble to toss a scoring strike to Michael Hayes that tied the game. Two Southern field goals clinched an improbable 37–31 victory.

The tables had turned by 2000. Williams had assembled the first of four consecutive Southwestern Athletic Conference and two straight National Black College Championship teams. The Tigers' lone loss was to Division I-A standout Louisville. They entered The Bayou Classic on an eight-game winning streak. Southern had been hanging around .500 all season and were ripe for defeat. Grambling had already clinched the Western Division championship, but that crown would mean little without a victory over the Jaguars. During his still-short stint at Southern, Richardson understood that mentality. "It's one of the most intense rivalries in the country—as fierce as Florida–Florida State, Michigan–Ohio State or Oklahoma–Nebraska," he said. "It's the cause of bad blood between friends and families. It's more than a football game. It's a way of life."[8]

A crowd of 72,000 packed the Superdome for the 2000 Bayou Classic. But those expecting Grambling to seize control from the start were stunned when Levy tossed an 86-yard touchdown pass and engineered two drives capped by Dain Lewis rushing scores, giving their team a 24–14 halftime lead. The battle came down to the final minute with the Jaguars leading 31–23. Hymes dramatically hit Scotty Anderson in the end zone with seven seconds remaining to cut it to 31–29, but his two-point conversion throw was tipped by Southern cornerback Lenny

Williams into the hands of teammate Edreece Brown, who sprinted 96 yards into the end zone. The wrong team had earned those two points in the minds of the Grambling coaches, players, and fans. Final score: Jaguars 33, Tigers 29.

Grambling avenged that defeat and ended their eight-game losing streak to Southern in 2001 but had its 10-game winning streak ended the following season with a lopsided loss to a mediocre Jaguars team. That game led to one of the most highly anticipated Bayou Classics ever in 2003. The Tigers entered as three-time defending conference champion and a 9–2 record. The Jaguars boasted a mark of 10–1 and their finest team since the late 1990s. Both teams boasted prolific quarterbacks. Grambling's Bruce Eugene was in the process of exceeding 3,000 yards and passing for 31 touchdowns. Southern counterpart Quincy Richard racked up 2,700 yards through the air and was the team's second-leading rusher.

A scoring explosion was expected and received. The two quarterbacks combined for a ridiculous 961 yards passing. Eugene fired scoring strikes of 76 and 71 yards and finished with 409 yards through the air, but he took a backseat to Richard, who set school single-game records with 552 yards passing and five touchdowns. And he had his team ahead, 44–41 with one minute left on the game clock. The Tigers could not take advantage of their last offensive possession. The result was their 10th defeat in the last 11 battles against Southern.

In the end, however, both programs lost. Violence marred the 2003 Bayou Classic. School officials were thrilled when an estimated 200,000 people converged on New Orleans for the game and other events. But three shootings that weekend shattered all feelings of sportsmanship between the fan bases. They were later left to speculate if those incidents entered into the decision by Williams to leave his coaching post for an executive position with the NFL Tampa Bay Buccaneers, though he returned in 2010 to coach Grambling with disastrous results. He was replaced in 2004 by offensive coordinator Melvin Spears.

Spears could not match the consistency of his predecessor, whose teams won 40 of 48 games in his last four seasons, but he did not receive much of an opportunity. After he began his tenure with a 6–5 season, he guided the Tigers to an 11–1 mark, conference title, and National Black College Championship. He groomed defensive end and future NFL players Kenneth Pettway and Jason Hatcher, but it was his offense that

proved special by scoring 44 or more in eight of 12 games, including a
50–35 defeat of Southern and 45–6 mauling of Alabama A&M in the
SWAC Championship Game. But the Tigers stunningly fell to 3–8 the
following season, after which Spears was dismissed.

The suddenness of his firing, which he believed to be unfair, motivated him to sue the university. He claimed he was canned without
cause, but the school countered with several charges, including that
Spears had wrongfully administered drug tests to some of his players
and had made insensitive remarks about a request from Alcorn State to
reschedule a game against Grambling in the wake of Hurricane Katrina.
Grambling won the lawsuit and hired North Carolina Central head
coach Rod Broadway to take his place.

Katrina had indeed wreaked havoc on the area just before the 2005
season. But it could not stop The Bayou Classic. The Superdome was a
mess, so the schools moved the game to Reliant Stadium in Houston.
And despite the comparative disinterest in the game among Texans, it
still drew 53,214 fans, who watched the powerful Grambling offense
run roughshod over the Jaguars.

By that time, the years of greatness at Southern under Richardson
were becoming a distant memory. His teams were never terrible—they
never finished more than one game under .500—but they lost at least
three in every year from 2004 to 2009. And it was after a 6–5 season in
2009 that he was fired. His fate was sealed by a 31–13 loss to Grambling, the most lopsided Bayou Classic defeat of his tenure.

Most college football programs do not boast a rivalry so intense and
important that defeat in it can cost a coach his job. But the annual
Grambling–Southern battle can be both a curse and a blessing to those
in that position.

Unless, of course, you were Eddie Robinson or Ace Mumford. To
those whose legends live on and without whom The Bayou Classic
would not exist, it was only a blessing.

Fact Box (through 2013)
   Nickname: The Bayou Classic
   Trophy: Waterford crystal
   Total meetings: 55 (1959 forward)
   Series record: Grambling leads, 29–26
   First meeting: 1959 (Southern 12, Grambling 6)

Figure 11.2.   Grambling State vs. Southern. *Courtesy of Southern University Athletics*

Largest margin of victory: Grambling, 1980 (Grambling 43, Southern 6)

Longest winning streak: Grambling, 9 (1970–1978)

Game Results, 1959 forward only (home team listed second unless at a neutral site)

1959: Southern 12, Grambling 6
1960: Southern 16, Grambling 6
1961: Southern 20, Grambling 9
1962: Grambling 13, Southern 3
1963: Southern 22, Grambling 21
1964: Grambling 20, Southern 17
1965: Grambling 34, Southern 14
1966: Southern 41, Grambling 13
1967: Grambling 27, Southern 20
1968: Grambling 34, Southern 32
1969: Southern 21, Grambling 17
1970: Grambling 37, Southern 24
1971: Grambling 31, Southern 3

1972: Grambling 2, Southern 0
1973: Grambling 19, Southern 14
1974: Grambling 21, Southern 0
1975: Grambling 33, Southern 17
1976: Grambling 10, Southern 2
1977: Grambling 55, Southern 20
1978: Grambling 28, Southern 15
1979: Southern 14, Grambling 7
1980: Grambling 43, Southern 6
1981: Southern 51, Grambling 20
1982: Southern 22, Grambling 17
1983: Grambling 24, Southern 10
1984: Grambling 31, Southern 29
1985: Grambling 29, Southern 0
1986: Grambling 30, Southern 3
1987: Southern 27, Grambling 21
1988: Southern 10, Grambling 3
1989: Grambling 44, Southern 30
1990: Grambling 25, Southern 13
1991: Southern 31, Grambling 30
1992: Grambling 30, Southern 27
1993: Southern 31, Grambling 13
1994: Southern 34, Grambling 7
1995: Southern 30, Grambling 14
1996: Southern 17, Grambling 12
1997: Southern 30, Grambling 7
1998: Southern 26, Grambling 14
1999: Southern 37, Grambling 31
2000: Southern 33, Grambling 29
2001: Grambling 30, Southern 20
2002: Southern 48, Grambling 24
2003: Southern 44, Grambling 41
2004: Grambling 24, Southern 13
2005: Grambling 50, Southern 35
2006: Southern 21, Grambling 17
2007: Southern 22, Grambling 13
2008: Grambling 29, Southern 14
2009: Grambling 31, Southern 13

2010: Grambling 38, Southern 17
2011: Grambling 36, Southern 12
2012: Southern 38, Grambling 33
2013: Southern 40, Grambling 17

Southern Bowl Game Appearances

1943 Flower Bowl: North Carolina A&T 14, Southern 12
1946 Yam Bowl: Southern 64, Tuskegee 7
1947 Yam Bowl: Southern 47, Fort Valley State 0
1948 Fruit Bowl: Southern 30, San Francisco State 0
1975 Pelican Bowl: Southern 15, South Carolina State 12
1994 Heritage Bowl: Southern 11, South Carolina State 0
1995 Heritage Bowl: Southern 30, Florida A&M 25
1996 Heritage Bowl: Howard 27, Southern 24
1997 Heritage Bowl: Southern 34, South Carolina State 28
1998 Heritage Bowl: Southern 28, Bethune-Cookman 2
1999 Heritage Bowl: Hampton 24, Southern 3

Grambling Bowl Game Appearances

1946 Flower Bowl: Grambling 19, Lane 6
1946 Lions Bowl: Grambling 70, Mississippi Industrial 12
1947 Lions Bowl: Grambling 47, Bethune-Cookman 6
1948 Vulcan Bowl: Central State 27, Grambling 21
1948 Lions Bowl: Grambling 26, Texas College 20
1949 Lions Bowl: Grambling 7, Texas College 0
1950 Lions Bowl: Bishop 38, Grambling 0
1951 Lions Bowl: Grambling 52, Bishop 0
1952 Lions Bowl: Grambling 27, Alcorn State 13
1955 Orange Blossom Classic: Grambling 28, Florida A&M 21
1964 Sugar Cup Classic: Grambling 42, Bishop 6
1964 Orange Blossom Classic: Florida A&M 42, Grambling 15
1965 Sugar Cup Classic: Grambling 54, Lincoln 18
1965 Pecan Bowl: North Dakota State 20, Grambling 7
1967 Orange Blossom Classic: Grambling 28, Florida A&M 25
1968 Pasadena Bowl: Grambling 34, Sacramento State 7
1969 Orange Blossom Classic: Florida A&M 23, Grambling 19
1972 Pelican Bowl: Grambling 56, North Carolina Central 6
1973 Boardwalk Bowl: Grambling 17, Delaware 8

1973 Grantland Rice Bowl: Western Kentucky 28, Grambling 20

1974 Pelican Bowl: Grambling 28, South Carolina State 7

1976 Mirage Bowl: Grambling 42, Morgan State 16

1977 Mirage Bowl: Grambling 35, Temple 32

1978 Orange Blossom Classic: Florida A&M 31, Grambling 7

1980 NCAA I-AA Playoff: Boise State 14, Grambling 9

1985 NCAA I-AA Playoff: Arkansas State 10, Grambling 7

1989 NCAA I-AA Playoff: Stephen F. Austin 59, Grambling 56

1992 Heritage Bowl: Grambling 45, Florida A&M 15

1994 Heritage Bowl: South Carolina State 31, Grambling 27

12

UTAH VS. BRIGHAM YOUNG:
THE HOLY WAR

It was November 28, 2009. Utah placekicker Joe Phillips had just kicked his fifth field goal of the game to give his team a 23–20 lead over Brigham Young in the annual Holy War. His boot minutes earlier had forced overtime.

This was no typical Cougars–Utes clash. Both teams were nationally ranked. Both had suffered just two losses heading into the traditional regular-season finale. Bowl games were at stake.

BYU needed to answer with a field goal to stay alive. But quarterback Max Hall did better than that. He found tight end Andrew George alone for a short pass over the middle. Nary a Utah jersey stood between George and pay dirt. He sprinted into the end zone for the winning touchdown, setting off a wild celebration at LaVell Edwards Stadium in Salt Lake City. Cougar fans joined their heroes on the field. George was buried in a pile of his teammates, but he didn't mind. "I couldn't breathe," he later exclaimed. "My shoulder was like up my head, but it's awesome. If that's what happens when you catch a game-winning TD, I'll take it."[1]

Hall took it as well. In fact, many believe he took it too far in his postgame comments. But his words were indicative of the passion and intensity fans of both teams have felt about The Holy War for more than a century. He claimed anger with how his family was treated by Utah fans a year earlier—and he really let them have it. "I don't like Utah," he said. "In fact, I hate them. I hate everything about them. I

Figure 12.1.   BYU vs. Utah. *Courtesy of BYU Photos*

hate their program, their fans, I hate everything. It felt really good to send those guys home."[2]

Why the hatred, which is prevalent on both sides? Religion is a primary component. Utah is a public school, while Brigham Young is the flagship university of the Church of Jesus Christ of Latter-Day Saints. Though both institutions have attempted to play down any animosity that exists between the students and players based on religion, some BYU supporters have accused their Utah counterparts of intentionally swearing or drinking excessively in their presence and otherwise acting antagonistically. On the other hand, Cougar fans have accused those of the Utes of arrogance or self-righteousness, as if to be morally superior. BYU students, including its football players, are sometimes chided for the strict behavioral rules imposed on them by the university, including a no-sex policy.

The hostility between the players and fans of the schools was evident more than 100 years earlier on April 6, 1896, when the two teams clashed for the first time. The battle was merely a prelude to a game scheduled for the following fall, but one wouldn't have understood its significance by the reaction of the fans. The Utah victory was marred by a fracas between about 100 fans of the school then known as Brigham Young Academy and those cheering on the host Utes. The former took exception to their treatment in Salt Lake City—just as Hall did more than a century hence—and fought back. "Afterwards, the hoodlums looked like they had been through a sausage mill," wrote one journalist following the battle.[3]

The Utes blanked the Cougars seven months later, but the latter won the next three meetings. Little did anyone know that the relative evenness of the programs in those early games would not reappear until the late 1980s. The Holy War has been marked by long stretches of dominance by one team, then the other. In fact, Brigham Young would win just twice more until embarking on a three-game winning streak in 1965.

There was an excuse from 1899 to 1921—the school did not field a team during those years. But when the Cougars returned to action, the Utes were far more developed. Utah had established a fine program in the first two decades of the 20th century under coaches Harvey Holmes, Joe Maddock, and Fred Bennion, first as an independent, then as a member of the Rocky Mountain Athletic Conference (RMAC). Their schedules were limited to no more than seven games, but they still managed just one losing season from 1898 to 1912.

It was the young Maddock who launched the program in earnest in 1905 after a successful playing career at the University of Michigan. He coached the team to a 28–9–1 record in six seasons and raised the level of interest in football at the university and throughout the state. So impressive was his work that the *Galveston Daily News* reported the following in 1905:

> He has the Mormons all football crazy. He has written here to say that his team now holds the championship of Utah, Montana, Wyoming, and the greater part of Colorado. When he won the hard-fought battle with Colorado College a week ago the Salt Lake City papers said: "Maddock" is a new way of saying success. The great Michigan tackle has taken boys who never saw a football before and made them the star players of the Rocky Mountain States. [4]

The departure of Maddock after the 1909 season and the beginning of conference competition the following year started did not slow the momentum. Players recruited and groomed by Maddock continued to thrive under Bennion, placing second in the league standings in both 1911 and 1912 before mediocrity set in. But the Utes rebounded in 1922 under coach Thomas Fitzpatrick, just in time to renew The Holy War. They finished that season 7–1, winning all five league games to snag their first title. Among the victories was a 49–0 thrashing of the fledgling Cougars that remained the most lopsided game in the history of the series until BYU turned the tables with a 56–6 triumph in 1980.

Brigham Young joined the Rocky Mountain Athletic Conference upon its gridiron rebirth in 1922 but proved to be the dregs of the league until coach G. Ott Romney (a distant relative of future presidential candidate Mitt Romney) began guiding the program in the right direction in the late 1920s. The Utes did not just win every Holy War clash from 1922 to 1927, but they also pitched four shutouts and yielded a mere 13 points in those six games. Even the blossoming of the Cougars under Romney could not stem the tide. BYU steamrolled to an 8–1 record in 1932, but its lone loss was a 29–0 shellacking at the hands of Utah.

Brigham Young was not alone in being victimized by the Utes of that era under Ike Armstrong, who also coached the basketball team for two seasons before establishing himself as the most storied football coach in school history. Armstrong guided the Utes to their first unbeaten season in 1926 and three more starting in 1928, which also marked the first of six consecutive conference championships. Utah managed a mark of 49–8–2 from 1925 to 1932, peaking in 1930, when it outscored its opponents, 340–20. The Utes teams of that era were led by such All-Americans as offensive linemen Jack Johnson, Alton Carman, and Marvin Jonas; end George Watkins; and running backs Earl "Powerhouse" Pomeroy and Frank Christensen, who scored a school-record 235 points before embarking on a career with the NFL Detroit Lions.

Their mastery of the RMAC ended as America sunk deeper into the Great Depression, but they continued on their run of 15 consecutive winning seasons while maintaining their dominance of the Cougars. The Utes pitched four consecutive shutouts of their hapless rivals from 1934 to 1937 despite comparable records. Aside from a scoreless tie in 1928, Brigham Young lost every Holy War from 1922 to 1937 by at least two touchdowns. By the time that period ended, another stretch of Utah greatness had begun. Led by such standouts as All-American tackle Bernard McGarry and future Cleveland Browns star receiver Mac Speedie, the Utes won another title in their first season in the Big Seven Conference and capped their season in 1938 with their first postseason triumph, a 26–0 dismantling of New Mexico in the Sun Bowl, then snagged three more BSC crowns from 1940 to 1942.

It was in the last of those seasons that the Cougars finally gained some satisfaction with a stunning 12–7 upset of the Utes. But Brigham Young could not take the momentum and run with it. The school shut down its football program the next year while Utah continued to play, though its winless 1943 season was partially due to the loss of talent to the battles overseas. And after the last shots had been fired and The Holy War resumed, so did the dominance of the Utes. Only a tie in 1950 prevented Utah from steamrolling to a 12-game winning streak against the Cougars, who sunk from mediocrity to wretchedness well into the 1950s. They won no more than four games in all but one season from 1947 to 1956, bottoming out at 0–11 in 1949 and compiling a pitiful mark of 28–69–3 during that period.

Despite their seemingly never-ending role as the Utes' personal punching bags, the Cougars did rise up occasionally to throw a scare into their Holy War rivals. Such an occasion was Thanksgiving Day in 1953. Another Utah rout was expected—and for good reason. The Utes were destined to win their second of three consecutive championships in what was now known as the Skyline Conference, while Brigham Young was in the midst of what had become an all-too-typical 2–7–1 season.

The showdown at Ute Stadium in Salt Lake City was nationally televised by NBC and handled by broadcasters Mel Allen and Lindsey Nelson, both of whom would eventually become legends of their field. Utah, now led by fourth-year head coach Jack Curtice, was favored by a whopping 24 points, but it became apparent quickly that such a margin would not be reached. Brigham Young trailed 33–26 with mere seconds remaining but scored a touchdown to chop its deficit to 33–32. The Cougars needed only an extra point to forge a tie, but their holder fumbled the snap and Utah recovered the ball to clinch its league title and frustrate its rival once again.

Curtice proved less successful than Armstrong, but he did recruit two of the finest players ever to don the Utah uniform in future NFL Hall of Fame safety Larry Wilson and consensus All-American quarterback Lee Grosscup, whose impact as a professional player after being selected 10th overall in the 1959 draft was dwarfed by that of his decades as a college football television analyst. Grosscup completed an amazing 69 percent of his passes in 1957 for 1,398 yards and 10 touchdowns.

It was during his time with the Utes that Brigham Young managed its first Holy War triumph in 16 years, a stunningly thorough 41–6 shellacking at Ute Stadium that proved to be a onetime wonder rather than the beginning of a trend. That would have to wait until the mid-1960s—Utah won the next six in a row to give it an absurd 37–5–4 all-time record against the Cougars.

But the writing was on the wall. The magic was gone for the Utes under coach Ray Nagel, who assumed control in 1958. They enjoyed one last spark of greatness in 1964, winning the Western Athletic Conference title, forging a 9–2 record overall, dominating West Virginia in the Liberty Bowl and making their first appearance in the national rankings at No. 14 behind the talent of future All-Pro wide receiver Roy Jefferson. But it would be 28 years before they earned another bowl berth and 31 before they snagged another league championship despite boasting such future NFL standout talent in the late 1960s and early 1970s as tight end Bob Trumpy, defensive tackle Manny Fernandez, cornerback Norm Thompson, and wide receiver Steve Odom.

While the Utes were beginning their descent, BYU was beginning its ascent under coach Tommy Hudspeth, who stopped the revolving door that had seen four coaches at the school in nine years. The Cougars managed their first three-game Holy War winning streak from 1965 to 1967. In the process, they planted the seeds for a reputation as a quarterback factory. Virgil Carter, who later served as a starting quarterback with the Cincinnati Bengals, passed for 3,971 yards and 41 touchdowns in 1965 and 1966 combined while leading his team to a 14–6 record and successive victories over the Utes in which the Cougars scored a total of 60 points. Not bad considering that BYU had scored more than 14 points against Utah a mere seven times in 46 previous meetings.

And even though Utah won the next four battles as the Hudspeth era came to an inglorious end, the generations of its Holy War dominance was over and would not return until the 21st century. One significant reason was the elevation of assistant LaVell Edwards to the position of head coach at Brigham Young. His promotion prompted little fanfare, as *Deseret News* sports columnist Doug Robinson recalled in the following excerpt from a 2000 article:

> There was nothing in this unpretentious, avuncular man to excite media or fans anyway—he was a low-key local who had grown up one of 14 kids on a farm in Orem [Utah]; he was part of the old coaching staff, which didn't exactly inspire confidence or hope; he had experienced little success in his 18 years as a coach, both at the prep and collegiate levels; and he was only the latest in a line of coaches passing quickly through Provo, losing season after losing season. What was one more coach?[5]

Little could anyone have imagined that, not only would Edwards not be just "one more coach," but he would blossom into one the most successful in college football history. He transformed a program that held steadfast to a traditional running attack into one of the most prolific passing teams in the sport. He lured premier high school quarterbacks to BYU with the promise that they would be given the opportunity to display their talents. And he began to, like no other coach in Cougars history, as soon as his recruits hit the field. A program that had wallowed among the dregs of the game was suddenly a perennial conference champion, annual bowl participant, and top-20 mainstay in the national rankings. The assistants he tutored have been scattered throughout the major college and professional game, including such Super Bowl coaches as Mike Holmgren, Brian Billick, and Andy Reid. And his hiring marked the beginning of a period of dominance in The Holy War that lasted a generation.

His first clash against Utah proved, however, that Edwards could maximize his talent without being married to the aerial circus he would eventually unleash. He inherited tailback "Fleet Pete" Van Valkenberg, who won the NCAA rushing title in 1972 with an average of 138.6 yards per game on the ground. Van Valkenberg keyed a 16–7 victory over the Utes that proved the turning point in The Holy War. But Edwards wasted no time attracting quarterbacks who could handle the workload. The first to thrive was Gary Sheide, who threw for 4,524 yards and 45 touchdowns in two seasons and led his team to a Western Athletic Conference championship in 1974 as well as the first bowl game in school history. Edwards was merely warming up. His first future NFL quarterback was Gifford Nielsen, who in 1976 helped launch an amazing run of 10 consecutive league championships during which time the Cougars compiled a record of 104–21 and played in nine bowl games, winning four.

The teeter-totter that has been The Holy War since its beginnings had swung in their direction not because of their greatness, but because of the collapse of the Utes, who managed a mark of 8–36 from 1974 to 1977 before coach Wayne Howard guided them to a surprising 8–3 record in 1978. In a series that has been marked by lopsided games between mismatched teams, the battle that season proved scintillating. The buildup began after the 1977 clash won by BYU, 38–8. The ire of the Utah football community was raised when Edwards kept prolific quarterback Marc Wilson in the game throughout to set an NCAA record with 571 passing yards in a game. It was perceived that the Cougars were running up the score. It was also alleged that one Brigham Young coach made disparaging remarks to Howard about his team during the midfield handshakes following the game, though the details remained unclear. What was clear was that Howard was upset—and he expressed his feelings at the postgame press conference. "The hatred between BYU and Utah is nothing compared to what it will be," he said. "It will be a crusade to beat BYU from now on."[6]

In the midst of an era of Utah football known as "The Dark Ages," a bright light shone through on November 18, 1978. The Utes had clinched their first winning season in five years but were not expected to upend a Cougars team that was en route to winning their third consecutive WAC title. Predictions of a BYU victory appeared justified when Cougars defensive back Dave Francis intercepted a pass from Utah quarterback Randy Gomez and sprinted 20 yards for a touchdown to stretch the lead to 22–7 heading into the fourth quarter. But when Gomez tossed a 19-yard touchdown pass to Frank Henry in the corner of the end zone on 4th-and-15 to complete a stirring comeback and 23–22 victory, revenge had been earned.

It would prove short lived. Edwards and his Cougars had established an era in which one quarterback after another would dominate the Utes and the rest of the conference. Nielsen and Wilson were followed by future Chicago Bears standout Jim McMahon, who bided his team behind Wilson before setting school-career marks by throwing for 9,356 yards and 84 touchdowns and leading his team to Holiday Bowl victories in his last two seasons. His departure provided an opportunity for Steve Young, who eventually blossomed into a perennial Super Bowl champion with the San Francisco 49ers and one of the finest quarterbacks in the history of the sport. Young guided the Cougars to an 11–1 overall record, unbeaten mark in the WAC, and Holiday Bowl triumph in 1983 as they soared to No. 7 in the nation, their highest ranking to date. Several of their targets over the years approached or exceeded 1,000 yards receiving, but none proved more successful at the NFL level than tight end Todd Christensen, who earned five consecutive Pro Bowl berths with the Oakland/Los Angeles Raiders.

But it was not an eventual NFL star that guided BYU to a magical season in 1984. Rather, it was Robbie Bosco, whose professional career fizzled from the start and ended due to a shoulder injury. Bosco led the nation with 3,875 yards passing and 33 touchdowns that year to finish third in the Heisman Trophy balloting. The Cougars opened the year ranked just 13th in the country but moved up to eighth after opening the year with a victory over No. 3 Pittsburgh and continued to climb. Surprisingly, it was the mediocre but plucky Utes that gave BYU one of its toughest games before falling. That triumph rocketed the Cougars into the No. 1 spot for the first time ever and they clinched the national championship with a 24–17 defeat of Michigan in the Holiday Bowl to complete a 13–0 season.

The hero of the game was Bosco, who was replaced in the first quarter after sustaining an injury on a late hit that was later diagnosed to be a medial collateral tear in his knee and grade 2 ankle sprain. Yet he yearned to return to the game, so he struck up a conversation with the medical staff. "After I was checked, I asked the trainers, 'If I get hit on it again, is it a career-ending injury? Can I play on this?' They said I could. I said, 'Wrap it up and let's go!'"[7]

His return did not result in immediate success. The Cougars were in the midst of blowing their shot at the championship with six turnovers and a blocked field goal. Yet their defense kept them alive and gave the offense a shot to win it with the ball on the Michigan 13-yard line and just over one minute remaining. Bosco dropped back to pass on third down. Running back Kelly Smith, who had already caught nine passes, was double teamed. Tight end David Mills, the second option on the play, was tackled, but no penalty was called. Smith sprinted down the sideline and snagged a lofted pass from Bosco for the go-ahead score. Defensive back Marv Allen secured the crown with an interception, setting off a raucous celebration and prompting Edwards to marvel at the guts of his quarterback. "Never have I seen a more courageous performance by a kid," he exclaimed after the game.[8]

That kid and the quarterbacks that preceded him at Brigham Young made certain that the inspired Utah victory in the 1978 Holy War battle was merely a brief interruption in an era of Cougar dominance. BYU not only responded by winning the next nine meetings, but they thrashed the Utes by such scores as 27–0, 56–6, 56–28, and 55–7 between 1979 and 1983 before their rivals began to lose more competitively.

It was no coincidence that a three-year period in which the Cougars did not boast a prized quarterback ended their run of Western Athletic Conference championships. Edwards coached his team to strong records and bowl appearances in each season from 1986 to 1988, but a 57–28 defeat to Utah in the last of those years signaled changing times. Ironically, it was the Utes that season that boasted a future NFL star quarterback in Scott Mitchell, who led the nation with 4,322 passing yards and 29 touchdowns. He exacted a modicum of revenge for all the prolific BYU quarterbacks that had buried Utah by throwing for 384 yards and three touchdowns in the shellacking of BYU.

So thorough was that lambasting that Edwards decided to test out freshman quarterback Ty Detmer. Little could anyone have imagined that Detmer would eventually surpass the likes of Nielsen, Wilson, McMahon, and Young in every statistical category en route to his own NFL career. Detmer helped the Cougars launch another era of WAC dominance. He guided his team to a 21–2–1 league record and three championships from 1989 to 1991 while maintaining its top-25 national ranking. Detmer helped set a Holy War record in 1989 by guiding BYU downfield for a whopping 70 points in 1989, though Edwards sat him in the second quarter in a vain attempt to prevent the Utes from further embarrassment. The Cougars still scored touchdowns in each of their first seven possessions. They tallied 163 points in three victories over Utah with Detmer as the starting quarterback.

Through the early 1990s, "parity" was not a word that could be seen in The Holy War dictionary. Brigham Young had answered the 46-game dominance of Utah with a 22–6 record and had won 19 of the last 21 games. Even Jim Fassel, who coached the Utes from 1985 to 1989 before embarking on an NFL career that earned him a Super Bowl berth with the New York Giants, couldn't stem the tide, losing four of five games to the Cougars and guiding his team to a 17–29 record in his last four seasons combined.

The scales of gridiron justice were finally about to even out for the only time in this storied rivalry. It did not come via a downturn in the fortunes of Brigham Young football. The Cougars continued their incredible run of non-losing seasons through the completion of Edwards's tenure in 2000. But the bold hiring at Utah of University of Arizona offensive line coach Ron McBride as a first-time head coach proved quite successful. McBride could not transform the Utes into national championships contenders upon his arrival in 1990, but he did turn them into consistent winners and frequent bowl participants.

Gaining a stalemate in The Holy War would have to wait a bit. His team lost its first three games to the Cougars before responding in kind from 1993 to 1995 for its first three-game winning streak in the series in more than two decades. McBride recruited a level of talent unseen at his school in a generation. Future NFL Pro Bowlers, such as running back Jamaal Anderson and defensive tackle Luther Ellis, as well as such eventual pro standouts as wide receiver Kevin Dyson and offensive lineman Barry Sims helped the Utes turn the tide in the mid-1990s.

They were followed by more top-level talent, such as wide receiver Steve Smith and offensive tackle Jordan Gross, both of whom emerged as All-Pros with the Carolina Panthers. The Utes finished the 20th century having won five of seven games against the team that had been tormenting them since 1972. They peaked in 1994 with a 10–2 record and Freedom Bowl triumph over Arizona that landed them at No. 8 in the nation, their first foray into the top 10. And for the first time ever, one could anticipate a close contest in The Holy War. Among the exceptions was a 37–17 BYU triumph in 1996, but such dominance was expected from a Cougars team that finished 14–1, won the Cotton Bowl, and finished the season ranked fifth in the nation. The point differential in every clash from 1997 to 2003 was seven or less. The result was several epic battles and exciting endings.

Perhaps the most memorable was played for the first time at new Rice-Eccles Stadium in Salt Lake City in 1998. A fantastic finish did not appear likely when Utah trailed 26–17 with 2:41 remaining. But a 95-yard kickoff return for a touchdown by Daniel Jones chopped the deficit to 26–24. The Ute defense forced a punt; then their offense embarked on what seemed destined to be a dramatic game-winning drive downfield. They marched to the BYU 15-yard line to set up what should have been an easy field goal attempt for placekicker Ryan Kaneshiro. But, alas, his boot clanked off the right goalpost. Game over.

Another thriller provided Edwards a fine parting gift in 2000. It did not seem appropriate that one of the winningest coaches in college football history would go out a loser, but that scenario seemed quite possible with the teams tied with two minutes left and the Cougars backed up inside their own 20-yard line on fourth down. But two long passes from Brandon Doman to Jonathan Pittman and an 11-yard touchdown run by the former gave BYU a 34–27 victory and sent Edwards out smiling.

The hiring of Chicago Bears offensive coordinator Gary Crowton to replace Edwards marked the beginning of a new era in The Holy War in which both programs traded short periods of greatness and supremacy. He arrived with a bang, guiding the Cougars to a 12–2 season and unbeaten record in the Mountain West Conference behind Doman and running back Luke Staley, who finished the season with 1,596 yards rushing. But their 24–21 defeat of Utah would prove to be their last in the Crowton era, which ended with three years of mediocrity and his firing in favor of Bronco Mendenhall.

While Crowton was attempting in vain to recapture the magic of 2001, new Utah coach Urban Meyer was forging a career that would make him a perennial national championship contender at Florida and Ohio State by guiding Utah to its best seasons ever. Behind the talents of such future NFL standouts as quarterback Alex Smith and defensive back Eric Weddle, the Utes won 10 games in 2003 and swept through the following season undefeated, winning MWC crowns both years. The 2004 edition peaked with a 35–7 victory over Pittsburgh in the Fiesta Bowl to finish the year ranked fourth in the country. But the fact that they received little national title consideration competing against no ranked opponents until the postseason helped convince Meyer to seek greener pastures. Utes fans lamented when Meyer, whom many accused of being a carpetbagger, bolted after two years to take over the Gators.

His departure and the emergence of a dominant Cougars team under Mendenhall resulted in a short period of success in the midst of an era of Utah dominance. BYU steamrolled through its MWC schedules unbeaten in both 2006 and 2007, but the Utes answered with their finest season ever in 2008 under Meyer replacement Kyle Whittingham with an explosive offense and a defense powered by future NFL players, such as cornerback Sean Smith, linebacker Paul Kruger, and lineman Koa Misi. Most impressive was their 48–24 thumping of the two-time defending champion Cougars, who were in the midst of a four-year run in which they compiled a 43–9 record. The Utes finished the year undefeated after a stunning 31–17 defeat of Alabama in which they held the Crimson Tide to a mere 31 yards rushing in 33 attempts and quarterback Brian Johnson threw for 336 yards and three touchdowns. The victory justified complaints after Utah was left out of the Bowl Championship Series in favor of more glorified teams, such as Florida and Oklahoma. And when it was over, Whittingham stated his case for Utah, the only undefeated team in the country, to be voted in as its national champion. "I know where I'm voting us," he said. "I'm voting us No. 1. End of story. . . . I don't know why they wouldn't deserve that consideration. Somebody has to explain to me why they wouldn't. There is only one undefeated team in the United States of

America right now in Division I football, and it's these guys right here."[9]

His words were for naught—the once-beaten Gators were handed the title, with Utah placing second. But the Utes continued to roll under Whittingham, particularly in The Holy War following their loss in the epic battle of 2009, winning the next four games, including a 20–13 defeat of the Cougars in 2013 that gave them a 57–34–4 record in the series and nine victories in the last 12 meetings.

That game, however, marked at least a temporary end to one of the most storied rivalries in college football. The move of Utah to the PAC-12 and BYU to independent status beginning in 2014 resulted in no game scheduled thereafter. The two schools arranged battles from 2016 to 2018, but none were to be played in 2014 and 2015. The hole on the schedules where The Holy War was supposed to be seemed as vast and empty as a Utah desert.

Fact Box (through 2013)
    Nickname: The Holy War
    Trophy: The Beehive Boot

Figure 12.2.   BYU vs. Utah. *Courtesy of BYU Photos*

Total meetings: 95
Series record: Utah leads, 57–34–4
First meeting: 1896 (Utah 12, BYU 4)
Largest margin of victory: BYU, 1980 (BYU 56, Utah 6)
Longest winning streak: BYU, 9 (1979–1987); Utah, 9 (1929–1937)

Game Results (home team listed second unless at a neutral site)
1896: BYU 4, Utah 12
1896: BYU 0, Utah 6
1896: Utah 6, BYU 8
1897: BYU 14, Utah 0
1897: Utah 0, BYU 22
1898: BYU 0, Utah 5
1922: BYU 0, Utah 49
1923: Utah 15, BYU 0
1924: BYU 6, Utah 35
1925: Utah 27, BYU 0
1926: BYU 7, Utah 40
1927: Utah 20, BYU 0
1928: BYU 0, Utah 0
1929: BYU 13, Utah 45
1930: BYU 7, Utah 34
1931: BYU 0, Utah 43
1932: BYU 0, Utah 29
1933: BYU 6, Utah 21
1934: BYU 0, Utah 43
1935: Utah 32, BYU 0
1936: BYU 0, Utah 18
1937: BYU 0, Utah 14
1938: BYU 7, Utah 7
1939: Utah 35, BYU 13
1940: BYU 6, Utah 12
1941: BYU 6, Utah 6
1942: BYU 12, Utah 7
1946: Utah 35, BYU 6
1947: BYU 6, Utah 28
1948: Utah 30, BYU 0

1949: BYU 0, Utah 38
1950: Utah 28, BYU 28
1951: BYU 6, Utah 7
1952: BYU 6, Utah 34
1953: BYU 32, Utah 33
1954: Utah 12, BYU 7
1955: BYU 9, Utah 41
1956: Utah 41, BYU 6
1957: BYU 0, Utah 27
1958: BYU 41, Utah 6
1959: BYU 6, Utah 20
1960: BYU 0, Utah 17
1961: BYU 20, Utah 21
1962: BYU 20, Utah 35
1963: BYU 6, Utah 15
1964: BYU 13, Utah 47
1965: Utah 20, BYU 25
1966: BYU 35, Utah 13
1967: Utah 13, BYU 17
1968: BYU 21, Utah 30
1969: Utah 16, BYU 6
1970: BYU 13, Utah 14
1971: Utah 17, BYU 15
1972: BYU 16, Utah 7
1973: BYU 46, Utah 22
1974: Utah 20, BYU 48
1975: Utah 20, BYU 51
1976: BYU 34, Utah 12
1977: Utah 8, BYU 38
1978: BYU 22, Utah 23
1979: Utah 0, BYU 27
1980: BYU 56, Utah 6
1981: Utah 28, BYU 56
1982: BYU 17, Utah 12
1983: Utah 7, BYU 55
1984: BYU 24, Utah 14
1985: Utah 28, BYU 38
1986: BYU 35, Utah 21

1987: Utah 18, BYU 21
1988: BYU 28, Utah 57
1989: Utah 31, BYU 70
1990: BYU 45, Utah 22
1991: Utah 17, BYU 48
1992: BYU 31, Utah 22
1993: Utah 34, BYU 31
1994: BYU 31, Utah 34
1995: Utah 31, BYU 17
1996: BYU 37, Utah 17
1997: Utah 20, BYU 14
1998: BYU 26, Utah 24
1999: Utah 20, BYU 17
2000: BYU 34, Utah 27
2001: Utah 21, BYU 24
2002: BYU 6, Utah 13
2003: Utah 3, BYU 0
2004: BYU 21, Utah 52
2005: Utah 41, BYU 34
2006: BYU 33, Utah 31
2007: Utah 10, BYU 17
2008: BYU 24, Utah 48
2009: Utah 23, BYU 26
2010: BYU 16, Utah 17
2011: Utah 54, BYU 10
2012: BYU 21, Utah 24
2013: Utah 20, BYU 13

Utah Bowl Game Appearances
1939 Sun Bowl: Utah 26, New Mexico 0
1947 Pineapple Bowl: Hawaii 19, Utah 16
1964 Liberty Bowl: Utah 32, West Virginia 6
1992 Copper Bowl: Washington State 31, Utah 28
1993 Freedom Bowl: USC 28, Utah 21
1994 Freedom Bowl: Utah 16, Arizona 13
1996 Copper Bowl: Wisconsin 38, Utah 10
1999 Las Vegas Bowl: Utah 17, Fresno State 16
2001 Las Vegas Bowl: Utah 10, USC 6

2003 Liberty Bowl: Utah 17, Southern Mississippi 0
2005 Fiesta Bowl: Utah 35, Pittsburgh 7
2005 Emerald Bowl: Utah 38, Georgia Tech 10
2006 Armed Forces Bowl: Utah 25, Tulsa 13
2007 Poinsettia Bowl: Utah 35, Navy 32
2009 Sugar Bowl: Utah 31, Alabama 17
2009 Poinsettia Bowl: Utah 37, California 27
2010 Maaco Bowl: Boise State 26, Utah 3
2011 Sun Bowl: Utah 30, Georgia Tech 27

BYU Bowl Game Appearances
1974 Fiesta Bowl: Oklahoma State 16, BYU 6
1976 Tangerine Bowl: Oklahoma State 49, BYU 21
1978 Holiday Bowl: Navy 23, BYU 16
1979 Holiday Bowl: Indiana 38, BYU 37
1980 Holiday Bowl: BYU 46, Southern Methodist 45
1981 Holiday Bowl: BYU 38, Washington State 36
1982 Holiday Bowl: Ohio State 47, BYU 17
1983 Holiday Bowl: BYU 21, Missouri 17
1984 Holiday Bowl: BYU 24, Michigan 17
1985 Citrus Bowl: Ohio State 10, BYU 7
1986 Freedom Bowl: UCLA 31, BYU 10
1987 All American Bowl: Virginia 22, BYU 16
1988 Freedom Bowl: BYU 20, Colorado 17
1989 Holiday Bowl: Penn State 50, BYU 39
1990 Holiday Bowl: Texas A&M 65, BYU 14
1991 Holiday Bowl: BYU 13, Iowa 13
1992 Aloha Bowl: Kansas 23, BYU 20
1993 Holiday Bowl: Ohio State 28, BYU 21
1994 Copper Bowl: BYU 31, Oklahoma 6
1997 Cotton Bowl: BYU 19, Kansas State 15
1998 Liberty Bowl: Tulane 41, BYU 27
1999 Motor City Bowl: Marshall 21, BYU 3
2001 Liberty Bowl: Louisville 28, BYU 10
2005 Las Vegas Bowl: California 35, BYU 28
2006 Las Vegas Bowl: BYU 38, Oregon 8
2007 Las Vegas Bowl: BYU 17, UCLA 16
2008 Las Vegas Bowl: Arizona 31, BYU 21

2009 Las Vegas Bowl: BYU 44, Oregon State 20
2010 New Mexico Bowl: BYU 52, UTEP 24
2011 Armed Forces Bowl: BYU 24, Tulsa 21
2012 Poinsettia Bowl: BYU 23, San Diego State 6
2013 Fight Hunger Bowl: Washington 31, BYU 16

13

OREGON VS. OREGON STATE: THE CIVIL WAR

The Oregon State team that took flight a month earlier had crashed and burned. It was November 29, 2013. Thanksgiving dinner had been devoured, but the Beavers were set to be the main course for a far superior Oregon that afternoon in Eugene.

That the Ducks would win their sixth straight in what is known as The Civil War seemed a foregone conclusion. The Beavers had lost four in a row, including a 69–27 shellacking at the hands of Washington a week earlier, after a 6–1 start. Their PAC-10 and in-state rivals had been ranked No. 2 in the country before falling to Stanford. An offense led by prolific quarterback Marcus Mariota was averaging nearly 50 points a game. Oregon State had experienced such explosiveness first-hand, having yielded 136 points to the Ducks in its previous five meetings.

Destiny seemed to be taking its course when Oregon jumped to a 14–0 lead in the first quarter. But the expected blowout never materialized. Oregon State forged a 17–17 tie at halftime on a touchdown pass from quarterback Sean Mannion and bolted ahead 35–30 with a mere 1:38 remaining in the game on a 25-yard scoring jaunt on an end around by fleet wide receiver Victor Bolden. Their team was on the verge of a stunning upset.

Mariota, who opened the game with six consecutive completions for 107 yards before missing on six in a row and throwing two interceptions to end the half, had rebounded after intermission. He led his team downfield, but time was running out. With just 29 seconds left, he hit wideout Josh Huff for a 12-yard touchdown that squelched the upset. "Quite frankly, it was a bad throw," Mariota said as his team celebrated its sixth consecutive 10-win season. "Huff made a great catch. I told him, 'Thank you, man, because that would've looked bad if you didn't catch it.'" Huff replied with a wide grin, "It's the best throw he's had this year."[1]

The spirit of that game has lived on for more than a century, from the time tiny Oregon Agricultural College blanked Oregon 16–0 in the inaugural Civil War clash in 1894. That spirit has shown itself not only on the gridiron but off the field as well with the following sampling of clashes:

> **1910:** A verbal spat between fans at a train station following the game motivated the Oregon Public Relations Department to spread rumors of OAC hooliganism, resulting in the suspension of the game the following year.
>
> **1937:** An invasion of the Oregon campus by 2,000 Oregon State fans caused an inevitable skirmish as Ducks fans pelted them with tomatoes and water balloons in the streets of Eugene.
>
> **1954:** A group of Oregon students were captured at a Beavers bonfire rally. The Oregon State revelers shaved their heads and painted them orange and black. One Ducks fan was forced to march through the Oregon State campus wearing a sign that read, "I'm a lame duck."
>
> **1972:** A brawl ensued after an Oregon win in 1972 in Corvallis when Beavers fans tried to prevent their Ducks counterparts from yanking down the goalposts.

The intensity and passion for The Civil War has followed a similar path at both institutions. The school known as Oregon Agricultural College or Oregon State College through 1960 launched its program in 1893 and Oregon followed suit a year later. Both remained stuck in mediocrity before and after the turn of the century. Though the team known at that time as the Webfoots forged a 14–3–4 record against the Beavers through 1916, most of the games were low scoring and close. Oregon State was shut out 14 times in those 21 clashes, including four times in a row from 1908 to 1912.

Both programs changed coaches with great frequency. No Oregon coach lasted longer than two seasons from 1894 to 1912, during which time 16 different coaches roamed its sideline. Oregon State featured a different coach every year from 1893 to 1904 and even played without one in 1898. No coach in either program well beyond that time was able to raise their teams into national prominence for longer than a year or two, leading to decades of average football. It was not until the 1990s that Oregon blossomed into a consistent winner. Oregon State has enjoyed only brief flourishes and forays into the national rankings. The result has been little national recognition for either team for more than than a century. While the finest high school players in the nation flocked to other West Coast schools, such as the University of Southern California (USC) and Stanford, the two Beaver State programs failed to consistently attract the same level of talent.

And though that has detracted from the focus on The Civil War outside Oregon, it has not cooled the intensity of the rivalry within its borders. Even games played between two losing teams have garnered the attention and passion of the students, players, coaches, and fans. And there were plenty of opportunities to prove it. Both teams have suffered through long stretches of inferiority. The most glaring example was a quarter-century period from 1972 to 1997 in which the Beavers compiled a troubling mark of 55–233, including a 16-year stretch in which they won no more than three games in any year. The Ducks never sunk to that depth but did go through five coaches from 1971 to 1979 while managing a mark of 28–71 in nine consecutive losing seasons. The ineptitude of both programs reached a nadir in 1983, when they played to the last scoreless tie (through 2013) in the history of Division I college football, combining for 11 fumbles, five interceptions, and four missed field goals in rain-soaked Eugene. The game has been forever known in Oregon as "The Toilet Bowl."

So what makes Oregon–Oregon State a classic rivalry outside of geographic proximity? It is the difference in what each represents. Oregon State excels in engineering and agriculture. Oregon is a liberal arts university. Oregon State has been known for its straitlaced students, Oregon for its hippies. Corvallis is conservative. Eugene is liberal. Though only 40 miles separate the two schools, they are as distant as the earth is from the moon in terms of life philosophies. All they have had in common until recent years has been poor football and one game to look forward to every season. That is, The Civil War.

And, oh yes, the Platypus Trophy, perhaps the oddest of all awards in college football. The story of that prized possession presented to the winner of the annual battle extends back to 1959, when Oregon undergraduate Warren Spady, inspired by a stuffed platypus, carved up two blocks of wood. He worked around the clock for a month with four mallets and six chisels until the beak resembled a duck and the tail a beaver. His handiwork was used as the spoils until it went missing in the early 1960s. Nobody seemed to know where it went until Spady stumbled upon it in a water polo case on the Oregon campus. It disappeared again for 18 more years until it was located in a closet in 2004. It has since been put to the use for which it was intended.

Both teams enjoyed brief successes long before Spady was born. Oregon State yielded just four points under coach F. S. Norcross in 1906, then followed up that year with perfection in more ways than one in 1907, not only winning all six of its games, but shutting out every foe. The Beavers compiled another unbeaten record in 1914 and outscored their opponents, 489–111 in 1925 and 1926 combined while winning 14 of 17 games. All-Americans, such as halfback Herman Abraham, fullback George "Gap" Powell, and quarterback Howard Maple, dotted their rosters in the first three decades of the 20th century.

Oregon thrived under coaches Hugo Bezdek and Charles A. Huntingon from 1914 to 1922, during which time they managed nine consecutive winning seasons. Bezdek guided his team to the first Pacific Coast Conference title in 1916, after which it put Western football on the map with a shocking 14–0 Rose Bowl defeat of powerful Penn. So confident was Penn coach Bob Folwell of a victory that he invited Bezdek to an open practice and showed him the Quakers' innovative reverse pass play. Folwell must have regretted it when Oregon used it to score its first touchdown, heaved by quarterback Shy Huntington, the school's first All-American. John Parsons set up the only other score of the game with a 42-yard run. Final score: Oregon 14, Penn 0. History had been made. According to a *Los Angeles Times* account, the Webfoots delighted in teaching the long-distance travelers a lesson as they were wrapping up the victory. "Are the city boys getting tired?" they asked derisively. "Came west to teach us football, did you?"[2]

Football historian Maxwell Stiles understood the importance of the Oregon triumph. "[It was] more than just one western victory in an ebb and flow of the intersectional tides," he wrote. "It is a dog-eared leaf in the history book of American football, the first significant victory of a Pacific Coast team over a big-time team admitted to be truly representative of eastern football at its best."[3]

Though the Ducks were generally stronger throughout the years preceding World War II, they did not dominate The Civil War. The strengths of the defenses and weaknesses of the offenses precluded blowouts—it was no wonder that six of the first 27 games played between the two teams finished tied and four of them were scoreless. The winning team tallied 14 points or fewer in all but one game from 1902 to 1924. The Beavers and Ducks traded short runs of dominance. The former won three straight from 1925 to 1927 and four consecutively from 1936 to 1939. The latter lost only once from 1903 to 1916 (with three ties tossed in) and four in a row from 1932 to 1935. Both teams featured several prominent players as the war approached. All-Americans, such as halfback Red Franklin and offensive lineman Ade Schwammel and Eberle Schultz, graced the Oregon State uniform in the 1930s, while Oregon boasted such All-Americans as tackle George Christenson, halfback Mike Mikulak, and end Raymond Morse.

It seemed the only major difference in the programs was continuity at the top. The Ducks went through coaches like they were shoulder pads, employing none more than six years into the mid-1950s. But the Beavers employed only Paul Schissler from 1924 to 1932 and Lon Stiner from 1933 to 1948 (though the program was dormant for two seasons during World War II). Both were only moderately successful, though the latter did coach his team to a 22–6–2 record from 1939 to 1941 powered by Schultz and All-American offensive linemen Vic Sears and Quentin Greenough.

Significant clashes between the two often-struggling programs were rare, but the stars aligned in 1933 before a crowd of 32,183 at Multnomah Stadium in Portland. Both teams arrived unbeaten, though Oregon State owned two ties. The hero of the afternoon was Mikulak, who rushed for 89 yards in a 13–3 victory before taking his talents to the NFL Chicago Cardinals. The Beavers performed well enough in the years before and just after Pearl Harbor forced American involvement in the war that they earned postseason berths in 1940 and 1942, beating

Hawaii in the 1940 Pineapple Bowl and Duke in the 1942 Rose Bowl, which was played in Durham, North Carolina, due to the fear of a Japanese attack in Pasadena.

Both programs ceased due to the war in 1943 and 1944. The mediocrity and inability to string more than one or two strong seasons together that plagued them through most of the prewar years dogged them upon the end of hostilities. Neither team won more than seven games in successive years until Oregon achieved that feat in 1989 and 1990. Its rival did not reach that goal until the turn of the 21st century.

In a way, their insignificance from a national perspective raised the level of importance of every annual Ducks–Beavers clash. The Civil War was generally all that either team and their fan bases had to look forward to. The teams were particularly bad in the late 1940s and early 1950s. A year after future NFL Hall of Fame quarterback Norm Van Brocklin ended his brilliant college career, leading the Ducks to a Cotton Bowl victory over Southern Methodist and 16–5 record overall, Oregon suffered through five consecutive losing seasons from 1949 to 1953, compiling a 13–35–2 mark during that stretch. Meanwhile, Oregon State managed a 10–33 record from 1950 to 1953 to cost coach Kip Taylor his job and usher in the Tommy Prothro era. Prothro brightened the fortunes of the Beavers during his 10-year tenure from 1955 to 1964, guiding the team to three eight-win seasons, just one losing campaign, three bowl appearances, and an overall mark of 63–37–2.

Prothro, who stressed defense, lured such All-American talent as tackles John Witte, Ted Bates, and Rich Koeper; split end Vern Burke; and linebacker Jack O'Billovich. But his prized recruit was quarterback Terry Baker, who racked up 2,276 yards and 24 touchdowns through the air and on the ground combined in 1962 to become the only Heisman Trophy winner in school history. He led the Beavers to seven consecutive wins to end the season, including a 6–0 defeat of Villanova in the Liberty Bowl.

The Ducks were not devoid of achievement during that same period. The school was rewarded for sticking it out with coach Len Casanova after three poor seasons with eight winning records and three bowl berths from 1954 to 1964. Their standouts of that era included quarterback George Shaw and Bob Berry and tackle Steve Barnett, but they boasted an eventual pro superstar in two-time All-American defensive back Mel Renfro, who blossomed into an NFL Hall of Famer with the Dallas Cowboys.

The relative parity of the two programs in the late 1950s and early 1960s resulted in close Civil War battles and evenness in results. The teams split eight games with two ties from 1954 to 1963. Included was one of the biggest upsets in the history of the rivalry in 1959. Oregon entered that game in the running for a Rose Bowl spot and was expected to beat a two-win Oregon State team handily. The Beavers fumbled away their first two possessions and fell behind 7–0 but dominated the rest of the game for a stunning 15–7 victory.

Little could anyone have imagined that the Ducks would win only one battle against the Beavers thereafter through 1971. After all, they boasted in 1970 and 1971 a future NFL Hall of Fame quarterback in Dan Fouts. But Fouts gave little indication of his future greatness while with the Ducks. He threw for 5,995 yards in three seasons as a starter but tossed just 37 touchdown passes and 54 interceptions and was forced to wait until the third round of the 1973 draft to be selected by the San Diego Chargers, with whom he developed into one of the most prolific passers in the history of the sport.

Oregon State embarked on what was then the longest Civil War winning streak of eight games in 1964 despite overall records that were not far superior to its rival. Coach Dee Andros, who replaced the UCLA-bound Prothro in 1965, suffered through nary a losing season from 1965 to 1970 and experienced no defeats to Oregon during that time. Even Lady Luck seemed to be on his side. With the score tied at 7–7 and less than a minute remaining in 1969, Oregon State placekicker Mike Nehl had a field goal blocked by Oregon's Jim Franklin. But the ball hit an official and eventually landed in the eager hands of Beavers tight end Bill Plumeau at the 4-yard line. That allowed Nehl to attempt a 21-yarder, which he booted through the uprights to clinch his team's sixth straight defeat of the Ducks.

That success against the Ducks—and the rest of the PAC-10— would end ingloriously in the mid-1970s. The Beavers then stumbled through one of the worst eras in the history of major college football. Their coaches attempted in vain to stop the flood of defeats. Victories over Oregon in 1973 and 1974 were more a reflection of the Ducks' wretchedness in those seasons because neither team won more than three games in either of those years. The Ducks thereafter remained the dominant team in The Civil War. They did not again lose to the Beavers until 1988—only the scoreless, mistake-filled tie in 1983 prevented them from winning 13 in a row. Oregon forged a record of 29–9–1 against its archrival from 1975 to 2013.

In fact, Oregon State was pretty much the only team the Ducks defeated consistently until the mid-1990s. The Beavers were shackled with losing records in all but one season from 1971 to 1982. They reached the level of stunning mediocrity under coach Rich Brooks in the 1980s, finishing with records within one game of .500 in all but two seasons from 1983 to 1993 despite such All-American talent as wide receiver Lew Barnes and cornerback Chris Oldham, as well as future Minnesota Vikings star guard and NFL Hall of Famer Gary Zimmerman.

The result of the foundering of both programs was that the annual Civil War spoils generally earned by the Ducks was little more than a moral victory. Not that the Beavers didn't gain occasional satisfaction. They managed to end a 13-game winless streak against Oregon in 1988 and avenge a 44–0 defeat from the year before—the largest margin in the history of The Civil War—by scoring two fourth-quarter touchdowns in a 21–10 victory. And in 1991, the winless Beavers actually practiced carrying their seniors off the field in triumph as a motivational tactic, then made that work worthwhile by upsetting the Ducks, 14–3, before hoisting their seniors on their shoulders in real celebration.

The end of the Brooks era that ushered in the promotion of offensive coordinator Mike Bellotti as head coach launched an era in which the Ducks soared to greatness. They gave Brooks a fine parting gift in 1994 by winning the PAC-10 title with a 9–4 mark before falling in the Rose Bowl and finishing the season ranked No. 11 in the country. They emerged as a perennial bowl participant under Bellotti, but it wasn't until the turn of the century that they blossomed into a national championship contender. Coincidentally, the Beavers finally awoke from their slumber simultaneously under new coach Dennis Erickson, who had spent his previous four seasons holding down the same post with the NFL Seattle Seahawks.

It all came together for both teams in 2000. The explosive Beavers, who racked up 5,266 passing yards that season and boasted a running back in Ken Simonton that rushed for 1,559 yards, featured two future star receivers with the NFL Cincinnati Bengals in brash Chad Johnson and T. J. Houshmandzadeh. They entered The Civil War fray with a 9–1 record, defeats over nationally ranked USC and UCLA, and a No. 8 national ranking. The fifth-ranked Ducks had notched victories over three ranked opponents, including one over a Washington team that had provided the Beavers with their lone loss, and were led by eventual Detroit Lions standout quarterback Joey Harrington.

Both teams needed a win to keep alive their Rose Bowl hopes. The heroes of the game proved to be Oregon State defensive back Jake Cookus, who recorded three of his team's five interceptions of Harrington. And, surprisingly, it was not Johnson or Houshmandzadeh assuming that role offensively for the Beavers. It was receiving mate Robert Prescott, who caught six passes for 109 yards and two touchdowns in a 23–13 victory.

Oregon State was denied a Rose Bowl berth in favor of Washington, but it did complete its finest season ever with a 41–9 blasting of Notre Dame in the Fiesta Bowl that earned them the No. 5 spot in the final national rankings. The hero was diminutive walk-on quarterback Jonathan Smith, who had been mistaken for the team manager when Erickson first saw him. Smith buried the Fighting Irish under the weight of 305 yards passing and three touchdowns. Beavers center Chris Gibson spoke years later about changing the culture of losing at his school and turning the attention in the state away from the Ducks. "The fact that we all bought into something together and we all came together being from everywhere and the different aspect of personalities that we had on the team, everyone was able to buy in and create success," he said. "Coach Erickson and his staff, I think he was able to get the maximum potential out of all those players because most weren't highly recruited from other teams."[4]

The Ducks not only avenged their defeat to the Beavers in 2001 with a 17–14 victory that was secured by a late rally and Keenan Howry punt return for a touchdown, but they battled for a national championship for the first time in school history. Only an upset loss to Stanford prevented them from snagging the title. They defeated nationally ranked Wisconsin, Washington State, and UCLA en route to a PAC-10 crown and Fiesta Bowl berth against third-ranked Colorado. The result was a 38–16 thrashing of the Buffaloes in which Harrington threw for 350 yards and four touchdowns, landing Oregon at No. 2 in the country. It was considered at the time the greatest victory in school history. "Not only was it the biggest win, but it was on the biggest stage and we did it in one of the most emphatic manners that a Duck team has ever played," Harrington said. "We made a statement today."[5]

The Ducks would make many more statements later in the decade under Bellotti, who was promoted to athletic director in 2009, and innovative replacement Chip Kelly. They continued to attract top athletes, including eventual Baltimore Ravens star nose tackle Haloti Ngata, who keyed a 2005 season in which they won 10 of 11 regular-season games before falling in the Holiday Bowl. But it was under Kelly that they blossomed into a perennial PAC-10 and PAC-12 champion and national title contender.

Kelly installed a zone read offensive scheme that confused defenses and transformed the Ducks into offensive juggernauts. NFL analyst and former Super Bowl–winning coach Jon Gruden explained the confusion the Kelly offense brought to opposing defenses. "They don't huddle," he said before the Ducks were to play Ohio State in the 2010 Rose Bowl. "I don't know where their pitch guy comes from. One time he came from underneath the Astroturf and showed up as the pitch guy. You don't know if they'll come out with an unbalanced line. You don't even know what uniform they're going to wear."[6]

The guys wearing Oregon uniforms were unstoppable on offense, particularly in 2010, when they steamrolled to a 12–0 record and led the nation at 47 points a game. Most impressive was the ability of Kelly to install such an explosive offense without premier skill position talent. The Ducks thrashed nationally ranked Stanford and USC by three touchdowns each, catapulted to No. 1 in the nation in mid-October, and won The Civil War to earn their first BCS National Championship Game berth. That exciting clash against powerful Auburn reached a crescendo when Oregon quarterback Darron Thomas threw a two-yard touchdown pass to running back LaMichael James with 2:33 remaining and added a two-point conversion strike to Jeff Maehl to forge a 19–19 tie. But, alas, the Tigers drove downfield against what had been a mediocre Ducks defense all season for the game-winning field goal. Oregon had lost its first shot at a national championship.

While the Ducks were flying high, the Beavers were also thriving under coach Mike Riley, who took over for Erickson in 2003. Though his teams could not soar to a conference crown or national title consideration, they did achieve winning records in six of seven seasons from

2003 to 2009 and Civil War triumphs in 2006 and 2007 before losing the next six to Oregon. Riley coached or recruited and coached such future NFL standouts as defensive back Brandon Browner and running backs Steven Jackson and Jacquizz Rodgers and guided his team to five bowl victories from 2003 to 2008 and another in 2013.

But it was the Ducks that earned most of the attention in the Beaver State. They ran their streak of league titles to four in 2012 after winning the Rose Bowl and placing fourth in the country a year earlier. They averaged nearly 50 points a game in 2012 while also grooming two eventual NFL star defenders in lineman Dion Jordan and linebacker Kiko Alonzo but were once again victimized by one defeat that killed their national championship dreams, this time to Stanford in the regular season.

Indeed, neither Oregon nor Oregon State had snagged a national title through 2013. But their emergence as top college programs after generations of mediocrity must be considered an achievement. And when The Civil War comes around, it doesn't really matter. Though success has spoiled some Oregon fans whose priorities have been swayed by a taste of title contention, pride has generally proven more important than record in the Beaver State for many years. Even when the only prize has been the rather silly Platypus Trophy.

Fact Box (through 2013)
   Nickname: The Civil War
   Trophy: The Platypus Trophy
   Total meetings: 117
   Series record: Oregon leads, 61–46–10
   First meeting: 1894 (Oregon Agricultural College 16, Oregon 0)
   Largest margin of victory: Oregon, 1895 (Oregon 44, Oregon Agricultural College 0); 1987 (Oregon 44, Oregon State 0)
   Longest winning streak: Oregon, 8 (1975–1982); Oregon State, 8 (1964–1971)

Game Results (home team listed second unless at a neutral site)
   1894: Oregon 0, Oregon State 16
   1895: Oregon State 0, Oregon 44
   1896: Oregon State 0, Oregon 2
   1896: Oregon 12, Oregon State 8

1897: Oregon State 26, Oregon 8

1898: Oregon 38, Oregon State 0

1899: Oregon State 0, Oregon 38

1902: Oregon 0, Oregon State 0

1903: Oregon State 0, Oregon 5

1904: Oregon 6, Oregon State 5

1905: Oregon State 0, Oregon 6

1906: Oregon 0, Oregon State 0

1907: Oregon State 4, Oregon 0

1908: Oregon 8, Oregon State 0

1909: Oregon State 0, Oregon 12

1910: Oregon 12, Oregon State 0

1912: Oregon 3, Oregon State 0

1913: Oregon State 10, Oregon 10

1914: Oregon 3, Oregon State 3

1915: Oregon State 0, Oregon 9

1916: Oregon 27, Oregon State 0

1917: Oregon State 14, Oregon 7

1918: Oregon 13, Oregon State 6

1919: Oregon State 0, Oregon 9

1920: Oregon 0, Oregon State 0

1921: Oregon State 0, Oregon 0

1922: Oregon 10, Oregon State 0

1923: Oregon State 6, Oregon 0

1924: Oregon 7, Oregon State 3

1925: Oregon State 24, Oregon 13

1926: Oregon 0, Oregon State 16

1927: Oregon State 21, Oregon 7

1928: Oregon 12, Oregon State 0

1929: Oregon State 0, Oregon 16

1930: Oregon 0, Oregon State 15

1931: Oregon State 0, Oregon 0

1932: Oregon 12, Oregon State 6

1933: Oregon 13, Oregon State 3

1934: Oregon 9, Oregon State 6

1935: Oregon State 0, Oregon 13

1936: Oregon 0, Oregon State 18

1937: Oregon State 14, Oregon 0

1938: Oregon State 14, Oregon 0
1939: Oregon State 19, Oregon 14
1940: Oregon 20, Oregon State 0
1941: Oregon State 12, Oregon 7
1942: Oregon State 39, Oregon 2
1945: Oregon 6, Oregon State 19
1945: Oregon State 13, Oregon 12
1946: Oregon State 13, Oregon 0
1947: Oregon 14, Oregon State 6
1948: Oregon State 0, Oregon 10
1949: Oregon State 20, Oregon 10
1950: Oregon State 14, Oregon 2
1951: Oregon State 14, Oregon 7
1952: Oregon State 22, Oregon 10
1953: Oregon State 7, Oregon 0
1954: Oregon 33, Oregon State 14
1955: Oregon State 0, Oregon 28
1956: Oregon 14, Oregon State 14
1957: Oregon State 10, Oregon 7
1958: Oregon 20, Oregon State 0
1959: Oregon State 15, Oregon 7
1960: Oregon 14, Oregon State 14
1961: Oregon State 6, Oregon 2
1962: Oregon 7, Oregon State 20
1963: Oregon State 14, Oregon 31
1964: Oregon 6, Oregon State 7
1965: Oregon State 19, Oregon 14
1966: Oregon State 20, Oregon 15
1967: Oregon 0, Oregon State 14
1968: Oregon State 41, Oregon 19
1969: Oregon 7, Oregon State 10
1970: Oregon State 24, Oregon 9
1971: Oregon 29, Oregon State 30
1972: Oregon State 3, Oregon 30
1973: Oregon 14, Oregon State 17
1974: Oregon State 35, Oregon 14
1975: Oregon 14, Oregon State 7
1976: Oregon State 14, Oregon 23

1977: Oregon 28, Oregon State 16
1978: Oregon State 3, Oregon 24
1979: Oregon 24, Oregon State 3
1980: Oregon State 21, Oregon 40
1981: Oregon 47, Oregon State 17
1982: Oregon State 6, Oregon 7
1983: Oregon 0, Oregon State 0
1984: Oregon State 6, Oregon 31
1985: Oregon 34, Oregon State 13
1986: Oregon State 28, Oregon 49
1987: Oregon 44, Oregon State 0
1988: Oregon State 21, Oregon 10
1989: Oregon 30, Oregon State 21
1990: Oregon State 3, Oregon 6
1991: Oregon 3, Oregon State 14
1992: Oregon State 0, Oregon 7
1993: Oregon 12, Oregon State 15
1994: Oregon State 13, Oregon 17
1995: Oregon 12, Oregon State 10
1996: Oregon State 13, Oregon 49
1997: Oregon 48, Oregon State 30
1998: Oregon State 44, Oregon 41
1999: Oregon 25, Oregon State 14
2000: Oregon State 23, Oregon 13
2001: Oregon 17, Oregon State 14
2002: Oregon State 45, Oregon 24
2003: Oregon 34, Oregon State 20
2004: Oregon State 50, Oregon 21
2005: Oregon 56, Oregon State 14
2006: Oregon State 30, Oregon 28
2007: Oregon 31, Oregon State 38
2008: Oregon State 38, Oregon 65
2009: Oregon 37, Oregon State 33
2010: Oregon State 20, Oregon 37
2011: Oregon 49, Oregon State 21
2012: Oregon State 24, Oregon 48
2013: Oregon 36, Oregon State 35

Oregon Bowl Game Appearances
1917 Rose Bowl: Oregon 14, Penn 0
1920 Rose Bowl: Harvard 7, Oregon 6
1949 Cotton Bowl: Southern Methodist 21, Oregon 13
1958 Rose Bowl: Ohio State 10, Oregon 7
1960 Liberty Bowl: Penn State 41, Oregon 12
1963 Sun Bowl: Oregon 21, Southern Methodist 14
1989 Independence Bowl: Oregon 27, Tulsa 24
1990 Freedom Bowl: Colorado State 32, Oregon 31
1992 Independence Bowl: Wake Forest 39, Oregon 35
1995 Rose Bowl: Penn State 38, Oregon 20
1996 Cotton Bowl: Colorado 36, Oregon 6
1997 Las Vegas Bowl: Oregon 41, Air Force 13
1998 Aloha Bowl: Colorado 51, Oregon 43
1999 Sun Bowl: Oregon 24, Minnesota 20
2000 Holiday Bowl: Oregon 35, Texas 30
2001 Fiesta Bowl: Oregon 38, Colorado 16
2002 Seattle Bowl: Wake Forest 38, Oregon 17
2003 Sun Bowl: Minnesota 31, Oregon 30
2005 Holiday Bowl: Oklahoma 17, Oregon 14
2006 Las Vegas Bowl: Brigham Young 38, Oregon 8
2007 Sun Bowl: Oregon 56, South Florida 21
2008 Holiday Bowl: Oklahoma State 42, Oregon 31
2010 Rose Bowl: Ohio State 26, Oregon 17
2011 BCS National Championship: Auburn 22, Oregon State 19
2012 Rose Bowl: Oregon 45, Wisconsin 38
2013 Fiesta Bowl: Oregon 35, Kansas State 17
2013 Alamo Bowl: Oregon 30, Texas 7

Oregon State Bowl Game Appearances
1940 Pineapple Bowl: Oregon State 39, Hawaii 6
1942 Rose Bowl: Oregon State 20, Duke 16
1949 Pineapple Bowl: Oregon State 47, Hawaii 27
1957 Rose Bowl: Iowa 35, Oregon State 19
1962 Liberty Bowl: Oregon State 6, Villanova 0
1965 Rose Bowl: Michigan 34, Oregon State 7
1999 Oahu Bowl: Hawaii 23, Oregon State 17
2001 Fiesta Bowl: Oregon State 41, Notre Dame 9

2002 Insight Bowl: Pittsburgh 38, Oregon State 13
2003 Las Vegas Bowl: Oregon State 55, New Mexico 14
2004 Insight Bowl: Oregon State 38, Notre Dame 21
2006 Sun Bowl: Oregon State 39, Missouri 38
2007 Emerald Bowl: Oregon State 21, Maryland 14
2008 Sun Bowl: Oregon State 3, Pittsburgh 0
2009 Maaco Bowl: Brigham Young 44, Oregon State 20
2012 Alamo Bowl: Texas 31, Oregon State 27
2013 Hawaii Bowl: Oregon State 38, Boise State 23

14

CLEMSON VS. SOUTH CAROLINA: THE PALMETTO BOWL

All indications were that South Carolina was doomed in their own stadium. They trailed Clemson, 24–0, in the third quarter. The Tigers were enjoying their finest season in nearly two decades and were ranked 15th in the nation. And the Gamecocks had proven once again in 1977 to be their typical mediocre selves. Their quarterback was Ron Bass, whose eventual fame as a main component in the high school team glorified in the film *Remember the Titans* far surpassed his production on the college gridiron. Their chance for a victory was about as great as Richard Nixon regaining the presidency.

But suddenly, stunningly, they launched a comeback for the ages. It began with a touchdown by running back Spencer Clark and two more by backfield mate Steve Dorsey. And when Bass fired a 40-yard scoring strike to favorite target Phillip Logan, they boasted a 27–24 lead against their stunned rival. They were setting the Tigers up to be turkeys five days before Thanksgiving.

Clemson battled back. Quarterback Steve Fuller fired a 26-yard pass to Rick Weddington and another for 18 yards to future San Francisco 49ers All-Pro Dwight Clark. The ball rested on the South Carolina 20-yard line with 49 seconds remaining in the game. Fuller eyed premier wideout Jerry Butler, whose black skin a decade earlier would have precluded him from wearing a Tigers uniform. He faked a break inside and turned left toward the corner of the end zone. Noticing that Fuller was being chased by Gamecocks defenders, he rushed back toward him.

Fuller heaved the ball to avoid what would have been a devastating sack. Two defensive backs were draped all over Butler, who leaped, reached toward the sky, snagged the ball, fell to the ground, and rolled over. Touchdown! Final score: Clemson 31, South Carolina 27. "I can still see that ball," Fuller later recalled. "It kind of looked white against the black sky. I didn't think it had a chance."[1]

The Tigers have generally had more than a chance to win The Palmetto Bowl. Periods of South Carolina dominance have been limited to the post–World War II years and the most recent era in the second decade of the 21st century. Clemson has won about 60 percent of all the battles in the intense interstate rivalry.

That rivalry was launched on November 12, 1896. The game was played on a Thursday morning to coincide with the South Carolina State Fair, and the tradition stuck. The date of future battles became known as Big Thursday until 1960, when the teams joined the rest of the college football world and began playing on Saturdays. The Gamecocks emerged with a 12–6 victory in 1896, but their success was short lived.

So was any camaraderie between the two teams and their fans. Clemson won the next four Palmetto Bowl clashes, pitching shutouts in the last three. An article in the *State* preached nothing more than healthy rooting as it described the scene at the county fair before the 1902 Palmetto Bowl:

> The friends and alumni of the respective colleges flock to the fair grounds on the day of the great game, and the college colors of each institution are very much in evidence on the day of the game. The garnet and black and the purple and orange cause no little comment when seen on the jackets of the fair ones who seem to take as much interest in the game as anyone else. The college girl, the society girl—all the girls—turn out in full force on Thursday, and very few are seen without the college colors of one of their rivals.[2]

When a South Carolina team that had won its first three games by a combined score of 98–0 used two Guy Gunter touchdowns to end their losing streak against a Tigers team coached by early football legend John Heisman, after whom the Heisman Trophy is named, tempers boiled over in the streets of Columbia. They were fueled by a store owner on Main Street that hung on his window a picture of a gamecock standing over a beaten tiger. Angered Clemson students reacted by arming themselves with brass knuckles and other weapons and marching to the center of town, where South Carolina students had barricaded themselves. Sporadic fighting was broken up by police, but the incident motivated the schools to end the rivalry. It would not be renewed until 1909 but has been played annually ever since.

There were many years thereafter in which the Gamecocks might have wished The Palmetto Ban had become permanent. The Tigers proved so dominant that their rivals were often fortunate to score. The 1902 victory was the only game of the seven played between 1898 and 1911 in which they managed to visit the end zone. And they fared little better as the 20th century marched on. After scoring 22 unanswered points in a defeat of Clemson in 1912, they managed just 25 points in their next seven games, which included six losses and a scoreless tie in which, it was later learned, nonroster ringers paid by the South Carolina alumni had suited up and played for the Gamecocks.

That domination comes as little surprise when examining the early records of the two programs. Though the Tigers were not tearing up the college football world, they did enjoy comparative success. They suffered through no losing seasons from 1907 and won 12 of 13 games combined under Heisman in 1900 and 1902 to capture Southern Intercollegiate Athletic Association championships. Heisman had already established himself as one of the great innovators of college football, though his invention of the forward pass would have to wait until he left Clemson for Georgia Tech. He authored a paper titled "Football at Clemson" in the 1902–1903 Clemson yearbook that stressed a

> greater demand than ever for scientifica and original coaches—coaches who can devise plays that will gain ground in spite of the best and most up-to-date knowledge of the principles of defense.

> At Clemson College we have a style of football play radically different than any other on earth. Its notoriety and the fear and the admiration of it have spread throughout the length and breadth of the entire Southern world of football and even further. There is not a single offensive play used that was ever learned from any other college, nor are the defensive formations any less different than those of other teams.[3]

Heisman, however, stuck around for just four years. Though their coaches came and went quickly—none lasted more than four years into the 1930s—their overall record stood at a fine 93–63–13 through 1919. The Gamecocks boasted a mark of 77–83–10 through that same season.

The tide turned briefly after South Carolina hired veteran coach Sol Metzger. The son of a Confederate captain in the Civil War, Metzger was a bit of a college football mercenary. He had toiled at six different schools before turning the Gamecocks around in 1920, sporting a winning record after the team had stumbled to a 1–7–1 record the year before. Metzger guided the program to four winning marks in five seasons and turned around their fortunes in The Palmetto Bowl. South Carolina won five of seven against Clemson from 1920 to 1926 before reverting to punching bag status through the prewar years. Only a three-game winning streak in the infancy of the Great Depression from 1931 to 1933 prevented the Gamecocks from losing 14 in a row to their archrivals.

It was in the latter years of the 1930s that the Tigers had clawed their way into national prominence behind future College Football Hall of Fame coach Jess Neely and halfback Banks McFadden, who was also an All-American basketball player. McFadden propelled Clemson to a 9–1 record in 1939 as a defensive back, running back, and punter. He batted down four passes in the second half of a 6–3 defeat of Boston College in the Cotton Bowl to cap his brilliant season. His 22 punts of at least 50 yards that year still stand as a school record. McFadden was selected with the fourth overall pick in the NFL draft and led the NFL in yards per carry in his only professional season.

McFadden's career was cut short by World War II, but the same could not be said about The Palmetto Bowl. The two teams continued to clash despite the loss of talent to the battles overseas as South Carolina began a period in which it exacted revenge for the all beatings it had endured over the years. The Gamecocks lost just twice to the Tigers from 1943 to 1954 as they gained continuity under longtime coach Rex Enright, who recruited such All-Americans as offensive linemen Bryant Meeks, Leon Cunningham, and Frank Mincevich; running back Steve Wadiak; defensive back Norris Mullis; and end Clyde Bennett.

Their dominance of Clemson was not a reflection of superior talent, however. South Carolina won no more than seven games in any season during that period. The only two noteworthy years during that era were achieved by the Tigers, who finished just 11th in the national rankings in 1948 despite an 11–0 record and defeat of Missouri in the Gator Bowl and missed out on a perfect season two years later on a 14–14 tie in The Palmetto Bowl. Just as the Gamecocks had found their coaching savior in Enright, the Tigers had replaced the popular and successful Neely with Frank Howard, who would emerge as their most legendary leader. Howard lured in many of the premier players in the history of the program, the earliest of which were tailback Bobby Gage and safety Jackie Calvert. The former was a three-way threat as a runner, passer, and defender who still ranks near the top in school history in total career yards and interceptions. The latter was an equally adept quarterback and safety who keyed a 1951 Orange Bowl victory over the University of Miami that catapulted Clemson into what was then an all-time-best No. 10 ranking in the national polls.

The 1950 tie that ruined Clemson's perfect season was not the most memorable Palmetto Bowl in the decade following World War II. Two others were more so, though they could be better termed as "notorious" for fan behavior. The 1946 clash was marred by a near riot instigated by two New York gangsters who printed counterfeit tickets to the game. Fans from both sides disallowed into the stadium became violent. They tore down fences and, joined by fans from the stands, stormed the field. One Clemson fan strangled a live rooster at midfield during halftime. Only the efforts of U.S. secretary of state James Byrnes and South Carolina senator Strom Thurmond to calm the crowd allowed the teams to complete the game, won by South Carolina.

George Bennett, a future Clemson cheerleader and fund-raiser, recalled the painful incident with clarity. He believed strongly that the violence was a reflection of the indoctrination to it received by those who had recently returned from battles in World War II. "It was the biggest fight I've ever seen in my life," he said. "The stands just erupted. It was all-out blood until one of the bands struck up the National Anthem. You've got to understand. A lot of these guys had just come back from war. They were trained to kill people. It was not uncommon to go to that game in '46, '47 and '48 and see people fighting all over the place. That was kind of the sideshow."[4]

A quite different scenario threated The Palmetto Bowl in 1952, when the Southern Conference ordered Clemson to limit its league schedule to Maryland as punishment for both schools accepting bowl bids against league mandates. But the South Carolina General Assembly usurped power in the matter, passing a resolution ordering the game between the two schools within its borders to continue their rivalry. The result was yet another victory for the Gamecocks.

The 1950s and 1960s marked an era of parity in the rivalry. The teams traded short winning streaks, but the games were generally close. In fact, only three games from 1952 to 1973 were decided by more than 14 points as both teams won eleven times. But aside from a five-season run by the Tigers in the late 1950s during which they compiled a 38–13 record and earned three bowl bids behind such talent as prolific running back Joel Wells and All-American tackle Lou Cordileone, neither team earned much national attention.

Rather, they gained more notoriety for the ingenuity of their fans. That creativity reached a peak in 1961 when members of the South Carolina fraternity Sigma Nu raced onto the field a few minutes before the Clemson players arrived for pregame warm-ups. The frat brothers jumped around and cheered in football uniforms resembling those worn by the Tigers, prompting the Clemson band to start playing their traditional "Tiger Rag." When the band struck up the tune, the pranksters began falling down as they faked their calisthenics, dropped passes in phony drills, and generally acted like gridiron clowns. Clemson fans finally realized they had been duped and some ran onto the field to confront the Sigma Nu members, but security stopped them before a fight could break out. The South Carolina frat boys also acquired a sickly cow they had planned to present as the "Clemson Homecoming Queen" at halftime, but old Bessie died on the way to the stadium. The final triumph for South Carolina came on the field, courtesy of a 21–14 victory.

Both teams joined the Atlantic Coast Conference in 1953. Clemson enjoyed more success against league foes. The Tigers won three consecutive ACC championships from 1965 to 1967, yet never finished with a better overall record than 6–4 during that period. The Gamecocks, on the other hand, fared better against conference competition until 1969, when they swept through the ACC unbeaten for their first crown behind premier fullback Warren Muir, yet lost four of five nonleague games.

On-field mediocrity remained a sad commentary of Palmetto State football through the first half of the 1970s. Not much was expected to change when Clemson promoted defensive coordinator Charley Pell to head coach in 1977. But after securing the job in December 1976, an incident he spoke about a quarter century later motivated him to transform the Tigers into an ACC power. "We went to an all-conference dinner at Greenville," he recalled. "And we're sitting there in that banquet and Clemson did not have a single player selected to the first or second team for all-conference in the ACC. . . . I was embarrassed and I was mad. I fumed all the way back to Clemson. . . . Clemson had zero. None. I was so angry and I wasn't angry at anybody. I was just fuming."[5]

Pell was determined to turn the program around—and he did. The Tigers rebounded from a 3–6–2 season to compile an 8–3–1 mark in his first season and an 11–1 record the following year behind Butler, Fuller, and fellow All-Americans, such as future NFL star guard Jeff Bostic (who won three Super Bowl rings as a member of the Washington Redskins) and defensive tackle Joe Stuckey (who won two Super Bowl rings as a member of the San Francisco 49ers). There was just one problem: Pell recruited illegally. Those revelations did not emerge until after Pell announced following the 1978 regular season that he was leaving to take an identical position at the University of Florida. Irked Clemson officials refused to allow him to coach the Gator Bowl that year. The Tigers' victory in that game was obscured by the notorious incident in which Woody Hayes punched Clemson defensive back Charlie Bauman after his interception, effectively ending the career of the legendary Ohio State coach.

Offensive line coach Danny Ford, who assumed the reins upon the departure of Pell, did something no Clemson coach could accomplish before or after—he won a national championship in 1981. And he did it with a defensive prowess that Pell instilled in the program. The Tigers that season boasted the premier defense in the country, yielding a mere 8.8 points a game. Future NFL standouts, such as free safety Terry Kinard, linebacker Jeff Davis, and defensive tackle William "Refrigerator" Perry, anchored a defense that held fourth-ranked Georgia to three points and nine of 12 opponents to 10 points or less. The Tigers capped their championship run with a 22–15 defeat of Nebraska in the Orange Bowl.

None of those defenders, however, was the premier player in The Palmetto Bowl in the early 1980s. That distinction belonged to South Carolina running back George Rogers, the only player at either school to win a Heisman Trophy. Rogers shattered a Gamecocks career mark by rushing for 5,091 yards and led the nation with 1,781 in earning the award in 1980. But, alas, he could not alone drag South Carolina out of the morass of mediocrity that had plagued its program since its inception.

He also could not prevent the Tigers from maintaining a domination of The Palmetto Bowl they reestablished in the late 1970s. They won seven of eight against the Gamecocks from 1976 to 1983. The Gamecocks finally and briefly ended that period of supremacy in 1984 when they steamrolled to the first 10-win season in program history. That elusive number would not have been reached without a dramatic comeback from a 21–3 deficit against their archrival. Quarterback Mike Hold completed it by engineering an 86-yard drive that gave his team a 22–21 victory. Their season-ending ranking of 11th in the country was the best in program history, but they lost an opportunity to soar higher with a Gator Bowl defeat to Oklahoma State.

They also lost an opportunity to run with their momentum, both in The Palmetto Bowl and in the national consciousness. South Carolina reverted to mediocrity in the mid-1980s and, despite a few strong seasons, remained an afterthought as an independent and as a member of the Southeastern Conference until coach Lou Holtz came to the rescue around the turn of the century.

Such was not the case with Clemson, which remained a national power throughout Ford's tenure and beyond. They won successive ACC titles from 1986 to 1988 and again in 1991 with replacement Ken Hatfield at the helm. They finished in the top 18 in the national rankings every year from 1986 to 1991 behind a wide array of All-American talent led by such future NFL standouts as linebacker Willie Kirkland, cornerback Donnell Woolford, and defensive tackle Michael Dean Perry. Their four-game winning streak against the Gamecocks from 1988 to 1991 was as thorough as any in The Palmetto Bowl since Clemson's dominant stretch in the mid-1930s.

In the midst of a two-generation period in which South Carolina would not win successive games against Clemson from 1971 to 2008, it was hard to imagine matters taking a downward turn from there. But indeed they did in the late 1990s when the Tigers again battered an even weaker Gamecocks team four straight. South Carolina won just once in 1998 and 1999 combined, the second year marking the beginning of the Holtz era and its first winless season since it lost all three of its games in 1897. But Holtz, who had been plucked from Notre Dame and was on the last leg of a notable coaching career, had yet to show his worth to the Gamecocks as a recruiter. He transformed his 0–11 squad into a winner in just one year, guiding them to an 8–4 record in 2000 and a 9–3 mark in 2001, beating powerful Ohio State in bowl games to cap both seasons.

His coaching talents, however, only helped to put a temporary halt to Clemson supremacy in The Palmetto Bowl in a 20–15 victory in 2001, which was followed by four more Tigers triumphs. The Gamecocks nearly snagged a win in 2000, but what became known as "The Catch II" prevented it. They led 14–13 when Clemson quarterback Woody Dantzler found wide receiver Rod Gardner for a 50-yard strike to the Carolina 8-yard line with 10 seconds remaining. The Gamecocks and their fans contended that Gardner pushed off on the play, but their opponents claimed the contact was incidental. Either way, it was followed by a game-winning field goal by Clemson placekicker Aaron Hunt.

Greater controversy erupted four years later in a meaningless Palmetto Bowl between two ordinary teams, the last game Holtz would ever coach. Hostilities began before the game when South Carolina players congregating in the end zone and Clemson players emerging from the tunnel scuffled briefly. Late in the game, Gamecocks quarterback Syvelle Newton took a hard shot to the head and Tigers players prevented him from rising off the ground. A brawl ensued. The most enduring and disturbing image was Clemson's Yusef Kelly kicking helmetless foe Woodley Telfort in the head. Kelly then picked up his victim's helmet and paraded it around the end zone before tossing it into the student section at Memorial Stadium. He later told reporters after state troopers had finally left the field and his team had concluded its 29–7 victory that Clemson fans should be proud of his actions. "I know the die-hard Clemson fans, they are going to love it," he said. "I think I kind of left an impression. They'll have something to remember me by."[6] Kelly later expressed regret and apologized for his actions.

That battle intensified the rivalry and an upgrade in talent as both schools launched a rare period of perennial winners competing in The Palmetto Bowl. Neither team threatened to capture a national championship as the new century gathered steam, but Clemson and South

Carolina enjoyed nothing but winning seasons every year from 2004 to 2013. Established coach Steve Spurrier assumed control of the Gamecocks in 2005 and recruited top-level athletes, such as defensive backs Stephon Gilmore and Antonio Allen, wide receiver Alshon Jeffery, and defensive ends Melvin Ingram and Jadeveon Clowney, who was regarded as the most talented defensive player in the nation and perhaps ever to grace a South Carolina uniform.

Clowney proved instrumental in extending the finest run in Gamecocks football history. The team finished 11–2 in three straight years from 2011 to 2013. They finished among the top 10 teams in the country all three seasons, soaring to No. 4 in the last of them after a bowl defeat of Wisconsin. Equally satisfying for their fans was their shedding of punching bag status to the Tigers, whom they tamed to the tune of five consecutive victories from 2009 to 2013, marking the longest winning streak ever against their archrivals.

Not bad considering Clemson boasted fine teams of its own during that time, including division champions in 2009, 2011, and 2012 and an 11–2 overall mark in 2013. Like their counterparts, the Tigers produced future NFL stars standouts during that era, including running back C. J. Spiller and defensive end Da'Quan Bowers.

But then, the Tigers had some payback coming after having proven their mastery over the Gamecocks through most of Palmetto Bowl history.

Fact Box (through 2013)
>   **Nickname:** The Palmetto Bowl
>   **Trophy:** Hardee's Trophy
>   **Total meetings:** 111
>   **Series record:** Clemson leads, 65–42–4
>   **First meeting:** 1896 (South Carolina 12, Clemson 6)
>   **Largest margin of victory:** Clemson, 1900 (Clemson 51, South Carolina 0)
>   **Longest winning streak:** Clemson, 7 (1934–1940)

Game Results (home team listed second unless at a neutral site)
>   1896: Clemson 6, South Carolina 12
>   1897: Clemson 20, South Carolina 6
>   1898: Clemson 24, South Carolina 0

1899: Clemson 34, South Carolina 0
1900: Clemson 51, South Carolina 0
1902: Clemson 6, South Carolina 12
1909: Clemson 6, South Carolina 0
1910: Clemson 24, South Carolina 0
1911: Clemson 27, South Carolina 0
1912: Clemson 7, South Carolina 22
1913: Clemson 32, South Carolina 0
1914: Clemson 29, South Carolina 6
1915: Clemson 0, South Carolina 0
1916: Clemson 27, South Carolina 0
1917: Clemson 21, South Carolina 13
1918: Clemson 39, South Carolina 0
1919: Clemson 19, South Carolina 6
1920: Clemson 0, South Carolina 3
1921: Clemson 0, South Carolina 21
1922: Clemson 3, South Carolina 0
1923: Clemson 7, South Carolina 6
1924: Clemson 0, South Carolina 3
1925: Clemson 7, South Carolina 33
1926: Clemson 0, South Carolina 24
1927: Clemson 20, South Carolina 0
1928: Clemson 32, South Carolina 0
1929: Clemson 21, South Carolina 14
1930: Clemson 20, South Carolina 7
1931: Clemson 0, South Carolina 21
1932: Clemson 0, South Carolina 14
1933: Clemson 0, South Carolina 7
1934: Clemson 19, South Carolina 0
1935: Clemson 44, South Carolina 0
1936: Clemson 19, South Carolina 0
1937: Clemson 34, South Carolina 6
1938: Clemson 34, South Carolina 12
1939: Clemson 27, South Carolina 0
1940: Clemson 21, South Carolina 13
1941: Clemson 14, South Carolina 18
1942: Clemson 18, South Carolina 6
1943: Clemson 6, South Carolina 33

1944: Clemson 20, South Carolina 13
1945: Clemson 0, South Carolina 0
1946: Clemson 14, South Carolina 26
1947: Clemson 19, South Carolina 21
1948: Clemson 13, South Carolina 7
1949: Clemson 13, South Carolina 27
1950: Clemson 14, South Carolina 14
1951: Clemson 0, South Carolina 20
1952: Clemson 0, South Carolina 6
1953: Clemson 7, South Carolina 14
1954: Clemson 8, South Carolina 13
1955: Clemson 28, South Carolina 14
1956: Clemson 7, South Carolina 0
1957: Clemson 13, South Carolina 0
1958: Clemson 6, South Carolina 26
1959: Clemson 27, South Carolina 0
1960: South Carolina 2, Clemson 12
1961: Clemson 14, South Carolina 21
1962: South Carolina 17, Clemson 20
1963: Clemson 24, South Carolina 20
1964: South Carolina 7, Clemson 3
1965: Clemson 16, South Carolina 17
1966: South Carolina 10, Clemson 35
1967: Clemson 23, South Carolina 12
1968: South Carolina 7, Clemson 3
1969: Clemson 13, South Carolina 27
1970: South Carolina 38, Clemson 32
1971: Clemson 17, South Carolina 7
1972: South Carolina 6, Clemson 7
1973: Clemson 20, South Carolina 32
1974: South Carolina 21, Clemson 39
1975: Clemson 20, South Carolina 56
1976: South Carolina 9, Clemson 28
1977: Clemson 31, South Carolina 27
1978: South Carolina 23, Clemson 41
1979: Clemson 9, South Carolina 13
1980: South Carolina 6, Clemson 27
1981: Clemson 29, South Carolina 13

1982: South Carolina 6, Clemson 24
1983: Clemson 27, South Carolina 13
1984: South Carolina 22, Clemson 21
1985: Clemson 24, South Carolina 17
1986: South Carolina 21, Clemson 21
1987: Clemson 7, South Carolina 20
1988: South Carolina 10, Clemson 29
1989: Clemson 45, South Carolina 0
1990: South Carolina 15, Clemson 24
1991: Clemson 41, South Carolina 24
1992: South Carolina 24, Clemson 13
1993: Clemson 16, South Carolina 13
1994: South Carolina 33, Clemson 7
1995: Clemson 38, South Carolina 17
1996: South Carolina 34, Clemson 31
1997: Clemson 47, South Carolina 21
1998: South Carolina 19, Clemson 28
1999: Clemson 31, South Carolina 21
2000: South Carolina 14, Clemson 16
2001: Clemson 15, South Carolina 20
2002: South Carolina 20, Clemson 27
2003: Clemson 63, South Carolina 17
2004: South Carolina 7, Clemson 29
2005: Clemson 13, South Carolina 9
2006: South Carolina 31, Clemson 28
2007: Clemson 23, South Carolina 21
2008: South Carolina 14, Clemson 31
2009: Clemson 17, South Carolina 34
2010: South Carolina 29, Clemson 7
2011: Clemson 13, South Carolina 34
2012: South Carolina 27, Clemson 17
2013: Clemson 17, South Carolina 31

Clemson Bowl Game Appearances

1940 Cotton Bowl: Clemson 6, Boston College 3
1949 Gator Bowl: Clemson 24, Missouri 23
1951 Orange Bowl: Clemson 15, Miami 14
1952 Gator Bowl: Miami 14, Clemson 0

1957 Orange Bowl: Colorado 27, Clemson 21
1959 Sugar Bowl: LSU 7, Clemson 0
1959 Bluebonnet Bowl: Clemson 7, Texas Christian 0
1977 Gator Bowl: Pittsburgh 34, Clemson 3
1978 Gator Bowl: Clemson 17, Ohio State 15
1979 Peach Bowl: Baylor 24, Clemson 18
1982 Orange Bowl: Clemson 22, Nebraska 15
1985 Independence Bowl: Minnesota 20, Clemson 13
1986 Gator Bowl: Clemson 27, Stanford 21
1988 Citrus Bowl: Clemson 35, Penn State 10
1989 Citrus Bowl: Clemson 13, Oklahoma 6
1989 Gator Bowl: Clemson 27, West Virginia 7
1991 Hall of Fame Bowl: Clemson 30, Illinois 0
1992 Citrus Bowl: California 37, Clemson 14
1993 Peach Bowl: Clemson 14, Kentucky 13
1996 Gator Bowl: Syracuse 41, Clemson 0
1996 Peach Bowl: LSU 10, Clemson 7
1998 Peach Bowl: Auburn 21, Clemson 17
1999 Peach Bowl: Mississippi 17, Clemson 7
2001 Gator Bowl: Virginia Tech 41, Clemson 20
2001 Humanitarian Bowl: Clemson 49, Louisiana Tech 24
2002 Tangerine Bowl: Texas Tech 55, Clemson 15
2004 Peach Bowl: Clemson 27, Tennessee 14
2005 Champs Sports Bowl: Clemson 19, Colorado 10
2006 Music City Bowl: Kentucky 28, Clemson 20
2007 Chick-fil-A Bowl: Auburn 23, Clemson 20
2009 Gator Bowl: Nebraska 26, Clemson 21
2009 Music City Bowl: Clemson 21, Kentucky 13
2010 Meineke Car Care Bowl: South Florida 31, Clemson 26
2012 Orange Bowl: West Virginia 70, Clemson 33
2012 Chick-fil-A Bowl: Clemson 25, LSU 24
2014 Orange Bowl: Clemson 40, Ohio State 35

South Carolina Bowl Appearances
1946 Gator Bowl: Wake Forest 26, South Carolina 14
1969 Peach Bowl: West Virginia 14, South Carolina 3
1975 Tangerine Bowl: Miami of Ohio 20, South Carolina 7
1979 Hall of Fame Bowl: Missouri 24, South Carolina 14

1980 Gator Bowl: Pittsburgh 37, South Carolina 9

1984 Gator Bowl: Oklahoma State 21, South Carolina 14

1987 Gator Bowl: LSU 30, South Carolina 13

1988 Liberty Bowl: Indiana 34, South Carolina 10

1995 Carquest Bowl: South Carolina 24, West Virginia 21

2001 Outback Bowl: South Carolina 24, Ohio State 7

2002 Outback Bowl: South Carolina 31, Ohio State 28

2005 Independence Bowl: Missouri 38, South Carolina 31

2006 Liberty Bowl: South Carolina 44, Houston 36

2009 Outback Bowl: Iowa 31, South Carolina 10

2010 PapaJohns.com Bowl: Connecticut 20, South Carolina 7

2010 Chick-fil-A Bowl: Florida State 26, South Carolina 17

2012 Capital One Bowl: South Carolina 30, Nebraska 13

2013 Outback Bowl: South Carolina 33, Michigan 28

2014 Capital One Bowl: South Carolina 34, Wisconsin 24

NOTES

I. OHIO STATE VS. MICHIGAN: WOODY, BO, AND BEYOND

1. Kaye Kessler and William F. Reed, "Bye-Bye, No. 1," *Sports Illustrated*, December 1, 1969, accessed September 26, 2013, http://sportsillustrated.cnn.com/vault/article/magazine/MAG1083094/1/index.htm.

2. Ed Chay, "Schembechler Upsets Mentor Hayes," in *Greatest Moments in Ohio State Football History* (Chicago: Triumph Books, 2002), 85.

3. Greg Emmanuel, *The 100-Yard War* (Hoboken, N.J.: Wiley, 2005), 91.

4. Emmanuel, *100-Yard War*, 95.

5. "Michigan vs. Ohio State: 1969 Game, Bo's Big Win," *Bentley Historical Library*, November 16, 2008, accessed September 26, 2013, http://bentley.umich.edu/athdept/football/umosu/1969game.htm.

6. Emmanuel, *100-Yard War*, 96.

7. Emmanuel, *100-Yard War*, 14.

8. Michael Bradley, *Big Games: College Football's Greatest Rivalries* (Dulles, Va.: Potomac Books, 2006), 293.

9. Emmanuel, *100-Yard War*, 38–39.

10. Willard Manus, "Passing Recognition," *Michigan Today* 36, no. 3 (Fall 2004), accessed September 28, 2013, http://michigantoday.umich.edu/04/Fall04/print.html?passing.

11. Ken Rappoport and Barry Wilner, *Football Feuds: The Greatest College Football Rivalries* (Guilford, Conn.: Lyons, 2007), 37.

12. Fredric Alan Maxwell, "The Late Great 98," *Michigan Today*, September 17, 2008, accessed September 29, 2013, http://michigantoday.umich.edu/2008/09/harmon.php.

13. Emmanuel, *100-Yard War*, 66–69.

14. Jay Hansen, "When Woody Was Hired," *Ohio State Alumni Association*, accessed September 30, 2013, http://www.ohiostatealumni.org/volunteer/celebratingalumni/Pages/WoodyHired.aspx.

15. Emmanuel, *100-Yard War*, 82.

16. Quoted in Larry Keith, "On Stage: Woody and Bo," *Sports Illustrated*, November 24, 1975, accessed September 30, 2013, http://sportsillustrated.cnn.com/vault/article/magazine/MAG1090511/index.htm.

17. Dan Jenkins, "Revival and Revenge," *Sports Illustrated*, November 30, 1970, accessed September 30, 2013, http://sportsillustrated.cnn.com/vault/article/magazine/MAG1084336/index.htm.

18. Emmanuel, *100-Yard War*, 82.

19. Emmanuel, *100-Yard War*, 99.

20. Emmanuel, *100-Yard War*, 100.

21. Michael Rosenberg, *War as They Knew It* (New York: Grand Central, 2008), Google Books online, accessed September 30, 2013, http://books.google.com/books?id=E5ScPqeQ2xIC&pg=PT212&lpg=PT212&dq=Bo+Schembechler+and+Woody+Hayes+punch&source=bl&ots=xDBsjmvOYJ&sig=tsGaPIayJRKLUWFT-EEnRKGmLfU&hl=en&sa=X&ei=Y85mUtOsHa-l4AO5hYHgBw&ved=0CEIQ6AEwAw#v=onepage&q=Bo%20Schembechler%20and%20Woody%20Hayes%20punch&f=false.

22. Ray Paprocki, "The Week the Town Went Crazy," *Columbus Monthly*, January 1988, accessed October 2, 2013, http://www.columbusmonthly.com/January-1988/The-week-the-town-went-crazy/.

23. Tim Layden, "Run for the Roses," *Sports Illustrated*, December 4, 1995, accessed October 2, 2013, http://sportsillustrated.cnn.com/vault/article/magazine/MAG1007496/1/index.htm.

24. Emmanuel, *100-Yard War*, 154–55.

25. Associated Press, "Cooper Is Gone," *ESPN.com*, Bowl Championship Series, December 13, 2002, accessed October 2, 2013, http://espn.go.com/abcsports/bcs/s/2001/0102/988788.html.

26. Austin Murphy, "The Buckeyes Have It," *Sports Illustrated*, November 27, 2006, accessed October 2, 2013, http://sportsillustrated.cnn.com/vault/article/magazine/MAG1114066/index.htm.

27. Rappoport and Wilner, *Football Feuds*, 38.

28. Associated Press, "Ohio State Survives When Michigan's 2-Point Attempt Fails," *ESPN.com*, November 30, 2013, accessed January 13, 2014, http://scores.espn.go.com/ncf/recap?gameId=333340130.

2. ALABAMA VS. AUBURN: THE IRON BOWL

1. Ken Rappoport and Barry Wilner, *Football Feuds: The Greatest College Football Rivalries* (Guilford, Conn.: Lyons, 2007), 82.

2. Roy Blount Jr., "A.D. Proves That 6 x 6 Equals No. 1," *Sports Illustrated*, December 11, 1972, accessed October 4, 2013, http://sportsillustrated.cnn.com/vault/article/magazine/MAG1086860/2/index.htm.

3. Blount, "A.D. Proves."

4. Michael Bradley, *Big Games: College Football's Greatest Rivalries* (Dulles, Va.: Potomac Books, 2006), 256.

5. David Shepard, *Bama, Bear Bryant and the Bible* (Lincoln, Neb.: Writer's Press Club, 2002), 103.

6. Bradley, *Big Games*, 253.

7. Keith Dunnavant, *The Missing Ring: How Bear Bryant and the 1966 Crimson Tide Were Denied College Football's Most Elusive Prize* (New York: St. Martin's, 2006). Excerpt (accessed October 4, 2013): http://goldenrankings.com/alabama1966.html.

8. Bradley, *Big Games*, 262–63.

9. Bradley, *Big Games*, 265.

10. Rappoport and Wilner, *Football Feuds*, 84.

11. Bradley, *Big Games*, 268.

12. Bradley, *Big Games*, 272–73.

13. Donald F. Staffo, *I Love Alabama* (Chicago: Triumph Books, 2012), Google Books online, accessed October 7, 2013, http://books.google.com/books?id=QYRT215O-kAC&pg=PT150&lpg=PT150&dq=Pat+Dye:+%22It+was+the+most+emotional+day+in+Auburn+history%22&source=bl&ots=jlgWKImg8_&sig=RBbjTkMwciCzC3MthK4EGRyDSlk&hl=en&sa=X&ei=hgBzUvDfINWysAS_r4HQCg&ved=0CEYQ6AEwBA#v=onepage&q=Pat%20Dye%3A%20%22It%20was%20the%20most%20emotional%20day%20in%20Auburn%20history%22&f=false.

14. Rappoport and Wilner, *Football Feuds*, 88.

15. Associated Press, "Alabama Takes Lead with 1:24 Left, Holds Off Late Auburn Drive," *ESPN.com*, November 27, 2009, accessed October 5, 2013, http://scores.espn.go.com/ncf/recap?gameId=293310002.

16. Bradley, *Big Games*, 252–53.

3. ARMY VS. NAVY: WAR ON THE GRIDIRON

1. Michael Bradley, *Big Games: College Football's Greatest Rivalries* (Dulles, Va.: Potomac Books, 2006), 328.

2. Quoted in Bradley, *Big Games*, 327–28.

3. Quoted in the Lost Century of Sports Collection, *The Lost Century of American Football: Reports from the Birth of a Game* (North Charleston, S.C.: BookSurge, 2011). Excerpt (accessed October 5, 2013): http://football1800. wordpress.com/2011/12/10/1st-army-navy-game-in-1891-by-walter-camp-120-years-ago.

4. Barry Wilner and Ken Rappoport, *Gridiron Glory: The Story of the Army–Navy Football Rivalry* (Lanham, Md.: Taylor Trade, 2005), 41.

5. William N. Wallace, "Earl (Red) Blaik, 92, Army's Top Football Coach," *New York Times*, May 7, 1989, accessed October 10, 2013, http://www. nytimes.com/1989/05/07/obituaries/earl-red-blaik-92-army-s-top-football-coach.html.

6. Bradley, *Big Games*, 350.

7. Bradley, *Big Games*, 350.

8. Quoted in Bradley, *Big Games*, 347.

9. Maury Allen, "The Middies Mock the Odds," *Sports Illustrated*, December 4, 1961, accessed October 10, 2013, http://si.com/vault/article/ magazine/MAG1073295/2/index.htm.

10. Ken Rappoport and Barry Wilner, *Football Feuds: The Greatest College Football Rivalries* (Guilford, Conn.: Lyons, 2007), 8.

11. Shirley Povich, foreword to *Football Scouting Methods*, by Steve Belichick (Mansfield Center, Conn.: Martino, 2008). Originally published by Ronald Press in 1962, Google Books online, accessed October 10, 2013. http:// books.google.com/books?id=9pkjHN2C4tUC&pg=PR3&lpg=PR3&dq=1957+ Navy+football+team&source=bl&ots=ZA1CyHxUBo&sig=X-QFKi7YxskXn2FIhvox2Xt6dno&hl=en&sa=X&ei= lml4UorzEKjisASAsYCABA&ved=0CE0Q6AEwBzgK#v=onepage&q= 1957%20Navy%20football%20team&f=false.

12. Bradley, *Big Games*, 336.

13. Gary Lambrecht, "50 Years Later the 1950 Navy Football Team Still Ranks as the Best in School History," *Navysports.com*, October 2, 2013, accessed October 11, 2013, http://www.navysports.com/sports/m-footbl/spec-rel/ 100213aaa.html.

14. Dave Caldwell, "Despite 10 Straight Wins in Series, Navy Reveres Army as an Equal," *New York Times*, December 6, 2012, accessed October 11, 2013, http://www.nytimes.com/2012/12/07/sports/ncaafootball/navy-dominates-its-rival-but-reveres-it-as-an-equal.html.

4. OKLAHOMA VS. TEXAS:
THE RED RIVER RIVALRY

1. Michael Bradley, *Big Games: College Football's Greatest Rivalries* (Dulles, Va.: Potomac Books, 2006), 89–90.

2. Bradley, *Big Games*, 72.

3. Bradley, *Big Games*, 76.

4. Ken Rappoport and Barry Wilner, *Football Feuds: The Greatest College Football Rivalries* (Guilford, Conn.: Lyons, 2007), 70.

5. Bob Carter, "Wilkinson Created Sooners Dynasty," *ESPN Classic*, accessed October 14, 2013, http://espn.go.com/classic/biography/s/wilkinson_bud.html.

6. Rappoport and Wilner, *Football Feuds*, 71.

7. Carter, "Wilkinson Created Sooners Dynasty."

8. News Services and Staff Reports, "Darrell Royal, Hall of Fame Texas Football Coach, Dies at 88," *Washington Post*, November 8, 2012, accessed October 17, 2013, http://articles.washingtonpost.com/2012-11-08/sports/35503951_1_football-coach-texas-teams-longhorns.

9. Bradley, *Big Games*, 96.

10. Joe Jares, "The Sooners Are the Better," *Sports Illustrated*, October 20, 1975, accessed October 17, 2013, http://sportsillustrated.cnn.com/vault/article/magazine/MAG1090368/2/index.htm.

11. Bradley, *Big Games*, 99.

12. Jon Finkel, "Ricky Williams' Magical Run in 1998: Wins Heisman Trophy, Sets All-Time Rushing Mark," *The Post Game*, September 19, 2013, accessed October 15, 2013, http://www.thepostgame.com/blog/loyalty-report/201309/mack-brown-ricky-williams-texas-longhorns-football-college-ncaa-heisman.

13. Associated Press, "Young Leads Texas to First OU Win in Five Years." *ESPN.com*, October 8, 2005, accessed October 15, 2013, http://espn.go.com/ncf/recap?id=252810251.

14. The Elusive Shadow, "Let's Do It: Let the Hate Flow through You," *Burnt Orange Nation*, October 9, 2013, accessed October 18, 2013, http://www.burntorangenation.com/2013/10/9/4819860/lets-do-it-let-the-hate-flow-through-you.

5. NOTRE DAME VS. SOUTHERN CALIFORNIA: THE CROSS-COUNTRY CLASH

1. Quoted in Steven Robert Travers, "Johnny Baker and USC's 1931 Comeback at South Bend," *Red Room* (blog), November 23, 2012, accessed October 20, 2013, http://redroom.com/member/steven-robert-travers/blog/johnny-baker-and-uscs-1931-comeback-at-south-bend.

2. Michael Bradley, *Big Games: College Football's Greatest Rivalries* (Dulles, Va.: Potomac Books, 2006), 115.

3. Grantland Rice, "The Four Horsemen," reprinted in *Sports Illustrated*, October 31, 1955, accessed October 20, 2013, http://sportsillustrated.cnn.com/vault/article/magazine/MAG1130404/index.htm.

4. Quoted in Bradley, *Big Games*, 113.

5. Esteban On, "9 Biggest Traitor Coaches in the History of College Football," *TotalProSports.com*, December 1, 2011, accessed October 20, 2013, http://www.totalprosports.com/2011/12/01/9-biggest-traitor-coaches-in-the-history-of-college-football.

6. Nick Selbe, "1962 National Champions Hold Reunion," *Daily Trojan*, October 9, 2012, accessed October 20, 2013, http://dailytrojan.com/2012/10/09/1962-national-champions-hold-reunion.

7. Jim Dent, *Resurrection: The Miracle Season That Saved Notre Dame* (New York: St. Martin's, 2009), 273.

8. Ken Rappoport and Barry Wilner, *Football Feuds: The Greatest College Football Rivalries* (Guilford, Conn.: Lyons, 2007), 23–24.

9. Pat Putnam, "'Twas a Great Day for the Irish," *Sports Illustrated*, November 5, 1973, accessed October 25, 2013, http://sportsillustrated.cnn.com/vault/article/magazine/MAG1087970/3/index.htm.

10. Douglas S. Looney, "They Were Dressed to Kill," *Sports Illustrated*, October 31, 1977, accessed October 25, 2013, http://sportsillustrated.cnn.com/vault/article/magazine/MAG1092955/2/index.htm.

11. Rick Telander, "Go Get 'Em, Men," *Sports Illustrated*, December 5, 1988, accessed October 25, 2013, http://sportsillustrated.cnn.com/vault/article/magazine/MAG1068048/2/index.htm.

12. Bradley, *Big Games*, 124.

13. Associated Press, "USC Win Streak Intact after Wild Fourth-Quarter Finish," *ESPN.com*, October 15, 2005, accessed November 1, 2013, http://scores.espn.go.com/ncf/recap?gameId=252880087.

14. Rappoport and Wilner, *Football Feuds*, 30.

6. HARVARD VS. YALE: THE GAME

1. Michael Bradley, *Big Games: College Football's Greatest Rivalries* (Dulles, Va.: Potomac Books, 2006), 6.

2. Quoted in "The Harvard–Yale Rivalry," *Harvard Athletics*, accessed November 2, 2013, http://www.gocrimson.com/sports/mcrew-hw/tradition/Harvard-Yale.

3. Mark F. Bernstein, *Football: The Ivy League Origins of an American Obsession* (Philadelphia: University of Pennsylvania Press, 2001), 74.

4. Bradley, *Big Games*, 10.

5. Quoted in "1923 College Football National Championship," *Tip Top 25*, accessed November 7, 2013, http://tiptop25.com/champ1923.html.

6. "Red Smith Heismans Get a Home," *New York Times*, November 23, 1981, accessed November 7, 2013, http://www.nytimes.com/1981/11/23/sports/red-smith-heismans-get-a-home.html.

7. "Red Smith Heismans."

8. Bradley, *Big Games*, 13.

9. Quoted in George Sullivan, "BackTalk; A Point Stuck in Harvard's Side," *New York Times*, November 17, 2002, accessed November 7, 2013, http://www.nytimes.com/2002/11/17/sports/backtalk-a-point-stuck-in-harvard-s-side.html.

10. Bradley, *Big Games*, 15.

11. Chip Malafronte, "Yale's Calvin Hill Becomes First Ivy League Player Selected in First Round of NFL Draft," *New Haven Register*, December 12, 2012, accessed November 7, 2013, http://www.nhregister.com/general-news/20121212/new-haven-200-yales-calvin-hill-becomes-first-ivy-league-player-selected-in-first-round-of-nfl-draft.

12. Ted Mandell, "Yale vs. Harvard," *Heart Stoppers and Hail Marys*, accessed November 7, 2013, http://www3.nd.edu/~tmandell/harvard.html.

13. Mandell, "Yale vs. Harvard."

14. Mandell, "Yale vs. Harvard."

15. Bradley, *Big Games*, 26.

16. Jeffrey R. Toobin, "What Does the Multiflex Mean?" *Harvard Crimson*, October 10, 1980, accessed November 11, 2013, http://www.thecrimson.com/article/1980/10/10/what-does-the-multiflex-mean-pthe.

17. Michael R. Vollonino, "Johnson's Grab Wins 116th Game for Yale," *Harvard Crimson*, November 22, 1999, accessed November 11, 2013, http://www.thecrimson.com/article/1999/11/22/johnsons-grab-wins-116th-game-for/#.

18. Bradley, *Big Games*, 24.

7. GEORGIA VS. FLORIDA: THE WORLD'S LARGEST OUTDOOR COCKTAIL PARTY

1. Michael DiRocco. "Georgia–Florida Game Needs a Name and a Trophy," *Florida Times-Union*, October 27, 2010, accessed November 13, 2013, http://members.jacksonville.com/sports/college/florida-gators/2010-10-28/story/revisiting-cocktail-party-Georgia–Florida-needs-name.

2. Michael Bradley, *Big Games: College Football's Greatest Rivalries* (Dulles, Va.: Potomac Books, 2006), 150.

3. Ryan Ferguson, "It's Still Important to Hate Georgia: A History Lesson," *AOLNews*, October 27, 2006, accessed November 13, 2013, http://archive.is/wYhhP.

4. C. J. Schexnayder, "Florida vs. Georgia Series History: Steve Spurrier, 1966 and Long Memories," *SB Nation*, October 28, 2011, accessed November 13, 2013, http://www.sbnation.com/ncaa-football/2011/10/28/2505359/Florida–Georgia-game-2011-series-history-steve-spurrier-1966.

5. Patrick Garbin, "Fourth and Dumb," *About Them Dawgs! Blawg* (blog), May 28, 2010, accessed November 18, 2013, http://patrickgarbin.blogspot.com/2010/05/fourth-and-dumb.html.

6. Joe Marshall, "How 'bout Them Dawgs?" *Sports Illustrated*, November 17, 1980, accessed November 18, 2013, http://sportsillustrated.cnn.com/vault/article/magazine/MAG1123953/1/index.htm.

7. Jeff Barlis, "Time Runs Out for Georgia's Senior Class," *Orlando Sentinel*, October 31, 1993, accessed November 14, 2013, http://articles.sun-sentinel.com/1993-10-31/sports/9310310151_1_georgia-s-first-victory-georgia-senior-linebacker-mitchell-and-davis.

8. Associated Press, "Gators Wreck Georgia's Perfect Season," *ESPN.com*, November 2, 2002, accessed November 22, 2013, http://espn.go.com/ncf/recap?id=223060061.

9. Mark Long, "Georgia Football: No. 3 Florida Falls to No. 12 Bulldogs 17–9," *Huffington Post*, October 27, 2012, accessed November 22, 2013, http://www.huffingtonpost.com/2012/10/27/Georgia–Florida-upset-bulldogs-gators-football_n_2031877.html.

8. LAFAYETTE VS. LEHIGH: THE FIRST RIVALRY

1. Ken Rappoport and Barry Wilner, *Football Feuds: The Greatest College Football Rivalries* (Guilford, Conn.: Lyons, 2007), 136.

2. Michael Bradley, *Big Games: College Football's Greatest Rivalries* (Dulles, Va.: Potomac Books, 2006), 188.

3. Walter R. Okeson, "Lehigh Winds Up Its Football Season with a Victory over Lafayette," *Lehigh Alumni Bulletin* 17, no. 3 (1929–1930), accessed November 27, 2013, http://archive.org/stream/lehighalumnibull1703/lehighalumnibull1703_djvu.txt.

4. "2 Lehigh Graduates Achieve Honor over the Philippines,"http://digital.lib.lehigh.edu/cgi-bin/showfile.exe?CISOROOT=/bw2&CISOMODE=print&CISOPTR=4125.

5. Jenna Marina, "The Greatest Game They Never Played," *Lafayette Official Athletic Site*, November 18, 2008, accessed December 2, 2013, http://www.goleopards.com/sports/m-footbl/spec-rel/111808aag.html.

6. *Lehigh University Brown and White* 49A, no. 2 (June 3, 1942), "Richard F. Doyne Is in the Lehigh Hall of Fame," accessed December 5, 2013, http://history.lehighsports.com/playerstats/display/5/1951/315.

7. Kim McQuilken, *The Road to Athletic Scholarship* (New York: New York University Press, 1996), 4, Google Books Online, http://books.google.com/books?id=vsa-rmIahfoC&pg=PA3&lpg=PA3&dq=Fred+Dunlap:+Lehigh&source=bl&ots=oHQDbThMBc&sig=SfwhTW2K8JqUnli8KhjNTNxf7V0&hl=en&sa=X&ei=EqG5UsyzG6TCywHPgoDIAg&ved=0CFwQ6AEwBw#v=onepage&q=Fred%20Dunlap%3A%20Lehigh&f=false.

8. *The Daily Inter Lake*, December 12, 1977, accessed December 10, 2013, http://www.newspapers.com/newspage/34824657.

9. Bradley, *Big Games*, 197.

9. CALIFORNIA VS. STANFORD:
THE BIG GAME

1. Michael Bradley, *Big Games: College Football's Greatest Rivalries* (Dulles, Va.: Potomac Books, 2006), 219.

2. "The Band Is Out on the Field!" *Real Clear Sports*, posted September 30, 2013, accessed December 14, 2013, http://www.realclearsports.com/lists/sports_broadcasting_calls/california_stanford_band_starkey.html.

3. Kelli Anderson, "An Oral History of the Play: Looking Back at Wild Finish 30 Years Later," *SI.com*, October 18, 2012, accessed December 14, 2013, http://sportsillustrated.cnn.com/2012/writers/the_bonus/10/18/the-play-Stanford–Cal/index.html.

4. Quoted in Hugh Wyatt, "Ernie Nevers—Has There Ever Been Better?" *coachwyatt.com*, accessed December 17, 2013, http://www.coachwyatt.com/ernienevers.htm.

5. Richard Goldstein, "Frankie Albert, a Pioneering Quarterback, Is Dead at 82," *New York Times*, September 9, 2002, accessed December 21, 2013, http://www.nytimes.com/2002/09/09/sports/frankie-albert-a-pioneering-quarterback-is-dead-at-82.html.

6. Bradley, *Big Games*, 245.

7. Gene Wojciechowski, "Stanford's Big Offense Makes Cal Eat Its Words," *Los Angeles Times*, November 24, 1991, accessed December 21, 2013, http://articles.latimes.com/1991-11-24/sports/sp-206_1_big-game-stuff.

8. Jeremy Ghassemi, "Ty Montgomery and Stanford Have Big Game, Demolish Cal 63–13," *Baysportsreport.com*, November 23, 2013, accessed December 21, 2013, http://www.baysportsreport.com/2013/11/23/ty-montgomery-and-stanford-have-big-game.

10. FLORIDA STATE VS. MIAMI:
THE GAME WITHOUT A NAME

1. Austin Murphy, "No. 1 by One," *Sports Illustrated*, November 25, 1991, accessed December 21, 2013, http://sportsillustrated.cnn.com/vault/article/magazine/MAG1140196/index.htm.

2. Murphy, "No. 1 by One."

3. Michael Bradley, *Big Games: College Football's Greatest Rivalries* (Dulles, Va.: Potomac Books, 2006), 44.

4. "Florida State: 1962 Seminoles," *Helmet Hut*, accessed December 28, 2013, http://www.helmethut.com/College/FloridaState/FLXFSU6262.html.

5. Pat Williams and Rob Wilson, *Bobby Bowden on Leadership* (Charleston, S.C.: Advantage Media Group, 2011), 45.

6. Bradley, *Big Games*, 48.

7. Dan O'Sullivan, "1984: Miami 31, Nebraska 30." *ESPN.com*, Bowl Championship Series, December 13, 2002, accessed December 28, 2013, http://espn.go.com/abcsports/bcs/orange/s/1984.html.

8. Rick Telander, "No More Rap or Rep," *Sports Illustrated*, September 12, 1988, accessed December 28, 2013, http://sportsillustrated.cnn.com/vault/article/magazine/MAG1067739/3/index.htm.

9. Rodney Page, "Florida State National Championship Years: 1993," *Tampa Bay Times*, November 30, 2009, accessed December 29, 2013, http://www.tampabay.com/sports/college/florida-state-national-championship-years-1993/1055407.

10. Williams and Wilson, *Bobby Bowden*, 49–50.

11. GRAMBLING STATE VS. SOUTHERN: THE BAYOU CLASSIC

1. Ken Rappoport and Barry Wilner, *Football Feuds: The Greatest College Football Rivalries* (Guilford, Conn.: Lyons, 2007), 145–46.

2. "Arnett 'Ace' Mumford," *Louisiana Sports Hall of Fame*, accessed January 4, 2014, http://www.lasportshall.com/inductees/football/arnett-ace-mumford/?back=inductee.

3. Eddie Robinson, *Never Before, Never Again* (New York: Thomas Dunne Books, 1999), 78, Google Books Online, http://books.google.com/books?id=TZ453RK7GXwC&pg=PA77&lpg=PA77&dq=Eddie+Robinson:+1946+loss+to+Southern&source=bl&ots=NE499srMxD&sig=7e-pADzFSUkZgppc36MMrF0D8eY&hl=en&sa=X&ei=sfvSUtTqOaLlyAGasoGYDg&ved=0CD0Q6AEwAw#v=onepage&q=Eddie%20Robinson%3A%201946%20loss%20to%20Southern&f=false.

4. Michael Bamberger, "Grambling Man," *Sports Illustrated*, October 21, 1996, accessed January 10, 2014, http://sportsillustrated.cnn.com/vault/article/magazine/MAG1008914/2/index.htm.

5. Ira Berkow, "White Player Gets a Chance at Black School," *New York Times*, December 29, 1996, accessed January 10, 2014, http://partners.nytimes.com/library/national/race/122996race-ra.html.

6. Allan Barra, "A History of Grambling University Football: The First Shot in Player Liberation," *Daily Beast*, November 9, 2013, accessed January 10, 2014, http://www.thedailybeast.com/articles/2013/11/09/a-history-of-grambling-university-football-the-first-shot-in-player-liberation.html.

7. Jim Kleinpeter, "A No-Nonsense Approach Helped Southern Coach Pete Richardson Lead the Jaguars to 4 National Titles, 5 SWAC Crowns," *New Orleans Times-Picayune*, June 22, 2012, accessed January 10, 2014, http://www.nola.com/sports/index.ssf/2012/06/a_no-nonsense_approach_helped.html.

8. Thomas Aiello, *Bayou Classic: The Grambling–Southern Football Rivalry* (Baton Rouge: Louisiana State University Press, 2010), 189.

12. UTAH VS. BRIGHAM YOUNG:
THE HOLY WAR

1. Associated Press, "Hall Connects with George to Lift BYU in OT; Disparages Utes," *ESPN.com*, November 28, 2009, accessed January 30, 2014, http://scores.espn.go.com/ncf/recap?gameId=293320252.

2. AP, "Hall Connects."

3. *"BYU vs. Utah: The So-Called Holy War," The Official Home of the BYU Cougars*, accessed January 30, 2014, http://byucougars.com/athletics/byu-vs-utah-so-called-holy-war.

4. "Progress of Teams: Football Coaches Watch with Interest Records of Players on the Gridiron," *Galveston Daily News*, November 12, 1905.

5. Doug Robinson, "Web Extra: LaVell Edwards Career Ending in Praise, Fanfare," *Deseret News*, November 18, 2000, accessed February 2, 2014, http://www.deseretnews.com/article/794007/LaVell-Edwards-career-ending-in-praise-fanfare.html?pg=all.

6. John Henderson, "Holy War Rages On . . . in Utah," *Denver Post*, November 21, 2008, accessed February 3, 2014, http://www.denverpost.com/colleges/ci_11036799.

7. Jeff Call, "BYU: Bowl Win Clinched National Title for Y," *Deseret News*, July 16, 2009, accessed February 3, 2014, http://www.deseretnews.com/article/705317199/BYU-football-Bowl-win-clinched-national-title-for-Y.html?pg=all.

8. Call, "BYU."

9. Associated Press, "Utah Secures Perfect Season with Sugar Bowl Win over Alabama," *ESPN.com*, January 2, 2009, accessed February 4, 2014, http://scores.espn.go.com/ncf/recap?gameId=290020333.

13. OREGON VS. OREGON STATE:
THE CIVIL WAR

1. Victor Flores, "Ducks Beat Oregon State 36–35 in Thrilling Civil War Game," *Daily Emerald*, November 29, 2013, accessed February 4, 2014, http://dailyemerald.com/2013/11/29/civil-war-recap.

2. Ben Bolch, "In 1917, Oregon Changed the Game," *Los Angeles Times*, January 1, 2010, accessed February 4, 2014, http://articles.latimes.com/2010/jan/01/sports/la-sp-rose-bowl-history1-2010jan01.

3. Quoted in Bolch, "In 1917."

4. Kevin Hampton, "2001 Fiesta Bowl Team Had Confidence, Swagger," *Gazette Times*, October 4, 2010, accessed February 9, 2014, http://www.gazettetimes.com/sports/beavers-sports/fiesta-bowl-team-had-confidence-swagger/article_4e926982-d027-11df-8b6b-001cc4c002e0.html.

5. Associated Press, "Oregon 38, Colorado 16," *Sports Illustrated*, January 1, 2002, accessed February 9, 2014, http://sportsillustrated.cnn.com/football/college/recaps/2002/01/01/ccn_ooe.

6. John Kampf, "Gruden Has High Praise for Oregon's Chip Kelly," *Lorain Morning Journal*, January 1, 2010, accessed February 9, 2014, http://www.morningjournal.com/general-news/20100101/gruden-has-high-praise-for-oregons-chip-kelly.

14. CLEMSON VS. SOUTH CAROLINA: THE PALMETTO BOWL

1. Ed McGranahan, "Butler Found End Zone and the Ball, and the Catch Is History," *The State*, November 22, 2012, accessed February 10, 2014, http://www.thestate.com/2012/11/22/2528024/butler-found-end-zone-and-the.html.

2. Quoted in Travis Haney and Larry Williams, *Classic Clashes of the Carolina–Clemson Football Rivalry: A State of Disunion* (Charleston, S.C.: History Press, 2011), 36, Google Books online, http://books.google.com/books?id=lymewh6L9T4C&pg=PP1&lpg=PP1&dq=Classic+Clashes+of+the+Carolina-Clemson+Football+Rivalry&source=bl&ots=peBrVd6xYf&sig=DVL9bgFbobGjStv5kYPyitXGGdc&hl=en&sa=X&ei=KrL5UtXSCuGSyAHUiIHYBA&ved=0CFcQ6AEwBg#v=onepage&q=Classic%20Clashes%20of%20the%20Carolina-Clemson%20Football%20Rivalry&f=false.

3. Haney and Williams, *Classic Clashes*, 38.

4. Haney and Williams, *Classic Clashes*, 55.

5. Tommy Hood, "Tiger Insider Sneak Peak: Charley Pell Turning Things Around Again," *TigerNet.com*, June 6, 2000, accessed February 11, 2014, http:/www.tigernet.com/view/story.do?id=518.

6. Associated Press, "Clemson Tailback Has No Regrets about Brawl," *USA Today*, November 25, 2004, accessed February 13, 2014, http://usatoday30.usatoday.com/sports/college/football/2004-11-25-kelly-clemson-brawl_x.htm.

BIBLIOGRAPHY

BOOKS

Aiello, Thomas. *Bayou Classic: The Grambling–Southern Football Rivalry*. Baton Rouge: Louisiana State University Press, 2010.

Bernstein, Mark F. *Football: The Ivy League Origins of an American Obsession*. Philadelphia: University of Pennsylvania Press, 2001.

Bradley, Michael. *Big Games: College Football's Greatest Rivalries*. Dulles, Va.: Potomac Books, 2006.

Chay, Ed. "Schembechler Upsets Mentor Hayes." In *Greatest Moments in Ohio State Football History*, 84–85. Chicago: Triumph Books, 2002.

Dent, Jim. *Resurrection: The Miracle Season That Saved Notre Dame*. New York: St. Martin's, 2009.

Dunnavant, Keith. *The Missing Ring: How Bear Bryant and the 1966 Crimson Tide Were Denied College Football's Most Elusive Prize*. New York: St. Martin's, 2006.

Emmanuel, Greg. *The 100-Yard War*. Hoboken, N.J.: Wiley, 2005.

Haney, Travis, and Larry Williams. *Classic Clashes of the Carolina–Clemson Football Rivalry: A State of Disunion*. Charleston, S.C.: History Press, 2011.

The Lost Century of Sports Collection. *The Lost Century of American Football: Reports from the Birth of a Game*. North Charleston, S.C.: BookSurge, 2011.

McQuilken, Kim. *The Road to Athletic Scholarship*. New York: New York University Press, 1996.

Povich, Shirley. Foreword. In *Football Scouting Methods* by Steve Belichick. Mansfield Center, Conn.: Martino, 2008. Originally published by Ronald Press in 1962.

Rappoport, Ken, and Barry Wilner. *Football Feuds: The Greatest College Football Rivalries*. Guilford, Conn.: Lyons, 2007.

Robinson, Eddie. *Never Before, Never Again*. New York: Thomas Dunne Books, 1999.

Rosenberg, Michael. *War as They Knew It*. New York: Grand Central, 2008.

Shepard, David. *Bama, Bear Bryant and the Bible*. Lincoln, Neb.: Writer's Press Club, 2002.

Shropshire, Mike. *Runnin' with the Big Dogs: The True, Unvarnished Story of the Texas–Oklahoma Football Wars*. New York: William Morrow, 2006.

Staffo, Donald F. *I Love Alabama*. Chicago: Triumph Books, 2012.

Williams, Pat, and Rob Wilson. *Bobby Bowden on Leadership*. Charleston, S.C.: Advantage Media Group, 2011.

Wilner, Barry, and Ken Rappoport. *Gridiron Glory: The Story of the Army–Navy Football Rivalry*. Lanham, Md.: Taylor Trade, 2005.

NEWSPAPERS/MAGAZINES

Allen, Maury. "The Middies Mock the Odds." *Sports Illustrated*, December 4, 1961. Accessed October 10, 2013. http://si.com/vault/article/magazine/MAG1073295/2/index.htm.

Anderson, Kelli. "An Oral History of the Play: Looking Back at Wild Finish 30 Years Later." *Sports Illustrated.com*, October 18, 2012. Accessed December 14, 2013. http://sportsillustrated.cnn.com/2012/writers/the_bonus/10/18/the-play-stanford-cal/index.html.

———. "Clemson Tailback Has No Regrets about Brawl." *USA Today*, November 25, 2004. Accessed February 13, 2014. http://usatoday30.usatoday.com/sports/college/football/2004-11-25-kelly-clemson-brawl_x.htm.

Associated Press. "Oregon 38, Colorado 16." *Sports Illustrated*, January 1, 2002. Accessed February 9, 2014. http://sportsillustrated.cnn.com/football/college/recaps/2002/01/01/ccn_ooe.

Bamberger, Michael. "Grambling Man." *Sports Illustrated*, October 21, 1996. Accessed January 10, 2014. http://sportsillustrated.cnn.com/vault/article/magazine/MAG1008914/2/index.htm.

Barlis, Jeff. "Time Runs Out for Georgia's Senior Class." *Orlando Sentinel*, October 31, 1993. Accessed November 14, 2013. http://articles.sun-sentinel.com/1993-10-31/sports/9310310151_1_georgia-s-first-victory-georgia-senior-linebacker-mitchell-and-davis.

Berkow, Ira. "White Player Gets a Chance at Black School." *New York Times*, December 29, 1996. Accessed January 10, 2014. http://partners.nytimes.com/library/national/race/122996race-ra.html.

Blount, Roy, Jr. "A.D. Proves That 6 x 6 Equals No. 1." *Sports Illustrated*, December 11, 1972. Accessed October 4, 2013. http://sportsillustrated.cnn.com/vault/article/magazine/MAG1086860/2/index.htm.

Bolch, Ben. "In 1917, Oregon Changed the Game." *Los Angeles Times*, January 1, 2010. Accessed February 4, 2014. http://articles.latimes.com/2010/jan/01/sports/la-sp-rose-bowl-history1-2010jan01.

Caldwell, Dave. "Despite 10 Straight Wins in Series, Navy Reveres Army as an Equal." *New York Times*. December 6, 2012. Accessed October 11, 2013. http://www.nytimes.com/2012/12/07/sports/ncaafootball/navy-dominates-its-rival-but-reveres-it-as-an-equal.html.

Call, Jeff. "BYU: Bowl Win Clinched National Title for Y." *Deseret News*, July 16, 2009. Accessed February 3, 2014. http://www.deseretnews.com/article/705317199/BYU-football-Bowl-win-clinched-national-title-for-Y.html?pg=all.

The Daily Inter Lake. December 12, 1977. Accessed December 10, 2013. http://www.newspapers.com/newspage/34824657.

DiRocco, Michael. "Georgia–Florida Game Needs a Name and a Trophy." *Florida Times-Union*, October 27, 2010. Accessed November 13, 2013. http://members.jacksonville.com/sports/college/florida-gators/2010-10-28/story/revisiting-cocktail-party-georgia-florida-needs-name.

Flores, Victor. "Ducks Beat Oregon State 36–35 in Thrilling Civil War Game." *Daily Emerald*, November 29, 2013. Accessed February 4, 2014. http://dailyemerald.com/2013/11/29/civil-war-recap.

Goldstein, Richard. "Frankie Albert, a Pioneering Quarterback, Is Dead at 82." *New York Times*, September 9, 2002. Accessed December 21, 2013. http://www.nytimes.com/2002/09/09/sports/frankie-albert-a-pioneering-quarterback-is-dead-at-82.html.

Hampton, Kevin. "2001 Fiesta Bowl Team Had Confidence, Swagger." *Gazette Times*, October 4, 2010. Accessed February 9, 2014. http://www.gazettetimes.com/sports/beavers-sports/fiesta-bowl-team-had-confidence-swagger/article_4e926982-d027-11df-8b6b-001cc4c002e0.html.

Henderson, John. "Holy War Rages On . . . in Utah." *Denver Post*, November 21, 2008. Accessed February 3, 2014. http://www.denverpost.com/colleges/ci_11036799.

Jares, Joe. "The Sooners Are the Better." *Sports Illustrated*, October 20, 1975. Accessed October 17, 2013. http://sportsillustrated.cnn.com/vault/article/magazine/MAG1090368/2/index.htm.

Jenkins, Dan. "Revival and Revenge." *Sports Illustrated*, November 30, 1970. Accessed September 30, 2013. http://sportsillustrated.cnn.com/vault/article/magazine/MAG1084336/index.htm.

Kampf, John. "Gruden Has High Praise for Oregon's Chip Kelly." *Lorain Morning Journal*, January 1, 2010. Accessed February 9, 2014. http://www.morningjournal.com/general-news/20100101/gruden-has-high-praise-for-oregons-chip-kelly.

Keith, Larry. "On Stage: Woody and Bo." *Sports Illustrated*, November 24, 1975. Accessed September 30, 2013. http://sportsillustrated.cnn.com/vault/article/magazine/MAG1090511/index.htm.

Kessler, Kaye, and William F. Reed. "Bye-Bye, No. 1." *Sports Illustrated*, December 1, 1969. Accessed September 26, 2013. http://sportsillustrated.cnn.com/vault/article/magazine/MAG1083094/1/index.htm.

Kleinpeter, Jim. "A No-Nonsense Approach Helped Southern Coach Pete Richardson Lead the Jaguars to 4 National Titles, 5 SWAC Crowns." *New Orleans Times-Picayune*, June 22, 2012. Accessed January 10, 2014. http://www.nola.com/sports/index.ssf/2012/06/a_no-nonsense_approach_helped.html.

Layden, Tim. "Run for the Roses." *Sports Illustrated*, December 4, 1995. Accessed October 2, 2013. http://sportsillustrated.cnn.com/vault/article/magazine/MAG1007496/1/index.htm.

Long, Mark. "Georgia Football: No. 3 Florida Falls to No. 12 Bulldogs 17–9." *Huffington Post*, October 27, 2012. Accessed November 22, 2013. http://www.huffingtonpost.com/2012/10/27/georgia-florida-upset-bulldogs-gators-football_n_2031877.html.

Looney, Douglas S. "They Were Dressed to Kill." *Sports Illustrated*, October 31, 1977. Accessed October 25, 2013. http://sportsillustrated.cnn.com/vault/article/magazine/MAG1092955/2/index.htm.

Malafronte, Chip. "Yale's Calvin Hill Becomes First Ivy League Player Selected in First Round of NFL Draft." *New Haven Register*, December 12, 2012. Accessed November 7, 2013. http://www.nhregister.com/general-news/20121212/new-haven-200-yales-calvin-hill-becomes-first-ivy-league-player-selected-in-first-round-of-nfl-draft.

Manus, Willard. "Passing Recognition." *Michigan Today* 36, no. 3 (Fall 2004). Accessed September 28, 2013. http://michigantoday.umich.edu/04/Fall04/print.html?passing.

Marshall, Joe. "How 'bout Them Dawgs?" *Sports Illustrated*, November 17, 1980. Accessed November 18, 2013. http://sportsillustrated.cnn.com/vault/article/magazine/MAG1123953/1/index.htm.

Maxwell, Fredric Alan. "The Late Great 98." *Michigan Today*, September 17, 2008. Accessed September 29, 2013. http://michigantoday.umich.edu/2008/09/harmon.php.

McGranahan, Ed. "Butler Found End Zone and the Ball, and the Catch Is History." *The State*, November 22, 2012. Accessed February 10, 2014. http://www.thestate.com/2012/11/22/2528024/butler-found-end-zone-and-the.html.

Murphy, Austin. "The Buckeyes Have It." *Sports Illustrated*, November 27, 2006. Accessed October 2, 2013. http://sportsillustrated.cnn.com/vault/article/magazine/MAG1114066/index.htm.

———. "No. 1 by One." *Sports Illustrated*, November 25, 1991. Accessed December 21, 2013. http://sportsillustrated.cnn.com/vault/article/magazine/MAG1140196/index.htm.

News Services and Staff Reports. "Darrell Royal, Hall of Fame Texas Football Coach, Dies at 88." *Washington Post*, November 8, 2012. Accessed October 17, 2013. http://articles.washingtonpost.com/2012-11-08/sports/35503951_1_football-coach-texas-teams-longhorns.

Okeson, Walter R. "Lehigh Winds Up Its Football Season with a Victory over Lafayette." *Lehigh Alumni Bulletin* 17, no. 3 (1929–1930). Accessed November 27, 2013. http://archive.org/stream/lehighalumnibull1703/lehighalumnibull1703_djvu.txt.

Page, Rodney. "Florida State National Championship Years: 1993." *Tampa Bay Times*, November 30, 2009. Accessed December 29, 2013. http://www.tampabay.com/sports/college/florida-state-national-championship-years-1993/1055407.

Paprocki, Ray. "The Week the Town Went Crazy." *Columbus Monthly*, January 1988. Accessed October 2, 2013. http://www.columbusmonthly.com/January-1988/The-week-the-town-went-crazy/.

"Progress of Teams: Football Coaches Watch with Interest Records of Players on the Gridiron." *Galveston Daily News*, November 12, 1905.

Putnam, Pat. " 'Twas a Great Day for the Irish." *Sports Illustrated*, November 5, 1973. Accessed October 25, 2013. http://sportsillustrated.cnn.com/vault/article/magazine/MAG1087970/3/index.htm.

"Red Smith Heismans Get a Home." *New York Times*, November 23, 1981. Accessed November 7, 2013. http://www.nytimes.com/1981/11/23/sports/red-smith-heismans-get-a-home.html.

Rice, Grantland. "The Four Horsemen." Reprinted in *Sports Illustrated*, October 31, 1955. Accessed October 20, 2013. http://sportsillustrated.cnn.com/vault/article/magazine/MAG1130404/index.htm.

Robinson, Doug. "Web Extra: LaVell Edwards Career Ending in Praise, Fanfare." *Deseret News*, November. 18, 2000. Accessed February 2, 2014. http://www.deseretnews.com/article/794007/LaVell-Edwards-career-ending-in-praise-fanfare.html?pg=all.

Selbe, Nick. "1962 National Champions Hold Reunion." *Daily Trojan*, October 9, 2012. Accessed October 20, 2013. http://dailytrojan.com/2012/10/09/1962-national-champions-hold-reunion.

Sullivan, George. "BackTalk; A Point Stuck in Harvard's Side." *New York Times*, November 17, 2002. Accessed November 7, 2013. http://www.nytimes.com/2002/11/17/sports/backtalk-a-point-stuck-in-harvard-s-side.html.

Telander, Rick. "Go Get 'Em, Men." *Sports Illustrated*, December 5, 1988. Accessed October 25, 2013. http://sportsillustrated.cnn.com/vault/article/magazine/MAG1068048/2/index.htm.

———. "No More Rap or Rep." *Sports Illustrated*, September 12, 1988. Accessed December 28, 2013. http://sportsillustrated.cnn.com/vault/article/magazine/MAG1067739/3/index.htm.

Toobin, Jeffrey R. "What Does the Multiflex Mean?" *Harvard Crimson*, October 10, 1980. Accessed November 11, 2013. http://www.thecrimson.com/article/1980/10/10/what-does-the-multiflex-mean-pthe.

Vollonino, Michael R. "Johnson's Grab Wins 116th Game for Yale." *Harvard Crimson*, November 22, 1999. Accessed November 11, 2013. http://www.thecrimson.com/article/1999/11/22/johnsons-grab-wins-116th-game-for/#.

Wallace, William N. "Earl (Red) Blaik, 92, Army's Top Football Coach." *New York Times*, May 7, 1989. Accessed October 10, 2013. http://www.nytimes.com/1989/05/07/obituaries/earl-red-blaik-92-army-s-top-football-coach.html.

Wojciechowski, Gene. "Stanford's Big Offense Makes Cal Eat Its Words." *Los Angeles Times*, November 24, 1991. Accessed December 21, 2013. http://articles.latimes.com/1991-11-24/sports/sp-206_1_big-game-stuff.

ONLINE

"1923 College Football National Championship." *Tip Top 25*, Accessed November 7, 2013. http://tiptop25.com/champ1923.html.

"Arnett 'Ace' Mumford." *Louisiana Sports Hall of Fame*, Accessed January 4, 2014. http://www.lasportshall.com/inductees/football/arnett-ace-mumford/?back=inductee.

Associated Press. "Alabama Takes Lead with 1:24 Left, Holds Off Late Auburn Drive." *ESPN.com*, November 27, 2009. Accessed October 5, 2013. http://scores.espn.go.com/ncf/recap?gameId=293310002.

———. "Cooper Is Gone." *ESPN.com*, Bowl Championship Series, December 13, 2002. Accessed October 2, 2013. http://espn.go.com/abcsports/bcs/s/2001/0102/988788.html.

———. "Gators Wreck Georgia's Perfect Season." *ESPN.com*, November 2, 2002. Accessed November 22, 2013. http://espn.go.com/ncf/recap?id=223060061.

———. "Hall Connects with George to Lift BYU in OT; Disparages Utes." *ESPN.com*, November 28, 2009. Accessed January 30, 2014. http://scores.espn.go.com/ncf/recap?gameId=293320252.

———. "Ohio State Survives When Michigan's 2-Point Attempt Fails." *ESPN.com*, November 30, 2013. Accessed January 13, 2014. http://scores.espn.go.com/ncf/recap?gameId=333340130.

———. "USC Win Streak Intact after Wild Fourth-Quarter Finish." *ESPN.com*, October 15, 2005. Accessed November 1, 2013. http://scores.espn.go.com/ncf/recap?gameId=252880087.

———. "Utah Secures Perfect Season with Sugar Bowl Win over Alabama." *ESPN.com*, January 2, 2009. Accessed February 4, 2014. http://scores.espn.go.com/ncf/recap?gameId=290020333.

———. "Young Leads Texas to First OU Win in Five Years." *ESPN.com*, October 8, 2005. Accessed October 15, 2013. http://espn.go.com/ncf/recap?id=252810251.

"The Band Is Out on the Field!" *Real Clear Sports*, Posted September 30, 2013. Accessed December 14, 2013. http://www.realclearsports.com/lists/sports_broadcasting_calls/california_stanford_band_starkey.html.

Barra, Allan. "A History of Grambling University Football: The First Shot in Player Liberation." *Daily Beast*, November 9, 2013. Accessed January 10, 2014. http://www.thedailybeast.com/articles/2013/11/09/a-history-of-grambling-university-football-the-first-shot-in-player-liberation.html.

"BYU vs. Utah: The So-Called Holy War." *The Official Home of the BYU Cougars*, Accessed January 30, 2014. http://byucougars.com/athletics/byu-vs-utah-so-called-holy-war.

Carter, Bob. "Wilkinson Created Sooners Dynasty." *ESPN Classic*. Accessed October 14, 2013. http://espn.go.com/classic/biography/s/wilkinson_bud.html.

The Elusive Shadow. "Let's Do It: Let the Hate Flow through You." *Burnt Orange Nation*, October 9, 2013. Accessed October 18, 2013. http://www.burntorangenation.com/2013/10/9/4819860/lets-do-it-let-the-hate-flow-through-you.

Ferguson, Ryan. "It's Still Important to Hate Georgia: A History Lesson." *AOLNews*, October 27, 2006. Accessed November 13, 2013. http://archive.is/wYhhP.

Finkel, Jon. "Ricky Williams' Magical Run in 1998: Wins Heisman Trophy, Sets All-Time Rushing Mark." *The Post Game*, September 19, 2013. Accessed October 15, 2013. http://www.thepostgame.com/blog/loyalty-report/201309/mack-brown-ricky-williams-texas-longhorns-football-college-ncaa-heisman.

"Florida State: 1962 Seminoles." *Helmet Hut*, Accessed December 28, 2013. http://www.helmethut.com/College/FloridaState/FLXFSU6262.html.

Garbin, Patrick. "Fourth and Dumb." *About Them Dawgs! Blawg* (blog), May 28, 2010. Accessed November 18, 2013. http://patrickgarbin.blogspot.com/2010/05/fourth-and-dumb.html.

Ghassemi, Jeremy. "Ty Montgomery and Stanford Have Big Game, Demolish Cal 63–13." *Baysportsreport.com*, November 23, 2013. Accessed December 21, 2013. http://www.baysportsreport.com/2013/11/23/ty-montgomery-and-stanford-have-big-game/.

Hansen, Jay. "When Woody Was Hired." *Ohio State Alumni Association*. Accessed September 30, 2013. http://www.ohiostatealumni.org/volunteer/celebratingalumni/Pages/WoodyHired.aspx.

"The Harvard–Yale Rivalry." *Harvard Athletics*, Accessed November 2, 2013. http://www.gocrimson.com/sports/mcrew-hw/tradition/harvard-yale.

Hood, Tommy. "Tiger Insider Sneak Peak: Charley Pell Turning Things Around Again." *TigerNet.com*, June 6, 2000. Accessed February 11, 2014. http://www.tigernet.com/view/story.do?id=518.

Lambrecht, Gary. "50 Years Later the 1950 Navy Football Team Still Ranks as the Best in School History." *Navysports.com*, October 2, 2013. Accessed October 11, 2013. http://www.navysports.com/sports/m-footbl/spec-rel/100213aaa.html.

Mandell, Ted. "Yale vs. Harvard." *Heart Stoppers and Hail Marys*. Accessed November 7, 2013. http://www3.nd.edu/~tmandell/harvard.html.

Marina, Jenna. "The Greatest Game They Never Played." *Lafayette Official Athletic Site*, November 18, 2008. Accessed December 2, 2013. http://www.goleopards.com/sports/m-footbl/spec-rel/111808aag.html.

"Michigan vs. Ohio State: 1969 Game, Bo's Big Win." *Bentley Historical Library*, November 16, 2008. Accessed September 26, 2013. http://bentley.umich.edu/athdept/football/umosu/1969game.htm.

On, Esteban. "9 Biggest Traitor Coaches in the History of College Football." *TotalProSports.com*, December 1, 2011. Accessed October 20, 2013. http://www.totalprosports.com/2011/12/01/9-biggest-traitor-coaches-in-the-history-of-college-football/.

O'Sullivan, Dan. "1984: Miami 31, Nebraska 30." *ESPN.com*, Bowl Championship Series, December 13, 2002. Accessed December 28, 2013. http://espn.go.com/abcsports/bcs/orange/s/1984.html .

"Richard F. Doyne Is in the Lehigh Hall of Fame." *Lehigh Sports*, Accessed December 5, 2013. http://history.lehighsports.com/playerstats/display/5/1951/315.

Schexnayder, C. J. "Florida vs. Georgia Series History: Steve Spurrier, 1966 and Long Memories." *SB Nation*, October 28, 2011. Accessed November 13, 2013. http://www.sbnation.com/ncaa-football/2011/10/28/2505359/florida-georgia-game-2011-series-history-steve-spurrier-1966.

Travers, Steven Robert. "Johnny Baker and USC's 1931 Comeback at South Bend." *Red Room* (blog), November 23, 2012. Accessed October 20, 2013. http://redroom.com/member/steven-robert-travers/blog/johnny-baker-and-uscs-1931-comeback-at-south-bend.

Wyatt, Hugh. "Ernie Nevers—Has There Ever Been Better?" *coachwyatt.com*. Accessed December 17, 2013. http://www.coachwyatt.com/ernienevers.htm.

INDEX

ABOUT THE AUTHOR

Marty Gitlin is a sportswriter and educational-book writer based in Cleveland, Ohio. He has had nearly 100 books published, mostly in the realm of sports, including works on the history of the Ohio State and Michigan football programs. He is also the author of *The Greatest Sitcoms of All Time*, which was published by Scarecrow Press, and *The Great American Cereal Book*, which has received national acclaim. He covered the Cleveland Browns for cbssports.com from 2009 to 2013 and is currently working for that website as a fantasy baseball and football writer. Gitlin is married and has three teenage children.